A B C D E F

G H I J K L M

N O P Q R S T

U V W X Y Z

1 2 3 4 5 6 7

8 9 0 !?;:&

I II III IV V VI

MASTERING THE ART OF
CALLIGRAPHY

everything you need to know about materials, equipment and techniques with 12 complete alphabets to copy and learn and over 50 beautiful step-by-step calligraphy projects to follow, shown in over 1000 photographs and artworks

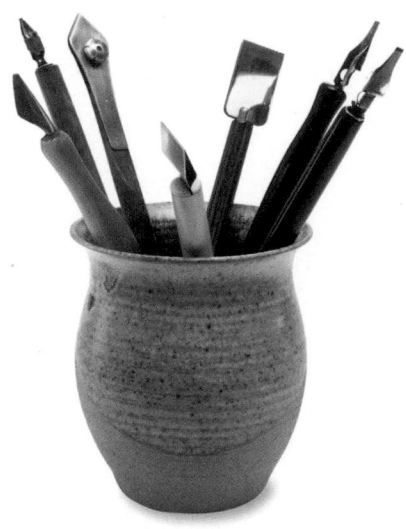

JANET MEHIGAN

LORENZ BOOKS

This edition is published by Lorenz Books,
an imprint of Anness Publishing Ltd, 108 Great Russell Street,
London WC1B 3NA; info@anness.com

www.lorenzbooks.com; www.annesspublishing.com

If you like the images in this book and would like to investigate
using them for publishing, promotions or advertising, please visit
our website www.practicalpictures.com for more information.

A CIP catalogue record for this book is available from the
British Library.

Designed and produced for Anness Publishing by
THE BRIDGEWATER BOOK COMPANY LTD.

Publisher: Joanna Lorenz
Editorial Director: Helen Sudell
Project Manager: Sarah Doughty
Editorial Assistance: Alison Hissey and Rachel Carter
Photography: wg photo
Designers: Jane Lanaway and Kevin Knight
Art Director: Michael Whitehead
Production Controller: Ben Worley

Contents

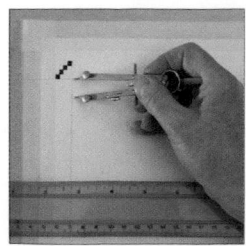
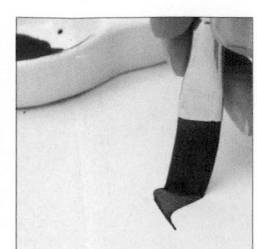

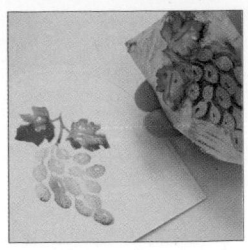
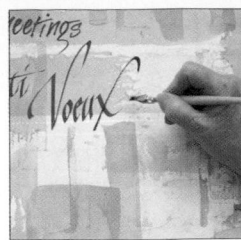
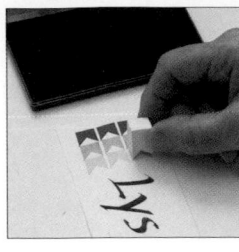
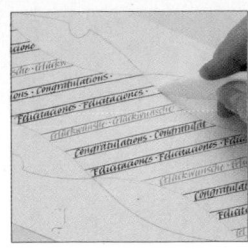

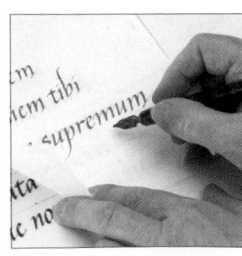
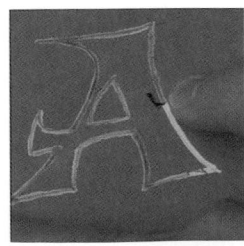
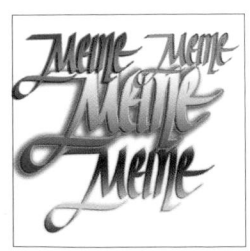
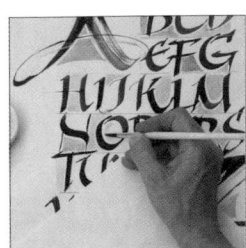

Introduction

Calligraphy is a fascinating and absorbing skill, which is as fresh and inventive today as it was at the time of its origin in the earliest human civilizations. This book draws from a rich calligraphic tradition, as well as from modern technological advances, in order to inform and inspire all those with an interest in beautiful lettering. The book provides instruction in the basic techniques and alphabets with practical exercises to reinforce knowlege. A variety of projects are designed to further the skills of the budding calligrapher as well as the more experienced lettering artist.

In order to fully appreciate the letterforms we use today, it is important to understand their origins. The book begins with an insight into the development of writing, its historical roots, and the practical uses to which it has been put. In the past, the calligrapher diligently recorded history, literature, documents and charters, but with the invention of printing by moveable type, his role was to change forever. Today, calligraphers, lettering artists and illuminators throughout the world are regarded not just as craftsmen but as artists. As well as taking writing to superb technical levels incorporating both new and old technologies, they also use words and calligraphic marks as images in their own right, creating a significant and exciting new art form.

A comprehensive section in *Getting Started* is devoted to details of materials and equipment needed to get going in calligraphy. In addition, there is an introduction to basic penmanship, and guidelines for layout and design – a useful reference for later work. Twelve calligraphic scripts or hands to be practised are presented in the *Alphabets* section, along with in-depth explanations of the scripts based on historical examples. For each script or hand, instructions are given on how to form the letters, which groups they fall into and how to avoid common mistakes. The exercises contained in this section will help you to develop a feel for the flow of the scripts and in time, select a script that complements the meaning of your text.

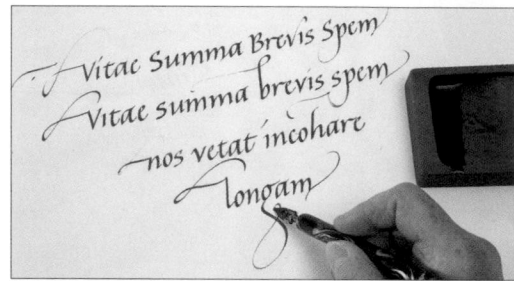

Tools of the trade ▼
A selection of the many dip pen nibs available for calligraphers. A variety of writing tools are used, but dip pens will give crisp and sharp letterforms. They can be used with a slip-on reservoir.

Sloping drawing board ▼
It is more comfortable to write on a sloping board. It keeps your back straight and helps to relax your shoulders and writing arm. It also makes the flow of ink more controllable.

Writing tools ▲
Almost any writing tool that makes a variety of strokes is suitable for calligraphy and there are many types available. A dip pen is charged with ink, and recharged often during writing.

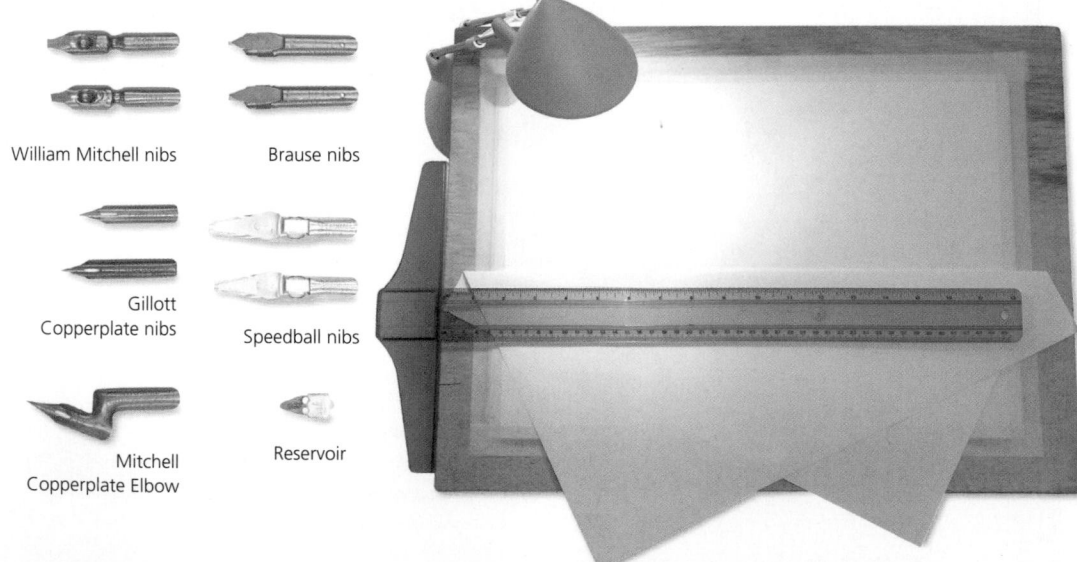

William Mitchell nibs

Brause nibs

Gillott
Copperplate nibs

Speedball nibs

Mitchell
Copperplate Elbow

Reservoir

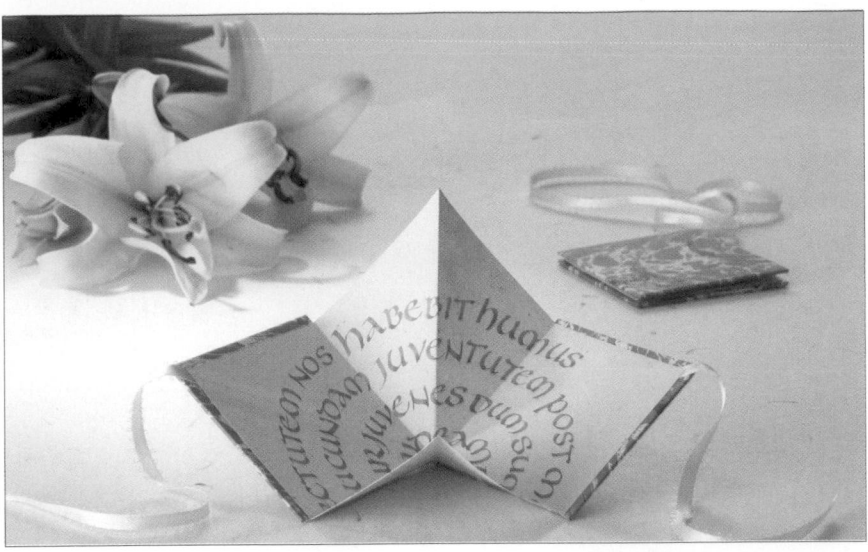

◀ The perfect gift
Calligraphic techniques can be employed to create a range of beautiful gifts and keepsakes such as this lotus book with a spiral script.

Creative projects to do ▼
Brown paper is transformed into stunning gift wrap with decorative lettering in white gouache paint.

Although mastery of the basic letterform is arguably the most important aspect of calligraphy, it is when this is combined with other skills that the true possibilities of calligraphy are revealed. The *Techniques* section features numerous ways to turn a piece of writing into a work of art, including an explanation and examples of brush lettering – which is a script in its own right. There are insights into useful skills including the use of colour washes, bookbinding techniques, cut letters and gilding. Also included is a section on digital calligraphy. Each technique is accompanied by practical, step-by-step exercises. Meanwhile, a *Gallery* of modern work offers inspirational ideas and illustrates the possibilities that are within reach of today's calligrapher.

The final section of this book is devoted to practical applications for calligraphy in the form of *Projects* – using both traditional and digital calligraphy. The projects begin with the least complicated tasks to inspire and promote confidence. For those with more calligraphic experience, the book moves on to projects that require greater competency. The most demanding of these are near the end of the book and cater for the accomplished calligrapher.

First, you need to practise the letterforms. Before embarking on a project, it is advisable to practise the chosen script until it can be written with some fluency and spontaneity – that is, until you can make letter shapes without continually referring to the alphabets. Good calligraphy relies primarily on well constructed letter shapes, secondly on freedom of execution and finally on individual expression.

Alternative scripts may be used on any of the projects given – change them to suit your own strengths. Work carefully from the step-by-step sequences trying not to cut corners. It is also worthwhile developing individual ideas and ways of working. However your skills develop, you will find calligraphy an immensely satisfying and rewarding pastime.

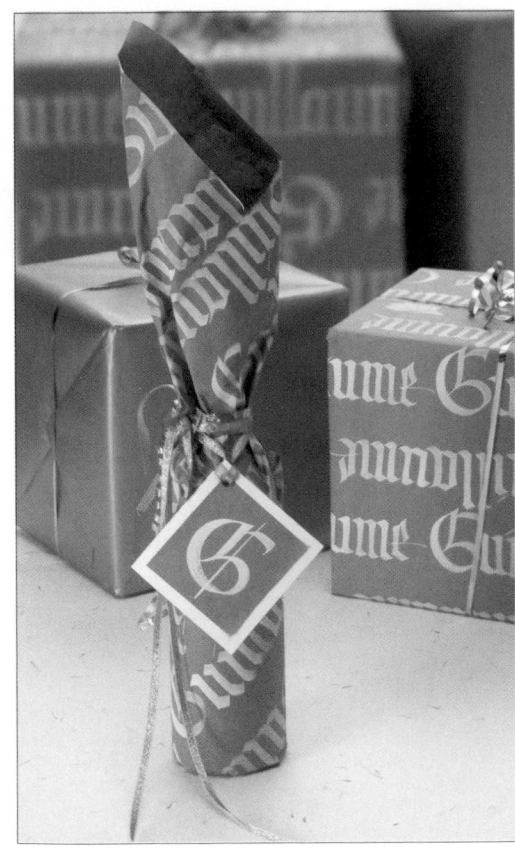

The origins of calligraphy

Writing is so basic that most of us take the written word for granted and barely take time to consider its fascinating origins and development. We look at hand-written, printed and computerized letters and only see the message or information that is conveyed. Yet words completely surround us in our everyday lives: they are used in road signs, advertisements, books, newspapers, magazines, television, computers, packaging, commodities and design. The list is endless and we could not function without these arranged alphabetic elements to express complex thoughts, ideas and information.

Early pictorial forms

The history of pictorial symbols is a long and complicated one beginning over 20,000 years ago with the cave paintings of early stone-age man, some wonderful examples of which are to be found in Lascaux in France and Altamira in Spain. These paintings may have been made to signify the triumphs in hunting animals, or perhaps executed for more subtle reasons, but what we can say with certainty is that they show humans were able to communicate their ideas by use of line and colour, thus presenting us with the first pictorial statements. These forms evolved over time, assimilated and modified by the social and technical changes that inevitably occurred. There are many gaps in our knowledge as we only have the evidence before us that has survived the ravages of time – the rest is conjecture.

The first writing system

In 3500BC the Sumerians, who lived in the fertile valley between the River Tigris and the River Euphrates (called Mesopotamia by the Greeks and part of modern Iraq today) represented the earliest civilization with evidence of a well-developed writing system. The Sumerians were highly organized, used domesticated animals for farming and irrigated land from the rivers. They invented the use of money and recorded business and agricultural transactions of everyday life on clay tablets, which were often baked hard in the sun to create a permanent record for future reference. The Sumerians used about 2,000 symbols, pictograms and drawings that represented objects. These eventually developed into ideograms, which were more abstract, representing words or sentences. Eventually the sounds of the

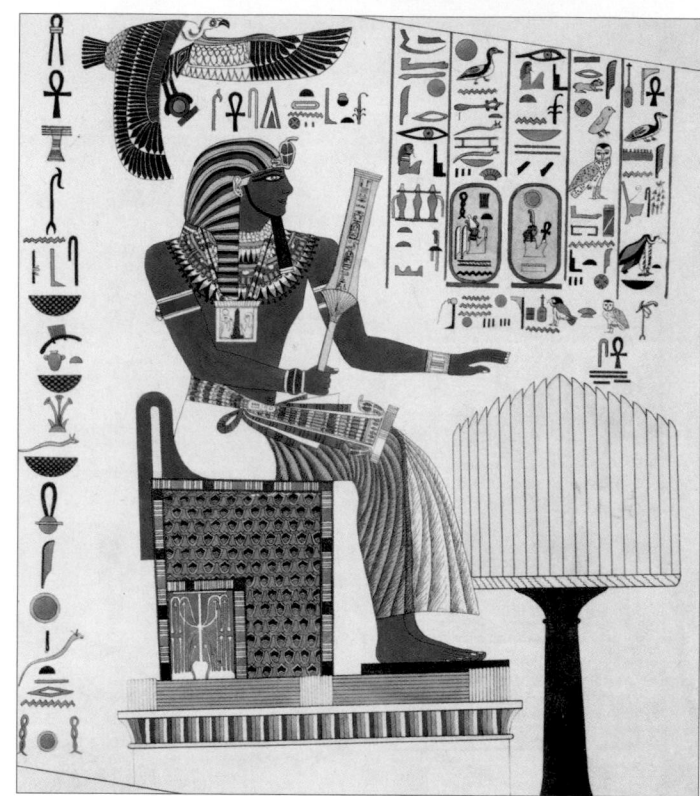

words themselves came to be used. The use of symbols or phonograms reduced the need for complicated illustrative text and reduced the number of symbols in the writing system to 600. The Sumerians used cuneiform script (from the Latin *cuneus* and *forma* – 'wedge-shaped'), which was inscribed on damp clay tablets with a sharpened wood or reed stylus. Over 20,000 tablets of this script have been preserved. Cuneiform was subsequently adopted by the Babylonians in 1720BC when they overran the Sumerians (and later by the Assyrians in 1200BC who succeeded them), eventually becoming a

Egyptian Hieroglyphics ▲
Illustration of a mural from the Tombs of the Kings of Thebes (Valley of the Kings) depicting Hieroglyphics (1550–1070BC).

syllabic alphabet. In the Egyptian civilization another type of picture writing was emerging: Hieroglyphics (from the Greek word *hieros* meaning 'sacred' and *glyphein*, 'to engrave'). About 700 characters were used, in the form of simplified pictures of animals and everyday objects. Simpler forms, beginning with hieratic writing, were developed and used with reed brush or pen on papyrus or linen.

First alphabets

Papyrus, from which the word paper derives, was grown in abundance in the fertile soil along the Nile. The stems were cut lengthwise in thin slivers and laid alongside each other. Another layer was placed at right angles on top of the first. When both layers were beaten, the inner pith bound them together to form a writing sheet. This was then laid in the sun to dry. By the year 2000BC writing was common all over western Asia, but it was the Phoenicians (who lived along the eastern Mediterranean coast near Byblos, now Lebanon and Syria) that gave us the rudiments of our own Western alphabet. The very word alphabet derives from the names given to the first two letters (*aleph* – 'ox', and *beth* – 'house'). The Phoenicians were outstanding seafarers and travelled throughout the Mediterranean from its eastern shores to Spain, North Africa and even to Britain. They traded wool, metals, gems, grain and livestock and took papyrus to the Greeks.

By 850BC the Greeks had adopted the alphabet. By 400BC a standardized alphabet, Ionic, had been developed. The Ionic alphabet had 24 signs, each representing a single consonantal sound in abstract form.

The Etruscans of Tuscany, northern Italy, invaded southern Italy in the 7th century BC, taking with them the Ionic Greek alphabet. They too were great traders and skilled craftsmen, and derived their alphabet from their neighbours in Greece. When the power of Rome eventually superseded their rule over 300 years later the Romans had also absorbed this alphabet modified with Latin.

The Roman alphabet

The alphabet used by the Romans contained 23 letters. 'I' and 'V' were dual purpose letters, serving also as 'J' and 'U' respectively, and 'W' did not exist. The letters 'Y' and 'Z' were used rarely, only in Greek place names. The letters 'J', 'U' and 'W' were added in the Middle Ages.

Roman Capitals were used in official inscriptions and were the original

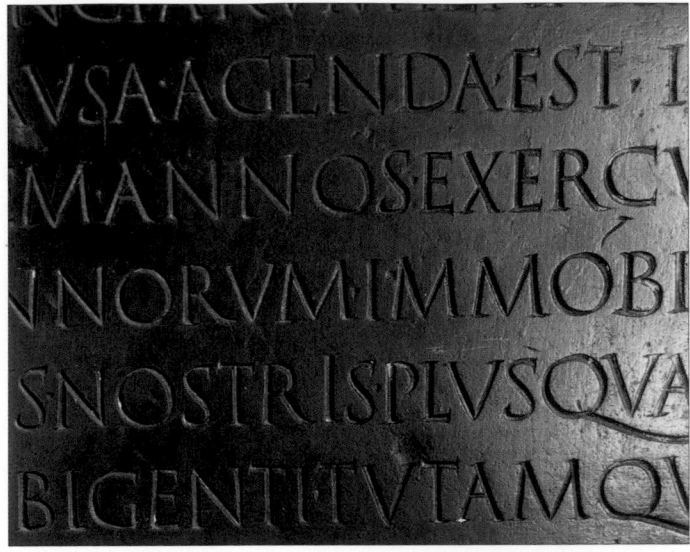

Roman Capitals ▲
Detail from the 'Claudian Table', written in bronze in Roman Capitals in the 1st century AD, and found in France.

models from which all formal Roman letterforms have descended. By the 1st century AD the Roman alphabet styles, of which there were many, had spread throughout the whole area of the powerful Roman Empire, from the Euphrates to northern Britain.

The Roman scripts have been in existence in the Western world for 2,000 years, and although their visual form has varied over time, the basic underlying letterforms have remained consistent. The Romans had the benefit of many alphabets at their disposal. They used cursive scripts for everyday wax tablets and papyrus scrolls, Rustic Capitals for manuscripts, documents and notices and for carving into marble or stone, and Roman Inscriptional Capitals for sign writing and incising on to monuments.

Roman Inscriptional Capitals (Imperial Capitals) were used both in brush form and on carved monuments, the most famous being the magnificent capitals on Trajan Column, AD113, commemorating the military victories of the Emperor Trajan. There are many examples of incised letters on the

remaining monuments of Rome and other western cities that were part of the great Roman Empire. These elegant letters were first painted with a brush and then chiselled expertly into the stone or bronze. Many inscriptions would have been filled with colour – often minium (an orange-brown colour reminiscent of burnt sienna), which over time has disappeared.

All subsequent Western scripts have evolved from the original Roman scripts. Rustic Capitals were written as a book hand during the 1st century AD and continued to be used up until the 6th century. Painted Rustic Capitals can be found on the ancient walls of Pompeii advertising the virtues of election candidates and announcing gladiator contests. Rustics were also used as display capitals up until the late 12th century as part of the 'hierarchy of scripts' on manuscript pages.

Square Capitals, written as a book hand, were evident by 4th century AD. Only two known examples of early Square Capitals written with a pen survive, and both manuscripts are texts of Virgil. Square Capitals are closely related to the Roman Inscriptional letters but the pen formation appears complex and time consuming, which may be why there is little evidence of their general use.

Scrolls and codices

Although parchment, prepared animal skin and other materials were used by scribes, undoubtedly the most common writing material used up until the 3rd century AD was papyrus. Papyrus scrolls, however, became increasingly expensive to import from Egypt. They were also brittle to handle, had an uneven surface, and only one side could be written upon. They were thus gradually replaced by the codex (book) and the use of animal skin. Parchment (sheep skin) and vellum (calf skin) became the standard writing surface, in the Western world for books, and the quill pen, usually goose, became the writing tool. The goose quill was easier to obtain than the reed in most of the Roman Empire and easier to use with ink on skins. The letter shapes produced with a quill pen on a smooth animal skin became rounder, finer and more fluid.

Uncials and Half-Uncials

From the 4th century AD the preferred writing style for religious texts was Uncial, composed of rounded curves, like the Roman architecture of the time. The letters were capitals, although on some variations it can be seen that letters 'D', 'H', 'I' and 'P' show the first suggestions of minuscule ascenders and descenders – the result of writing with a pen at speed. The evolution of these letters occurred over a long period of time, and was influenced by many social and religious changes that took place during this period. Uncials remained the main hand for books until the 8th century and for headings up until the 12th century. Their origins are to be found in the integration of Roman Capitals with scripts from North Africa and the surrounding Mediterranean. Many variations were produced, which subsequently spread throughout

Europe. The script was brought to Britain by Augustine's missions between AD550 and 600.

Half-Uncial is an 18th-century name given to a script first used in the 6th century. It is composed of a mixture of characteristics of both capital and minuscule alphabets and is often used with Uncial and Rustic Capitals. The letter shapes are probably written with a 'right oblique' pen nib to enable the scribe to write the more flattened angles of the letters with confidence.

Insular Half-Uncial

The Christian communities of Wearmouth and Jarrow in north-east England were founded by Benedict Biscop in AD674 and 681. On his many visits to Rome he returned with manuscripts from which the monasteries developed their own Roman Uncial script. Three huge bibles were commissioned, one for each monastery and one for the Pope: *The Codex Amiatinus.*

Insular Half-Uncial derives its name from the Latin for 'island'. The Insular Half-Uncials of Britain were first used in Ireland and brought to northern England by the monks where the script predominated until the 10th century. The Lindisfarne Gospels and Book of Kells are two fine examples. The St Cuthbert (formerly Stoneyhurst) Gospel was written by a scribe of the Wearmouth and Jarrow monasteries at the end of the 7th and the beginning of the 8th century. It was laid in St Cuthbert's coffin, and discovered in 1104 when his tomb was opened so that his relics could be transferred to a new shrine. It is a good example for a modern Uncial hand as the pen angle is consistent, with little pen manipulation. As more and more books were produced, writing became less formal, and with speed, ascenders and descenders became progressively longer creating the beginnings of the first minuscule writing.

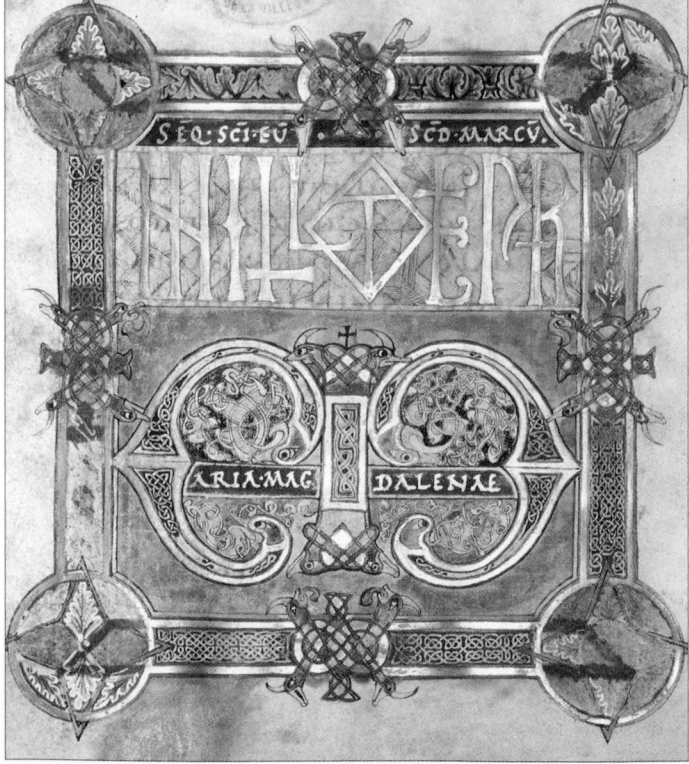

◀ **Gospel with gold Uncials**
Extract from a 9th-century gospel from Saint-Vaast, with Uncials written in gold on vellum.

Carolingian minuscule

Charlemagne was crowned King of the Franks in AD768 and during his 46-year reign he created a Christian Empire that stretched throughout Europe – from the Baltic to Italy, Spain and Germany. Pope Leo III made him Emperor of Rome in AD800. Charlemagne ruled successfully, and encouraged the spread of learning throughout his kingdom. He united France, Germany, northern Spain and northern Italy and was a devoted Christian and a skilled administrator. He issued a decree to reform all liturgical books and to this purpose invited all learned men to his court. These scholars were set the task of accurately revising bibles, gospels, liturgical books and works from the classical writers using only authentic sources from the libraries of Rome. Among the many he appointed was Alcuin of York, an eminent scholar, the Librarian of York Cathedral and also head of the York Scriptorium, to become Master of the Court School of Aix-la-Chapelle (Aachen). For ten years Alcuin directed the revival of classical culture inspiring the Carolingian Renaissance until he retired, becoming abbot of St Martin's Abbey at Tours in AD796 where he continued the work he had begun.

The script used at the Court of Charlemagne was written at speed with an elegant forward slant, full of rhythm and beauty. This was Carolingian or Carolingian hand, and was used into the 11th century. By the middle of the 9th century, Tours had become renowned for the richly illuminated bibles using this hand. The Moutier Grandval Bible (AD840), written in St Martin's Abbey, was one of nearly a hundred produced at the scriptorium along with other liturgical and classical texts. Also from Tours came the First Bible of Charles the Bald, Charlemagne's grandson, commissioned by Abbott Vivian to present to the King in AD846. The use of 'hierarchical scripts' in texts, featuring the use of Roman Capitals, Rustics or Uncials for page titles and chapter openings was highly developed during this period and the letter 'i' is not dotted.

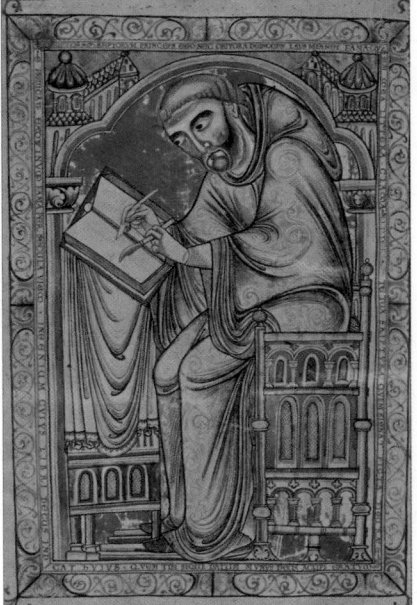

Eadwine Psalter (c.1150) ▲
Influenced by the Carolingian hand, Benedictine monks such as Eadwine were also painters and illuminators. (f.283v)

English Carolingian minuscules

It was after the Danish invasions of the 9th century that Carolingian script finally reached the shores of England. There was a significant increase in the production of lavish books at English monasteries, which was at its peak in the 12th century. There were libraries and scriptoria at Durham, Peterborough Abbey, Canterbury and Winchester. A beautiful example of Carolingian script is contained within the lavishly illuminated Benedictional of Aethelwold, written in southern England for Aethelwold the Bishop of Winchester during the late 10th century. The Ramsey Psalter, also written in southern England between AD974 and 986, probably in the Cathedral Priory of Winchester, is another example of English Carolingian script. This was the distinctive manuscript on which Edward Johnston chose to base his 'Foundational' script in the 19th century.

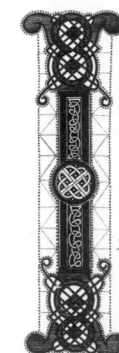

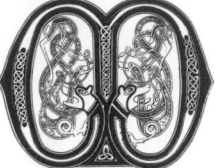

Second Bible of Charles the Bald ▲
A large decorative initial letter followed by Uncial 'Display' capitals marks the beginning of this paragraph. (AD846)

Versals

The earliest manuscripts contained continuous writing in capital letters with few spaces. Later, larger pen-drawn Roman Capitals were used to give importance to headings and to mark the beginnings of verses. It was the Carolingian scribes of St Martin's and other scriptoria that perfected the use of Versals in manuscripts. The elegant proportions of these majestic built-up pen letters show that they were based on the monumental lettering used on Roman inscriptions of the 1st century and in the earlier Roman manuscripts of the 6th century. These outstandingly beautiful letters can be found throughout the Benedictional of Aethelwold and in the Second Bible of Charles the Bald as well as in many other Carolingian manuscripts. Many of the Versals were penned in gold. Later 'Lombardic' Versals in red, blue and green can be found in the Winchester Bible of AD1160.

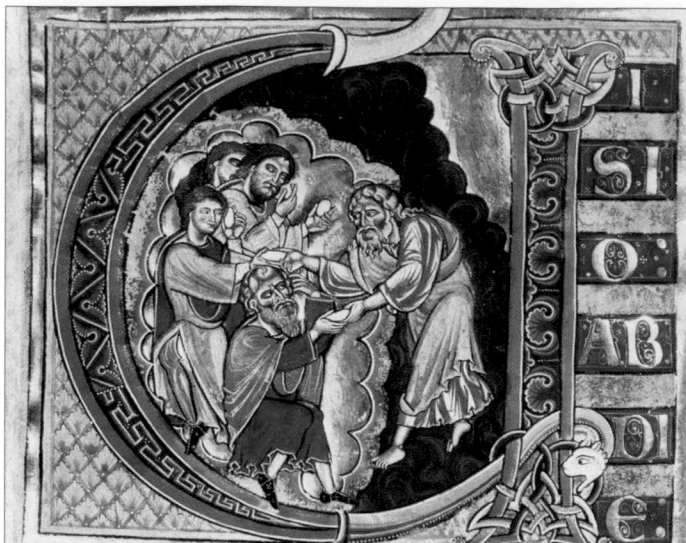

Gothic

At the end of the 11th century the written Carolingian script became more compressed and slightly more angular, eventually evolving into Gothic Black Letter. During the transitional period from Carolingian to Gothic two notable books were written in England: The Arundel Psalter (at Christ Church Cathedral Priory, Canterbury 1212–23) and The Winchester Bible (Cathedral Priory, Winchester, 1160–75). The Winchester Bible is the biggest of the 12th-century bibles surviving today. The writing is regular and beautifully executed, virtually by a single scribe, and the Romanesque gold and painted illuminations throughout are breathtaking. The 48 large illuminated initials were made by several artists. In both of these manuscripts the compression of the Carolingian hand towards Early Gothic script can be seen.

There was a great demand for books not only from the Church but from universities, rich merchants and aristocrats, on philosophy, medicine and poetry. By the 13th century, craft workshops had been established to meet the demand and cities such as Bologna, Paris, Winchester, Oxford and York were employing professional scriveners, colour men and associated

The Winchester Bible (1160–75) ▲
The Book of Obadiah (f.203v). An illuminated and historiated initial letter 'V' – illustrated by a scene of taking food to the hiding Prophets in the cave (3 Kings 18.4).

artisans. The trend towards compressed letter shapes was probably influenced by artistic fashions and innovations, but is also likely to have resulted from the need to economize on the cost of materials such as skins, as well as a reduction in the size of the individual books. Many of these books would have been used by the laity and scholars of cathedral schools and universities. These people required books that were easily transportable, rather than huge tomes. Not only did the writing become compressed but many abbreviations were to be found in the text rendering them difficult to read. Gothic, a term also applied to the architecture of the period, was written in a great variety of styles, both formal and informal, and its use spanned over three hundred years from the late 12th century through to the Renaissance of the 15th century continuing into the 16th century. The characteristics of Gothic script are lateral compression, heavyweight pen strokes and angular shapes. Earlier Gothic Quadrata was less compressed and

more graceful, retaining some of the roundness of earlier Carolingian scripts, and with diamond-shaped terminations to the letters. There were often fine pen hairlines attached to letters adding to the graceful appearance of a manuscript, such as in the Metz Pontifical (Fitzwilliam Museum, Cambridge), written and illuminated in northern France about 1300.

Textura, written between the 13th and 15th centuries, is the most widely known of the Gothic scripts because its dense grid-like appearance is so easily recognizable. The spacing between the letters in Textura is no more than the width of the letter stem, which created a heavy even black and white texture to the page. The script was slow to write and difficult to read.

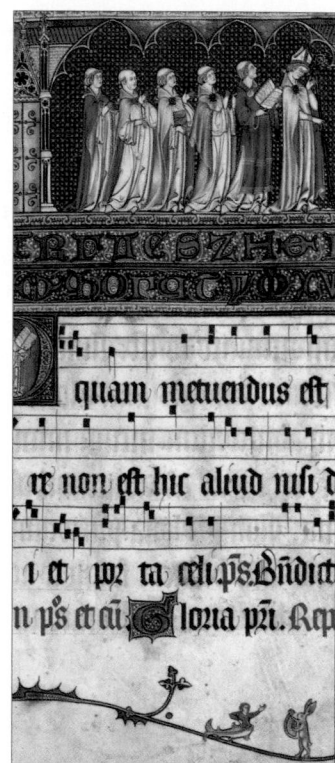

Metz Pontifical ▲
Written on vellum in Gothic script, in the early 14th century, this is an elegant French liturgical manuscript. The script used is Gothic Quadrata.

The Gothic Prescissus (with 'flat feet' letters) was written during the 13th to 14th centuries. The script consists of very compressed letter shapes with pen manipulation to create 'flattened feet' or straight endings to the lower stem on certain letters; notably 'a', 'i', 'f', 'n', 'm', 'p' and 'q'. The stems begin with a diamond 'head' or top, which adds to the heavy texture of the writing. The flat feet would have been constructed with a twist of the pen to flatten the angle or filled in at the end with the corner of the nib. The Queen Mary Psalter and the Luttrell Psalter are written in this script. The Luttrell Psalter was written and illuminated for Sir Geoffrey Luttrell in Lincolnshire between 1335–40, and depicts scenes from everyday life in the lavish marginal decoration.

Rotunda Gothic

In Italy and Spain a more rounded Gothic script evolved. Rotunda was used for very large manuscripts for the Church where it accompanied musical notes. Rotunda was also used in the small Books of Hours, which were gaining popularity at that time. Gothic continued in Germany as a modern hand in a more rounded version through to the last century.

Batarde

During the 14th century, the French cursive Gothic known as Batarde was developed. This was a vigorous flowing script used extensively in the Books of Hours. It was introduced into England in the late 14th century as Bastard Secretary. Books written in this hand for rich merchants were full of border decoration and small miniature paintings, which were becoming popular. The hand was variable depending on where it had been written. Generally executed with a slight forward lilt it was an expressive hand and full of vitality. From the middle of the 15th century the most beautiful specimens of this script are known as Flemish Bastarda, written by Flemish calligraphers and illuminators who produced hundreds of handwritten and illuminated books containing lavishly

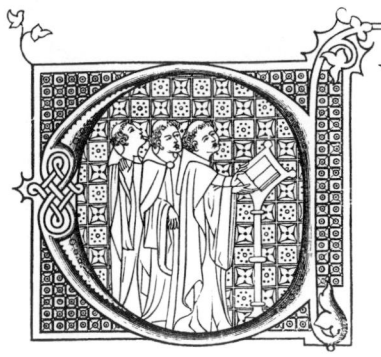

Decorative border ▲
Detail of a decoration from a 14th-century manuscript, now to be found in the British Museum.

painted miniatures and richly decorated borders and initials. These devotional and liturgical manuscripts provide valuable evidence of the secular life and culture of the Middle Ages.

Renaissance scripts

The 15th century marked the beginning of the Renaissance, a cultural movement that was to spread throughout western Europe during the 16th century reviving a great interest in classical learning and

Luttrell Psalter (1335–40) ▼
Scenes of everyday life, with text in Gothic Prescissus. The text stands flat and unserifed on the baseline (f.84).

the artistic culture of Rome. It was a time of new education and new freedoms. The Humanistic Script of the Italian Renaissance was the last development of script before printing. It reached its peak of perfection as a result of the efforts of Poggio Bracciolini (1380–1459). Born in Terranuova, Tuscany, Bracciolini travelled widely in Europe as a Papal official and rediscovered classical Latin manuscripts in monastic libraries which were later translated. In addition, he not only trained scribes but wrote texts himself. His script was based on the Carolingian hand for its simplicity and purity, which harmonized with the ideals of the Renaissance. This script soon became an excellent model for the metal fonts of the printing press.

The Italian Humanist scribes also revived the Roman Square Capitals which, in turn, were based on the Roman Inscriptional letters. Many of the manuscripts written in Italy from 1450 onwards contained these elegant letters. The Paduan scribe Bartolomeo San Vito (1435–1512), who worked in Padua and Rome, created his own distinctive style by alternating coloured capital letters with gold letters to add to the richness of the text. The letters were well spaced and the accompanying Italic letters beautifully executed.

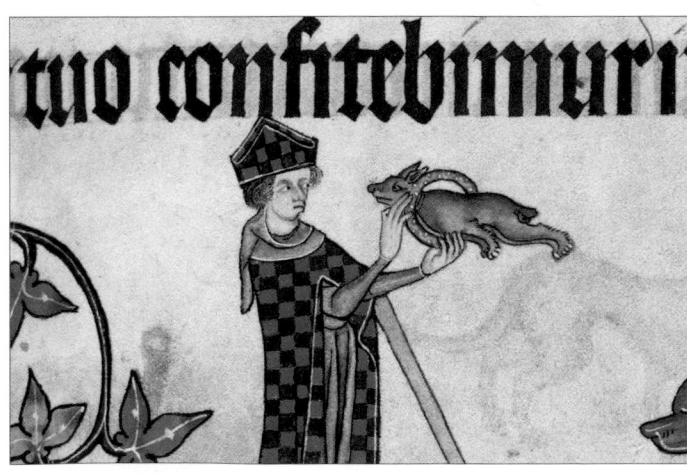

Italic

In its simplest form, Italic, or Chancery Cursive (*Canellaresca Corsiva*) is a descendant of Humanist minuscule. It was invented by Niccolo Niccoli in 1420 to replace Humanist hand, which he found too slow. Within 20 years his new script had been adopted as the official hand of the Papal Chancery.

Ludovico degli Arrighi was born at the end of the 15th century in a small village in Vicenza. He began to study calligraphy and typography at a very early age, and by 1522 he had written a manual, *La Operina,* which he was able to publish. Within this publication were the rules of how to construct Chancery script, its oval forms, the slant of the letter and the correct ascenders and descenders. The fine script that he created is a model that is still used today for Italic calligraphy. The advent of printing and movable type meant that scribes such as Bernardino Cantaneo, Giovanni Francesco Cresci and Palatino were all able to publish writing manuals, in addition to Arrighi.

German manuscripts dating from about 1400 show a slightly different hand which is now called Fraktur. It was a cursive hand like Batarde but written upright with the heaviness and rigid feel of Textura Gothic.

Craftsmen and scribes in particular were not generally paid well for their art during this time, although there were some notable exceptions, such as the Limbourg Brothers, who wrote and illuminated the *Tres Riches Heures* for their wealthy and influential Patron the Duc de Berry in 1409.

The arrival of the printing press, pioneered by Johann Gutenberg of Mainz around 1450, saw an increase in the speed of book production, but a decline in work for the scribe, although decoration was still added by hand.

Copperplate

After the Renaissance, writing with the edged pen declined. With the advent of printing and the printed manuals of fine writing, which had been etched into the copper plates for the printing examples, a new pen hand was ready to evolve.

It was the writing masters of Flanders and the Netherlands that developed the use of Copperplate in the early 16th century. Calligraphy was taught in primary schools and it was not long before many gifted calligraphers emerged. Among the great masters, one of the most copied was Van den Velde, who was born in Antwerp in 1569 and died 1623. He taught at a Latin school in Rotterdam and published several books containing his calligraphic work. Most of Van den Velde's books were printed using copper plates. Holland was thriving commercially and when some of the Dutch calligraphers established themselves in London, English calligraphers found that they could address themselves to rich Dutch traders who were wealthy enough to give them lots of work. In 1651 the domination of Holland's commercial fleet declined and the English navy expanded. This brought about more work for English calligraphers. The first English writing manual appeared in 1571. By the 17th and 18th centuries English Round hand (Copperplate) was well established. George Bickham's *Universal Penman*, engraved and published in 1741, includes the work of 24 eminent English calligraphers.

The development of modern scripts

William Morris (1834–96) was one of the most important artistic, literary and political figures of the late 19th century. A prolific designer, typographer and calligrapher, he founded the Arts and Crafts movement in a bid to improve art and design during the Industrial Revolution, when it seemed that fine art had been lost to the mechanics of manufacturing. Among his close friends was William Richard Lethaby, architect, designer and Principal of the Central School of Art. When Edward Johnston, one of the most famous pioneers of modern calligraphy, went to London he was introduced to Lethaby.

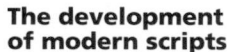

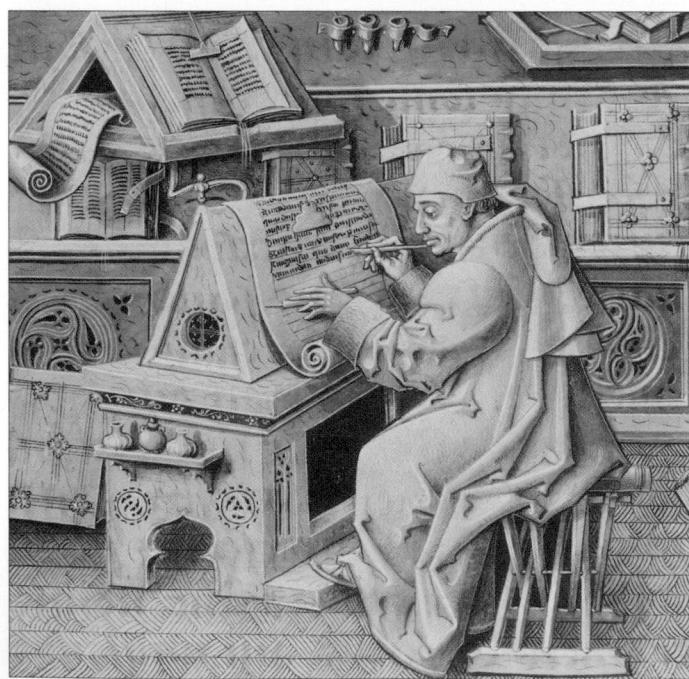

15th-century scribe ◄
Flemish author, scribe and translator Jean Miélot (fl.1448–68), in a scriptorium typical of the period.

He commissioned Johnston to write a manuscript, and when it was completed he asked him if he would teach at the Central School. Johnston was given access to the manuscripts at the British Museum, and his study of these led to his development of the Foundational hand. The more Johnston learned, the more he could teach his students. At about the same time a revival of calligraphic skills was occurring in Austria, led by Rudolf von Larisch (1856–1934) and in Germany led by Rudolph Koch (1874–1934). So began the 20th century revival of calligraphy.

Neuland

One of the most iconic typefaces of the early 20th century is Neuland, designed and cut by Rudolph Koch for the Klingspor Foundry, Germany, in 1923. Today, Neuland has become a popular alphabet to write with an edged pen because of its fairly simple execution and modern appearance. It is written with two pen angles, horizontal and vertical, to maintain the almost even weight of its letterform. It is a sans serif letter and only simple rules of execution are needed for its formation. Neuland provides a good opportunity for calligraphers to write in a modern interpretive way using heavyweight letters that create texture.

The future of calligraphy

A new interest in calligraphy appeared in the 1970s with Ann Camp, Ann Hechle, Donald Jackson and Sheila Waters in England, and Hermann Zapf, Werner Schneider, Friedrich Poppl, Gottfried Pott, and Katharina Peiper in Germany, plus Villu Toots from Estonia to name just a few. In America the revival of interest in calligraphy was due to William A. Dwiggins, James Hayes, Arnold Bank and Lloyd Reynolds among others. The list of influential calligraphers today from Europe, American and Australasia is endless and impressive. The art of calligraphy is flourishing!

The role of the calligrapher in the 21st century is to continue to enrich letterforms. Most calligraphers now

William Morris designs ▼
Ornamental initial letters from the *Kelmscott Chaucer*, published at the end of the 19th century.

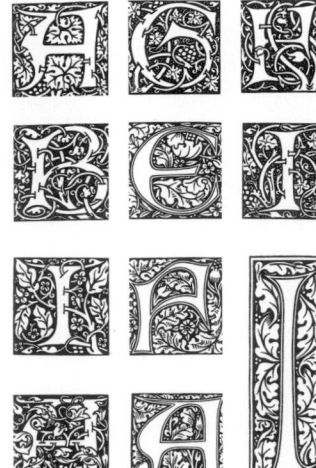

Modern techniques ▼
21st-century copy of an illuminated initial 'V' showing Jeremiah receiving the word from God, from the Book of Jeremiah (f.148) from The Winchester Bible (1160–75).

have at their disposal the ability to assimilate scripts from historical manuscripts, but that does not mean that they must stringently copy them. Rather, calligraphers should study them carefully, practise them diligently, adapt them sensitively and adopt their own creative styles. It is important to understand the tools and materials (including new technology), colour, design, space, rhythm and all the individual marks and gestures that can be made.

In the new millennium, technology for creating, designing and reproducing letterforms, calligraphy and illustration for advertising, commissions or personal pleasure, is developing at an ever-increasing rate. There are computer programs that can completely change the written word, twisting and altering it at a touch of a button. With the application of different tools the whole concept of creating exciting letterforms and creative, expressive lines becomes exhilarating. Results can be stunning. However, this new technology does not mean that traditional skills are no longer necessary – in fact, there is even more of a need to ensure that our basic learning of letterform and calligraphy remains sound.

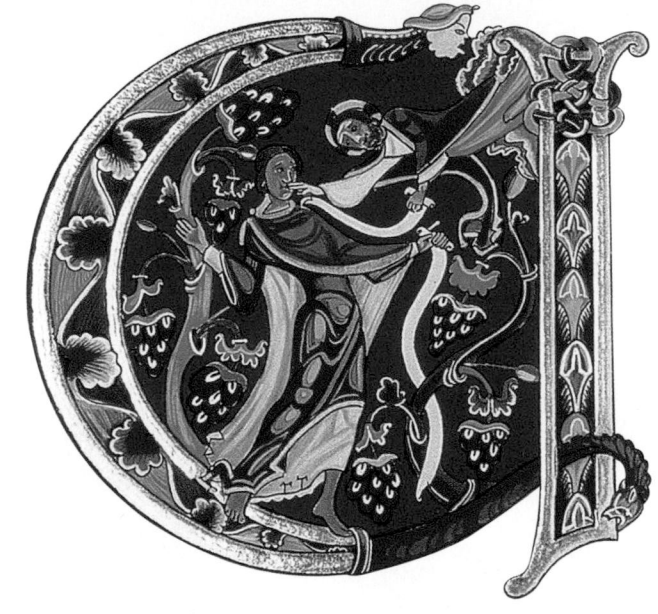

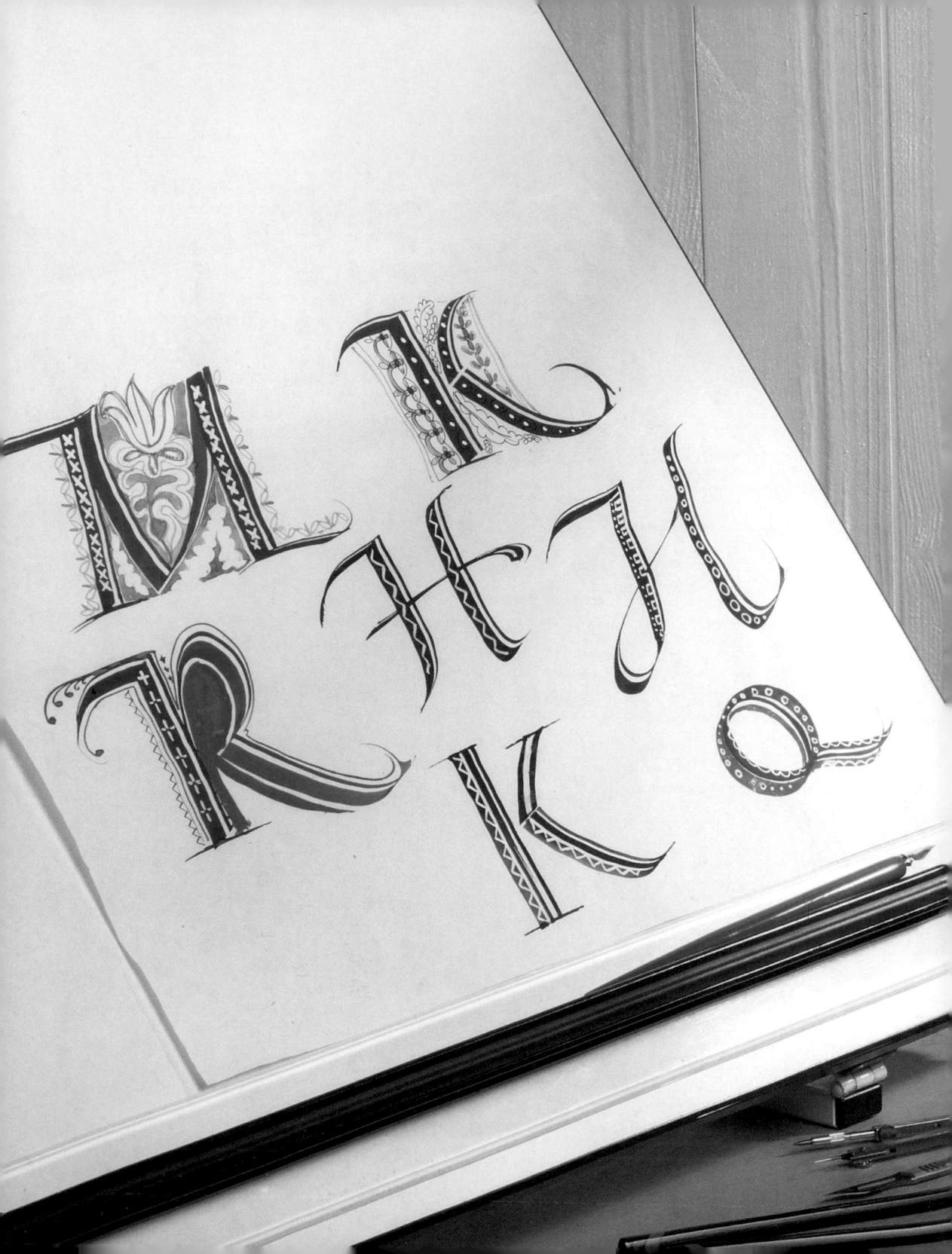

Getting Started

Putting pen to paper, or beginning any form of calligraphy practice requires some simple yet essential preparation. This section outlines the materials and equipment you will need to get started, explains the best way to set up your working space and teaches the fundamentals of penmanship, layout and design. As your enthusiasm grows, so will your interest in trying variants on the basics and this may require a variety of equipment. Visit a local supplier for art materials and before you buy be sure that the materials on offer will meet your needs. Use calligraphy suppliers' websites for details of more specialist tools.

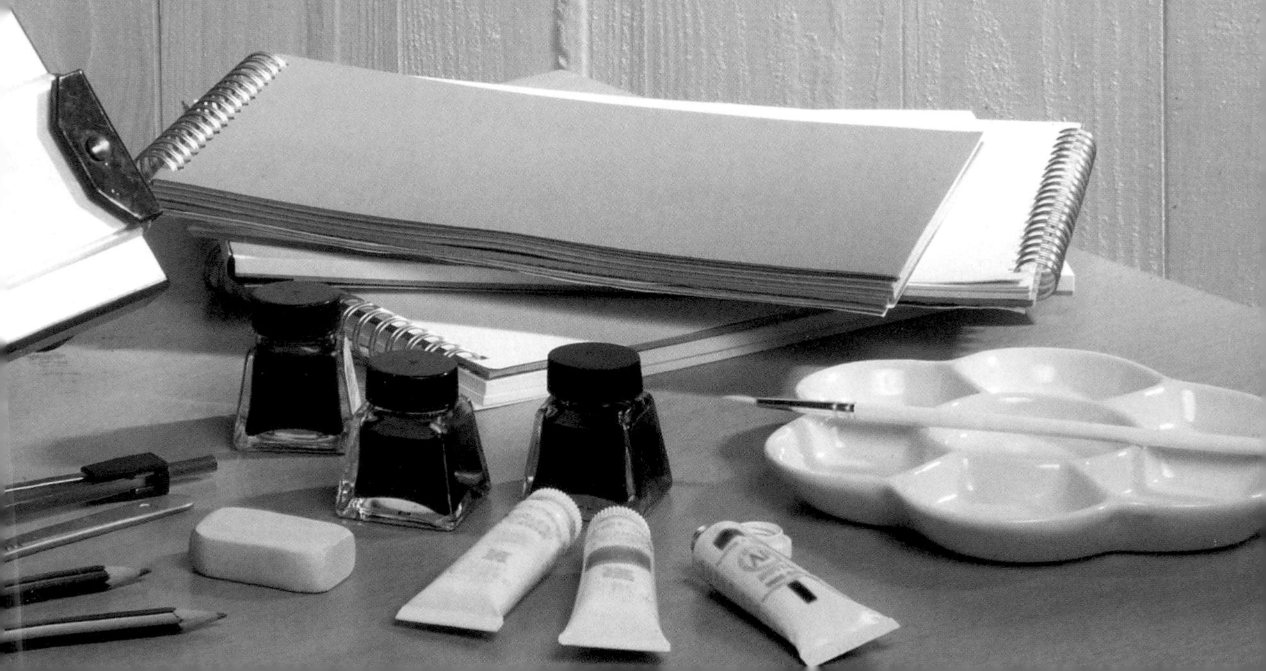

Pens

There are many different sizes and shapes of calligraphy pen, although the nearest supplier may only have a limited range. Check the pen has a wide nib at least 2mm (5/64in) in size. Left-handers should look for square-ended or left-oblique nibs.

Many calligraphers prefer a metal dip pen because it can be used with all kinds of paints and inks mixed to different colours and consistencies. While its name implies that it is dipped in ink, this is not always the case; feeding it with a paintbrush of mixed gouache paint allows good control of paint flow and consistency of colour density. The best metal nibs are modelled on the profile of the traditional quill, combining flexibility with sharpness. The dip pen is the nearest convenient equivalent to the quill, saving modern calligraphers the time and skill needed to cut and maintain that revered ancestor.

Pen sizes vary enormously, allowing large poster writing with perhaps a 2.5cm (1in) pen that demands a bold arm movement across the page; in contrast, small, delicate writing in a manuscript book would instead need a tiny nib, maybe just 1mm (3/64in) wide or smaller, and if choosing to write elegant Copperplate, then a flexible pointed nib is the only answer. In general, however, and certainly when starting out, it is best to begin in the middle range of these extremes, and study the letterforms at a size that allows you to see all the detail of construction, before going too small; a nib about 2.5mm (7/64in) is ideal. Other pens available to the calligrapher include larger poster pens, automatic pens, which come in many sizes, and ruling pens.

Felt-tipped pens and fountain pens are the most convenient of all calligraphic tools. They are available in bright colours and provide instant results with non-clogging inks. As the dye-based inks may fade in time they are best for practice and for short-term projects where the results will not be exposed to light for too long. The nibs flow well across smooth paper. Felt-tips will soften and lose their sharpness over time, so replace them frequently and before the writing suffers.

Pen manufacturers have not standardized their size coding, making instant comparisons difficult. One maker's smallest size is size 6, with its largest size 0, whereas most other makes increase their numbers with their size. This discrepancy only becomes apparent when working with different makes, so start with one complete set or just be prepared to make visual comparisons. Do not order by size number alone.

Dip pens ▶
A handle and a range of differently sized nibs make up the dip pen. There are several manufacturers. Some nibs have an integral reservoir, others have a slip-on version. Whatever pen collection is chosen, there will be a variety of nib sizes available, although the sizes may vary between manufacturers. Some makes are slightly right oblique, which will not suit left-handers, who should look out for square-ended or preferably left-oblique versions. Copperplate nibs are fine and can have a very distinctive elbow shape. For large, bold writing, explore the fun of enormous pens; they use a lot of ink, and dipping may be preferable to feeding with a brush.

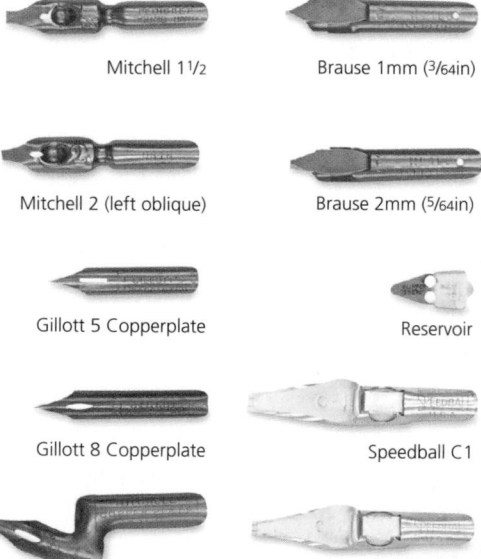

Mitchell 1 1/2

Brause 1mm (3/64in)

Mitchell 2 (left oblique)

Brause 2mm (5/64in)

Gillott 5 Copperplate

Reservoir

Gillott 8 Copperplate

Speedball C1

Mitchell Copperplate elbow

Speedball C2

Tip: New dip pens may need to be degreased at the writing edge. Clean the end with detergent or use saliva and a tissue until the ink coats the underside of the pen.

Tip: Push the nib firmly into the pen holder so that the dip pen does not shake when you write. Ensure the nib sits securely between any metal prongs inside the holder, and its outer shell.

Handle of pen

Larger pens ▶

There are nibs that are designed for the large writing found on posters, which are sometimes called poster pens. Automatic pens can be moved in any direction with continuous ink flow, and produce both very thin and contrasting thick lines. Each pen nib has a serrated side and a smooth side, and is used with the smooth side against the paper. It can be used either full width, or when worked in can also produce lines by turning on its thin edge. Ruling pens were traditionally used for drawing straight lines against a ruler, but calligraphers also use them for freer writing and wider versions have been invented specifically for creative calligraphy. The screw adjustment allows for cleaning and for varying line width.

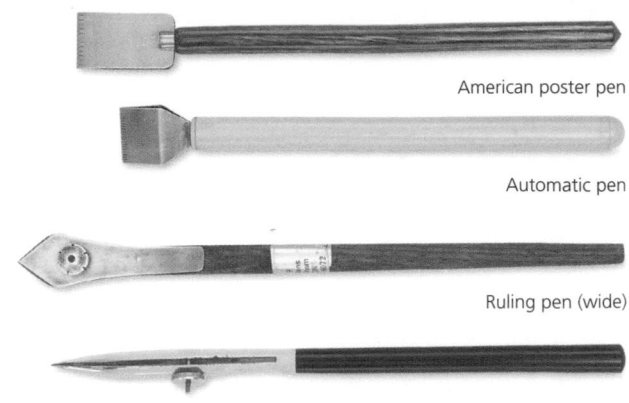

American poster pen

Automatic pen

Ruling pen (wide)

Ruling pen (technical drawing pen)

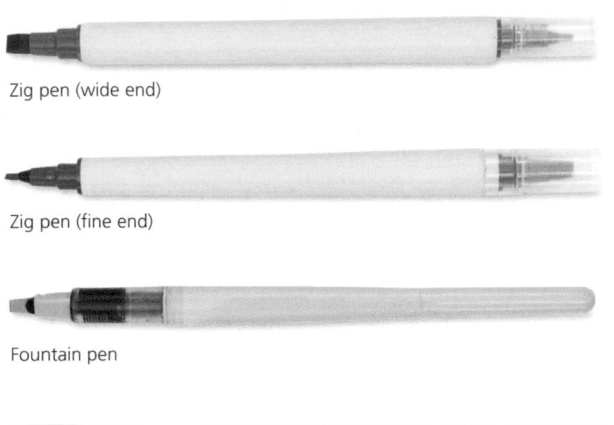

Zig pen (wide end)

Zig pen (fine end)

Fountain pen

Broad-edged brush

◀ Other types of pen

Personal taste will determine the other types of pen used. Felt-tipped pens are especially useful for quick work, and will travel well in a pocket. The ones with a nib at each end, in different sizes, are especially useful. Fountain pens are convenient; the ink is in cartridges so refilling is quick. Choose a make that supplies a flushing tool for washing out if the colours are to be changed frequently. Broad-edged brushes need to be nylon for springiness, not sable (too floppy) or bristle (too stiff).

Tip: If reading the nib size is a problem when changing nibs, buy a handle for every nib and label the handle with a sliver of paper fixed with transparent sticky tape.

Caring for your pens

Dip pens will last a very long time if they are cleaned after use. Do not allow them to rust. Store the spare nibs in a container that will allow some air circulation in case any are damp from cleaning. If nibs are kept attached to their handles, check them to see they have not rusted in. Store pens flat while drying, to prevent water causing rusting.

Materials
- *Water pot*
- *Old toothbrush*
- *Kitchen paper*

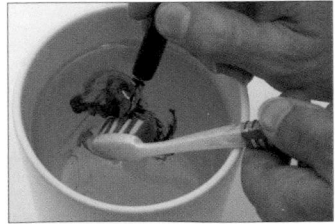

1 Clean the nib (while still attached to the handle) over your water pot, using a toothbrush, or water will run up the handle and cause rusting.

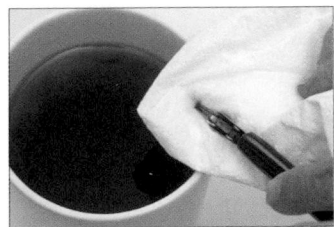

2 Once the nib has been cleaned, dry it (and the reservoir, if is a slip-on one) using kitchen paper.

Inks and paints

There are many inks available to the calligrapher. The most important quality of an ink or paint in the pen is that it should flow easily and not spread on the surface. Density of colour and light-fastness are important factors for finished work. Thus many calligraphers use Chinese or Japanese stick inks, or gouache paint, both of which are dense and opaque, or watercolours for more transparent effects. Bottled fountain pen inks are good for practising as they flow well. Waterproof inks are not recommended in the pen as they clog, and do not give sharp writing. They are better used much diluted for background washes. For beginners, fountain pens with broad calligraphy nibs provide inks in convenient cartridges and with a continuous flow. Felt-tipped pens are very successful for practising and have a range of calligraphy nibs. In both cases these inks are dye-based so they are free-flowing and translucent, but may fade on exposure to light.

Black inks

For black ink, Japanese or Chinese stick ink is recommended, purchased from a reliable source. Inks supplied for the tourist market will be for novelty value, not for ink quality. Be aware that whereas many stick inks are manufactured for the quality of their greys, Western calligraphers value black opacity in their inks. Some ink is supplied with helpful shade cards showing how black it is, and whether when thinner it is blue-grey or warm-grey. An alternative bottled version, known as Sumi Ink, is available for those who need their black ink constantly or instantly available.

Japanese stick ink ▼
Ready-to-use, Japanese stick ink comes, either in a bottle (water it down a little), or matured in a stick for grinding.

> **Tip:** When starting a new tube of gouache, you should discard the first squeeze of paint if it oozes any transparent liquid, as this can interfere with smooth writing qualities.

Gouache

Designers' gouache is an important choice when using colour. Gouache is opaque, so the colour will show up when writing on coloured backgrounds. Most colours are lightproof so ideal for finished pieces that will be on display. The choice of colours is vast, but by experimentation with mixing, only six colours are needed. They are: two reds – a pinkish one (magenta) and an orangey one (scarlet); two blues – ultramarine (makes purple with magenta) and cerulean, or a cheaper phthalo blue (makes bright greens); and two yellows – lemon (for bright greens) and a warmer hint of orange yellow. Imitation gold paint is most successful for calligraphy in gouache form; bottled versions will be fine for other applications but separate too quickly for pen work.

Colour wheel ▶
The three primary colours are red, yellow and blue. They are the only colours that cannot be made by mixing two other colours. The three secondary colours are green, orange and violet and they are each a mixture of two primary colours. The secondary colours are positioned between the colours

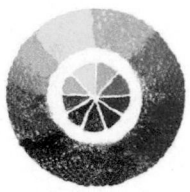

from which they are made. The six tertiary colours (red-orange, red-violet, yellow-green, yellow-orange, blue-green and blue-violet) are made by mixing a primary colour with an adjacent secondary colour. The tertiary colours are positioned between the primary and secondary colours from which they are made.

Tubes of gouache ▼
Designers' gouaches come in tubes. Squeeze out 1cm (1/2in) in a palette and add water by the brush full until a single (light) cream consistency is achieved, or until it flows well in the pen.

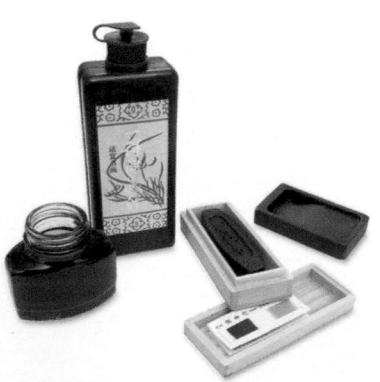

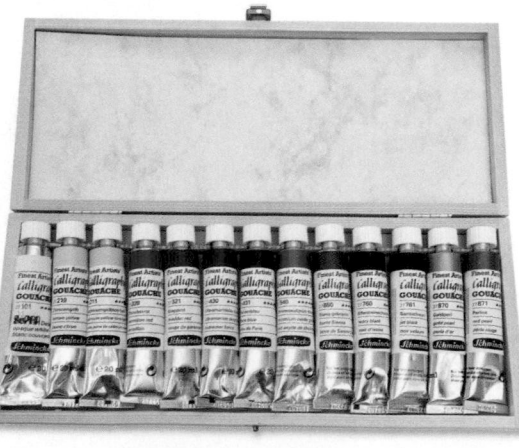

Watercolour paints

These paints are transparent and economical to use. Their transparency makes them ideal for use on white paper, which shows off their true colours. Watercolour paint can be effectively used when writing one letter on top of another. If a wet letter touches another the colours will blend. Writing in watercolour is easy to do because the paint flows easily from the pen. However, care should be taken when writing in watercolour on to coloured paper as its transparency will encourage it to disappear. As with gouaches, only six colours are required if they are mixed. In some watercolour paintboxes the selection has already been made.

Mixing watercolour paint ▼
Watercolours come in tubes and in pans. Tubes are useful when mixing up a large quantity, perhaps for a series of background washes. Brushes for fine painting need to keep their fine point, with no stray hairs. Choose size 0 or 1, springy acrylic or more absorbent sable.

Tip: Always replace the tops of paints immediately, as oxidation will occur and the paint will harden.

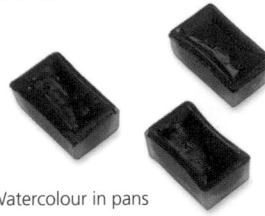

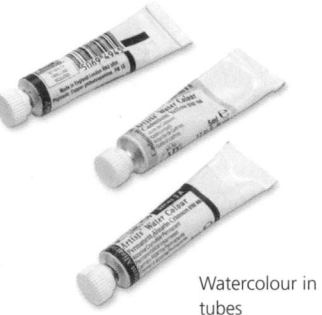

Watercolour in pans

Watercolour in tubes

Other types of paint

Bottled acrylic inks are ideal for making wash backgrounds for calligraphy. This is because they dry waterproof, making a non-porous surface on which to write. Do not try putting acrylic ink in the pen, however, as it will not give sharp writing and the pen will need to be cleaned before it dries. Casein-based paints are bright colours that behave like household emulsion (latex) paint. Use these only as backgrounds. 'Bleedproof white' is like a gouache in a bottle and is very opaque. Once water is added it works well in a dip pen fed with a brush, producing very sharp writing.

Bottled acrylic ink ▼
This type of paint works well for creating wash backgrounds.

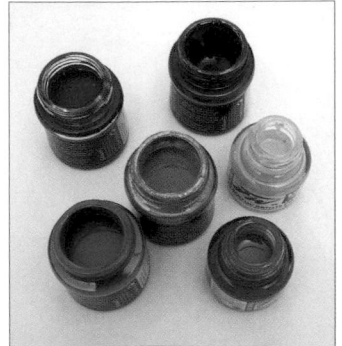

Practice exercise: **Using an inkstone**

An inkstone is a small sloping block with raised sides and a slightly abrasive surface. The ink is rubbed down with a stick and water to produce ink in small quantities as needed. In this way the calligrapher controls the density of colour and texture. The consistency of the ink can be controlled by fixing the amount of water and the rubbing time.

Materials
• *Water: distilled or boiled tap water*
• *Inkstone and stick*
• *Brush*
• *Cloth*

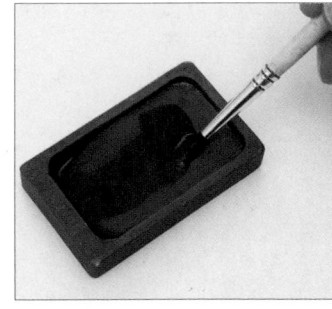

1 Put a few drops of water on the flat surface of the inkstone with a brush.

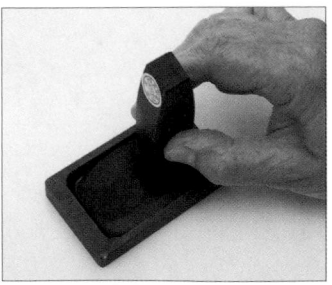

2 Rub the ink stick firmly in a circular motion for a minute or two to mix some of the ink with the water.

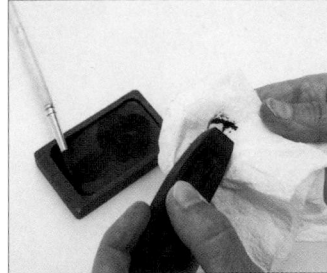

3 When it feels sticky, use a wet paintbrush to move the ink into the trough and repeat the grinding with fresh water until you have sufficient. Do not leave the stick to soak, or it will crack; dry it with a cloth.

Papers

There are many different papers on the market. They are intended more for watercolour artists than for calligraphers, so it is helpful to know which papers are most suitable for writing. A large supply of practice paper is probably the best investment, in order to try out designs and revise the writing many times before using 'best' paper.

Practice or layout paper conveniently comes in pads, in several sizes. Choose a size that has enough space to do paste-ups and expansive writing. Layout paper is very white and is about 50gsm (23lb). This is thin enough to see through and to have a grid of ruled lines placed underneath as guidelines. Photocopy paper is a good alternative that is available from office suppliers, and comes in large packs. It is 80gsm (39lb) making it thicker than layout paper, and therefore it may not be possible to see fine lines drawn underneath.

Paper for a final, 'best' piece needs to be thicker. Thicker paper will wrinkle less when written on, and will not be so easily bruised – thin paper poorly handled will show every little crease, and may take on more creases when erasing lines. A first 'best' paper might be cartridge, as this is available in pads and is very inexpensive. Choose at least 150gsm (71lb) and look for acid free, so it will not go brown.

Better quality papers have some rag content, with various surface treatments and a wide sizing range, which affects the absorbency. Thus, blotting paper is unsized. Hot-pressed watercolour papers are suitable for calligraphy as they have a very smooth surface and are well-sized so the ink will stay where it is placed, resulting in sharp writing. The paper accepts paint well when drawing or painting additional features. Choose 200gsm (95lb) or thicker, if planning to get the paper wet. Craft suppliers usually stock hot-pressed watercolour paper in a limited range. Internally sized print-making paper has a softer surface, accepts writing very well and is popular with calligraphers, but care should be taken when using an eraser because this disturbs its surface.

Papers with a texture, such as the more popular 'not' (meaning 'not hot-pressed') and 'rough' watercolour papers can impart an interesting broken effect to large writing but are an impeding factor when trying to write in small pens. As a general rule, look for smooth surfaced papers. These surfaces are, however, ideal for background washes as the texture gives added character. With experience, it becomes worth searching out more specialist suppliers with a wider range of papers that have different characteristics.

Types of paper ▼
From left to right: layout paper is thin, white paper used for practice. Cartridge paper is an inexpensive high-quality paper. Hot-pressed watercolour paper is a good quality paper used for finished work, while watercolour paper comes in a variety of qualities and may be textured.

Tip: If paper is absorbent and makes the ink bleed, try spraying it first with a cheap hairspray.

Other papers

There is a whole range of coloured papers which are useful for making small artefacts and for taking the place of coloured washes. Some surfaces have a 'laid' effect of parallel lines; one side will be smoother, check to see which is easier for writing. Pastel papers – bright and subtle colours for use with pastels – accept ink very well (but not small writing). Investigate handmade Indian papers – not all accept ink without bleeding but some are fun to try.

Layout paper   Cartridge paper   Hot-pressed watercolour paper   Textured watercolour paper

Practice exercise: **Removing a mistake**

It is worth investing in thicker, good quality paper for important work, as small corrections can be made by scraping and smoothing down.

Materials
- *Good quality paper*
- *Dip pen*
- *Ink*
- *Scalpel or craft (utility) knife*
- *Putty eraser or similar*
- *Fixative or hairspray*

> **Tip:** Always store paper flat. Try not to over-handle it as damage can occur easily, making tiny creases that are impossible to remove.

> **Tip:** For washes, if paper is under 300gsm (142lb) stretch it. Soak it in water for 5–10 minutes, then smooth over a board with a sponge, before securing the edges with brown tape.

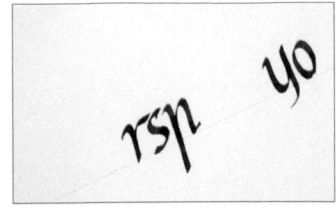

1 If a mistake has been made, all is not lost. First wait for the ink to dry completely.

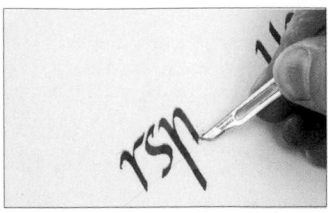

2 Gently scrape with a curved blade to remove the error.

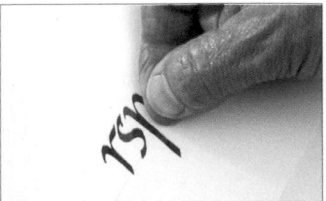

3 Lift off residue with a putty eraser or similar. Rub the surface with a hard smooth object or your fingernail to repair the surface, and lightly spray with fixative or hairspray to seal it.

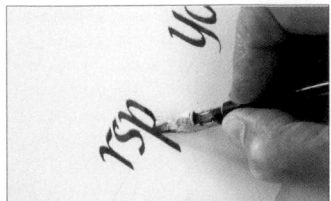

4 Rewrite when the repaired surface is completely dry.

Other types of paper ▼
Pastel papers such as Canson mi-teintes are heavy French papers in a series of colours, with a 'vellum' texture on one side and smooth on the other. Canson Ingres papers are a lighter weight than the mi-teintes and come in a series of colours. Khadi are heavy Indian handmade papers in a huge range of qualities and textures.

Vellum ▼
Writing material made from animal skins is called vellum. It costs more than paper, but offcuts can be found in specialist stores. This type of material is valued for prestige items such as illuminated manuscripts as it behaves well with gesso gilding. If you are using vellum for illumination it should need no extra preparation, but a final sanding with 400 grade 'wet and dry' abrasive paper may be necessary for sharp writing.

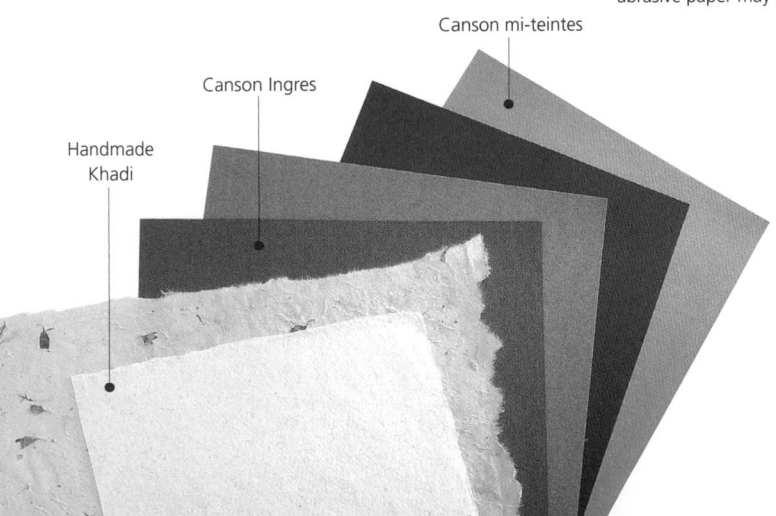

Canson mi-teintes

Canson Ingres

Handmade Khadi

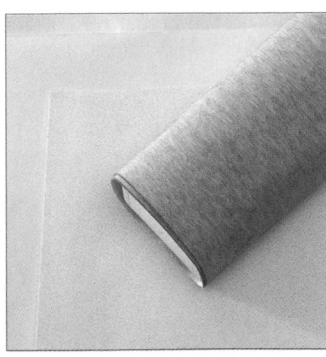

Abrasive paper block and vellum

Gilding materials

Gold leaf has a special attraction for calligraphers because it adds a sumptuous touch to lettering. It is useful to accumulate all the accoutrements available for developing this branch of decoration.

Loose leaf and transfer gold

A sheet of gold is thinner than paper and as delicate to handle as gossamer, so it is supplied interleaved in books of 25 leaves. The most flimsy to handle is the loose form ('loose leaf'). There is another version attached to a backing paper; most suppliers call this form 'transfer gold' but be aware there are differences between countries on this labelling. Gold leaf should be at least 23¼ carat as lower carats could tarnish with time. Gold also comes in two thicknesses, single and double (or extra thick). Double is useful for building up layers after the first layer has stuck to the base glue; layering will add depth to the shine. Gold leaf needs to be treated with care as it is expensive. It can be obtained from specialist art suppliers.

Other golds

Dutch metals or schlag are made from brass and other metals and are thicker, so they will not behave in the same way as gold leaf. They are much cheaper than gold and are available in unusual colours. They need to be applied with acrylic glues.

Gold and silver powders need to be mixed with glue and painted; imitation gold gouache can be very successful and works well in the pen, whereas bottled gold inks are only good for painting. Real gold for painting or writing comes as a tablet, originally supplied in a small shell and known as shell gold.

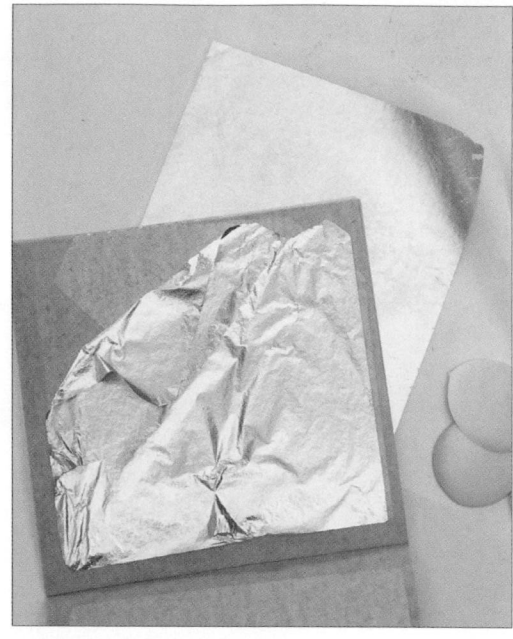

Loose leaf and transfer gold ▲
Laying gold leaf or gold transfer is a very delicate process as it is a fine, clinging material that needs to be placed on an adhesive background. Loose leaf or transfer gold is ideal for decorating a page with a highlighted initial letter or filling in an ornament.

Tip: It is useful to experiment with other forms of metallic leaf that are available. These include palladium leaf, derived from platinum, and silver leaf.

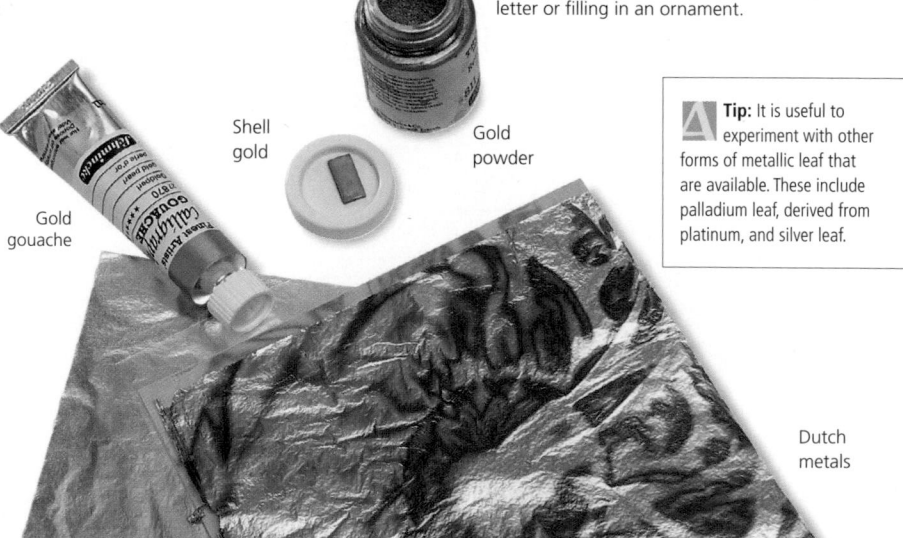

Shell gold

Gold powder

Gold gouache

Dutch metals

Gesso

Gold leaf needs a glue base in order to attach it to paper or vellum; the form familiar from historical illuminated manuscripts is gesso, which gives a cushioned or raised effect. The ancient skills for making and using gesso have been passed down through generations and remain the most successful and yet the most exacting of techniques. The gesso used for gilding is not the same as that manufactured for gilding wooden frames – the latter are oil-based and would stain paper or vellum. Gesso used in calligraphy may be applied with a quill or a brush. The substance has a slightly sticky surface once it has been activated.

Gesso is an ideal choice of platform for creating raised gold – by placing golf leaf on top of a raised surface to create a very shiny three-dimensional effect. It can take a while to prepare gesso if created from its raw materials but the results are well worth the effort.

Gesso ▶
Essentially a mixture of plaster and glue, gesso is solid but fairly flexible when dry. It is the ideal base for gold decoration, providing an even surface for gilding to take place.

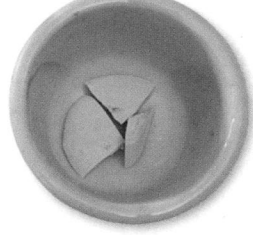

Gesso

Other glues

A number of other glues can be used for gilding. Gum ammoniac is a traditional sticky plant residue, sometimes available ready made. Modern glues include PVA or 'white glue', and acrylic gloss medium – a vehicle intended for extending and imparting shine to acrylic paints – but ideal as a glue base for gilding. Acrylic gold size stays sticky when dry (like adhesive tape), and is useful for sticking the Dutch metals.

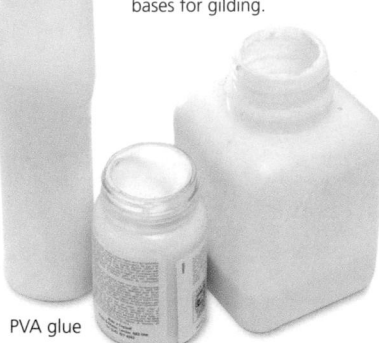

Bases for gilding ▼
PVA (white) glue, acrylic gloss medium and water gold size can all be used as bases for gilding.

PVA glue

Water gold size   Acrylic gloss medium

Tools

A number of tools are needed for successful gilding, including a small pair of scissors (keep them polished and clean or they will stick to the gold), tweezers and a burnisher. Special burnishers are available with different shaped ends for polishing the gold and persuading it to stick in awkward corners. Agate burnishers, which are 'dog-tooth' in shape, are the most commonly available; their tips must be protected in a soft sleeve to prevent scratches, which would damage the gold. Psilomelanite burnishers have generally replaced the more valued haematite burnishers – a lipstick-shaped tool and the highest prized tool for getting the gold to stick and obtaining a good shine when polishing. Laying of the gold and the initial polishing is generally done through a sheet of glassine paper, which is a shiny paper sometimes seen in photograph albums. A dry, soft brush is useful for removing the excess gold leaf surrounding a gilded letter.

Tip: Take care when handling the flimsy gold leaf. Clean your scissors with silk before cutting so that the leaf does not stick to the scissors.

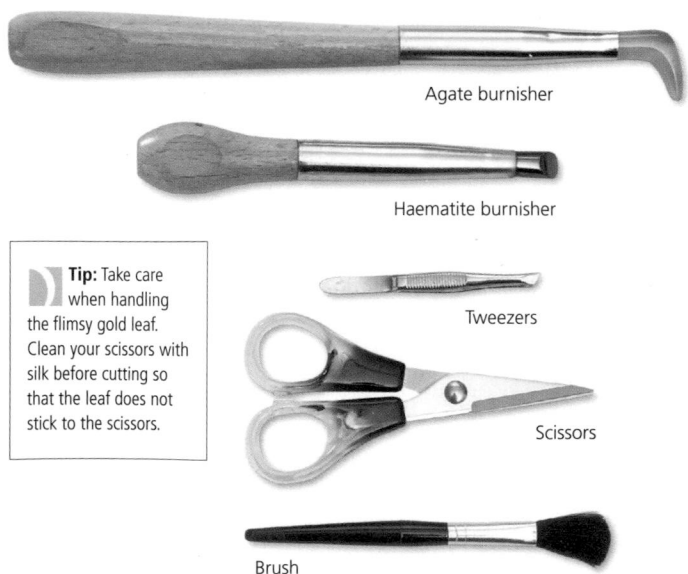

Agate burnisher

Haematite burnisher

Tweezers

Scissors

Brush

Setting up

To get the best results from calligraphy, a comfortable work surface is needed and a desk with a slope is the best option. Choose a chair that is the correct height so that it will support your back. A relaxed posture will encourage a consistent ink flow. Once you begin work, remember to take frequent breaks. You may find it helpful to do some stretches during this time.

The drawing board

Make a drawing-board out of a sheet of plywood, or MDF (medium-density fiberboard). Do not use hardboard as this will bend. Have it cut to size, if possible at approximately 60 x 45cm (24 x 18in). Customize this to your own needs by applying a padded writing surface. The simplest method is to iron at least six sheets of newspaper to remove all creases, attach this to the board with masking tape, then attach a final white cover of cartridge paper, or better still, white blotting paper. Tape the paper all around the board with masking tape, but ensure the tape does not go over the edges of the board, as this could hinder the use of a T-square.

There are many ways of positioning the board. It can be positioned on a table of comfortable height, propped up with some books. Alternatively, two boards hinged together with piano hinges can be used, so that the book props provide infinite adjustment without slipping.

If the single board slips on the table, try attaching it at the base with white-tack or a strip of non-slip rug underlay. If a steeper board is preferred, position the narrow side on your lap, rest it on the table edge, and adjust the distance between chair and table. If possible, sit near a window or good light source, with the light coming from the left if right-handed, or from the right if left-handed. For evening work, a lamp that can be adjusted to spotlight the writing area would be a major advantage. If intending to work at night using colour, consider using a daylight bulb as it will show the colours in a more realistic light.

The final refinement of the board is made by attaching a guard sheet. Take a strip of paper – fold a sheet diagonally to make it wider if necessary – and attach it left and right of the board so that the top edge sits where you would be writing. This ensures your hand will always rest on the guard sheet and not on the writing paper, preventing the paper from becoming greasy. If you forget to use a guard sheet, it may become harder to write – as you meet the greasier part of the paper, the ink will resist.

Prepared drawing board ▼
Whether using a simple sheet of wood, or a commerically produced drawing board, it needs to be well padded, with the padding taped down. Note the gap between the tape and the edge, allowing the T-square to operate. Attach the guard sheet or keep it free.

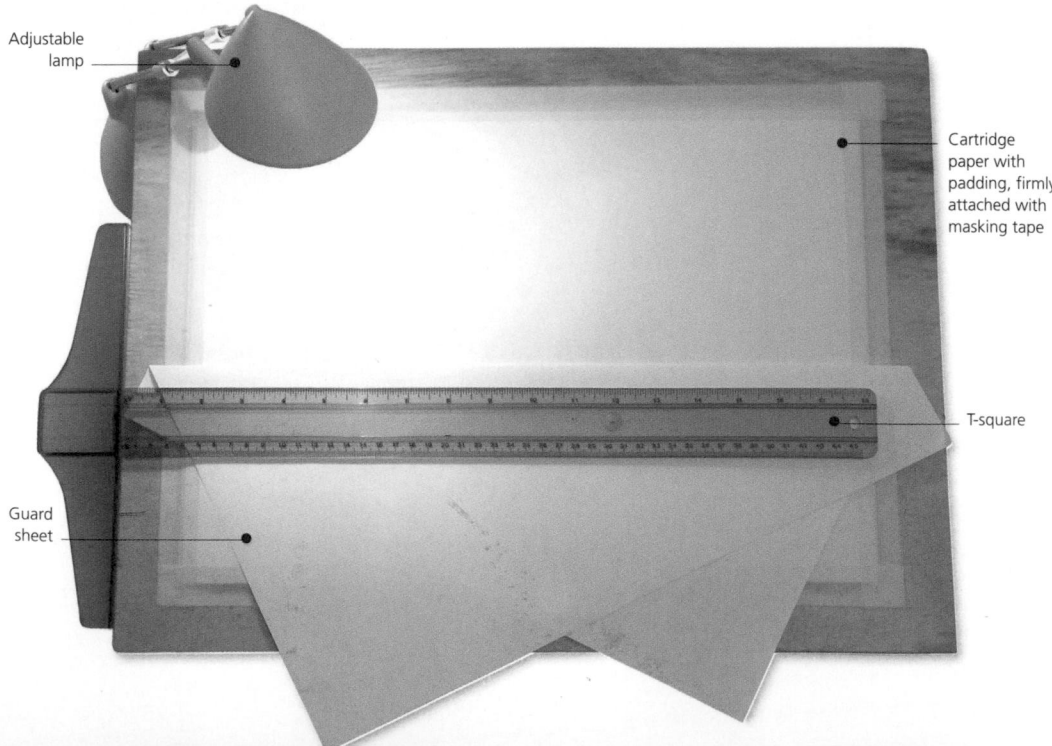

Adjustable lamp

Cartridge paper with padding, firmly attached with masking tape

T-square

Guard sheet

Useful tools

A ruler with clear markings for the accurate mark-up of lines is one of the most essential items. A metal edge is also a useful tool. A ruler or metal edge can be used when cutting paper; work on a self-healing cutting mat or use thick cardboard. Bone folders may be used for scoring and making crisp and accurate folds.

A T-square is a useful, time-saving luxury, as line markings need only be made down one side; parallel lines can then be ruled across. This is why the edge of the board should not be inhibited by masking tape. A set square (triangle) can be used to rule right angles and helps maintain pen angles of 45, 30 or 60 degrees. A protractor is used for measuring letter angles.

Masking tape can be used to attach paper to a sloping board to prevent it from sliding off. Tape can also be stuck in place to preserve a clean strip of paper when using colour washes.

It is useful to have a supply of 2H and 4H pencils for ruling lines and HB pencils for making notes. It is important that the pencils used for ruling lines are well sharpened. Always keep a soft eraser at hand.

> **Tip:** Using scissors, cut a bottle-sized hole in a small bath sponge to keep your ink bottle safe from tipping. If ink does spill, some will be absorbed by the sponge.

Basic techniques

These are techniques that you are likely to use repeatedly. It is important to do them correctly to avoid damaging materials and equipment.

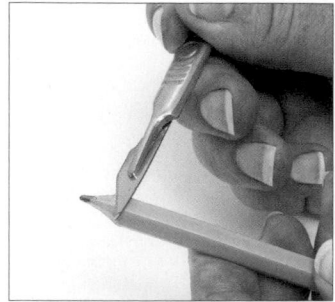

Sharpening a pencil ▲
Hard pencils (2H, 3H, 4H) will stay sharp for longer than soft pencils. Soft pencils (HB, B, 2B etc.) will break under pressure and become blunt quickly. A standard pencil sharpener will do most of the job (if it is new), but the final touch is to shave away the tip with a craft knife.

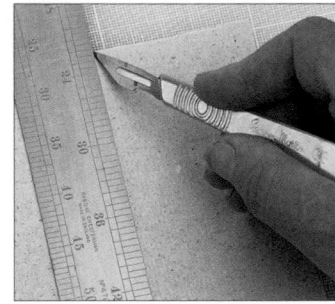

Cutting paper ▲
Always use a sharp blade. If it is blunt the blade will need to be pressed harder and the chances of it slipping are higher, with possible resultant injury. Cut against a metal ruler, or a plastic ruler with a cutting edge. Use a cutting mat or thick cardboard, such as the back of a layout pad. Cut with several light strokes rather than one heavy one, and arrange the paper so you can make cutting strokes towards your body. Cutting from left to right is less controlled and the knife may slip.

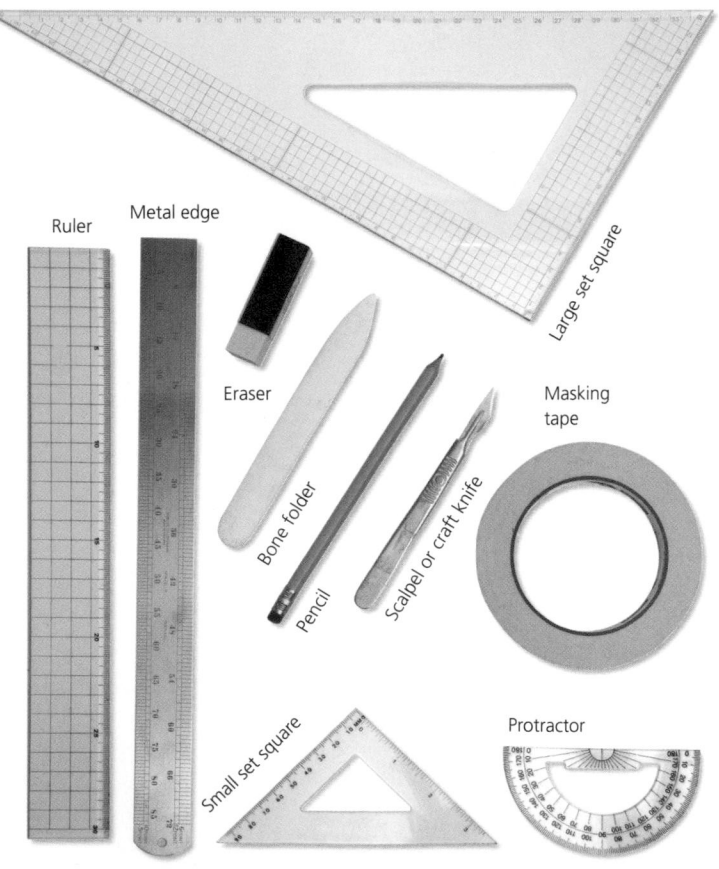

Ruler
Metal edge
Large set square
Eraser
Bone folder
Pencil
Scalpel or craft knife
Masking tape
Small set square
Protractor

Basic penmanship

Once all the necessary equipment has been assembled, you can prepare to begin your calligraphy. To produce good work a relaxed posture is needed, as well as an arm position that encourages a steady flow of ink. Spend some time adjusting your position so that you are comfortable – learning calligraphy should always be an enjoyable experience, but it also requires much concentration. Work is more likely to be successful if calligraphy is practised on a regular basis and all the equipment is kept in one place. You may prefer to work on a drawing board resting on a table top, or secured to the edge of a table. Alternatively, the drawing board can be rested in your lap, or flat on a table, resting your weight on the non-writing arm so you have free movement with your pen. Remember to lay padding underneath your paper as this will help the flexibility of the nib, and prevent it from scratching on the paper. Make sure that the writing sheets are fixed to the board securely. Light should fall evenly on the working area, and although daylight is best, an adjustable lamp will illuminate the page.

Terminology

Calligraphy uses special terminology to describe the constituent parts of letters and words, and the way they are written. The style or 'hand' in which the writing is created is composed of letterforms. These are divided into capital, or upper-case letters, and smaller, lower-case letters (traditionally called majuscule and minuscule). Text is usually written in lower-case letters because they are easier to read than solid blocks of capital letters. The x-height is the term used for the height of the full letter in capitals (the space an 'X' occupies) and for the main body of the letter for lower case, excluding ascenders and descenders. In lines of text, the gap between x-heights, which accomodates ascenders or descenders, is known as the interlinear space. The spaces enclosed within letters are called counters.

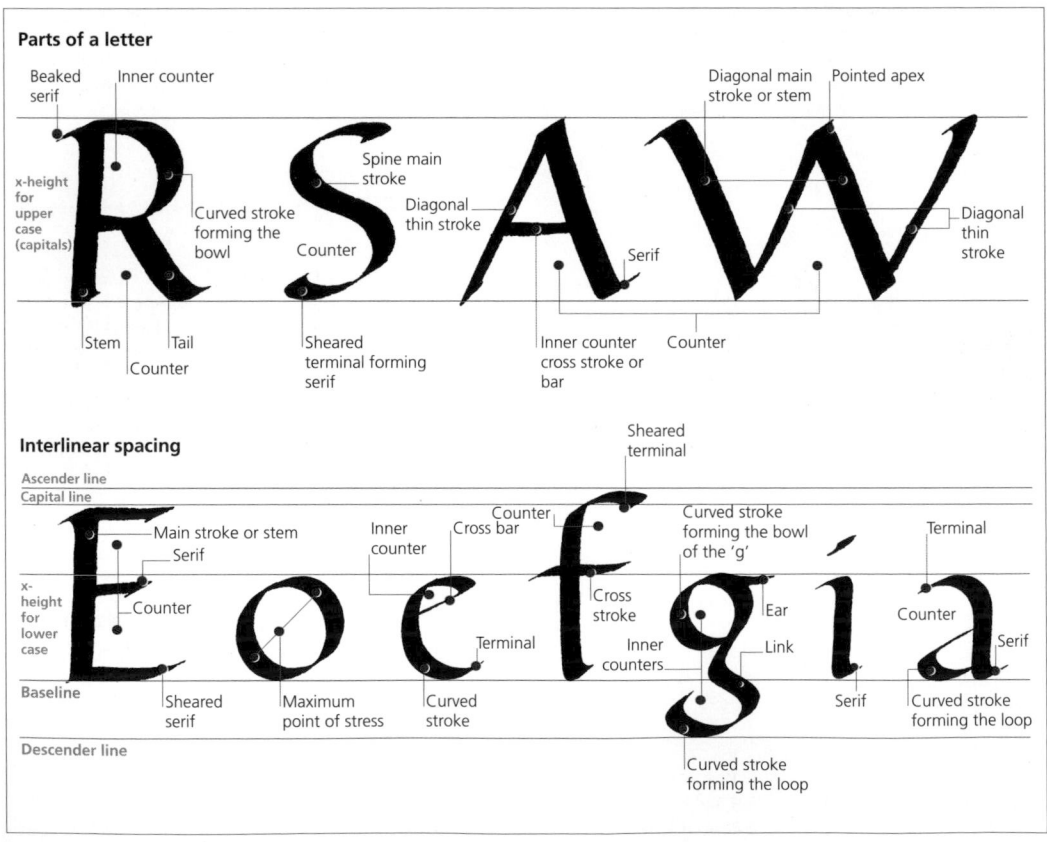

Parts of a letter

Beaked serif · Inner counter · Diagonal main stroke or stem · Pointed apex · x-height for upper case (capitals) · Spine main stroke · Curved stroke forming the bowl · Diagonal thin stroke · Counter · Serif · Diagonal thin stroke · Stem · Tail · Counter · Sheared terminal forming serif · Inner counter cross stroke or bar · Counter

Interlinear spacing

Ascender line · Capital line · Main stroke or stem · Serif · Inner counter · Cross bar · Counter · Sheared terminal · Curved stroke forming the bowl of the 'g' · Terminal · x-height for lower case · Counter · Cross stroke · Ear · Counter · Terminal · Inner counters · Link · Serif · Baseline · Sheared serif · Maximum point of stress · Curved stroke · Serif · Curved stroke forming the loop · Descender line · Curved stroke forming the loop

Essential techniques

The techniques detailed below are essential to creating good calligraphy. Carrying them out properly will ensure that letterforms are properly proportioned, well spaced and at the correct angle. It is important to practise some of these, such as using a broad nib and holding the pen at a constant angle, before you begin to write letters and words.

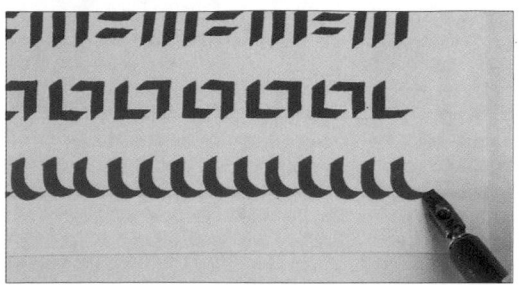

Using a broad nib ▲
A broad nib, pen or brush is the essential tool for calligraphy. When the pen is held in the hand it forms an angle to the horizontal writing line, known as the pen angle. It takes some adjustment to use this sort of tool after using pointed pens and pencils. It is helpful to pay careful attention to just keeping the whole nib edge against the paper when writing to avoid ragged strokes. Try some zig-zags – aim to create the thinnest and thickest of the marks by moving the pen along its side and along its width to appreciate its extremes.

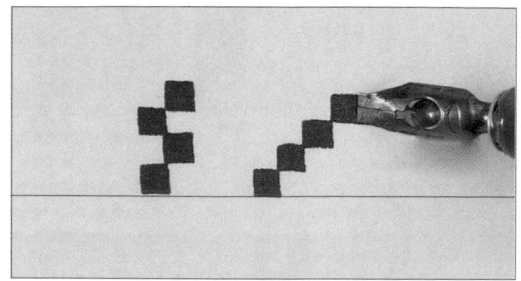

Measuring nib widths ▲
Whatever nib size is used, the height of the letter is determined by using a 'ladder' of nib widths. A baseline is ruled first and a broad-edged pen held at right angles (90 degrees) to the line. A clear mark should be made, long enough to be a square. The pen is moved upwards and marks are drawn so that they just touch; forming a 'stairway' shape or a 'ladder'. An alphabet exemplar will indicate the number of nib-widths needed for the x-height of a hand. Use that measurement for ruling all the lines.

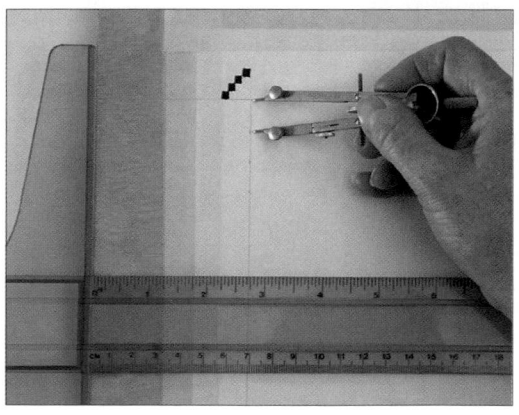

Ruling the lines ▲
The standard method is to mark repeat measurements (taken from the nib width exercise above) down both sides of the paper, then join them up with a ruler. Another way is to use a scrap of paper with a straight edge, mark a short series of accurate measurements and transfer these across (this is not suitable for measurements below 4mm (5/32in) but is accurate enough in larger sizes). Marking down just one side of the paper is sufficient if using a T-square. Attach the marked sheet to the board top and bottom to prevent movement. The T-square is used to rule parallel lines across the page.

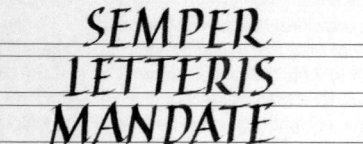

Leaving enough spaces ▲
Take the measurement of the required number of nib-widths for the x-height. For lower case letters such as Italic, rule all the lines to this measurement and leave two gaps between x-heights, to allow for ascenders and descenders. When ruling up for writing entirely capitals, it is sufficient to use a single gap, or even less, as there are no extensions.

Layout and design

The skill of how and where to place a piece of text or an illustration on a page is paramount. Deciding how the work is displayed, how much space there is for margins or how text is aligned, is as much a skill as the calligraphy itself, and good design can really transform the appearance of a piece of calligraphy. A good formula for the measurement of margins is to make the top margin twice the size of the largest interlinear space in the finished design, the side margins about 1 1/2 times

the size of the top margin and the bottom margin twice the size of the top margin. The design of the page is influenced by letterform size and the length of the written line. Other factors to be considered are the amount of colour or illustrative content, the creative stamp the calligrapher wishes to place on the design, and the function or purpose of the final artwork. It is extremely important to plan the design of a piece thoroughly before you start writing the text.

Different styles of layout

The ideas shown here offer some layout options that could be used for a piece of simple text. These designs can easily be altered or combined to produce many artistic variations. Think about the meaning of the text and the flow of the words and how this could be reflected in the layout of the piece.

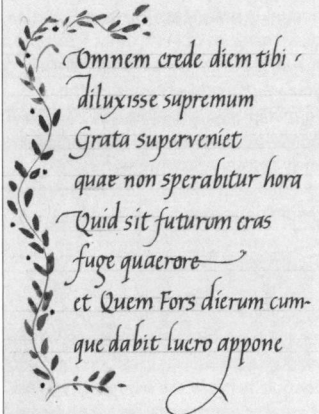

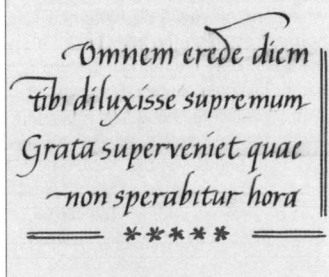

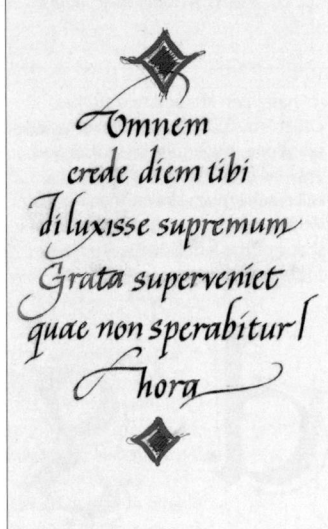

Aligned left ▲
This text has been aligned or ranged left with a margin, which has a decorative design of foliage. The text is slightly ragged on the right-hand side, but because the lines are around the same length the space on the right hand is acceptable. Left alignment is commonly used, particularly in practice work, as it requires very little line adjustment and planning. The text always starts in the same place.

Aligned right ▲
This text is right aligned, or ranged right. The layout is not often chosen as it is difficult to achieve – but can be effective when used with short lines. The ending of each line must be accurate for the text to align. Right aligned text is often used with other right-ranged elements such as illustrations or photographs.

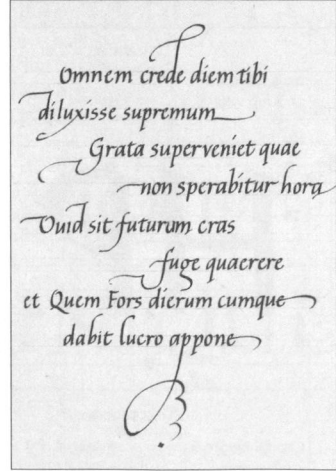

Centred ▲
This is a centred layout that features a small design top and bottom. This is an acceptable standard layout because it looks balanced and is very suitable for both long and short lines of writing. However, producing a centred piece of work requires both accuracy and patience because the length of the individual lines must be established first before the layout can be finalized.

Asymmetrical ▶
This is an asymmetric layout, which looks centred on the paper but the lines are of varying lengths. This is a useful layout for poetry or prose that has extra long lines which need to be incorporated into a space. The top line and the bottom line are centred, and the intermediate lines are ranged from right to left in a way that makes the whole piece look balanced.

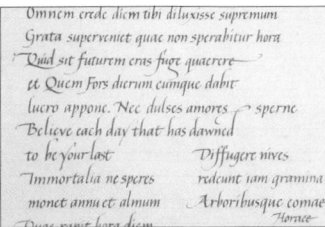

Quid sit futurim cras fuge quarere
et Quem fors dierum cumque dabit lucro appone
Nec dulcis amores sperne puer neque tu choreas
Horace *Donec virenti canities abest morosa*

◀ **Focal point to the left**

◀ **Focal point to the left**

This is also an asymmetrical layout with a focal point to the left, which carries the weight and colour of the image. It gives a feeling of freedom to the writing. This layout can create atmosphere and give a feel to the design in hand. However, its use is entirely dependent on the individual calligrapher's feel for balance and the shape of the composition.

Marking up

Making a rough or mock-up of the layout is a good method of transcribing the text and finalizing the design. This is called 'cut and paste' or 'paste-up'.

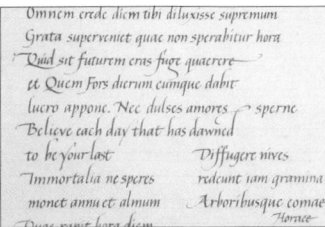

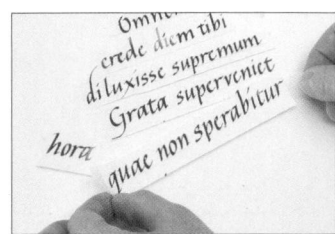

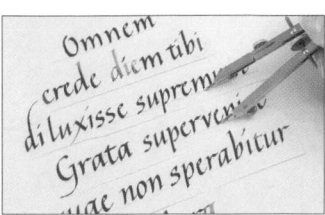

1 Choose the preferred text, the letter size and the script that will be used. Measure the pen nib widths and rule up the page. Write the text carefully. If a mistake is made write the word again correctly and proceed with the rest of the text.

2 Cut the text into strips and place into a layout. Remove any incorrect words and replace with the correct text. Paste the strips into an ordered layout using re-positional tape or glue. Do not use a ruler or lines at this stage – just use your 'eye' to place the strips.

3 Measure the distances between the baselines of the writing. They will vary from line to line but not significantly. Choose the most suitable distance (interlinear space) which should not be too close or too spaced as the text will not read well. Once the distance from baseline to baseline has been chosen, rule up a sheet of practice paper with all the required baselines, equidistant from each other.

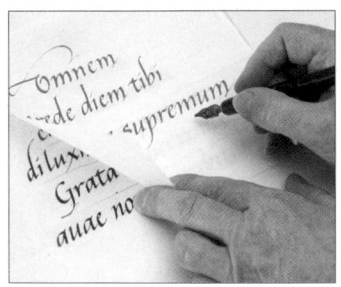

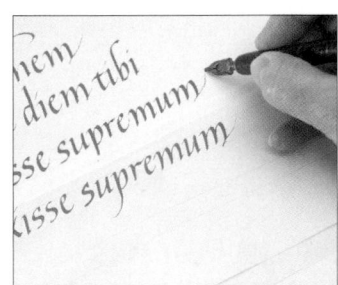

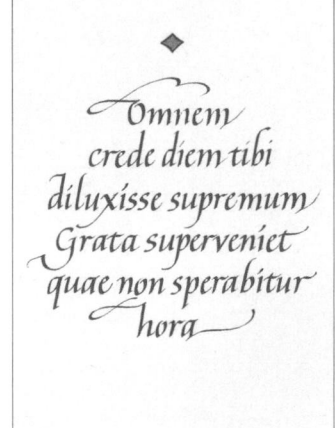

4 Overlay your paste-up work with the newly lined paper and write it out once more. Refine the letterforms and adjust the spacing.

> **Tip:** Always write the first 'practice' text in dark coloured ink so that it is easily seen through the practice paper.

5 This is the penultimate piece of work. Rule up on good quality paper using this last sheet as a line guide. You are now ready to write. Fold over the written piece line by line, to place as a guide under each new writing line. This ensures no spelling mistakes are made and each line that you write will start and end in the correct place.

6 The finished calligraphy can be decorated at the top with a little gilded diamond.

DEFG
KLMN   1 2 3 4 5 6
PQRSTU   7 8 9 10
PQRSTU   Æ Å Ø Ê Ë É
VWXYZ&   &!?ß

124 0 0 E

MRSEH

Alphabets

One of the joys of calligraphy is being able to choose a script that in some way expresses the meaning of the text. Hundreds of beautiful calligraphic alphabets have been developed over the centuries, and in this section 12 of the most popular are presented in detail. To enable you to accurately construct the individual letters, the alphabets are demonstrated in upper and lower case along with helpful markers to indicate the direction and order of the strokes used. Calligraphy, however, is not just a matter of mechanically following rules – it requires a feel for the style and flow of the scripts, and following the exercises that accompany each alphabet will help you to develop this. Practise the scripts, taking care to avoid the common mistakes, until you can write them fluently.

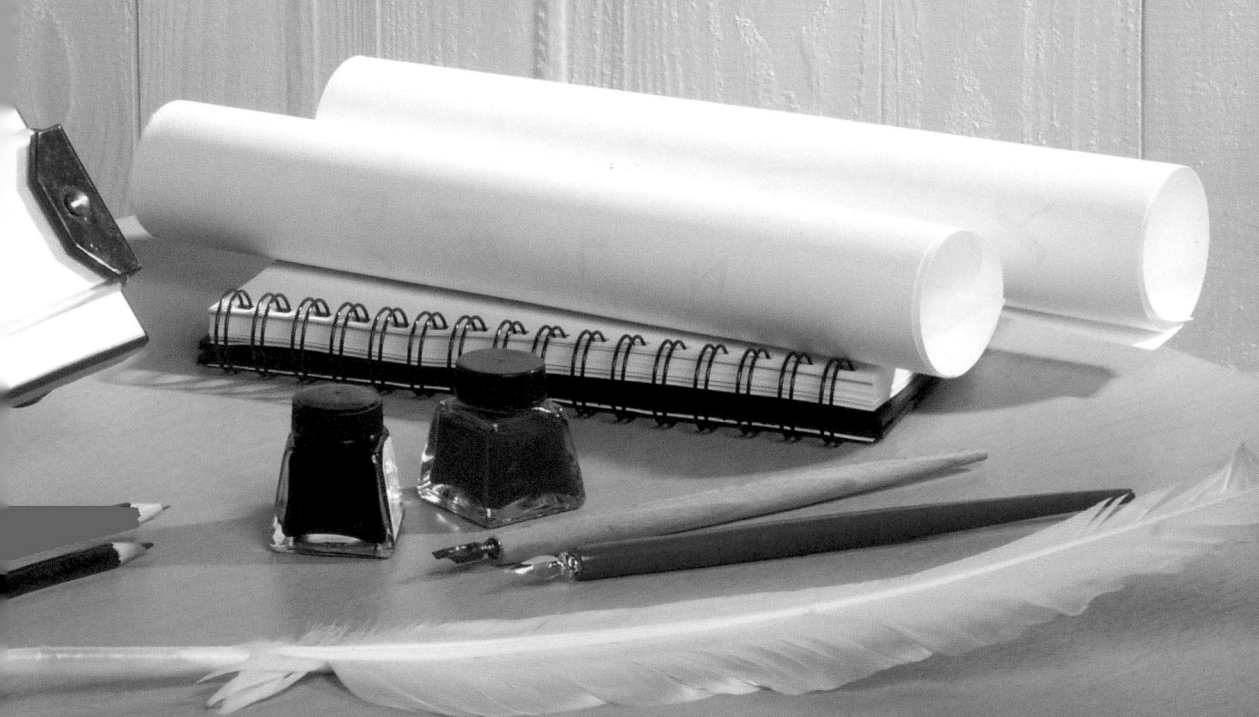

Foundational hand

The Foundational hand, also known as Round hand, was devised by Edward Johnston (1872–1944) following his studies of medieval manuscripts in the British Library. He based this hand on the writing of the Ramsey Psalter – an English Carolingian script with well-formed and consistent letterforms that was written around the end of the 10th century.

The Foundational hand is based on the circle made by two overlapping strokes of the pen. This cursive hand is written with a constant pen angle and few pen lifts. It is this constant angle that produces the characteristic 'thick' and 'thin' strokes of the letterforms.

In the 9th and 10th centuries either Uncial or Versal letters would have been used at the beginning of the Carolingian scripts on which Foundational hand is based. However, Roman Capitals are now used in conjunction with the Foundational hand. These capitals are based on the carved inscriptional letters used in Ancient Rome and their elegant proportions relate to the geometric proportions of a circle within a square. The Foundational alphabet can be divided into several groups, and the circle within a square construction is used as the guidelines for the proportions of the letters within each group.

Circular letters follow the circle, rectangular letters are three-quarters the width of the square and narrow letters are half the width of the square. The only letters that do not fall into a group are the two wide capital letters 'M' and 'W'. The central part of the letter 'M' is constructed in the same way as 'V' and the legs extend right into the corners of the square. The letter 'W' is constructed as two 'V's side by side, making a very wide letter that extends beyond the boundaries of the square.

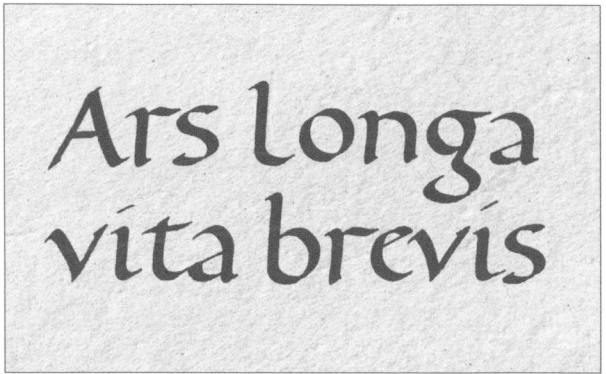

The basic rules

Foundational hand is a formal, upright script where each letter is made up of two or more strokes, which means that it has more pen lifts than a cursive script. The constant pen angle of 30 degrees controls the distribution of weight, creating thick and thin strokes. This pen angle must be maintained throughout in order to create good, rounded letterforms and strong arches.

The letters should be evenly spaced for easy reading. An important characteristic of this hand is that the top curves of 'c' and 'r' are slightly flattened to help the eye travel along the line of writing.

LETTER HEIGHT
The Foundational letter height is four times the width of the nib. Turn the pen sideways to make squares with the nib, then rule the lines that far apart.

LETTER SLOPE
Foundational letters are upright and should not lean.

PEN ANGLES
Hold the nib at a constant angle of 30 degrees for all letters except for diagonals, where the first stroke is made with a pen angle of 45 degrees.

45°

30°

Practice exercise: **Foundational hand**

Almost all the letterforms of this hand relate to the circle and arches, so practise by drawing controlled crescent moon shapes, beginning and ending on a thin point. Once this has been mastered, these semicircles can be attached to upright stems to create rounded letterforms or they can be extended into a downstroke to form arches. Begin high up and inside the stem to produce a strong rounded arch. Rounded serifs are used on entry and exit of strokes.

Group	Strokes (1st = red, 2nd = blue, 3rd = green)	

Round or circular

cbpoedq

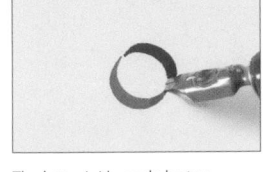 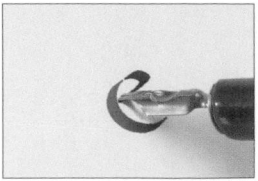

Note where the thin parts of the letters are. The first stroke of these letters should be a clean semicircular sweep, producing a shape like a crescent moon. Start at the top and move the pen downwards. The left and right edges of the pen form the circles.

The letter 'o' is made by two overlapping semicircular strokes which produce the characteristic oval shape of the counter.

The back of the 'e' does not quite follow the circular 'o' but is flattened so it appears balanced. The top joins just above halfway.

Arched

lmnrhau

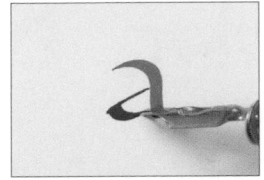 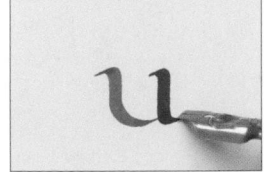

The arch joins the stem high up. Beginning with the pen in the stem, draw outwards in a wide curve, following the 'o' form. Start the letters with a strong, curved serif and end with a smaller curved serif. Keep the pen angle at 30 degrees throughout.

Draw an arch continuing into a straight stroke. The bowl of the letter begins halfway down the stem with the pen at 30 degrees.

The 'u' follows the same line as an 'n' but upside down, producing a strong arch with no thin hairlines. Add the stem last.

Diagonal

wxkvyz

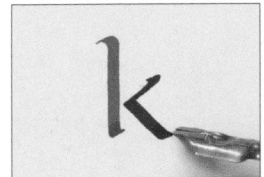 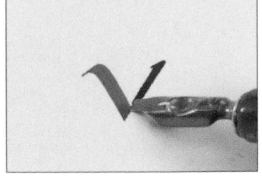

For the first stroke, hold the pen at the steeper angle of 45 degrees. This will prevent the stroke from being too thick. Take care not to make any curve on this stroke. Revert to a pen angle of 30 degrees for the second stroke.

Start the ascender three nib widths above the body height. The second stroke is made in one continuous movement forming a right angle.

The pen angle is steepened for the thick stroke and the strokes should sit upright. The second stroke begins with a small, hooked serif.

Ungrouped

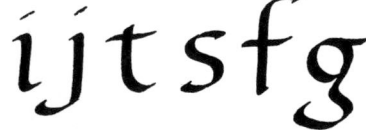 ijtsfg

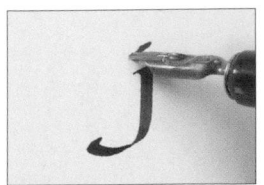 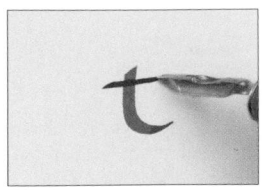

Keep the pen angle at 30 degrees for these letters. Remember to follow the smooth shape of the 'o' when drawing curves, rather than simply flicking the pen. Crossbars should sit just below the top line, and should protrude to nearly the width of the curve.

The base of the first stroke curves to relate to the 'i'. The second stroke begins with a small serif and neatly joins to this base.

Start just above the top line. The crossbar forms the second stroke and is made by placing the nib at an angle just below the top line.

Foundational hand

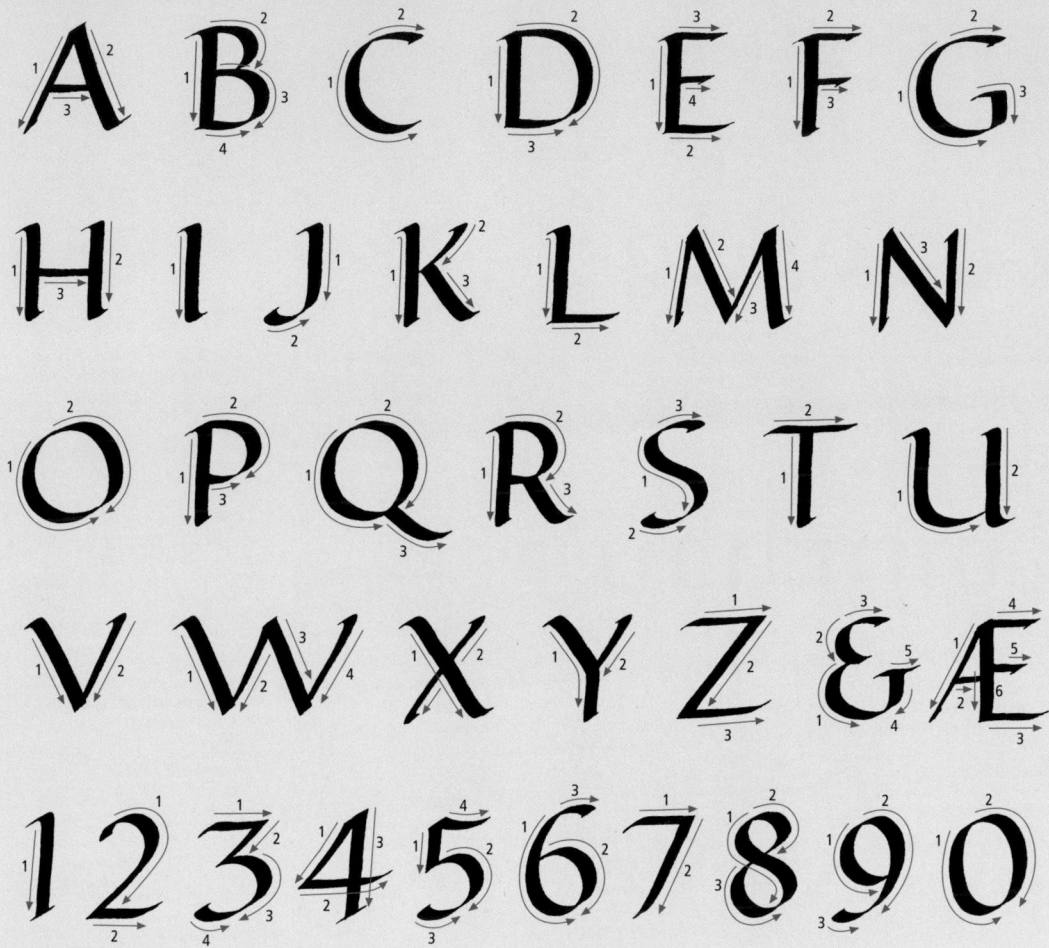

COMMON MISTAKES – CAPITALS

Often people start calligraphy with the Foundational hand and it is easy to establish incorrect letterforms. The most common place to go wrong with capitals is on the width of the letters and in keeping a correct pen angle. In addition to this, overlapping can cause unsightly dense areas.

The outer legs are too splayed and the 'v' is too narrow.

The top curve should be slightly flattened.

The bottom bowl should be slightly larger than the top with a smooth curve at the base.

Fatten the base of the bowl to avoid a dense join.

The diagonal stroke should be straight and not curved.

Strokes should cross slightly above half way up.

a b c d e f g

h i j k l m n

o p q r s t u

v w x y z &

? æ ĕ ü é ß .,

COMMON MISTAKES – LOWER CASE

A common mistake is to give letters the wrong shape. This is usually caused by not following the shape of the 'o'. As a result, the bowls of the letters will be too small, and arches will be weak and uneven.

Both arches should be evenly spaced.

The bowl is a little too small.

The top curve should be slightly flattened.

The bowl is too small.

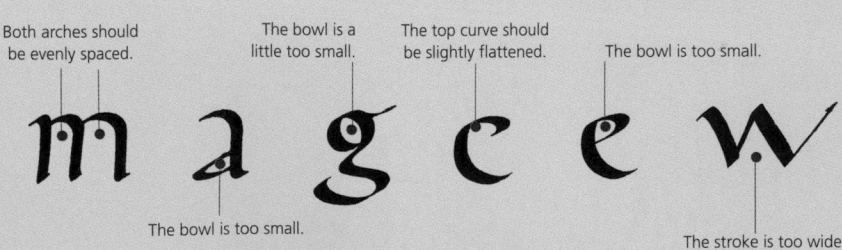

The bowl is too small.

The stroke is too wide and unevenly spaced.

Roman Capitals

Roman Capitals are arguably the most important early ancestors of Western calligraphy. Two thousand years old, and originating from the beautiful letters inscribed in stone or marble in ancient Rome, they are now revered as classical models. Even today, the work of Roman craftsmen still exists throughout what used to be the Roman Empire for all to see.

The version of Roman Capitals shown here is lightweight, with small, elegant serifs. The letters maintain the classical Roman proportions, but are modelled on a more recent pen version developed in the medieval period by the famous Italian scribe Bartholomeo San Vito.

The Roman Capital letterforms are based in structure on the geometric proportions of the circle and the square. They can be divided into four groups: the circle within the square, three-quarter width, half width and the whole square or larger. It is helpful to try out these proportions first in pencil, making just skeleton monoline letters, perhaps on graph paper. Try them in width groups (as shown opposite) to familiarize yourself with the proportions before you begin to write using the edged pen. When you do write with the edged pen, ensure that you maintain the pen angle at 30 degrees. This angle can be flatter for the serifs if aiming for elegance. The serif endings may need to be finished off by using the corner of the nib. Diagonal strokes demand a 45-degree pen angle.

Close attention must be paid to the height and width of the letters if they are to be recreated with their true proportions. The letters need some space around them, so avoid crowding them too closely together.

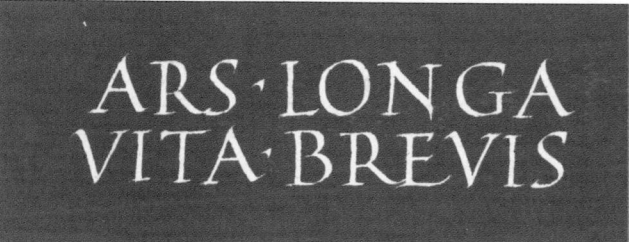

The basic rules

It is important to retain good pen control when writing Roman Capitals. In general, maintain a constant pen angle of 30 degrees. There are, however, a few exceptions to this rule that add elegance to the letterform. The upright strokes in 'N', and the first stroke in 'M', need a steeper pen angle of 60 degrees in order to make a thinner stroke. 'Z' needs a stronger diagonal stroke than 30 degrees will confer, so cheat and flatten the pen completely for a thicker stroke. You may find that in order to blend the serifs into the uprights, your pen needs to be well filled with ink; this helps the strokes flow together. In order to create serifs, a pen angle of 5 degrees may be adopted. Several different types of serif can be produced, requiring different levels of competence.

LETTER HEIGHT
The letters shown here are eight nib-widths, giving light elegance. You could try seven or even six nib widths, but take care not to allow the serifs to become too dominant.

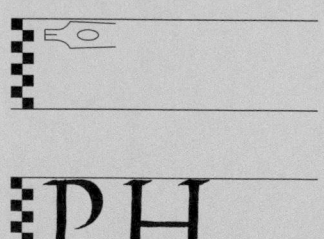

LETTER SLOPE
The letters are upright, and should have no forward slope. Check that letters have not developed a lean by looking at the writing upside down.

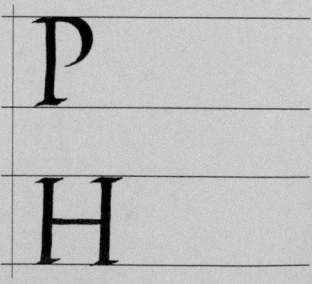

PEN ANGLES
Thirty degrees is maintained overall, maybe a little flatter for elegance of serifs, a little steeper for the uprights of 'N' (to make them thinner) and flatter for the diagonal of 'Z' to make it thicker.

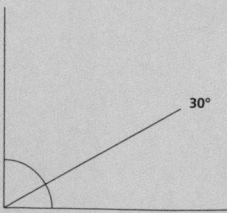

Practice exercise: **Roman Capitals**

Unlike all lower-case (minuscule) hands, Roman Capitals rely for their elegance on their geometry, and in particular on their widths relative to the circle and square. These widths are the basis upon which the groups of letters are formed. It is important to have a sound understanding of how Roman Capital letters are constructed before embarking upon reproducing the whole alphabet. An edged or broad pen may be used when writing this script.

Group

Strokes (1st = red, 2nd = blue, 3rd = green, 4th = mauve)

Circular

OCGDQ

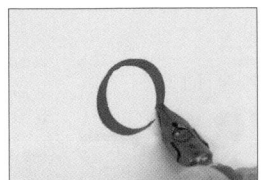 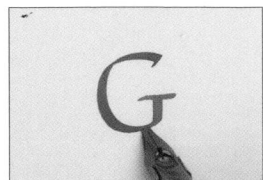

All are formed as all or part of a circle. Make sure that your circle really is round and not oval, and that the letters that belong to this group have a round shape overall. 'D' is difficult to make rounded – you may find it helps if you pencil in the circle first.

This letter is made in two 'half-moon' strokes pulled downwards and joined at the thin points.

This letter has more parts; ensure it echoes the 'O' in shape, and blend the last stroke into the bottom without leaving a thin stroke.

Three-quarter width

HAVNTUXYZ

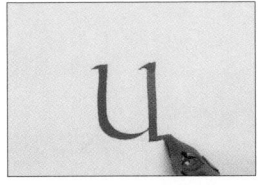 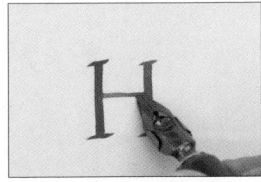

In geometric terms, these letters occupy the area where a circle in a square meets the two diagonal lines that cross it – equal to three-quarters of the width of the square. All the letters in this group occupy the same width – three-quarters of their height.

Make a confident curve finishing on a thin stroke, and bring the second stroke down to make an overlapped join.

Judging the distance between the two uprights will need practice; ensure the crossbar is a little above the centre.

Half-width

BPRKSELFIJ

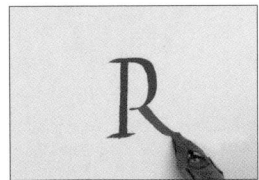 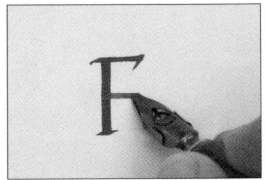

These letters are grouped together because, in geometric terms, the major part of the letter occupies just half of the square. In the case of 'R' and 'K', the tails of the letters will extend beyond the half of the square, and the letter 'I' is narrower than this.

The top serif is made as part of the stroke that carries on to make the curve. The tail does not start from the stem, but from the curve.

The top stroke starts as a serif to the left, and continues across with a slight twisting of the pen. Repeat for the central crossbar.

Broad-width

MW

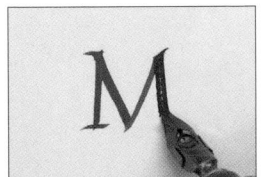 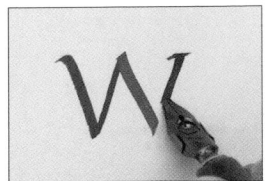

There are just two letters remaining: 'M' and 'W'. They are not upside-down versions of each other, so do not overdo the very slight splaying of 'M's legs. In geometric terms, 'M' mainly fits the shape of a square, whereas 'W' is two 'V's, making it very wide.

Make the first stroke with a steeper pen angle for a fine line; try not to allow the outer strokes to splay too much.

Put two 'V' shapes together, blending the joins by careful overlapping, especially at the bottom points.

Roman Capitals

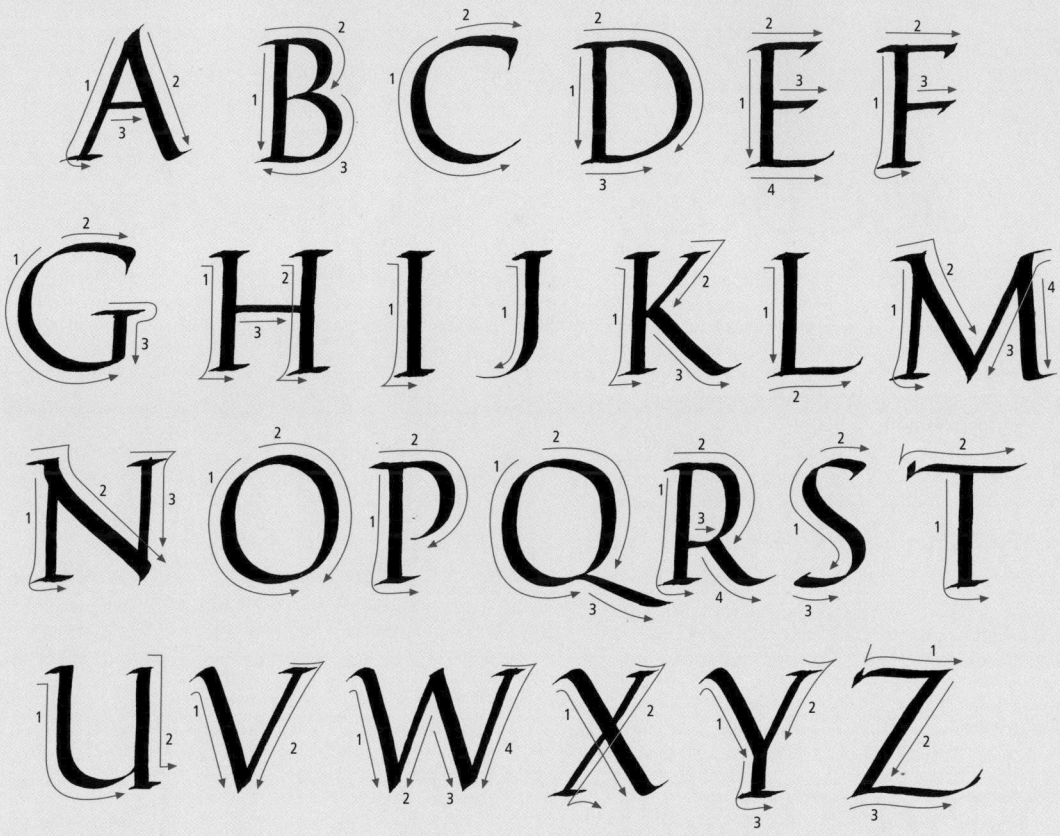

COMMON MISTAKES – CAPITALS

Mistakes of proportion are the most common problem with Roman Capitals, so you may prefer to trace the letters the first time, to help get the 'feel' of the balance of forms.

Bottom bowl should be larger than top, for visual balance.

Too narrow, this looks like half a circle – it should have a straight top to assist in gaining the width.

Too long; the horizontals should be a similar width.

Too wide; this is a half-width letter.

If the first stroke is sloping too much, the whole letter becomes an upside-down 'W'.

Crossbar too low; throws the letter out of balance.

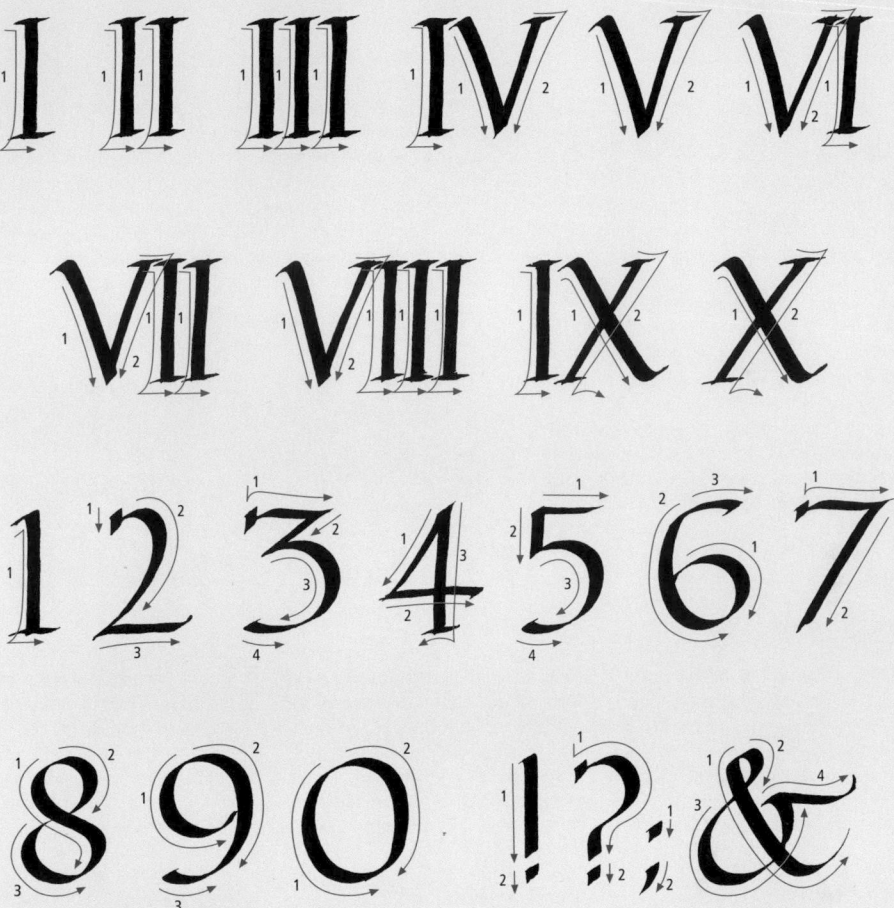

COMMON MISTAKES – NUMERALS AND SYMBOLS

Originally, of course, only Roman numerals would have been used with Roman Capitals. For speed, some writers join all the top and bottom serifs into horizontal bars. Arabic numerals were assimilated into the alphabet at a later date. They should generally be bottom-heavy so that they look balanced.

Divided too low, bottom bowl too small.

Top heavy; larger bowl should be at bottom for visual balance.

Top and bottom bowls too similar, make top bowl smaller.

Crossbar too high; makes it very small.

Small bowl, with lower stroke extending too far to bottom left.

Leaning backwards; start the first diagonal more upright.

Uncial hand

This script has a long history, developed around the 4th century AD or earlier. It is composed entirely of majuscules (capitals) which have no corresponding minuscules (lower-case letters) to accompany them. Minuscule forms had not yet evolved when Uncial was developed, but the few letters which extend above or below the body height ('D', 'H' and 'Q' for example) are the first signs of ascenders and descenders to come.

The precise origin of Uncials is uncertain, but they may have originated from north African scripts. They appear to combine Latin and Greek shapes – look at 'A', 'D' and 'E' (version with crossbar), 'H' and 'M', which seem to have Greek parentage. The early versions of Uncial appear to be quick to write, and this will have endeared them to scriptoria where dissemination of religious writings (including the bible) was the focus. They are known as 'book hands', or hands that were specifically evolved to suit writing at small scale.

Uncials became associated with Christianity, as they accompanied the spread of this 'religion of the book'. Luxury books of the time often incorporated very large writing (sometimes for practical purposes of being readable at a distance during a religious service). It is thought the term 'Uncial', which literally means 'inch-high', was an affectionate exaggeration of that size, and in the 19th century that name became the accepted name of the script.

Later versions of Uncial, used from the 7th to 9th centuries, became more complex, requiring twisting or 'manipulation' of the pen to obtain subtle wedged serifs, which would have slowed down the writing speed. Both forms are shown on the following pages, but follow the simple form before attempting the manipulated version, which requires more concentration.

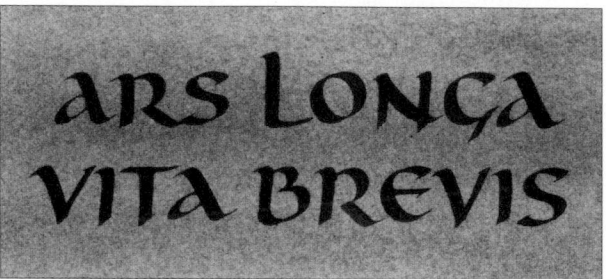

The basic rules

These letters are all very rounded, and may not come naturally to anyone who normally writes compressed forms. If this is the case, draw a row of circles lightly in pencil and write the letters on top, checking that each one maintains the rounded shape. All arches follow the round arches of 'O'. Even the diagonal letters correspond to the circle shape in width (except 'W', which incorporates two 'O's overlapped). Check that you have the pen at a flat pen angle, as steeper angles invite the pen to make narrower marks. Some letters have slight ascenders that are higher than the body height, or descenders that fall below the baseline, but these should be minimal in height, extending only between one and two nib widths. 'I' and 'J' are not dotted, because all Uncials are capital letters.

LETTER HEIGHT
The Uncials shown here are three and a half nib widths high, which provides the historically correct weight. However, they can also be written at four or more nib widths for lighter versions. The extensions are minimal, and must not exceed two nib widths.

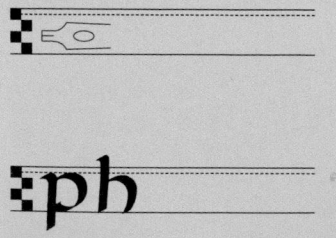

LETTER SLOPE
These are upright letters and should not have a slope. Speed of writing occasionally creates a slight forward lean, but this is not good practice, so slow down if a slope creeps in.

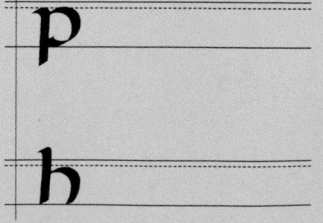

PEN ANGLES
A comparatively flat angle is necessary for these letters, between 15 and 25 degrees. Check where your thinnest part in a curved letter comes – it should be very near the top, with the accompanying danger of weak arch joins.

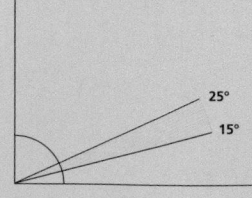

Practice exercise: **Uncial hand**

For this script think 'fat and flat': very rounded, wide letters written with the pen at a very flat pen angle. They are fairly comfortable for left-handers; right-handers should tuck their elbow into their waist if having trouble with this pen angle. Keep checking that the thin strokes are near the top and bottom on curved letters, and that the horizontal strokes are much narrower than the upright strokes on straight letters.

Groups   Strokes (1st = red, 2nd = blue, 3rd = green)

Round or circular

ocdeeçpqs

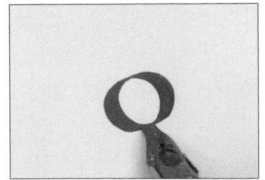 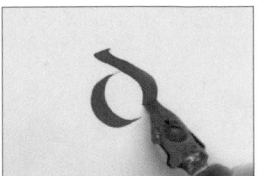

Most Uncial letters are rounded in shape. Try to see the secret 'O' in every letter, but remember that the Uncial 'O' is slightly wider than a circle. It may help to draw pencil circles to write over. There are two 'E's; the first 'E' in this group is Greek in origin.

Make a half-moon curve from top to bottom, then blend in the second curve using a clockwise movement.

Start just like the 'O', then begin the second stroke above the line, completing the 'O' shape. Beware of flattening the right-hand side.

Diagonal

kvwxyzna

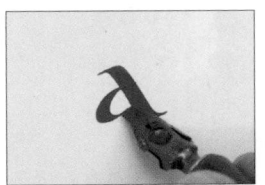 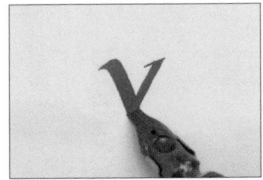

These letters still maintain the width of the 'O'. Watch your pen angle carefully so as not to make the diagonal strokes very much thicker than the upright strokes. The right-to-left diagonals should be thinner than their left-to-right counterparts.

Make the first stroke a diagonal stroke, then, starting inside the diagonal, make a sweeping but tight curve.

Pull the diagonal down at the shallow angle, and bring the second stroke down to overlap for a neat corner; check its thickness.

Arched

hmurb

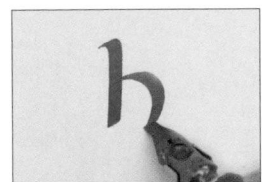 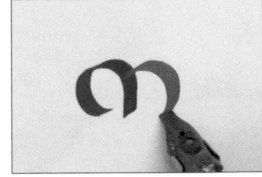

A very flat pen angle puts the thinnest point of a curved letter near the top – just where it would join an upright for an arched letter. This can weaken the letter, so take care to start the curve inside the upright to make it look well attached.

Start the upright stroke above the line, and firmly lock the curved stroke into it by starting within the stem. Note its roundness.

The first stroke is like 'O', the second forms an upright, and the last stroke repeats the curve with a firmly attached branching arch.

Straight

ijltf

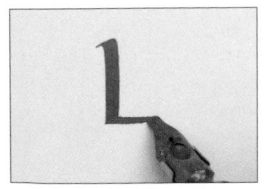 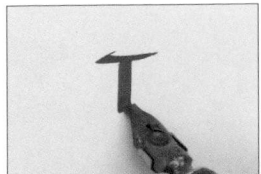

These letters are the simplest, but they are useful for practising writing with the correct pen angle, as you can pay attention solely to attaining the desired difference in thickness between horizontals and verticals.

Start above the line with a minimal serif, and pull down for a strong vertical stroke, changing direction but not pen angle at the base.

Start with the crossbar, as this will help when spacing text. Make a downstroke much thicker than the crossbar with the same pen angle.

Uncial hand

EARLY

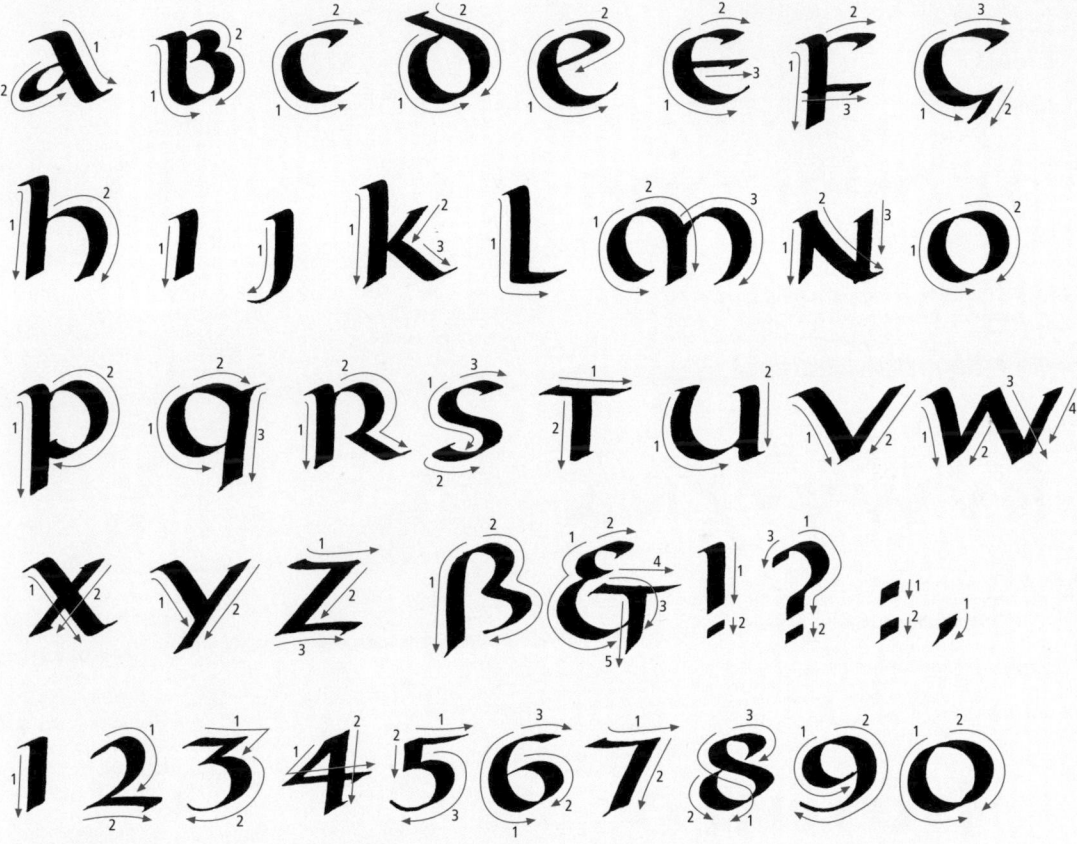

COMMON MISTAKES – EARLY UNCIALS

The main problem encountered with Uncials is not maintaining the roundness of every letter. It is this roundness that characterizes the overall texture in a block of Uncial writing – without it, the text loses its rhythm. Another mistake is to make ascenders too high and to place crossbars too high up the stem.

Diagonal should be straight, resembling the right-hand side of a standard capital 'A'.

Second stroke starts too high and cuts off the top right curve of the 'O' shape it needs.

Left and right 'drooping leaves' should be same distance away from the stem.

Too narrow, no echo of the rounded letters.

Ascender too high.

Join goes too far into the stem giving a heavy look.

Too narrow, ends curled up enhance this narrowness.

LATE

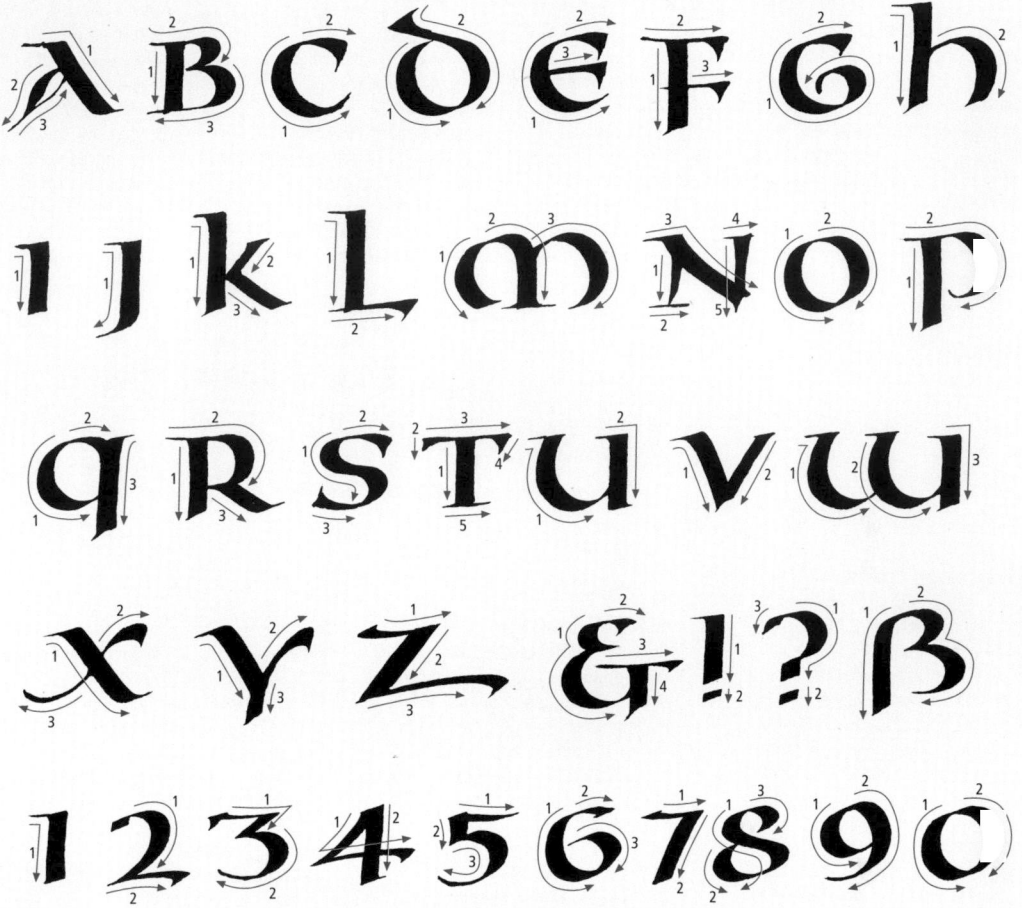

COMMON MISTAKES – LATE UNCIALS

The very flat pen angle is even more essential for these manipulated letters, as it creates contrasts of thickness, but take care with the twisted serifs which are its feature. These wedge shapes are made in a flowing movement twisting the pen from horizontal to near-vertical.

Top-heavy, give it a fatter body and a smaller head.

Too steep a pen angle, so both strokes are very similar in thickness – lacks contrast.

Horizontal stroke uncontrolled and wavy, manipulation required both ends.

Too narrow, not echoing the 'O' in width.

All strokes heavy, the uprights need manipulating for thinner strokes.

Extra serif on left unnecessary and in danger of looking like 'T'.

Gothic hand

Gothic was much despised by calligraphers in the early part of the 20th century, due no doubt in part to the previous generation's mistaken idea that it was first drawn and then 'filled-in'. Many bizarre versions of this writing appeared in the form of loyal addresses and freedoms of the city, which still emerge from time to time in manuscript sales. If influential calligrapher Edward Johnston had given as much attention to the Metz Pontifical as he gave to the Ramsey Psalter, the history of calligraphy might have been very different. Then instead of basing the introduction to calligraphy on the very circular shaped latter, with all the inherent problems of spacing, he could have inspired beginners to obtain the skill needed for control of the broad-edged pen with an easily spaced, simply constructed, straight-sided alphabet. Luckily Gothic, in all its various forms, is far too attractive and decorative a script for it to be consigned to obscurity for any length of time. The American calligrapher Ward Dunham was the champion of 'modern Gothic', a strong fierce hand that dominates all around it, or harmonizes beautifully with a more rhapsodic script, such as a delicate Italic – and where the attribute of script illegibility is shown to be a falsehood.

The defining characteristic of Gothic is the extreme density that has also earned it the name 'Blackletter'. Writing this hand is like beginning a war between the paper and the writing medium, one which the paper must lose. While the upper-case letters in Gothic are more decorative, the lower-case letters are almost geometric; the white spaces inside the letters should be kept the same width as the black strokes and the ascenders and descenders shallow. The sides of Gothic letters are very straight with many lines parallel to one another. Several Gothic letters are produced using identical strokes.

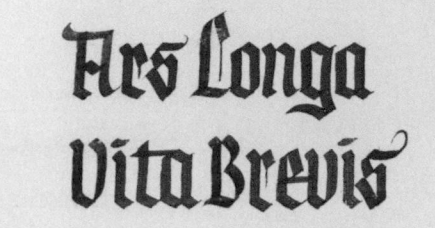

The basic rules

This is a modern version of a Gothic script and it is essential to bear in mind the importance of the writing's dominance over the area it covers, therefore a fairly flat pen angle of 30 degrees should be used. Medieval scribes had no 'official' majuscule letters for their Gothic scripts and so they borrowed heavily from the Roman Capitals and the Uncial forms. When these appeared too lightweight, they decorated them with diamonds, hairlines and small quill flicks to 'fill in' the white spaces. These letters seem over-elaborate for current use. However, the capitals chosen still maintain their link to the Roman and Uncial forms. If preferred, a simple weighted Roman capital is an effective alternative. Gothic majuscules should be used only sparingly. Keep them for the beginning of sentences and proper nouns – written in a block they become completely illegible.

LETTER HEIGHT
The x-height for this script is five nib widths. Height lines should be ruled before practising Gothic.

LETTER SLOPE
The Gothic hand is written without a slope. Gothic letters should remain upright and not be created with even the slightest of slants.

PEN ANGLES
This script is written with a pen angle of 30 degrees. The hairlines are drawn with the pen at an angle of 90 degrees or, for the letters 's' and 'x', with the left hand point of the nib.

Practice exercise: **Gothic hand**

Practise the dominant strokes of this hand: with an x-height of five nib widths and a pen angle of 30 degrees, draw the pen across and downwards to the right for one nib width. Without lifting the pen, draw it straight down the page for three nib widths and finally downwards to the right again for one nib width. Repeat this exercise several times; there should be only the space of one nib width between the vertical strokes. Do this before practising the letters described below.

Group

Strokes (1st = red, 2nd = blue, 3rd = green)

Oval

o a b c d e g q

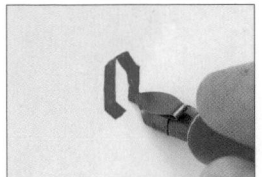 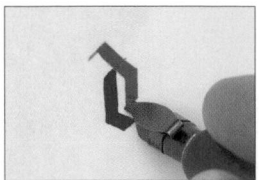

A constant angle of 30 degrees is maintained while writing these letters except for when drawing the hairlines. Vertical lines are created close together.

Both strokes are drawn with a pen angle of 30 degrees. The counter space needs to be the same width as the pen strokes.

The second stroke (the ascender) starts above the x-height and to the left of the first stroke.

Arched

n m h k r u v w y

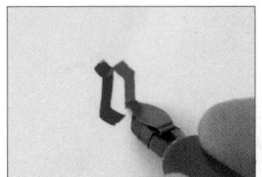 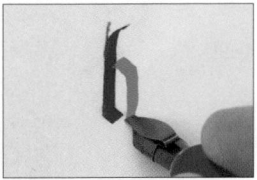

Note that the last stroke of 'n' and 'm' has an upwards curved finish while the last stroke of 'h' curves below the line. The letter 'r' needs its base serif in order to limit the amount of white space around it.

The letter 'n' is made from two strokes that are almost identical. The second stroke ends with a curved serif.

After the first stroke, draw a hairline at 90 degrees. The third stroke returns to 30 degrees finishing with a nib slide to the left.

Straight

i f j l t x

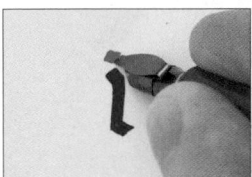 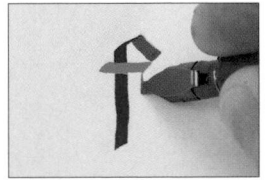

It was only with the introduction of Gothic writing that 'i' and 'j' acquired their dots, to aid legibility. To create the fine hairline for the letter 'x', place a spot of ink within the downstroke before attempting to draw out the line.

Draw the first stroke at 30 degrees, and keep the same angle of pen when drawing the dot.

The first stroke starts as an ascender, finishing as a descender. The second stays above x-height, the crossbar hangs from x-height.

Ungrouped

p s z

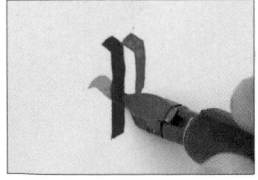 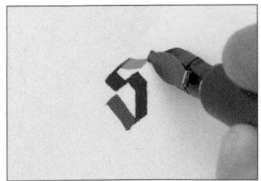

While these letters relate well to the rest of the alphabet, their complex construction keeps them in this separate category. None are difficult, although at first sight the 's' seems a little daunting.

Make the descender, and repeat the style for the second stroke. The third stroke slides to the right and down to meet the second stroke.

At x-height move one nib width following the path, then straight down. Touch with second stroke, and hang third stroke from x-height.

Gothic hand

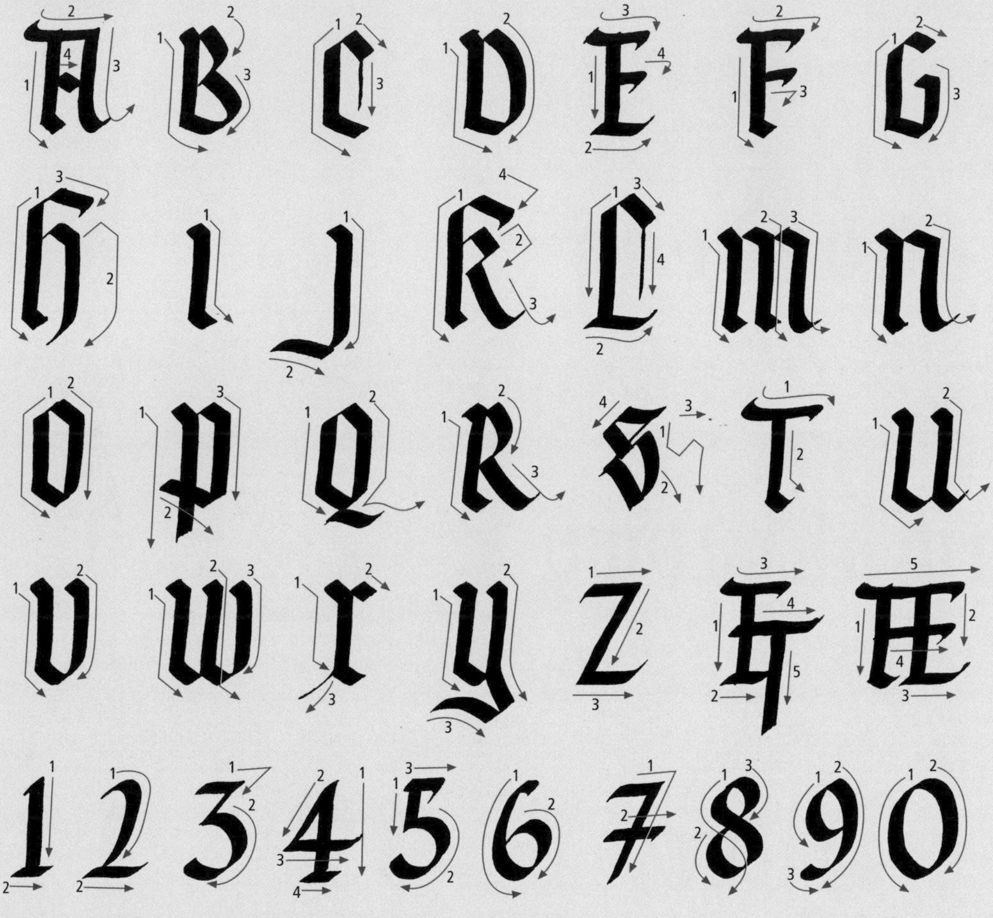

(alphabet chart showing Gothic capital letters A through Z with stroke-order numbers and arrows, followed by ligatures and numerals 1 2 3 4 5 6 7 8 9 0)

COMMON MISTAKES – CAPITALS

Having mastered the main structural elements of Gothic capital letters, they are not as difficult to recreate as they appear. Unlike, lower-case Gothic, capital letters are spacious and elegant. However, whole words should not be written in Gothic capitals as they are extremely hard to read. Common errors include groups of letters that do not appear consistent, and unbalanced letters.

Too curved – the stroke should be flatter.

Letter is too narrow and should be in proportion to other capitals.

Letter too short. It should be at least one nib width higher than the x-height of the lower case.

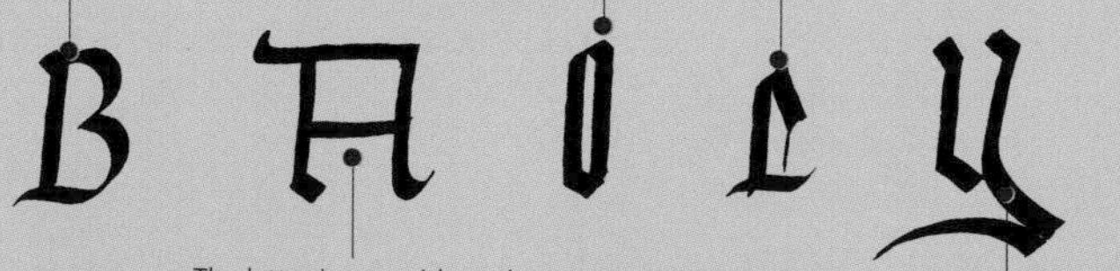

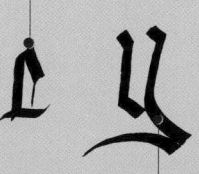

The letter is too wide and out of proportion.

Downstroke is curving too soon.

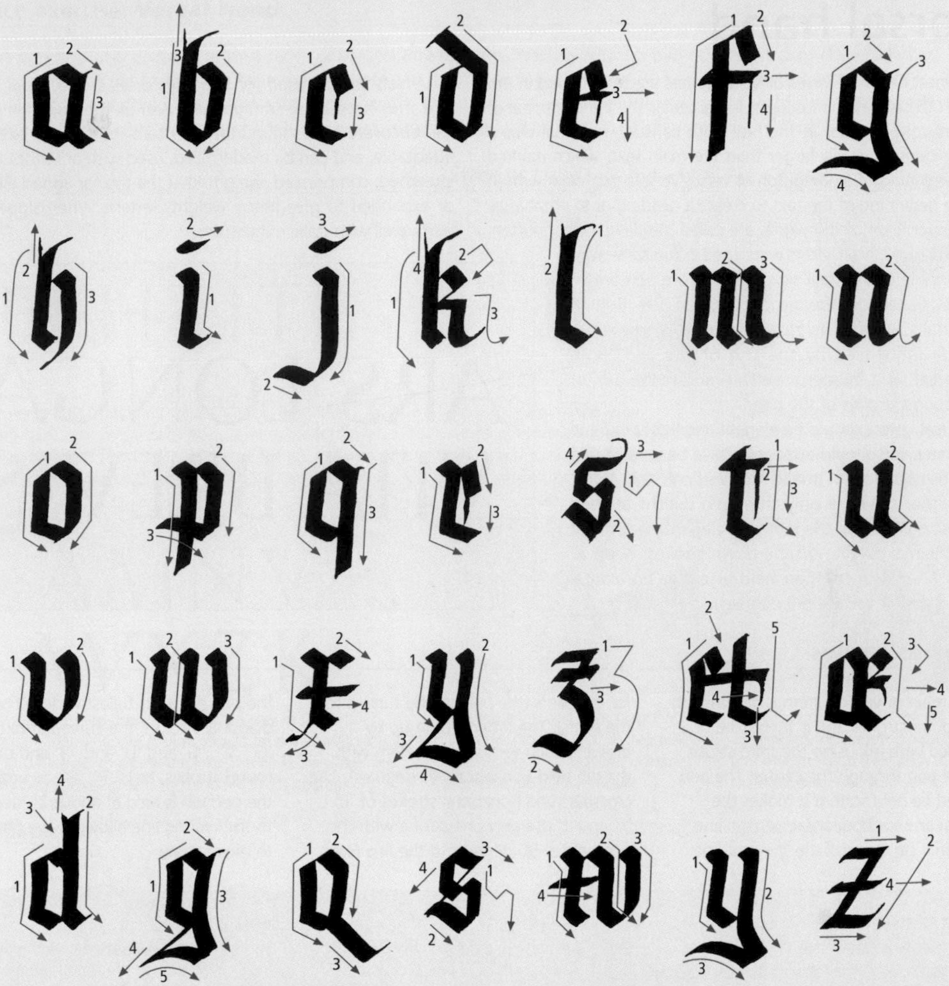

a b c d e f g
h i j k l m n
o p q r s t u
v w x y z et x
d g q s w y z

COMMON MISTAKES – LOWER CASE

With lower-case letters, spaces between words and lines should be as small as possible. A common mistake is the inclusion of a thin sideways stroke to make letters wider, or over-extension of ascenders and descenders. It may take time to adjust to such narrow letters without slim strokes and with few curves.

The crossbar is too high – it should hang from the x-height not sit upon it.

The ascender is too short.

Arches are uneven in width.

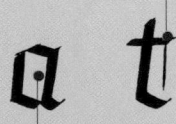 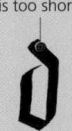 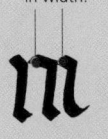 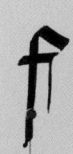

Letter is too wide, the counter space should be only the width of one nib.

The pen angle is too steep.

Versal hand

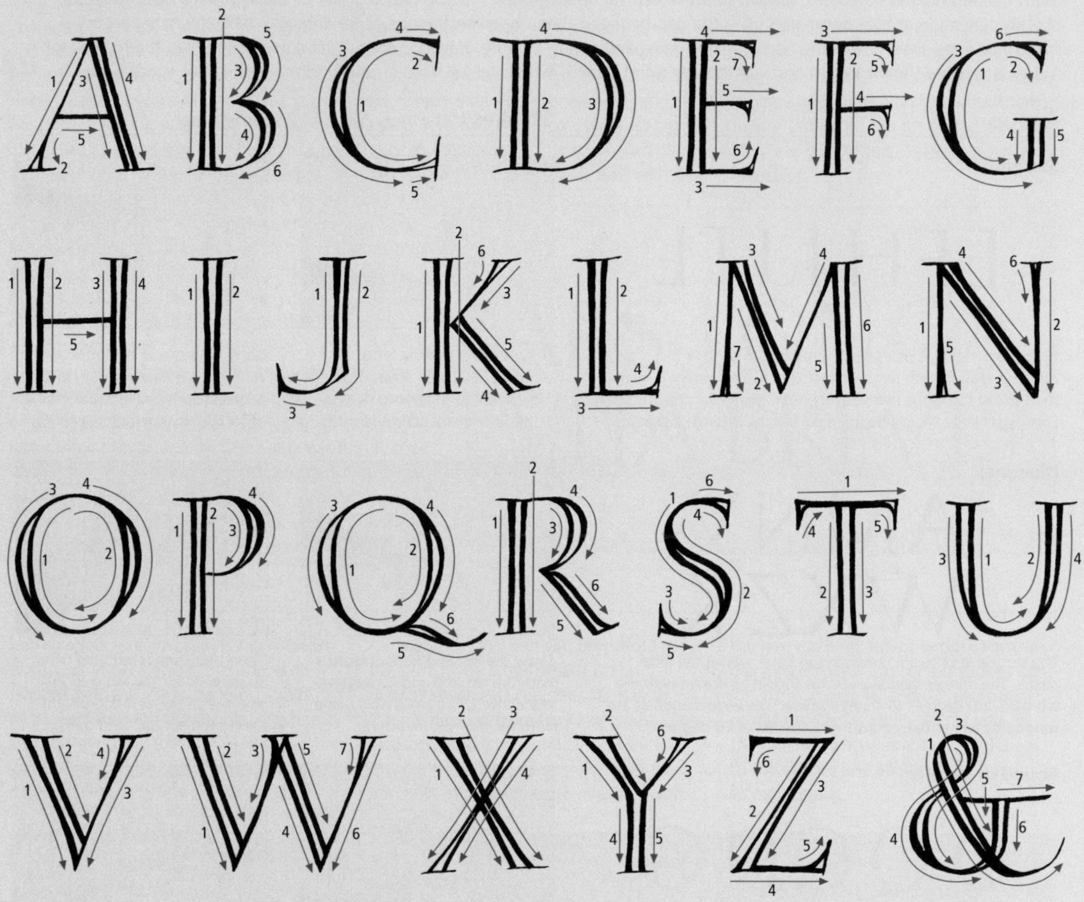

ABCDEFG
HIJKLMN
OPQRSTU
VWXYZ&

Outer strokes are splayed too wide.

Serif on the second stroke is not fine enough.

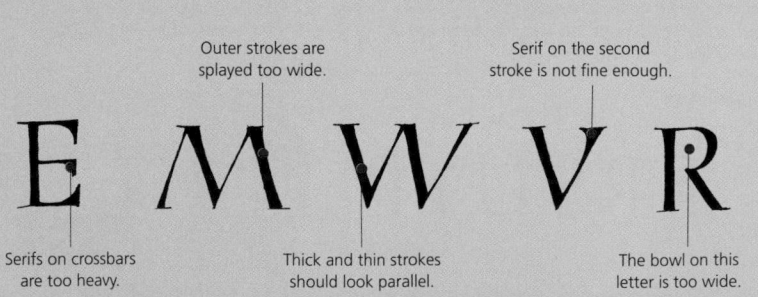

Serifs on crossbars are too heavy.

Thick and thin strokes should look parallel.

The bowl on this letter is too wide.

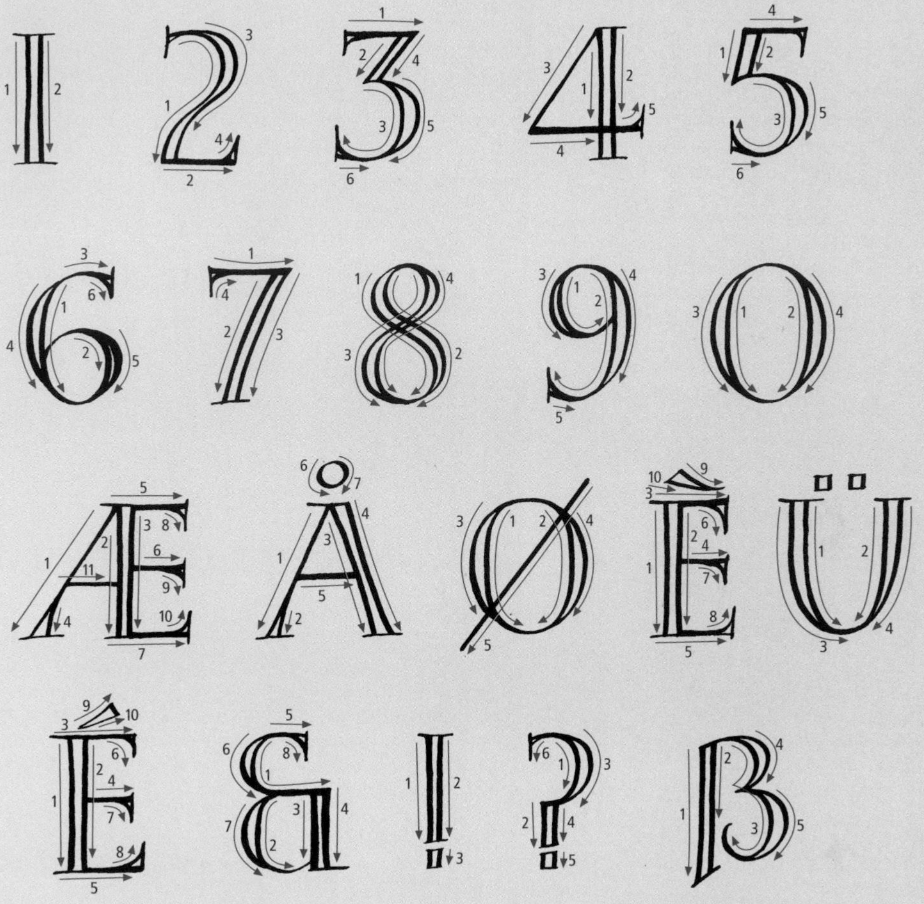

1 2 3 4 5

6 7 8 9 0

Æ Å Ø Ë Ü

E Ɛ ¡ ¿ ß

COMMON MISTAKES – NUMERALS AND SYMBOLS

Numbers should not appear too heavy or squat. As with the Versal letters, the lines and shapes should be elegant and rhythmic, and 'waisting' should not be too pronounced. Those numbers and figures that follow a circular shape should be slightly vertically elongated rather than completely round.

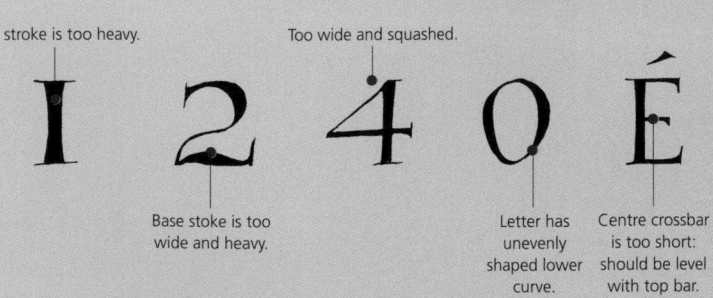

This stroke is too heavy.

Too wide and squashed.

Base stoke is too wide and heavy.

Letter has unevenly shaped lower curve.

Centre crossbar is too short: should be level with top bar.

Italic hand

The name 'Italic' reveals this script's country of origin. It developed in Italy during the early Renaissance period of the 15th century. While the arts flourished, calligraphy manifested itself in painted and illuminated books of the period. The Italic hand was adopted by Pope Nicholas V for the papal chancery in the 15th century, and became known as Cancellaresca Corsiva, or Chancery Cursive.

Today, Italic is beloved of modern scribes. It is a flowing script that is created swiftly and demands few lifts of the pen. Italic differs from many other hands, being oval-shaped with a forward slope. It is written using a pen angle of between 35 and 45 degrees, which should remain constant.

This hand is a form of calligraphy that closely relates to handwriting, as the letters are formed with a rhythmic up-and-down movement, occasioned by one stroke developing from where the last stroke ended; this contrasts with Roman Capitals, for example, where each stroke is separate and often starts back at the top of the letter. The Italic script is very adaptable to variations, owing to its branching construction, and is ideal for flourishing (see Flourished Italics). Regular practice is recommended

in order to develop a consistency in slope and width, and it is important to master the basic formal version before progressing to more complex Italic forms. In typography, any letterform that slopes is called italic, whereas in calligraphy a letter is only Italic if it conforms to the branching arch that is the defining feature of the Italic hand.

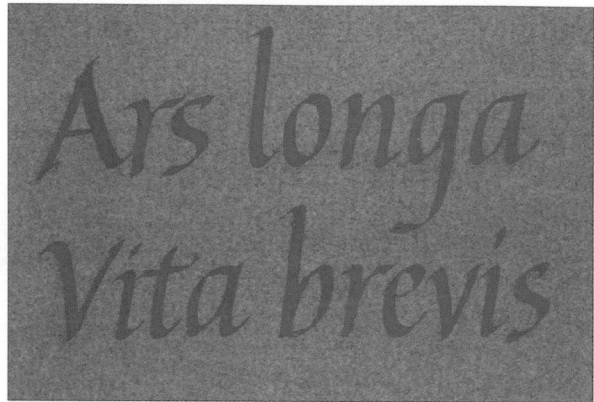

The basic rules

This is a slightly sloping, oval-shaped letterform with springing arches. The arch formation is the most important feature, and it distinguishes Italic from many other hands. You may wish to practise some pen patterns so that you become used to working with a pen angle of 30 to 45 degrees and a slope of 5 to 12 degrees. Practise with a pencil first, to develop the up-and-down rhythm used in 'm's and 'n's, and check where the arch emerges from the stem – it should be halfway. Look closely at 'u' – this needs to be identical in arch formation to 'n', branching halfway from the stem. All the arch shapes of the letters should be asymmetrical, and not too rounded.

LETTER HEIGHT
Five nib widths are the standard x-height for these letters, with ascenders and descenders extending up to five more nib widths above and below, although four is acceptable.

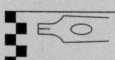

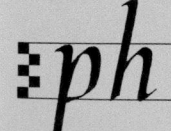

LETTER SLOPE
Between five and 12 degrees forward slope from the vertical is average for Italic, just ensure it is consistently the same throughout one piece of work.

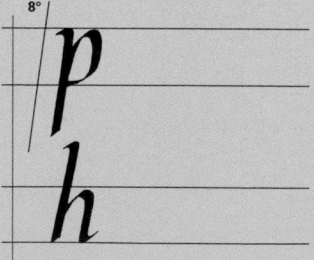

PEN ANGLES
Forty to forty-five degrees is the recommended angle for Italic lower case. However, it should be 30 degrees for the capitals, as 45 degrees will provide no difference in thickness of horizontals against vertical strokes.

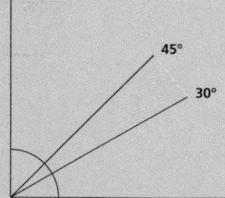

Practice exercise: **Italic hand**

If your pen resists the upward movement of the branching arches, lighten the pressure so that it does not dig into the paper – do not allow the pen to stop halfway. With 'n' and 'm' shapes, the pen moves from one stroke to the next without coming off the paper, and the arch emerges halfway up the stem. If your pen comes off, go back and try it again. When 'n' comes naturally, focus on the branching effect of 'u' and 'a' shapes which are the same format, upside down.

Group

Strokes (1st = red, 2nd = blue, 3rd = green)

Arched

n mrhpb

Practise with a pencil first if necessary, to make an 'n' shape without taking the tool off the paper. With 'p', where travelling all the way from a descender is too far, take the pen off the descender and start again on the baseline as if making an 'n'.

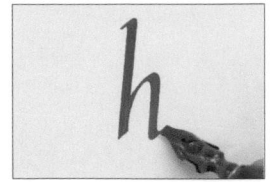

Start the ascender above the line, pause at baseline then move uphill, emerging halfway up the stem. Complete the downwards curve.

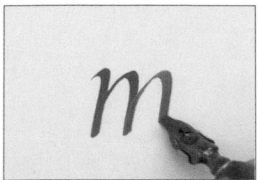

Make the first stem, pause at the baseline, rise and emerge halfway, make a tight corner down. Repeat stroke ending with an exit serif.

Base-arched

adgquy

These arches mimic the first group, but are upside down. The adding of a 'lid' can be left to the end. If it helps to maintain a rhythm of up-and-down, keep going without releasing the pen until the end.

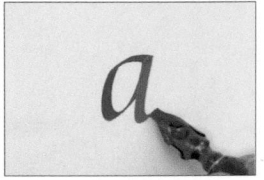

A tight stroke curves round and up to the topline. The lid is drawn next. The downstroke carries on where the upward curve finished.

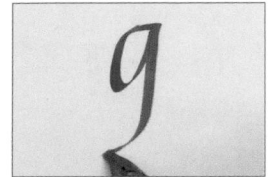

As in 'a', but with an extended downstroke that curves at the bottom. Finish with a horizontal, or add a stroke from the left.

Diagonals

vwxyzk

The angle in the top-left to bottom-right stroke needs to be adjusted to prevent it becoming thicker than any upright stroke. Use a steeper pen angle of about 50 degrees. The other diagonal must be thinner – try a 30-degree angle.

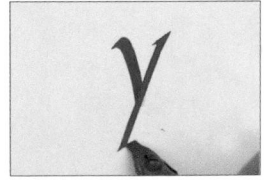

Steepen the pen angle to 50 degrees for the first stroke; flatten it to 30 degrees for the second. The descender should not bend.

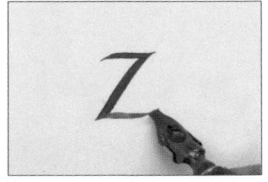

Make the horizontal stroke then completely flatten the pen angle for a thick diagonal. Complete the horizontal at the usual angle.

Ungrouped

ocesijfflt

'O' is frequently the governing letter of a hand, but in Italic it takes second place to 'n' and 'a'. However, it is essential to understand the smooth oval shape of the 'o', so that it can be matched to 'e' and 'c'. 'S' should also fit into a secret 'o' shape.

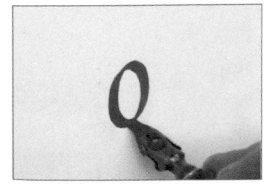

Start with a half-moon beginning and ending at the thinnest point. The second curve blends into the bottom curve.

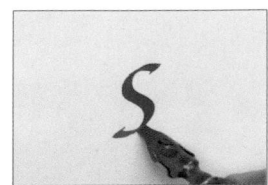

Start below the topline and flow left and right of two imaginary circles. Add end strokes with serifs that are straight rather than curved.

Italic hand

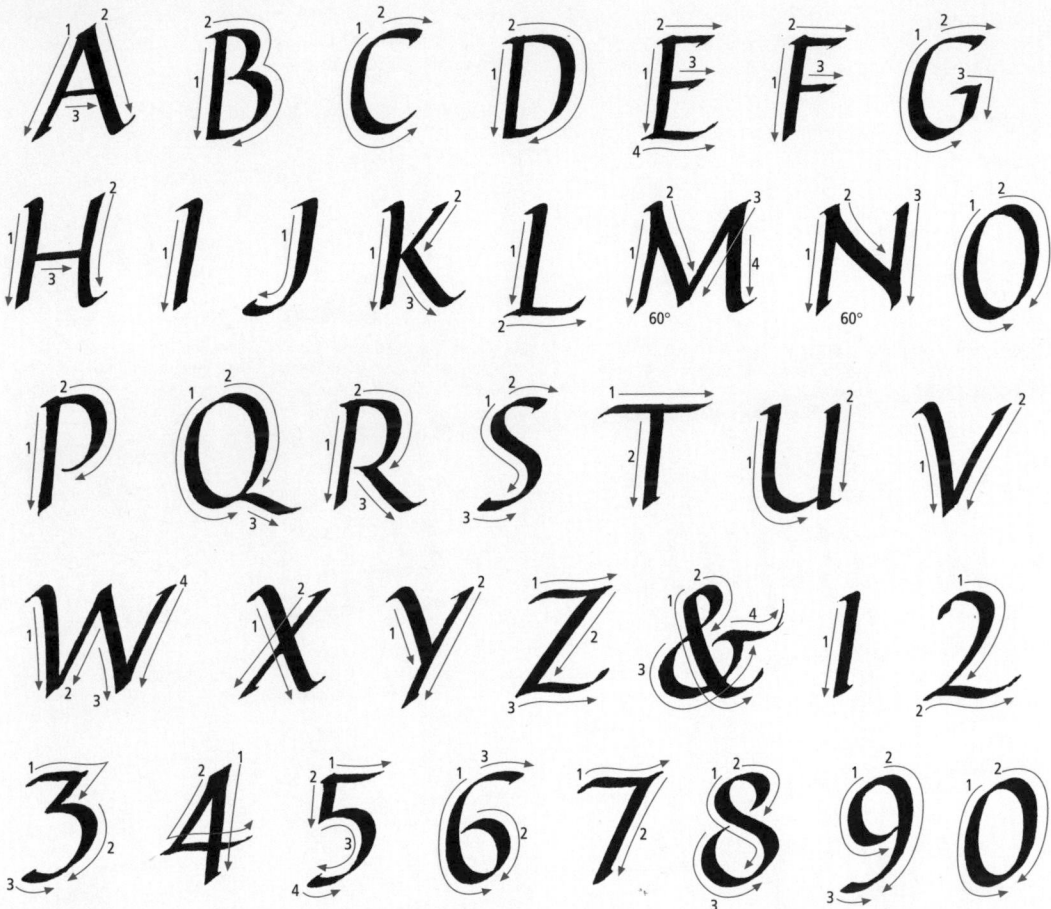

COMMON MISTAKES – CAPITALS

Italic letters are a compressed form of the Roman Capital but they should not be made either too wide or too narrow. Keep letters at a consistent forward slope and make firm joins by starting the next stroke inside the stem it joins.

Too narrow, with the top sloping forward too soon – uplift before curving round.

Uneven in widths, caused by the second stroke going too wide.

Three strokes all the same thickness – steepen pen angle to make the uprights thinner.

Sloping backwards instead of forwards.

Diagonal too thin – need to flatten the pen to thicken this stroke

Top heavy; better to be bottom-heavy for visual stability.

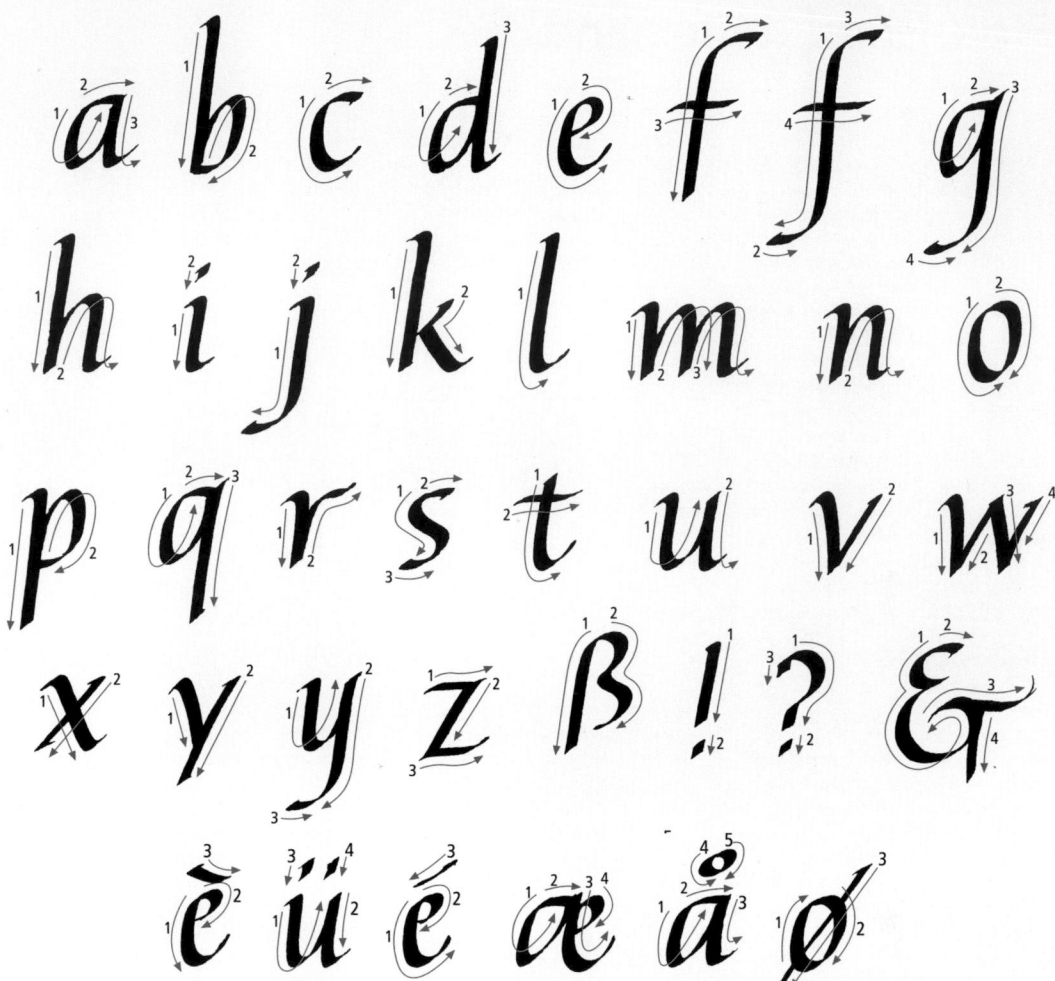

COMMON MISTAKES – LOWER CASE

Branching arches are a key part of this alphabet. They should not begin too high up the letter. The letters should be kept at a consistent forward slope (not more than 12 degrees from upright) throughout a piece of work. Do not make letters too rounded as they should be kept narrow.

Arch is not branching; should start from the baseline and emerge half way.

Not at the correct angle, and crossbar should sit higher.

Loop should be smaller and not pulled down which causes letter to fall backwards.

Lacks essential upward branching arch – pen has come off at the bottom instead of going to the top.

Ascender is a little short, making it look squat.

Uneven in shape, with corners.

Flourished Italic hand

The Italic hand was developed during the Italian Renaissance and was more elegant and rhythmically written than the Gothic hand of northern Europe at that time. Flourished Italic is a slightly more modern and exuberant version of formal Italic and one that is more adaptable for today's calligraphy. It is lightweight and elegant in its execution and has an energy that comes from being written with speed. The letters have a forward slope and springing arches. The basic letter shapes are that of Formal Italic but with fewer pen lifts. The proportions are the same: five nib widths for the body height of the minuscule letter and seven nib widths for the capitals. The actual stroke that forms the letter tends to be straight. The only strokes that curve into a flourish are the first and last strokes.

The Flourished Italic capitals, which are based on compressed sloped Roman Capitals, are also called swash capitals. The ascenders and descenders are the easiest to flourish and extend. The greater the decoration, the more space is required.

When executing more exuberant writing, extra consideration is needed for layout and design space. Be careful not to over-flourish the letters, as less is definitely better. Too many flourishes will make the words difficult to read. You may find it helps to decide on where to flourish by using a pencil.

The basic flourished letters shown on these pages are fairly restrained so that it is easy to see how they are constructed. As you gain more confidence and greater control over the pen, flourishing can become more adventurous, and innovative and exciting effects can be produced.

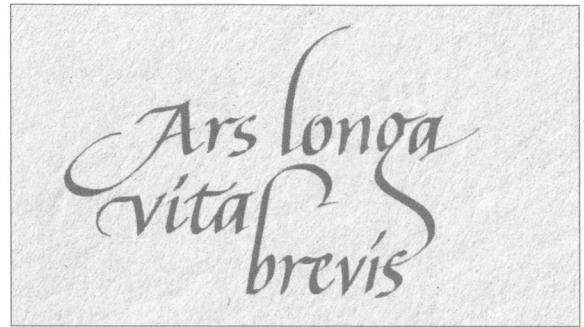

The basic rules

Attention needs to be given to the choice of paper. This should be easy to write on, with a surface that will not hinder the flow of the pen and ink. The pen nib should be smooth and easy to manipulate. For small writing the reservoir can be detached, giving the pen more flex. For the larger nib push the reservoir back from the edge allowing more of the nib to show. Load the pen before each flourish to ensure a good flow of ink. Ensure that the body height of the letter remains at five nib widths and continue to keep the Italic capitals at seven nib widths high or slightly less. The width of the letter forms are two-thirds body height to keep the proportions elegant. Modern Italic can sometimes be written in a more compressed and even pointed style to add interest to the writing.

LETTER HEIGHT
The x-height is five nib widths for the minuscules and seven nib widths for the capitals. The ascenders and descenders are normally three widths extra but can be more.

LETTER SLOPE
The letters are usually sloped between three and five degrees. They can slope 12 degrees or more but care will have to be taken over the angle of the pen nib to ensure that the letter weights are correct.

PEN ANGLES
The pen angles range between 30 and 45 degrees. There is some pen manipulation when flourishing to ensure easy movement on the paper. The average pen angle is about 40 degrees.

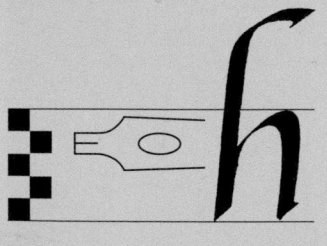

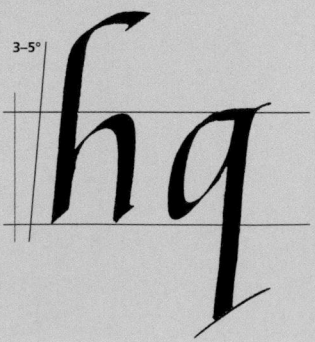

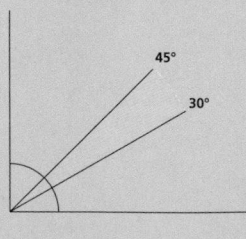

Practice exercise: **Flourished Italic hand**

Begin by writing in formal Italic. Lead into the chosen letters by extending the first serif before beginning the letter. Extend the exit stroke, for example with 'k' and 'z'. Try writing the ascenders taller and the descenders longer. Use a whole arm movement to create the letter, sweeping the pen off the paper at the end. Hold the pen lightly and write the shapes quite speedily. If you can do one or two letters well keep practising them to gain familiarity with the movements and confidence in what you are writing.

Group

Strokes (1st = red, 2nd = blue, 3rd = green)

Arched

nmhbkpr

The letter 'n' is the key letter in this alphabet. The asymmetrical arch that springs from about two-thirds up the stem is the shape of all of the arched letters in Italic. Practise this stroke until you are confident writing it.

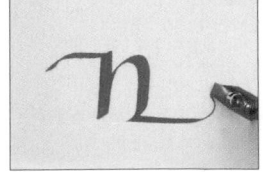

This letter is written in two strokes starting from the serif at the top, going down and springing up, round and down, with a flourish.

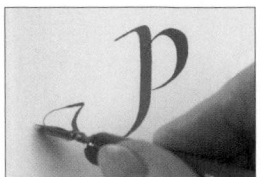

The downward stroke sweeps round to the left. Spring the second stroke from two thirds up the stem and round at the bottom. Flourish.

Base-arched

uyqgad

With arched letters, a variety of flourishes can be produced. Use a pen angle of 40 degrees and employ the whole hand to create the flourish on the first stroke.

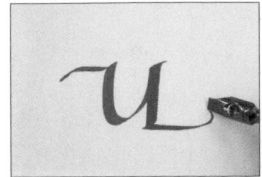

The 'u' follows the shape of the 'n' but in reverse. Start with the arch, then draw the stem, finishing with the flourish at the baseline.

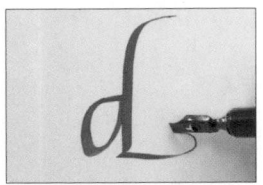

Create the bowl of 'd' with a lid. Curve in from the top right to start the ascender, down to the baseline and flourish outwards.

Round

vecsijltfg

The round letters in this group begin with a downwards stroke. With 'e', the pen is moved downwards to create an oval shape with straight sides that curve when reaching the bottom.

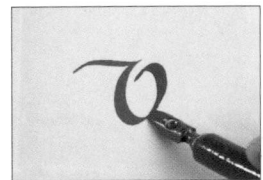

Lead in with a long serif to do the top of the letter and create the bowl. Add the second stroke from the top right.

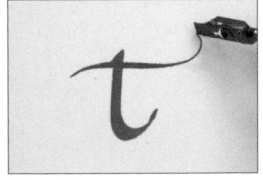

Create the descender. The crossbar of the 't' can be flourished a long way depending on the space available either side.

Diagonal

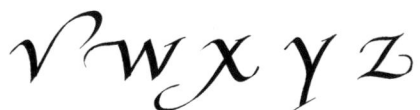

vwxyz

The nib may be flattened to 10 degrees in order to create the second diagonal in these letters. The flourishes can either be kept small or they can be extended to form quite elaborate designs.

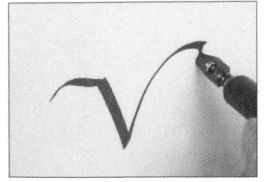

The first stroke can be extended from the front serif, and the second can be drawn up into a sweeping flourished curve.

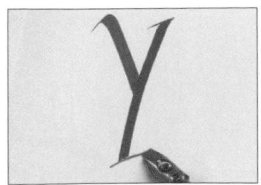

Pull down diagonally for the first stroke. Bring down the second stroke and flatten the pen angle. Add a third stroke to finish.

Flourished Italic hand

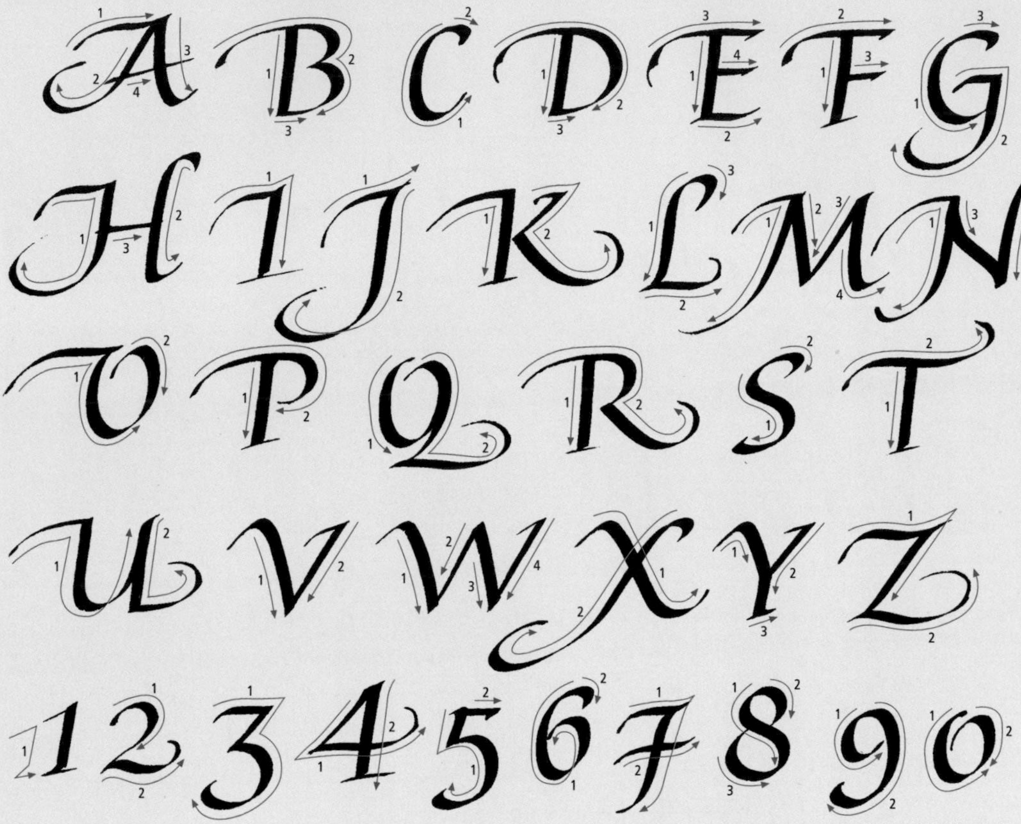

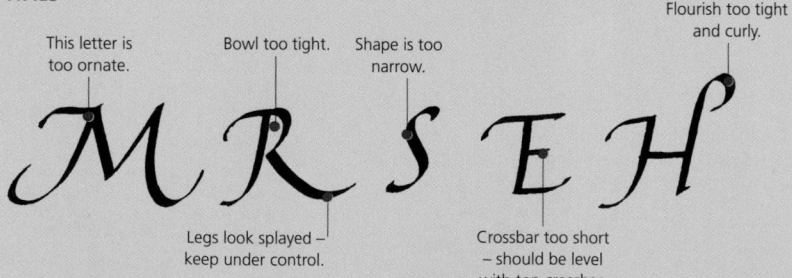

COMMON MISTAKES – CAPITALS

Flourished Italic capital letters should use the same spacing as the Italic script. Large flourishes will demand a greater distance between lines. Do not allow the letters to become too cramped. It may be a good idea to pencil in the path of any extending ascenders and descenders.

This letter is too ornate.

Bowl too tight.

Shape is too narrow.

Flourish too tight and curly.

Legs look splayed – keep under control.

Crossbar too short – should be level with top crossbar.

COMMON MISTAKES – LOWER CASE

The springing arches are the key to this alphabet. Do not start the arch too high on the stem because it will look like the round arch of Foundational hand. The arches in Flourished Italic spring from about two-thirds up the stem of the letter and are asymmetrical in shape.

The bowl is too round. Continue first stroke down, then lift stroke upwards to the top of the writing line.

The top part is too high.

The bottom stroke is too tightly curved, making it look contrived.

The second stroke is too short.

The letter shape is too mannered or curved.

The tail is too narrow.

Rustic hand

The Rustic script, which was widely used in the Roman Empire, was originally thought to have been a development of Roman Square Capitals. The discovery of early documents, however, has proved that it in fact pre-dates this script.

'Rustic' is perhaps something of a misnomer as it brings with it the whiff of country air and all things rural and casual. The Romans did have a script that relates to today's idea of 'bad handwriting', which they would use to 'scribble' on a wax tablet or write a quick note to a friend. However, this has nothing in common with the Rustic hand, which requires considerable calligraphic skill in order to obtain the changes of pen angle that are required on the majority of letters.

Rustic letters are both elongated and refined, with particularly slim stems. They were probably written with a reed or brush – certainly very large brushes must have been used to write the graffiti that can still be seen on the walls of Pompeii and Herculaneum. The script's rhythm is lively due to its weighty diagonals and serif strokes.

Although second only to Roman Capitals in its position of importance within a document, the Rustic

script seems to have been relatively unpopular with medieval scribes and most examples appear to be poorly written. In manuscripts, Rustic was often written in a continuous stream, without spaces. By the 15th century it had ceased to be used, and it was only during the 20th century that an interest in this singular script fuelled a mini Rustic revival.

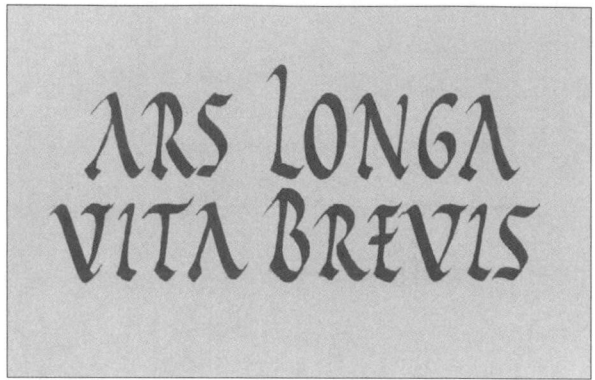

The basic rules

Rustic script is written at a relatively quick speed, and uses considerable variations in pen angle. In its original form the flexibility of the writing tool, probably a reed or a brush, would have allowed the change of pen angle and

weight of stems to happen in one stroke. However, the modern metal nib is not as flexible and the effect is best achieved by using separate strokes. Many of the letterforms such as 'E' and 'T' are extremely narrow, and the

difference in size between them and the wider letters such as 'M' and 'W' appears much greater than in classic Roman Capital letters. The interlinear space is minimal, probably no more than four nib widths.

LETTER HEIGHT
Seven nib widths for all letters except for 'B', 'F' and 'L'. These are written at eight nib widths.

LETTER SLOPE
This script should be written completely upright, without any slope.

PEN ANGLES
These vary from 80 degrees to 30 degrees. Right-handed calligraphers may find it easier to use a left-hand oblique nib.

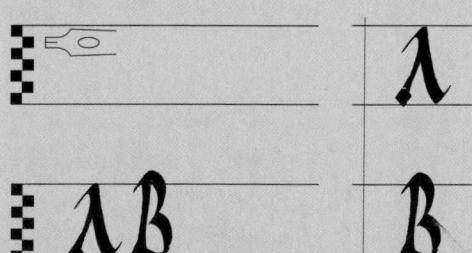

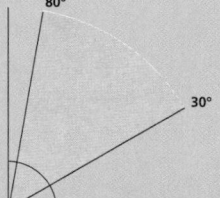

Practice exercise: **Rustic hand**

It may take a little practice to retain the extremely steep pen angle used for this script. Before starting to write letters try making several hooked downstrokes to obtain the correct rhythm. The spacing between these strokes should be even and should reflect the normal letter spacing of this hand. Next, try holding the pen at 60 degrees and creating a series of oval shapes – drawing first the left side and then the right side. This will help to establish the hand movements needed for the rounded and oval parts of letters.

Group	Strokes (1st = red, 2nd = blue, 3rd = green)

Diagonal

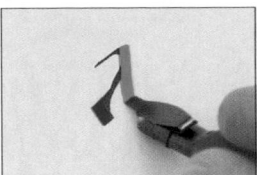 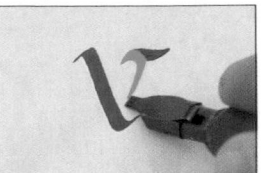

While at first glance these letters may not appear to have much in common, practice will underline their family characteristics. Note that the third stroke of 'A' appears in all of these letters.

Swing the first diagonal stroke's base right. From the first stroke pull left, then right to produce the foot. Add the final diagonal stroke.

The first stroke is similar to the last stroke of 'A'. The right-hand serif is formed slightly flat. The final stroke should leave a finishing lift visible.

Straight

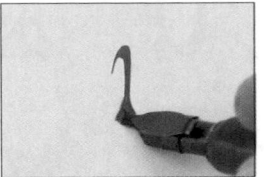 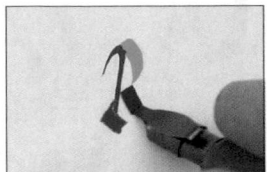

The letter 'I' is the parent of this family. Note that the foot serif is elongated for the letters 'B', 'D', 'E' and 'L' and that the bowls of 'B', 'D', 'P' and 'R' continue the curve of the original serif in a downward movement.

Emphasize the hooked serif and make a well-defined swing to the right at the end of the stroke. The second stroke starts within the first.

Construct a letter 'I', then with the pen within the curved serif, draw a bowl that meets the stem. Keep the angle to make the final stroke.

Oval

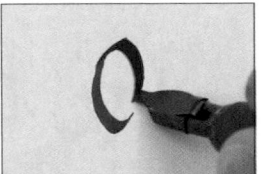 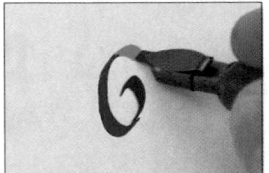

'O' is the parent of this family. Note how narrow it is. A pen angle of around 60 degrees is used to create these oval letters, and this angle needs to be maintained throughout the letter.

With a steep pen angle make the curved stroke. The second stroke reflects this shape and starts and finishes within the first stroke.

The first stroke is as for 'O'. The second starts just above the middle of the letter. For the top of the 'G' pull to the right, then lift slightly.

Ungrouped

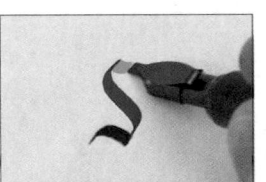 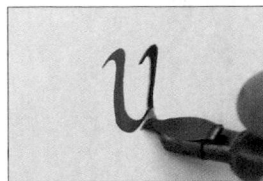

Of these letters 'J' and 'U' have been designed to complement the rest of the alphabet as they did not exist in Roman times. Do ensure that the top and bottom strokes of 'S' are written with a concave curve, and that the letter appears upright.

First draw the diagonal stroke with curved serifs to the right and left. The concave strokes at the head and tail should be kept short.

Begin the first stroke as for 'I' but finish with a curved bowl. The second and third strokes are the same as for a letter 'I'.

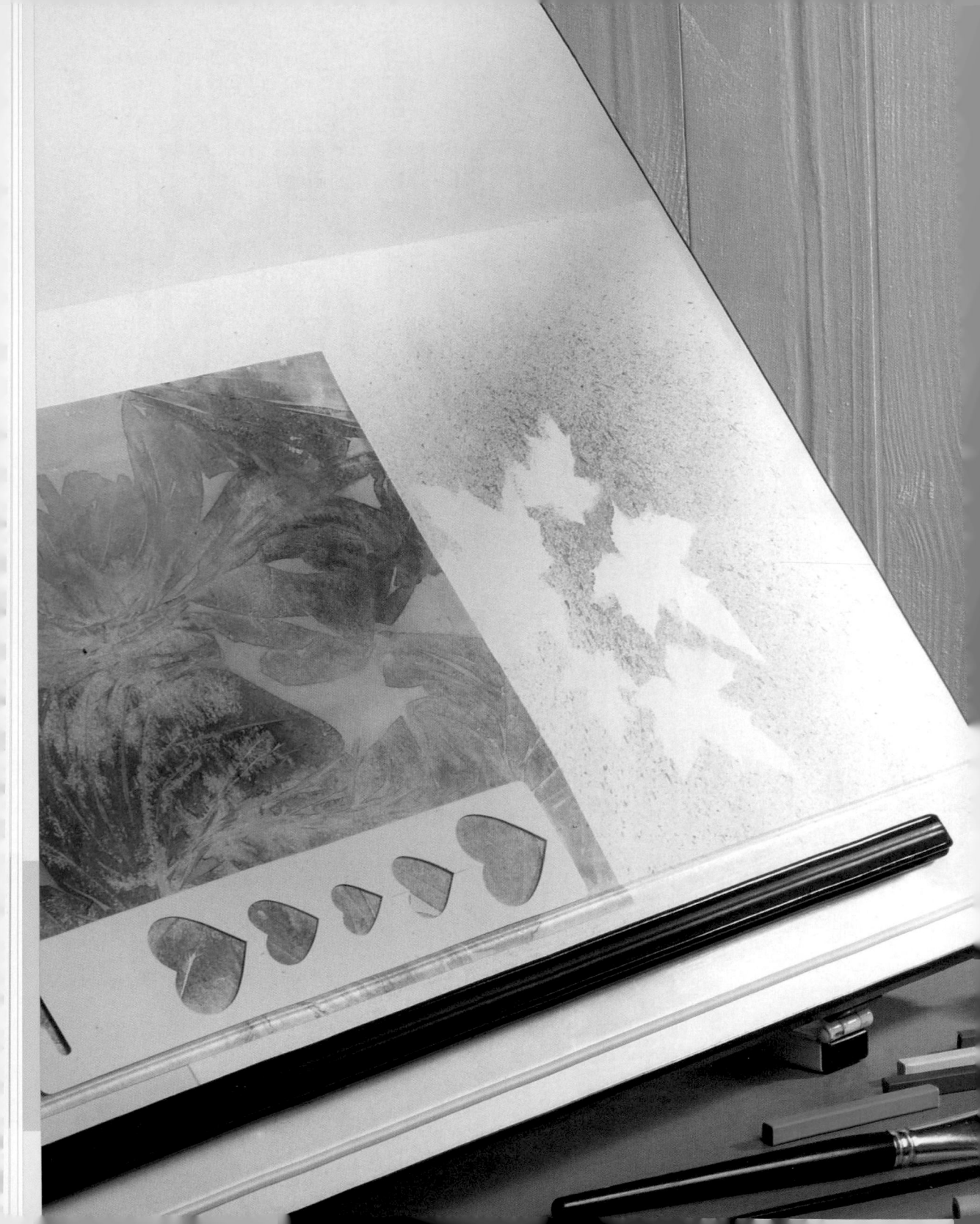

Calligraphic Techniques

There are numerous techniques, both traditional and modern, that can be combined with calligraphic lettering to create wonderful visual effects. This part of the book guides you through a number of these methods of decoration and embellishment, from the elegant simplicity of embossing to the more complicated but richly satisfying technique of gilding, and shows how they can be put into practice. At the end of this section an introduction to digital calligraphy demonstrates the exciting possibilities presented by this new art form, and outlines all you need to create calligraphic art on your home computer.

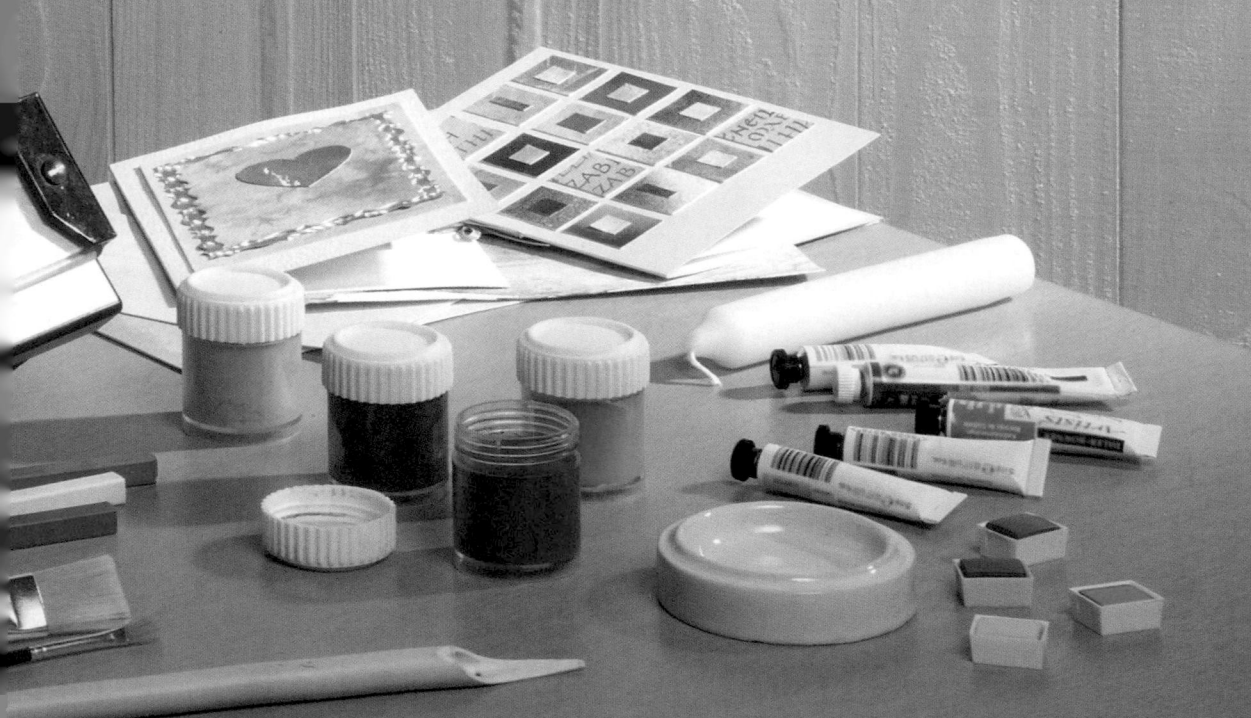

Flourished Italic and Italic swash capitals

Flourishes are extensions applied to the beginning and ending of letters. The variations produced by flourishing Italic letters are fun to do and the possibilities are endless. Practising will give you confidence in handling the pen. Some letters are easier to flourish than others, and there are some letters that cannot be flourished. Swash or flourished Italic capitals have simple extensions to the letter. A swash should be a simple flourish that is not too ornate, so as not to alter the character of the whole piece.

Practising letters

The letters are written and spaced as for formal Italic hand with the same x-height of 5 nib widths. The interlinear space will need to be greater to accommodate the flowing upward and downward flourishes. Care should be taken to keep a good basic Italic letterform throughout. The flowing movement of the letter extensions should not appear to be too constricted or too tight as flourished letters do not look good if they are too cramped. When deciding on the route of the extensions on the ascenders and descenders, a finely drawn pencil line is often helpful. Use a dip pen and keep it well loaded with ink as this helps the flow. Try writing the letters using some different sized nibs and a range of nib widths. Experiment with different letters of the alphabet to discover which flourishes work best.

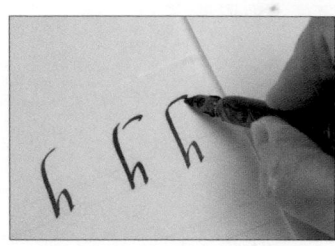

1 Rule writing lines as for formal Italic but make the interlinear space much larger to allow more space for the flourished ascenders and descenders. Begin flourishing by making the ascenders a little taller than usual. Try a simple lead-in stroke from the right of the letter 'h', completing it as normal. Go back to the top of the ascender and add the second stroke.

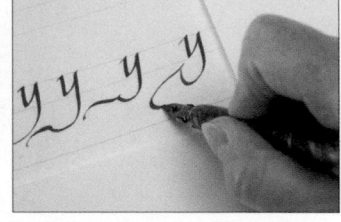

2 Try flourishing the letter 'y'. Remember to keep the underlying letterform. If the flourishes seem awkward to do then it is best not to pursue them. Practise the shapes that flow easily from the pen.

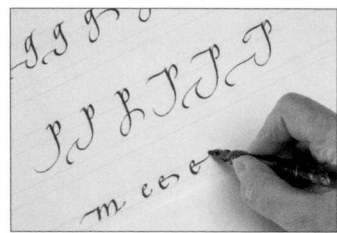

3 Try some different flourishes – be adventurous. Sometimes it is useful to extend the letter along the line (as in the case of 'm' and 'n'). Try elongating the central bar of 'e'. By trial and error you will discover which flourishes are the most successful.

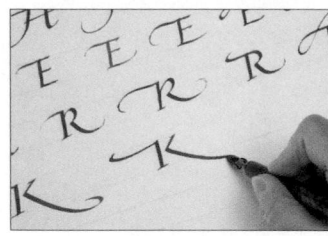

4 Flourished Italic capitals or swash capitals are also exciting to do and look very smart as a single letter to introduce a line of lower-case Italic writing. Practise adding some simple extensions first.

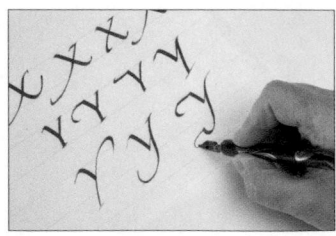

5 Try to relax when writing these shapes. The pen angle can change as you are working: moving from 40 degrees through to 5 degrees to enable you to manoeuvre the pen in a fluid way. Here the pen has been turned on its tip. It can be tilted on its side to add fine detail. This pen manipulation is quite acceptable.

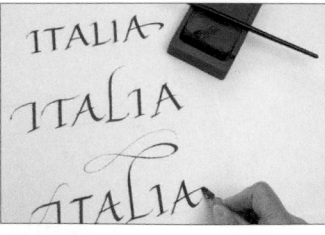

6 Practise three variations of Italic capitals with flourishes added. Note that not every letter is flourished. Less is better and has more impact.

Planning flourished letters

When flourishing letters, the action of the hand holding the pen should come from an arm movement rather than just the fingers or the hand. To practise these arm movements take a large sheet of practice paper and make some expansive, gestural movements with a loaded pen. This exercise will help you to create sweeping flourishes.

In a line of writing it is best to plan the letters that can be flourished. Resist the temptation to flourish every ascender and descender as this will look crowded and over ornate, making the writing unpleasant to read. On a short line of text, you should only flourish the first and last letter. Flourished capitals allow room for lots of creativity and can

look very striking, but do not be tempted to use them for whole pieces of text – too many will not work well together as they make the text appear overly busy. Flourishes should always have a specific purpose – as decoration, to balance a design, or to emphasize the flow of the line. They should be lively but applied cautiously.

Practice exercise: **Name tags and place labels**

Show off flourished Italics and swash capitals by writing the names of friends and family for an event or party.

Materials
- *Layout or practice paper*
- *Black ink or gouache*
- *Good quality paper or thin card (stock), in a variety of colours*
- *Gouache paint in white*
- *Dip pens*
- *Scissors or craft (utility) knife*
- *Hole punch*
- *Ribbon*

> **Tip:** Have fun writing in colour or adorn your place cards with flourished pen patterns.

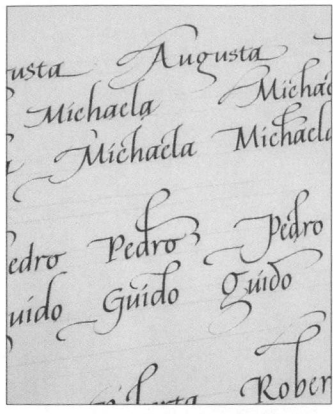

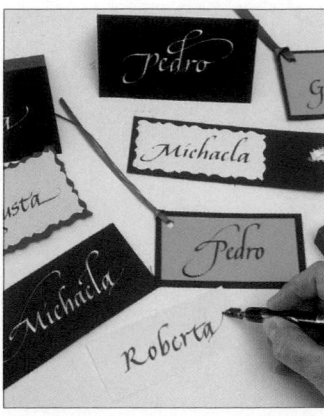

1 Name tags are a wonderful way to enjoy flourished Italic. Practise writing the names of people that you wish to invite on layout paper. Do a swash capital first followed by flourished Italic minuscules.

2 Make the gift tags by writing the names on coloured paper or thin card, then cut to size. Embellish decoratively and punch a hole to thread a ribbon, if required.

Practice exercise: **Quotation or poem**

Try writing a favourite quotation or poem and plan where the flourishes and swash letters should fall.

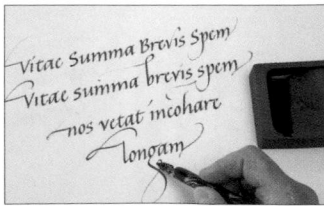

1 Practise writing the small quotation or poem and carefully plan the route of the flourishes to enhance and complement the layout of the design.

Materials
- *Layout or practice paper*
- *Black ink*
- *Dip pen*
- *Good quality paper*
- *Gouache paint in various colours*

2 Transfer to good quality paper. Decorate the project with colour, such as red and gold.

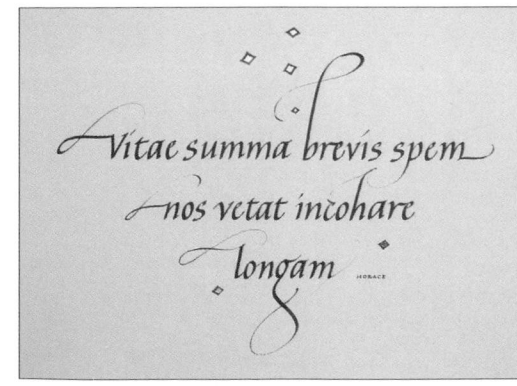

Pen patterns

Trying out different pen patterns is an excellent way to establish what your pen can do. These patterns help develop the skills that are required for calligraphy, as well as being an end in themselves. There are many decorative devices that can be copied and then developed as you build up a repertoire. The repetitive nature of pen patterns is also important because it enables you to build up a rhythm in writing.

Felt-tipped pens are ideal to use for pen patterns as they move freely across the paper without resistance. Choose two sizes of pen, in two colours, or the kind with a nib at each end in two sizes. This gives much more opportunity for variety in pattern-making at little cost. Once you are confident in using the felt-tipped pens, try creating the patterns using different sizes of broad-edged brushes.

Practising strokes

Many of the strokes that can be practised are parts of letterform strokes. Pen angles have to be consistent, or the pattern will be uneven, and this is a good discipline to learn. Notice any change in angle, and train your hand-eye coordination to maintain that angle. Measuring and ruling lines to accommodate the pattern is good practice for preparing lines for writing.

> **Tip:** When using patterns try to achieve complete harmony throughout your work. Pattens should be planned before a piece of calligraphy is begun and not simply added in on a whim. By using a square grid at 45 degrees to the horizontal, you can create the diamond which forms the basis of the zig-zag pattern.

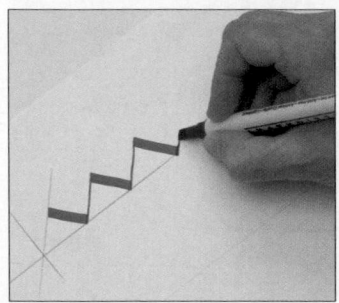

1 Practise holding the pen at a constant 45-degree angle. Control the pen by making equal-sized zig-zags. Practise making very thick and very thin lines in the zig-zags.

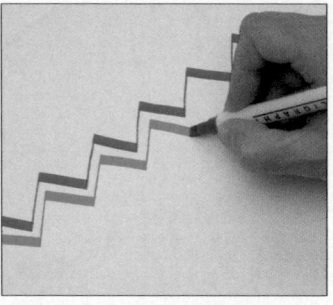

2 Put another row next to the first in a different colour to make parallel zig-zag marks. This will help develop coordination.

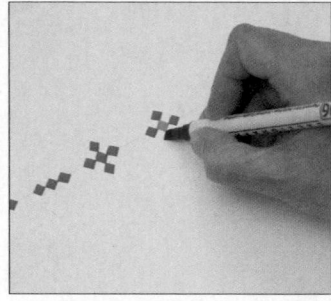

3 Make smaller, more concise marks just by making squares; make their edges touch – this takes more care.

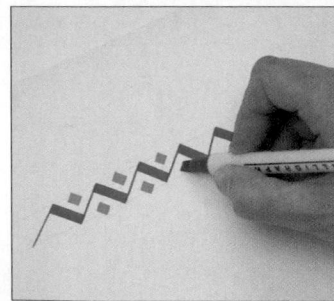

4 Do another zig-zag, then add squares using the other colour.

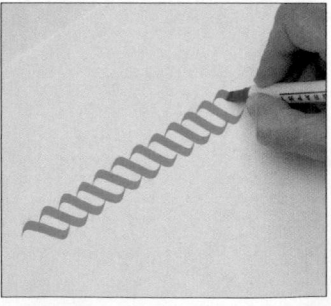

5 Curves are next; but do not be deceived, this is a small curve at each end of a straight stroke, which is repeated to build up the design.

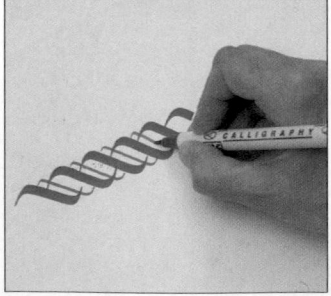

6 The appearance of the 'rope' created can be varied by opening up the white spaces between the curves and adding a narrower side stroke.

Practice exercise: **Building up pen patterns**

Continue to practise with more complex pen patterns created by using two colours of felt-tipped pen, each in large and small sizes, such as 5mm (1/4in) and 2mm (5/64in). Alternatively, use two sizes of broad-edged pen and two colours of ink. When you have perfected drawing the patterns in pen, try using brushes. Alter the pressure on the brush to change the thickness of the line.

Materials
- *Plain white paper*
- *Pens in two sizes*
- *Inks in two colours*

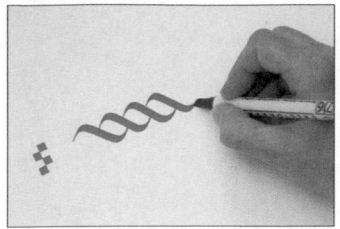

1 In one colour, make wide curves, paying attention to keeping the white spaces inside an even distance apart. Use a constant 45-degree pen angle.

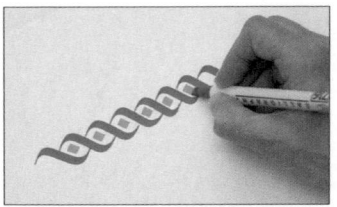

2 In another colour, add squares inside the curves, maintaining the 45-degree pen angle.

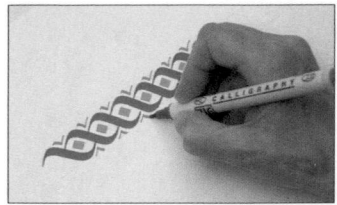

3 In one of the two colours already used, build up the pattern with a thinner pen on the outside.

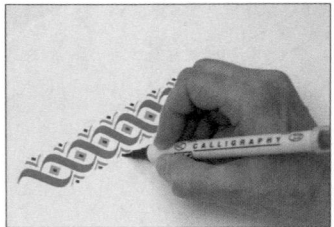

4 Complete the decoration with small squares using the narrower pen in the other colour.

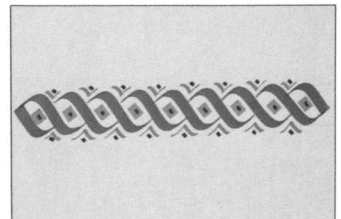

5 The finished design: repeated strokes develop a rhythm that makes a lively pattern. The two sizes add visual interest.

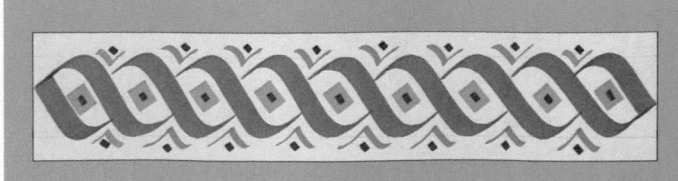

6 This would make an attractive border to a piece of work, or it could be given a frame and mounted by itself.

Other patterns

These decorative patterns will help you to practise different pen strokes.

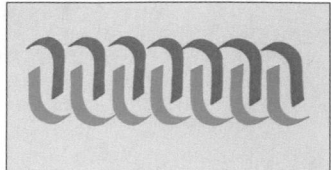

Curves ▲
It can be helpful to turn the page the other way up for the second row so that the marks are being repeated in the same way.

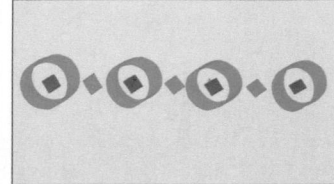

Circles and diamonds ▲
If all the circles are made first, judging the gap for the diamonds will be difficult, so make the diamonds as you progress.

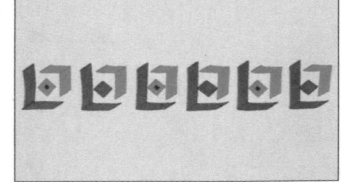

Build up 'L' shapes ▲
Make all the 'L's, then go back and make inverted 'L's in another colour. Add the diamonds last.

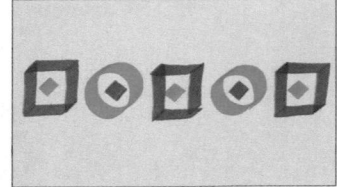

Squares and circles ▲
Alternate colours create added visual interest in this pattern.

Ruling pen

The ruling pen is a tool made up of a pen holder with two stainless-steel blades attached at the writing end. One of the pen's blades is straight and flat and the other bows slightly outwards. The tips of the pen almost meet and the space between them forms the reservoir for the ink or paint. The pen is loaded with ink or paint using a brush or the dipper that is supplied with bottles of ink. The thumbscrew on its bowed blade alters the distance between the tips and finely adjusts the amount of ink that flows, thereby changing the width of the line. The further apart the tips, the thicker the line made by the pen.

The original purpose of the ruling pen was for ruling accurate lines of uniform thickness. Technical drawing has now been overtaken by the use of technical pens, and in more recent years, by computer technology, which is able to produce ruled lines much more quickly. However, calligraphers have adopted the ruling pen as an artistic tool, and have found new ways to make marks, both conventional and more experimental. The attraction of this pen in calligraphy is its freedom of movement in any direction, unimpeded by a broad edge, which means it flows freely across the paper. Although the ruling pen is still frequently used for creating straight lines, it also presents possibilities for making calligraphy exciting for those who prefer expressive, gestural writing.

Practising ruling lines and making marks

Drawing neat straight lines is one way of using the ruling pen, but there is so much more that it can be used for. It is also an ideal tool for creating free, fine strokes for either writing or drawing, and if it is held in a less conventional way, flattened over the paper, with its open side pressed towards the paper, more ink will escape, making a thicker mark. When used in this way the ruling pen produces a heavy line rather like a brush. Once this technique has been mastered, the pen can be manipulated and bold marks of various thicknesses can be developed.

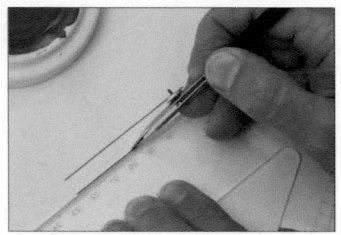

1 To rule lines conventionally, place the rule with its bevelled edge up, to prevent ink seepage. Dip the pen in ink and rule a straight line. Adjust the thickness with the screw thread.

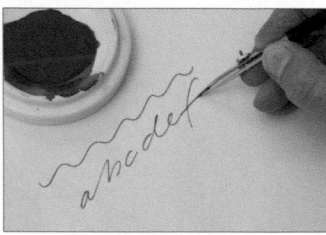

2 Without the ruler, use the ruling pen as an adaptable tool for sketching, scribbling, or writing a quick, flowing line.

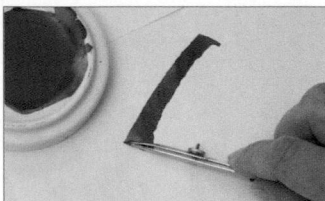

3 Held on its side, well charged with ink and with the open edge against the paper, the ruling pen will discharge its ink very dramatically.

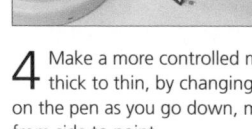

4 Make a more controlled mark from thick to thin, by changing the hold on the pen as you go down, moving from side to point.

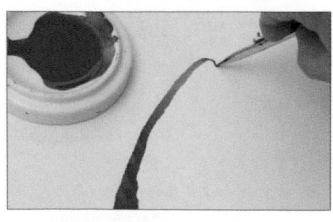

5 Dramatic upward strokes are also fun to try for lively ascenders.

6 Combining a thick stroke with a thin one takes a little more practice. Use a flick of the wrist as you change from holding the pen flat to riding back up to its point; thick stroke down, thin stroke up.

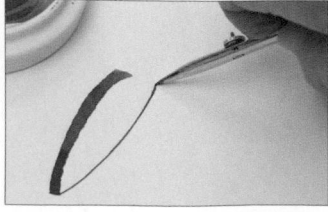

> **Tip:** A ruling pen attachment is often included in a compass set. The attachment can be inserted into the compass instead of a pencil, and can be used to draw circular lines, either as guidelines for writing or as decoration.

Practice exercise: **Core letters (a, b, c)**

Practise the first letters of the alphabet using contrasting thick and thin strokes.

Materials
• *Technical ruling pen*
• *Plain white paper*
• *Free-flowing ink or paint*

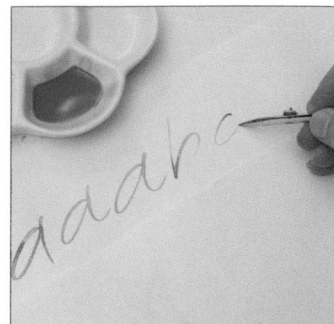

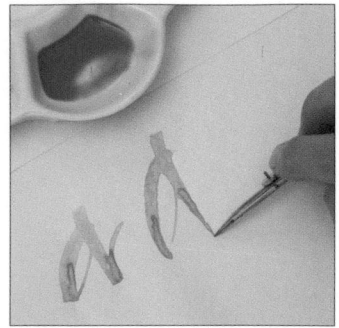

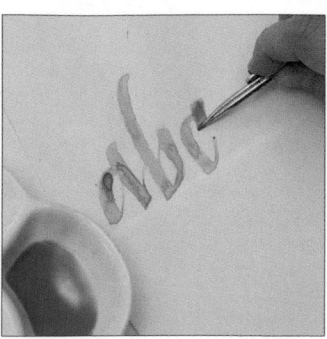

2 Repeat the structure of the letter, but this time manipulate the pen to create a thick downwards stroke and a thin upwards stroke.

3 Follow the 'thick down, thin up' process for 'a, b, c' and keep writing these three letters until a successful set has been created.

1 Write the core letter shapes in monoline first, holding the pen like a pencil and moving down, up, down to create this Italic form of 'a'.

Tip: Do not unscrew the ruling pen very much. Start with the points just touching, then loosen a hair's breadth – if the gap is too wide it will not allow for surface tension to hold the ink in place and it will not flow properly.

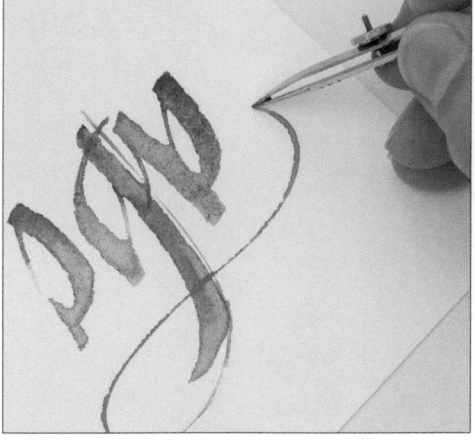

4 Make a thin-lined flourish to complete the design – it may help to complete this flourish by turning the work upside down.

Practice exercise: **Core letters (x, y, z)**

Just three letters create an attractive design in their own right. Placing any three letters together needs practice to avoid forming unsightly holes.

Materials
• *Technical ruling pen*
• *Plain white paper*
• *Free-flowing ink or paint*

Tip: Always make sure both tips of the ruling pen are on the paper, otherwise the ink will not flow.

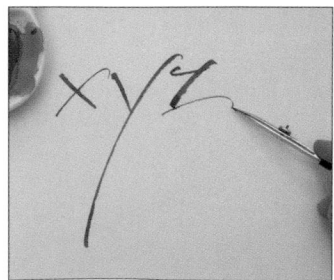

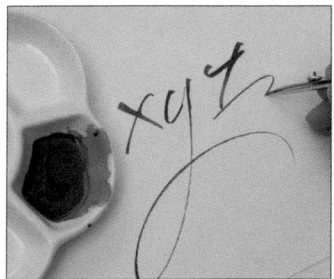

1 Write 'X, Y, Z' using all diagonals. Hold the pen flat to create the thick lines usually made by an edged pen.

2 Try another version of the same letters, combining diagonals with curves and a bold flourish.

Brush lettering

The broad-edged brush is an underused calligraphic tool. The benefit of using a brush is that it allows writing to be carried out on surfaces that would be difficult for a pen. Brushes are also particularly useful for large-scale writing as they come in much larger sizes than pens. Beginners sometimes find the most difficult part of using the brush is controlling the hairs, as there is no definite pressure to be felt as when putting pen to paper. The secret is not to hold the brush in the same way as a pen. Instead, hold it perpendicular to the paper – this will feel unnatural at first. Position your fingers with the thumb one side and the first two fingers on the other; test if you can twist the brush with those fingers. Use the rest of your hand to steady the brush by resting on the paper. Slide your hand around to make the letterform – do not try to do it all using the fingers.

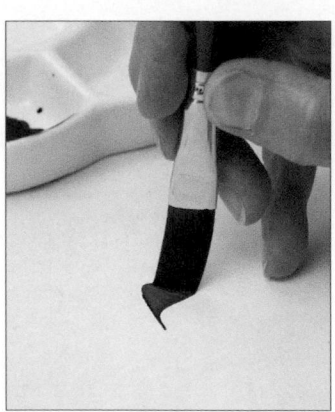

5 Check your fingers are either side of the handle and that you can twist the brush by moving your thumb, not your wrist. Try twisting a quarter turn.

> **Tip:** Even if you make a mistake, do not stop work on a piece as it is good practice and helps you get used to the brush. With time, it will become easier to know the best brush to use in order to achieve the required effect.

Practising with the brush

The brush techniques shown here will help control lettering with the paint.

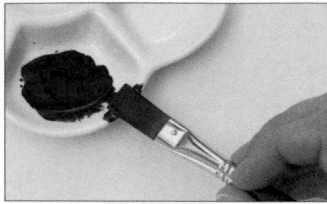

1 Practise preserving the chisel edge of the brush, by filling it with paint then wiping most of it off against the flat edge.

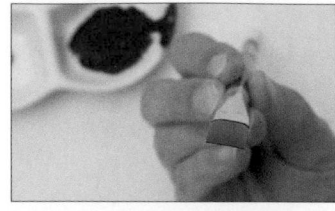

2 Get into the habit of checking closely that sufficient paint has been wiped off the brush to create a sharp chisel edge.

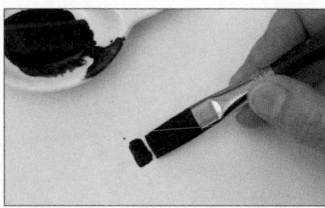

3 Keeping the brush overcharged with paint will result in an unattractive blobby mark.

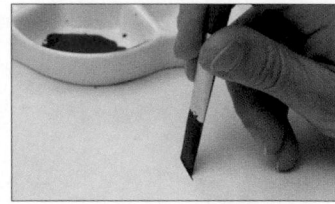

4 For best results, hold the brush perpendicular to the paper, not like a normal pen; this way you will be able to make fine lines as well as broad ones.

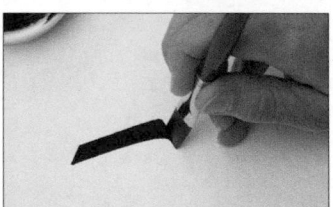

6 Twisting gives subtlety to strokes. Here the brush starts with its edge at 45 degrees to the writing line, then is smoothly twisted to 90 degrees.

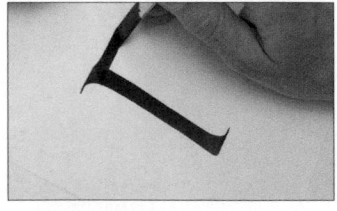

7 Blend adjoining strokes by starting the second stroke within the first. This is important with large letters, as thin joins weaken the structure.

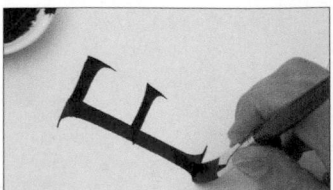

8 The final serif on this 'F' starts entirely within the upright stroke and twists clockwise as it emerges.

Practical exercise: **Making an Uncial 'E'**

This exercise uses the brush and two colours of paint to make an Uncial 'E'. Uncials are upper case letters and very rounded. Keep the brush at a flat angle or the letters will become too narrow.

Materials
- *Gouache paints e.g. ultramarine and magenta*
- *Paper with slightly rough surface*
- *Paint palette or saucers*
- *Water pot*
- *Broad-edged brush*
- *Handmade and Ingres papers*
- *Kitchen paper*

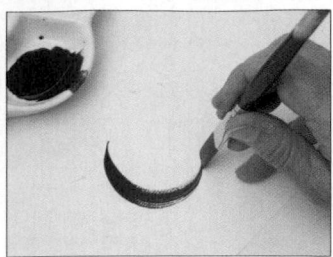

1 In the blue gouache, make a smooth half-moon curve by holding the brush perpendicular to the paper and moving your arm round in a sweeping movement.

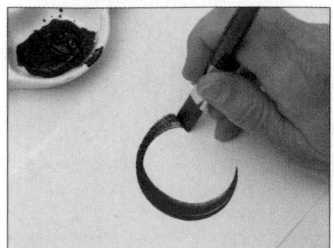

2 Without cleaning the brush, replenish with magenta paint at the same consistency; check you have wiped to a chisel edge. Start this stroke inside the first, and manipulate the serif by twisting.

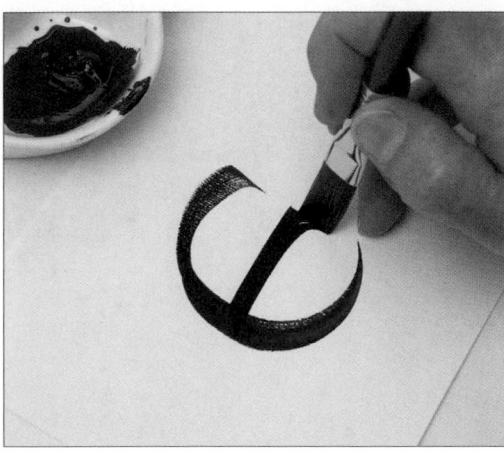

3 Replenish with more magenta (remember to wipe it sharp), hold the brush at 45 degrees to the writing line, pull a straight stroke and finish with a twist for the serif.

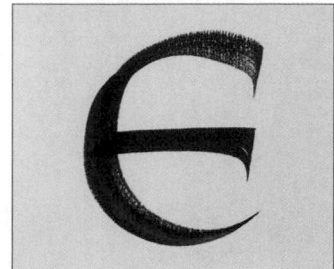

4 Using a large brush on paper with a 'tooth' can give a pleasing granular effect in places, adding texture. Here the colour changes highlight the structure of the letter, making it an object of visual interest.

Special surfaces

One big advantage of the brush is its ability to write on special surfaces such as quite rough-surfaced paper, which would be unsuitable for writing on with a metal pen. Experiment with any forms you can find.

> **Tip:** Brush lettering is suitable for a huge range of designs and can be particularly effective when used as a headline. By placing a piece of paper underneath your working hand, you can help ensure the paper remains clean.

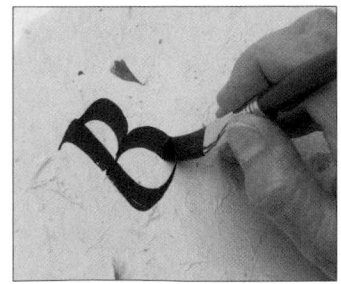

Handmade Indian petal paper ▲
This rough-textured paper has fibres and petals embedded in it which give the paint a slightly granular effect.

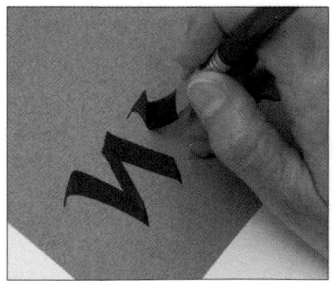

Ingres pastel paper ▲
This paper is lightly textured which creates plenty of 'drag', enabling controlled brush work.

Cutting balsa, reed and quill pens

Early writers used natural materials such as reeds and feathers for nibs. These materials have been used successfully for thousands of years as alphabets developed requiring a fine balance of thick and thin strokes. The modern calligrapher has access to an enormous range of modern equipment. However, elaborate effects may call for the use of more adventurous tools on traditional papers and surfaces such as vellum. It is well worth trying to create tools using traditional materials, and they are inexpensive to make and easy to replace.

Making a balsa pen

Balsa wood pens are enjoyable to use. They are quick and easy to make and many can be made from one sheet of balsa wood. Try a variety of sizes by varying the width of the pen. Balsa wood is a very lightweight wood and is often used in model-making because it is easy to cut and shape. There is a grain to the wood and it is best to follow the grain when cutting the length of the pen.

Materials
• *Sheet of balsa wood*
• *Self-healing cutting mat*
• *Scalpel and craft (utility) knife*

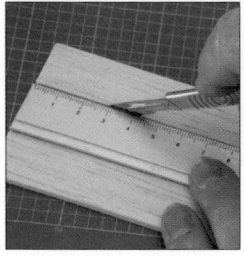

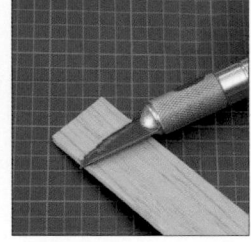

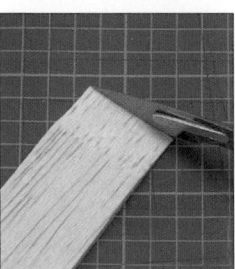

1 Cut the wood into a rectangle approximately 10–12cm (4½in) in length. The width can be varied to suit your needs, but about 2.5cm (1in) is a good guide.

2 Starting 1cm (½in) away from one of the narrow ends, use a sharp craft knife to shave a bevelled cut. A left-hander should make a left-oblique cut.

3 Make a cut straight down at 90 degrees, using the scalpel. The edge will need to be sharp to do this.

Making a reed pen

Reed pens date back even further in history than the quill. They were used by Middle Eastern scribes because reeds were in plentiful supply. They were sturdy and hollow-centred which made them very suitable to cut as a writing tool. Reed pens are still used by calligraphers today. Bamboo cane is often used as a substitute and is readily available. It is possible to cut reed pens with a thicker nib and they are used for larger writing.

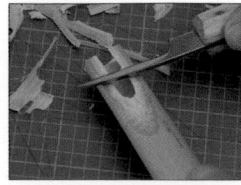

Materials
• *Sharp knife*
• *Length of reed or bamboo*
• *Self-healing cutting mat*
• *Drinks can*

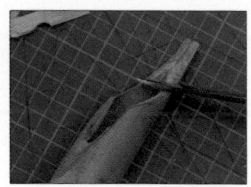

1 Using a sharp knife, cut the reed to about 20cm (8in). Cut a downward stroke, beginning 2.5cm (1in) from the end of the reed curving sharply to mid-way, and then bring the curve parallel with the reed shaft. Scrape away the soft pith.

2 Cut the side sections to form the shoulders of the nib.

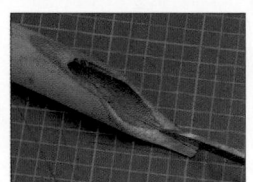

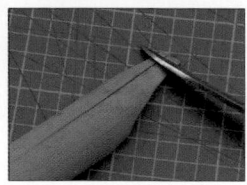

3 Make a vertical slit up the centre. Do not make this too long or the nib will separate when writing.

4 Cut across the top at an oblique angle of 30 degrees to shape the nib.

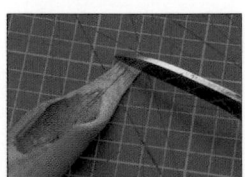

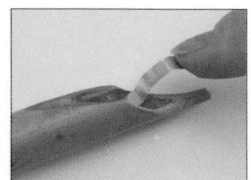

5 Cut the tip cleanly across to form a sharp writing edge at 90 degrees.

6 To make a reservoir, cut a strip of metal from a drinks can, bend it and insert it in the barrel. The ink sits behind the reservoir.

Curing and cutting a quill

Quills have been used for hundreds of years. Most calligraphers frequently use metals pens, but quills are still the preferred choice for writing on vellum because of their sensitivity and flexibility. Calligraphers mainly use goose, turkey and swan feathers, and crow for very fine writing. The best feathers for use with the right hand come from the first five flights of the left wing of the bird, and for a left-handed scribe, from the right wing of the bird. This is because the natural curve of the feather gives the correct balance in the hand.

Once prepared, the quill pen does not quite live up to its image of the beautiful plume – the quill is cut to a manageable length of about 20cm (8in) and stripped of its barbs, which makes it easier to handle.

Materials
- *Silver sand*
- *Cooker and pan*
- *Feather*
- *Sharp knife*
- *Self-healing cutting mat*

Tip: The drying process eliminates oils. Ideally, this should be carried out naturally, but this could take many months of drying. Instead an artificial heat source is used with a pan, but this needs to be kept gentle and very brief or the barrel becomes too brittle. The heating alters the quill from being soft textured and opaque to becoming harder.

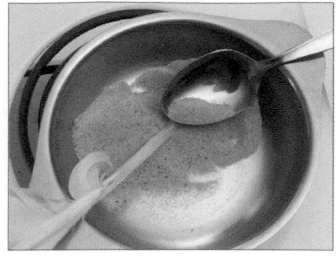

1 The quill needs to be cured so that the barrel is hardened. Before this is done, cut the sealed end of the barrel, then soak in water overnight. The next day heat the silver sand in a pan for about 15 minutes until really hot. Temper the quill by pouring hot sand down the upturned barrel. Insert the quill into the hot sand and leave for about 10–15 seconds (this is trial and error). If it is left too long, the nib will not crack cleanly and if under-cured, will be too rubbery. Cool the quill quickly by dipping it into cold water then shake it dry. The outer membrane is then scraped away using the back of a sharp knife.

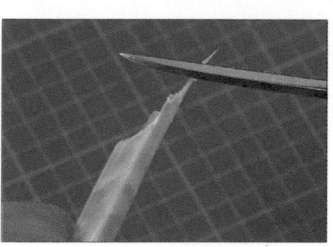

4 Scoop out the shoulders, matching both sides equally.

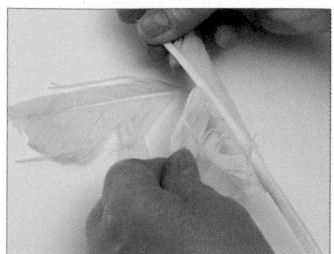

2 Use a sharp knife to cut the quill. Cut the feathers to about 20cm (8in) in length and strip away the barbs.

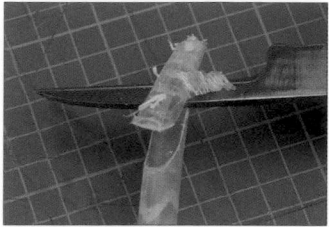

3 Make a long scoop on the underside of the barrel.

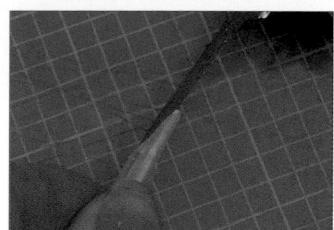

5 Place the top of the quill on a cutting mat. Place the knife blade in the centre of the nib and make a slit of one and a half times the nib width.

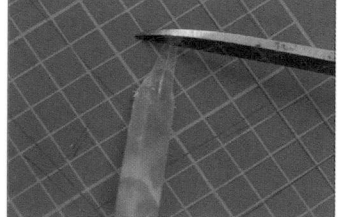

6 Trim the end of the quill with a small cut off the tip.

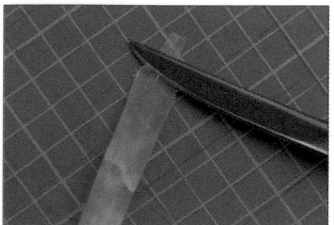

7 Scoop a thin sliver off the top of the nib.

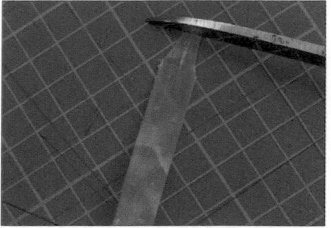

8 To square the nib, make a 90-degree clean cut.

Cut-paper lettering

Paper cutting has been a folk art ever since paper was invented in AD105 by Ts'ai Lun, an official in the court of Ho Ti, Emperor of Cathay in China. However, it has not been widely recognized as an art form, although artists and historians are becomingly increasingly aware of its valuable folk heritage. Traditional techniques using cut paper include German *scherenschnitte*, Chinese *chien-chih*, Japanese *kirigami* or *mon-kiri,* Polish *wycinanki* and French *silhouettes.*

The craft of paper cutting is easily adapted to cut letters and may be used in conjunction with a piece of calligraphy or as a stand-alone design. The basic technique of cutting letters out of paper may be separated into two distinct categories – stencil and silhouette images. While similar, they each have their own 'rules'. These refer to whether it is the letter or the background that is cut out. For stencils, the letter is cut away, while for silhouettes it is the background that is lost.

Silhouette and stencil letters

On the left of this card is a silhouette, or positive letter, which is best thought of as a letter within a frame, ideally touching in at least three places. The letter stays while the background is cut away. On the right is a stencil or negative letter, which is removed from the paper leaving the letter-shaped hole, with the background firmly in place.

With practice it is possible to develop skills that allow elaborate lettering and designs to be cut out. It is important to remember when cutting around the curves of a shape or letter only to cut in small arcs, before stopping and moving the paper. Do not lift the knife, but keep it in the same position and continue cutting when the paper has been repositioned. This may seem a slow technique, but it will ensure a smoother shape to your cuts. Keep the blade upright – without slanting it to one side or the other – and make sure that the sharp edge is facing towards you. A sharp blade makes a great deal of difference to the quality of the cuts as well as the amount of effort that is needed to make them. A blade that is not sharp will produce uneven edges and poor curves so change the blade frequently. Choose the paper carefully because the thickness of the paper and the amount of detail in the letters also play a role in how successfully the letters are cut.

> **Tip:** For crisp cutting, work in two directions – downwards and to the right. Turn the work to accommodate these directions. Left-handers should reverse the latter directions to work to the left and anticlockwise. At all times keep your free hand away from the cutting direction.

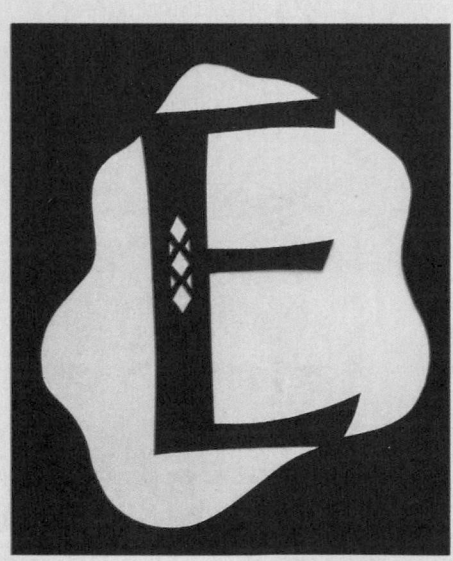

Silhouette letter

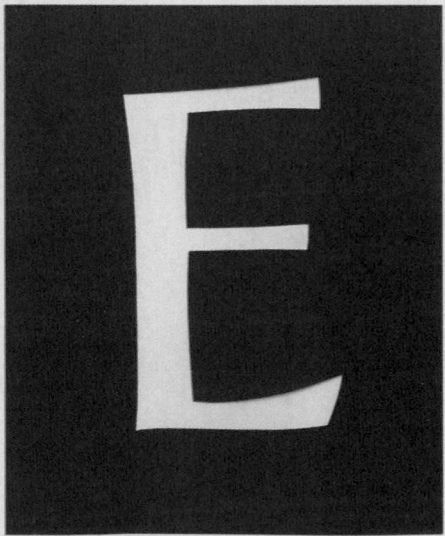

Stencil letter

Making stencil letters

When cutting these stencils careful thought needs to be given to letters with enclosed areas that could simply fall out. If the stencil letter has a 'counter' or enclosed space, there needs to be a way to keep this 'island' in place as the letter is cut away. The letters with counters are: 'A', 'B', 'D', 'O', 'P', 'Q' and 'R' and 'a', 'b', 'd', 'e', 'g', 'o', 'p' and 'q'.

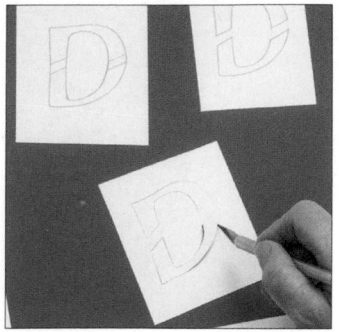

Cutting the counter ▲
Draw in pencil before you cut, to show where the letter will be cut. The addition of a 'pathway' such as a chevron can hold the middle of a letter, such as a 'D'.

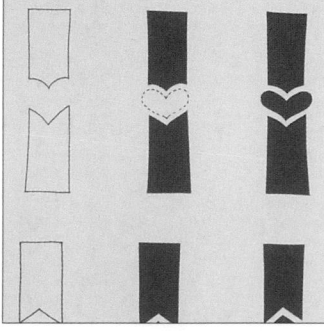

Using designs to create pathways ▲
Make use of designs to create 'pathways' of safety. Including shapes such as hearts or diamonds midway across the letter can create a pathway. Rub out any overlap points to avoid cutting and making mistakes.

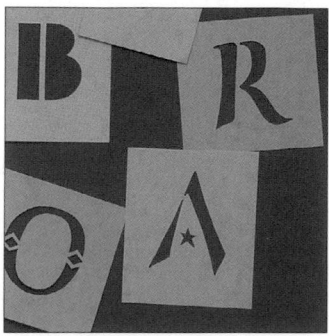

The finished letters ▲
These are some of the ways of making safe pathways on letters. When combining stencil letters within words, it is also important not to let them touch each other as the design will become physically unstable.

Practice exercise: **Making a stencil and silhouette letter**

When cutting silhouette letters, counter shapes and backgrounds are removed, but it is important that letters physically touch each other and their frame at overlap points, so that the design will be stable and hold together.

Materials
- *2H pencil*
- *Lightweight watercolour paper*
- *Craft (utility) knife or scalpel with a long, pointed blade*

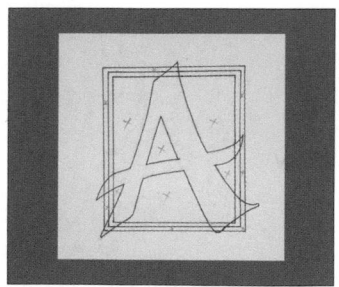

1 Draw the letter 'A' on to watercolour paper. Be very clear about where the cut is to be made, marking the spaces where the card can be cut away with an 'x'. To add a border around a silhouette letter, draw three lines in tandem, ensuring the letter protrudes beyond the outer line in at least three places and rubbing out the overlap areas.

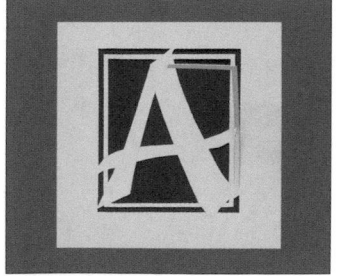

2 Cut a channel between the outer and middle lines and all other marked areas. Leave the border intact, because it keeps a pathway of safety.

Tip: Mark the areas to be cut and rub out overlap points. Do not just cut out the letter profile, or it will fall out.

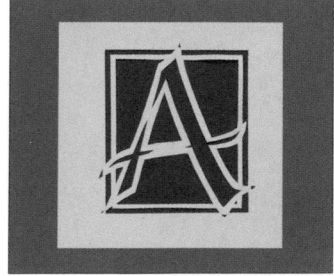

3 It is possible to combine both silhouette and stencil techniques, by further cutting into a silhouette letter. When doing so it must be remembered that stencil rules now apply, and care must again be taken to save the middles of letters.

Embossing

This is a technique that is sometimes described as 'white on white'. Unlike usual calligraphy it does not use colour against a contrasting surface to make itself legible. Instead it uses shadows. The effect is achieved by stretching the paper through a stencil using a specialized embossing tool or a substitute such as a pointed bone folder. With practise, it is possible to cut very elaborate stencils for this purpose but it is best to start with a simple design, which should be relatively heavy as, when embossed, the shapes will appear narrower.

Always use a sharp blade when cutting your stencil. If the stencil is very complicated, the blade may need to be replaced several times. When cutting, keep your fingers well away from the blade. If you have an assortment of different sized embossing tools always start with the largest and progress to the smallest. This way the paper will gradually be stretched and will not be pierced. Do not emboss all the way around the stencil in the same direction as this will tear the paper. Start at the middle of one side and work part way around then go back to the beginning and work in the opposite direction. Take care of your stencils as they can be used many times. The cardboard of cereal boxes is an ideal material for making stencils. Remember to always stencil from the reversed side. You need a light box or light source for embossing, which should be secured with tape.

Making a stencil and embossing

The technique involves making two embossed letters in Foundational script, 'a' and 'n'. To form the letters use a double pencil (two pencils taped together). The letters are traced and the counter of the 'a' is glued in the correct position. Work on a light box or against a window to give you the best light. Go over the outline of the shapes with the embossing tool.

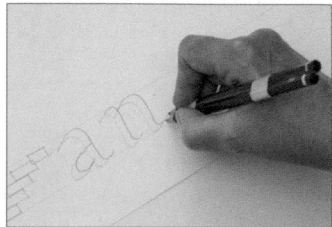

1 With double pencils and on layout paper, write two letters, one of which should have an internal counter.

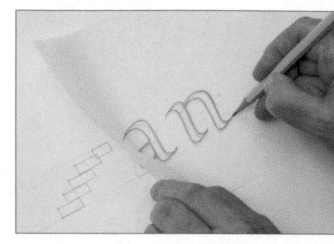

2 With tracing paper and a B pencil, trace the outline of these letters. Reverse the tracing paper and fix to a piece of lightweight card with masking tape.

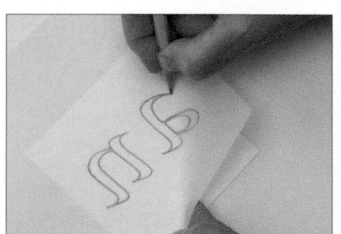

3 To transfer the design, carefully trace over the reversed letters with an H pencil onto the piece of lightweight card.

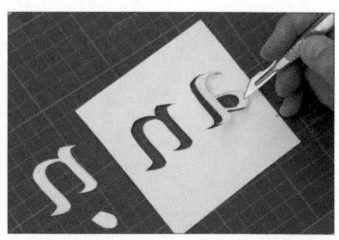

4 Remove the tracing paper and, with a scalpel on a self-healing cutting mat, carefully cut around the shapes. The counter space will come loose.

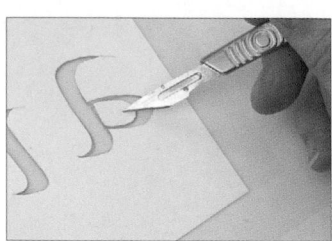

5 Erase any pencil marks and glue the stencil, with the correct letterforms face down, on tracing paper. Lay this over the original tracing and glue the loose counter space in position.

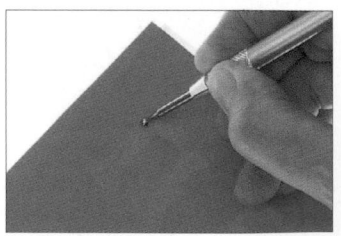

6 Place the stencil on a light box. Lay the good paper over this and tape the top edge to the light source. Using the embossing tool, carefully go around the outline of the shapes.

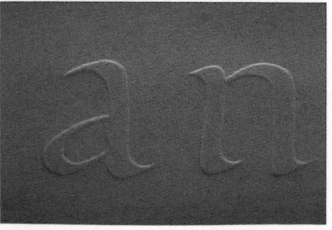

7 Remove your paper and turn over to appreciate the embossing.

Practice exercise: **Making an embossed bookmark**

This simple but effective bookmark uses a technique of overlapping using a series of hearts to portray a love of books, or it can be made as a special present for a friend.

Materials
- Pencil
- Tracing paper
- Lightweight card (stock)
- Scalpel or craft (utility) knife
- Self-healing cutting mat
- Lightweight watercolour or pastel paper
- Light box
- Masking tape
- Embossing tool
- Scrap paper
- Glue stick

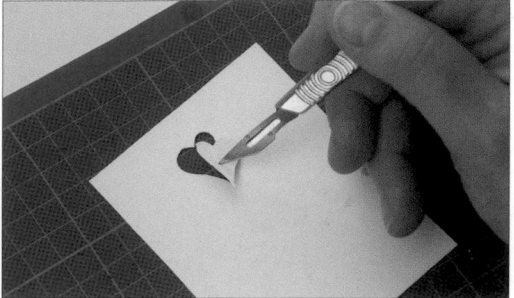

1 Draw a simple heart. Trace and transfer this to a piece of card. On a cutting mat, cut the stencil by taking out the heart using a scalpel or craft knife.

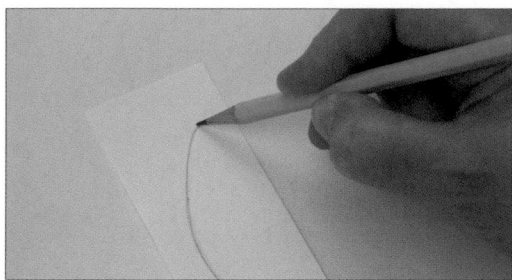

2 Cut a piece of lightweight paper to the dimensions of a bookmark. Lightly pencil a flowing line along the length.

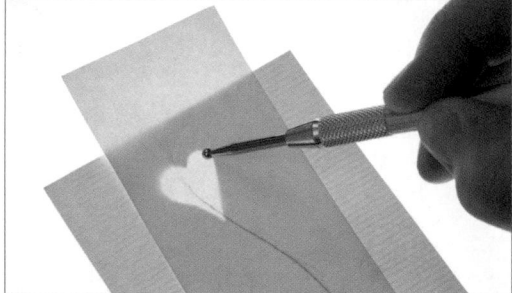

3 Secure the stencil to a light source using masking tape and, using the line as a guide, emboss hearts all the way along, making sure they overlap. Do not erase the pencil line as this will flatten the embossing.

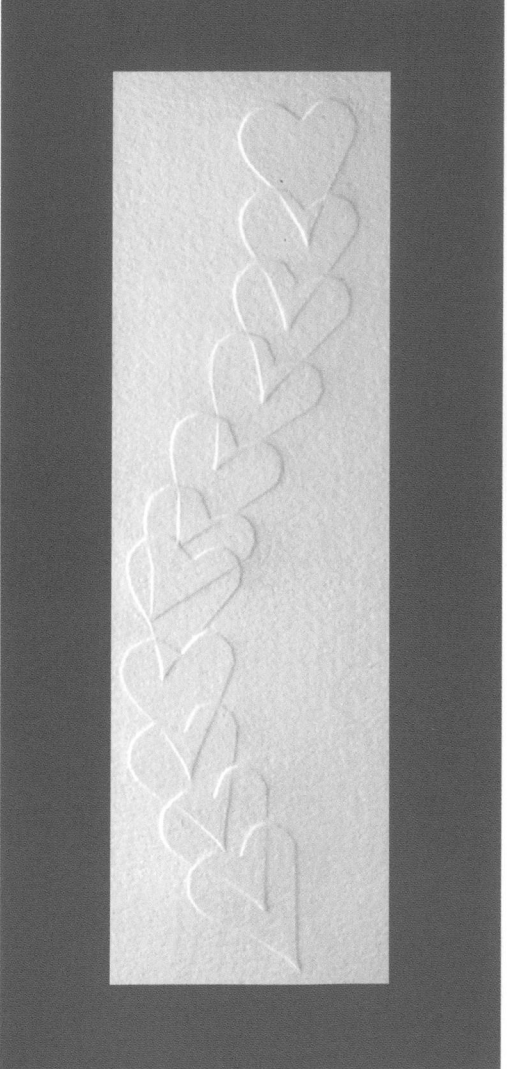

4 Remove from the light source and place on a piece of shiny scrap paper for protection. Glue around the edges before turning the embossed paper over and fixing it to a contrasting piece of card.

Washes and backgrounds

There are many different effects that you can create with background washes. There is a wealth of possibilities if you consider using different media and tools. Dry brush techniques, clear film, spattering, spraying, rollers, sponge and textured cloth all produce different marks when used with paint or acrylic inks. With experimentation and practise, texture and visual excitement, mood and atmosphere can be achieved in the backgrounds to calligraphic work. There are lots of creative possibilities to be explored using washes, single or variegated, with dropped-in colour on the paper.

Before making washes and backgrounds it is wise to stretch the paper if it is under 300gsm (140lb) in weight. This means saturating the paper with water and then securing it on to a wooden board with brown paper tape. Overlap the tape at the corners, keep the board flat for drying and leave the paper attached until all the colour work is finished. When dry, the paper becomes taut and accepts any amount of watercolour without buckling or becoming wrinkled.

> **Tip:** For best results use hot-pressed or cold-pressed papers for colour washes. Mix up enough paint to ensure you do not run short during an application. Thinly diluted watercolour paint will produce a more subtle wash effect, and applying the wash quickly will help avoid streaks and runs from forming.

Different effects

Try these washes and paint effects to create different backgrounds and patterns on paper.

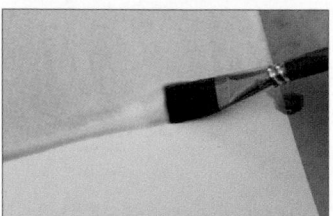

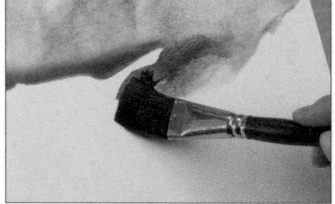

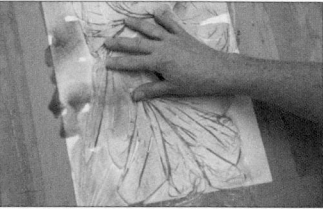

A single wash ▲
Raise the board at one end to apply the wash to the paper. Mix the watercolour paint or acrylic ink to a watery consistency. Dip a large brush in the paint draw it across the paper to create a smooth wash.

A variegated wash ▲
Mix up three separate colours. Dip the brush into the first colour and apply to the paper randomly. Rinse the brush and load with the second colour, adding it to the paper and blending into the spaces. Rinse the brush and add the final colour.

Using clear film or plastic wrap ▲
Paint a variegated wash on the paper, dropping in extra colour while it is still very wet. Drape a large piece of clear film on to the wet wash and drag it into different patterns. Leave to dry thoroughly before removing the film. This will create patterns in the colours.

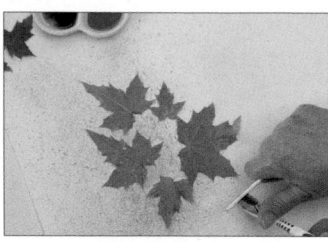

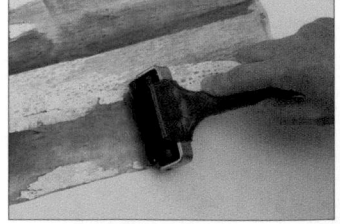

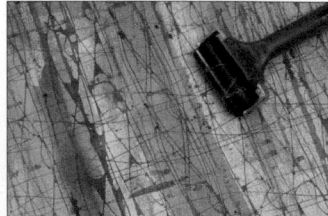

Spatter colour ▲
Use an old toothbrush loaded with paint. To spatter the paint drag a piece of card (stock) or a metal rule over the bristles towards yourself. Use a second brush for another colour. Alternatively, a spray bottle filled with paint can be used to create a similar effect.

Using a roller ▲
A printmaking roller or commercial paint roller can be used. Each will create a different effect. Squeeze two different colours into a flat wide container and add water. Roller the colours together slightly before applying them in broad bands.

String around the roller ▲
The string creates interesting random patterns when it is used to roll ink or paint on to the paper. Thin string on a print roller has been used to create the effect shown here. For a different effect try strands of cotton around the roller.

Practice exercise: **A decorative card**

Practise background colours by blending washes and creating different effects on paper. Use a limited range of paint or ink colours to help you to remember the paint mixes. By using acrylic inks or casein paint in the background, your paper will have the added advantages of it being waterproof when dry, giving a soft pleasant surface on which to work and allowing easy removal of writing mistakes. If the paper is 300gsm (140lb) and small in size then it is not necessary to stretch it. The larger the piece of paper, the more water it will hold and the more buckled it will become if it is not taped to a board.

Materials
- *A selection of practice sheets*
- *Coloured card (stock)*
- *Decorative paper*
- *Craft glue*
- *White photocopy paper*
- *Ribbon*
- *A sequin or decorative motif or beads (optional)*

Tip: When using washes, varying the length of time that each colour is allowed to dry before adding another can create a more complex design with greater depth. Always wait until all the paint is completely dry before you start to write on the paper.

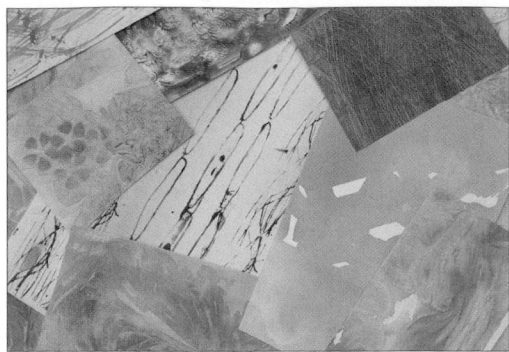

1 Create a variety of different textured and coloured paper, including different washes, patterns made with clear film (plastic wrap), spatter and coloured paper.

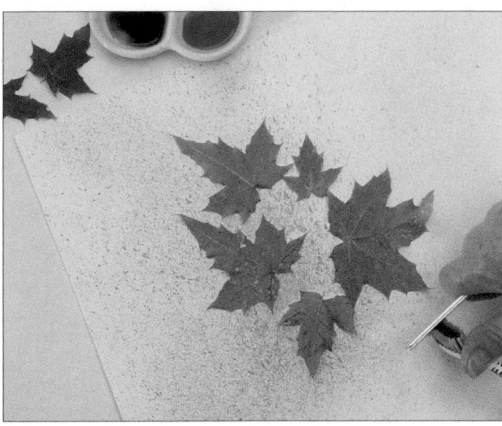

2 Cut a small sheet of coloured card in half, then fold each piece in half to create two separate cards. Cut some of the decorative pieces of paper into small rectangle or square shapes. Choose colour patterns that work harmoniously together and stick them to the cards with craft glue, piling different shapes on top of one another.

3 Finish the cards by adding a paper insert. For each card fold a small sheet of white photocopy paper in half and trim around the edges. Write your own message inside the folded paper and stick each one carefully into a card. Add a ribbon around the back spine making a neat bow on the outside. A sequin or decorative motif or beads can be added as a final decoration on the front of the cards.

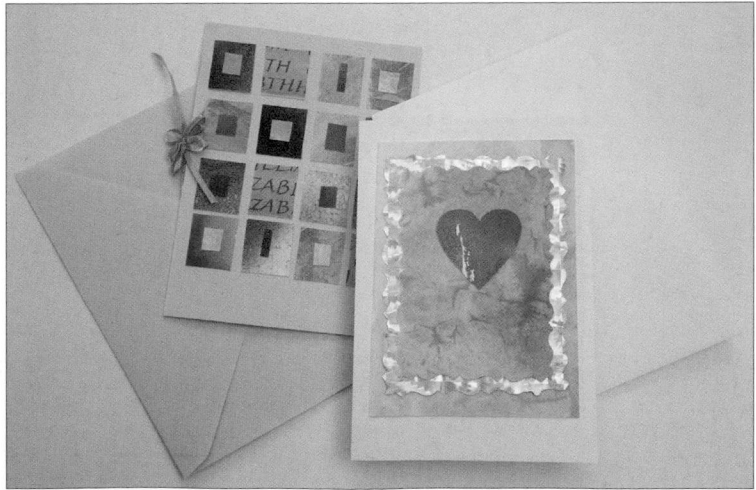

Resists

Methods that are used to protect areas of work are called resists. This allows work to eventually appear through any processes that have covered them. The definition of 'resist' is 'to stop from reaching'. White gouache, a white candle and masking fluid can all be used to create a resist, and each will produce a different result. When using resist techniques, ensure each step has dried completely before going on to the next. If speed is important, work may be gently dried using a hairdryer. Make sure that your paper can withstand the resist soaking and sponging before you start your main work.

Experimenting with gouache

This resist is made by using dilute gouache on water-colour paper, covering it with colour and dissolving the gouache in hot water.

Materials
- *Bleed proof/permanent white gouache*
- *Watercolour paper*
- *Automatic pens*
- *Large brush or hake*
- *Waterproof ink or acrylic colour*
- *Bath of water*
- *Natural sponge*
- *Drawing board*
- *Brown paper gum strip*

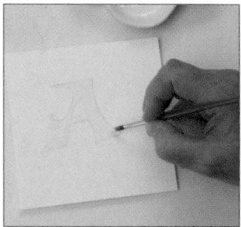 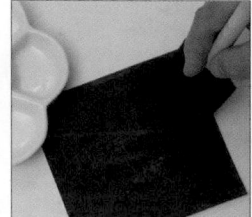 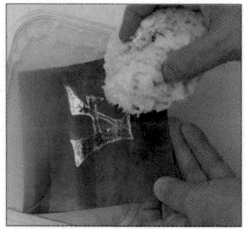 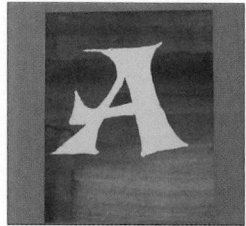

1 Using dilute white gouache (but not too dilute) on a piece of watercolour paper, write a large capital letter with the automatic pen. Allow to dry.

2 Fill a large wide brush with waterproof ink or acrylic colour and, with even strokes, cover the paper. Do not go back over a stroke as the gouache could dissolve. Allow to dry.

3 Soak the paper in water, either in a bath or under a tap. Gently rub the surface with a natural sponge. The gouache will dissolve and lift away taking the waterproof covering with it.

4 Place on a drawing board or similar and stretch with gum strip. Allow to dry before removing.

Experimenting with white candle wax

This method of resist uses the wax of a candle to form a resist against paint that is rolled over it.

Materials
- *Watercolour paper*
- *Waterproof ink*
- *Gouache paint in two colours diluted with water and washing-up liquid (liquid soap)*
- *Low-tack masking tape*
- *White candle*
- *Foam paint roller or equivalent*

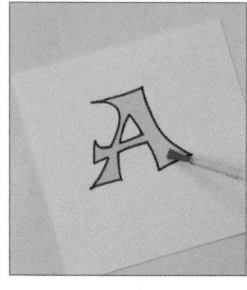 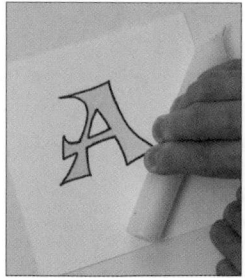 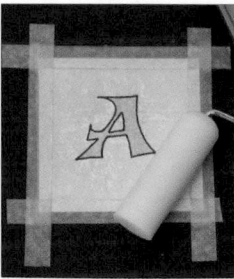

1 On a piece of watercolour paper draw the outline of a letter in waterproof ink. Fill in the shape with the darker of the gouache mixtures and leave to dry.

2 Outline the area of the design with low-tack masking tape, press down well to prevent seepage and vigorously rub the entire surface with the candle making sure that everything is well covered.

3 Using the foam paint roller, cover the surface with the paler gouache mixture; this should be very diluted. Leave to dry before carefully removing the masking tape.

Experimenting with masking fluid

This method of resist uses masking fluid to form a resist against watercolour that is brushed over it. This technique can be used to create quite intricate or delicate designs.

Materials
• *Watercolour paper*
• *Pencil*
• *Masking fluid*
• *Small and large paint brush*
• *Watercolour paint*

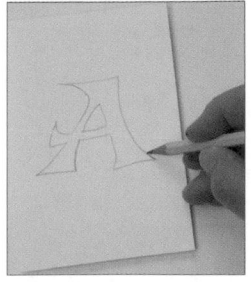

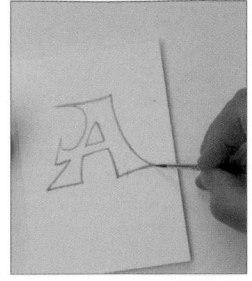

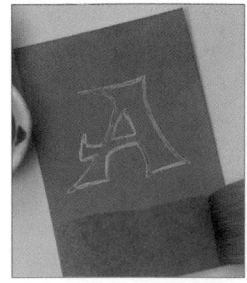

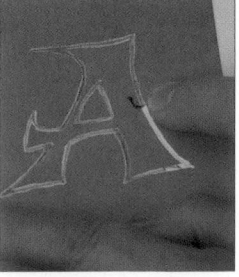

1 On a piece of watercolour paper draw an outline of the letter 'A'.

2 Paint over the outline of the letter with masking fluid. Allow to dry.

3 Using a large brush wash colour over the surface of the paper. Leave to dry.

4 Gently remove the masking fluid by rubbing it with your finger.

Practice exercise: **AZ**

This exercise uses gouache to create an interesting layered resist. Two colours of paint are used, which mix to form a third, apart from in the places where the gouache resist has been applied. It is possible to use many different layers of colour.

Materials
• *White gouache*
• *Watercolour paper*
• *Small brush*
• *Large brush or hake*
• *Waterproof or acrylic paint (two colours – one darker than the other)*
• *Natural sponge*

Tip: If you do not want any white to appear on the page, paint a coloured wash on to the paper before adding the first resist. Leave this wash to dry thoroughly before adding the resist. The 'blank' area will then be the colour of the first wash.

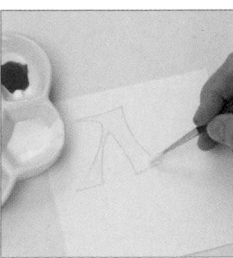

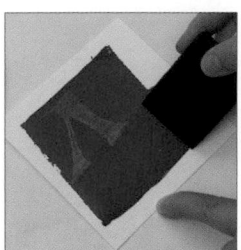

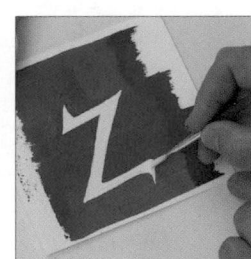

1 Using white gouache write a capital letter 'A' on to watercolour paper. Allow this to dry.

2 With a hake or similar wide brush, cover the surface of the paper with a wash of light coloured paint. Leave to dry.

3 Using white gouache, write a capital letter 'Z' over the obliterated 'A' and once again leave to dry.

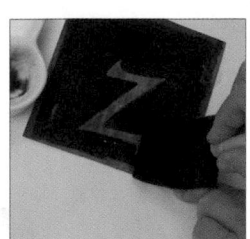

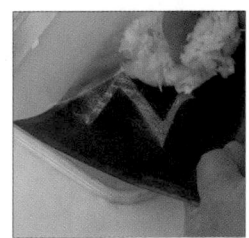

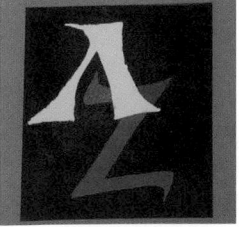

4 Cover the surface with a darker wash of waterproof or acrylic colour. Take more time over this than before, because the two colours need to dry.

5 Allow the paint to dry before washing it off the area of resist and stretching.

6 The finished resist before being removed from the board.

Gilding

Gold imparts a sense of richness and splendour to the page. It is a unique commodity and its specific qualities have been recognized by artists and artisans for thousands of years. It is pure, non-tarnishable and is one of the most malleable metals – which means it can be beaten into leaf by virtually the same methods as used in antiquity.

There are three methods of gilding: using powdered gold, applying gold leaf on to a gum base and burnishing gold leaf on a raised gesso base. Both flat and raised gold can be produced. Some techniques are easy and some are a little more technically demanding but most people will find a method which suits them and the piece they are working on.

Powdered gold

This type of gold is mixed with distilled water and gum arabic before being applied to the paper or other surface. It is often referred to as 'shell' gold (so called because the gold was originally sold in mussel shells), and is painted with a fine brush, or loaded into a pen. It dries flat and can be burnished, and patterns of lines and dots may be impressed into its surface with a pointed burnisher. The gold needs to be stirred from time to time to keep the particles well mixed. Powdered gold does not have the high brilliance of gold leaf, but using the two types of gold together can make a stunning contrast.

Gilding with gold leaf

This is quite a simple technique whereby wafer-thin sheets of gold are applied to a layer of gum. Traditionally only natural gums were used such as gum ammoniac, glair, parchment or vellum size. There are now synthetic adhesives which are equally suitable for gilding such as PVA (white) glue, acrylic gloss medium and gold water size. Gum ammoniac is easy to use. It can either be bought ready prepared or it can be made up and mixed with a little water and colour. Gesso, which is made mainly from plaster, can be made up or bought in cakes, and is the ideal base for gilding with loose leaf gold.

Practice exercise: **Using gum ammoniac to apply loose leaf gold**

This technique uses gum ammoniac, made from resin, as the base for laying loose leaf gold.

Materials
- *Gum ammoniac resin*
- *Plastic bag*
- *Rolling pin or hammer*
- *Small jars*
- *Distilled water*
- *Dish*
- *Muslin (cheesecloth)*
- *Liquid watercolour*
- *Brush*
- *Rolled paper*
- *Loose leaf gold*
- *Glassine paper*
- *Burnisher*
- *Clean cotton rag*
- *Paint and brush*

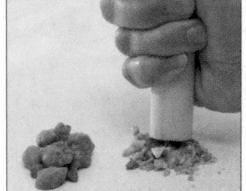

1 Put the gum ammoniac on a hard surface and crush the gum into fine pieces with a rolling pin or hammer.

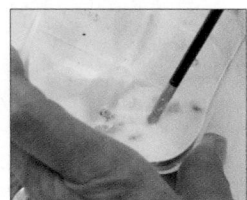

2 Transfer the pieces of crushed gum ammoniac to a small jar. Fill the jar with just enough distilled water to cover the gum, stir and leave overnight to dissolve.

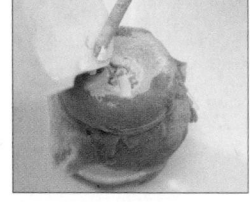

3 Strain the milky liquid through some muslin into another jar. Transfer to a dish. (Instead of using muslin you can use a piece of fabric cut from some old tights.)

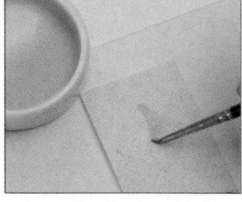

4 Add a couple of drops of liquid watercolour to the gum ammoniac and it is ready to use. Apply the gum to the surface using a paintbrush. Wash this brush.

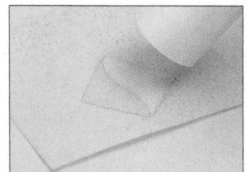

5 Using a piece of rolled-up paper, breathe on the letter to create a tacky surface.

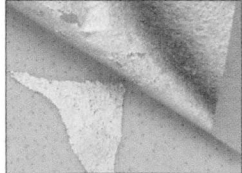

6 Apply a sheet of loose leaf gold and press down. Apply more gold on top if necessary.

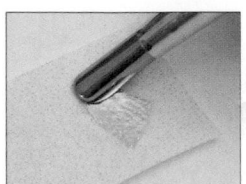

7 Brush away the excess gold and use the burnisher. Polish the gold with a clean cotton rag.

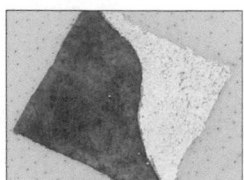

8 Complete the decoration. The gum ammoniac produces a flat layer of gold.

Practice exercise: **Using gesso to apply loose leaf gold**

This technique uses gesso to lay loose leaf gold. Gesso needs to be reconstituted before use, adding water to break up the pieces of gesso.

Materials
- *Distilled water*
- *Gesso*
- *Paintbrush*
- *Craft (utility) knife*
- *Burnisher*
- *Glassine paper*
- *Rolled paper*
- *Loose leaf gold*
- *Paint and brush*
- *Soft brush*
- *Clean cotton rag*

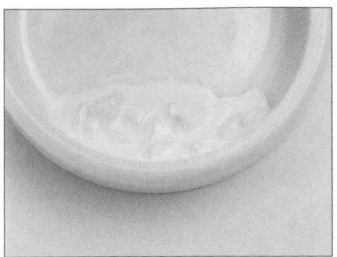

1 Add drops of distilled water to the gesso until it is the consistency of thin cream. Stir very gently to avoid air bubbles. If bubbles appear, blot them with a tissue.

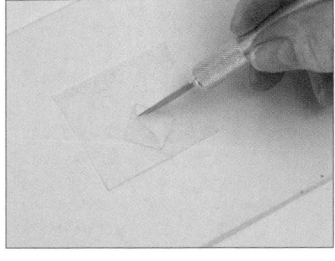

2 Load a paintbrush with this mixture and 'tease' the gesso into the shape. Leave to dry overnight. If it does not have an even surface, gently scrape it with a craft knife.

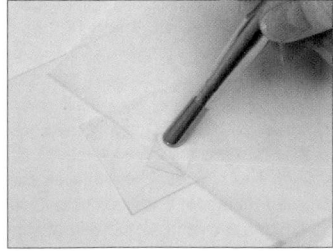

3 Burnish the gesso with a burnisher through glassine paper until the surface is completely smooth. This will encourage the gold leaf to adhere to the gesso.

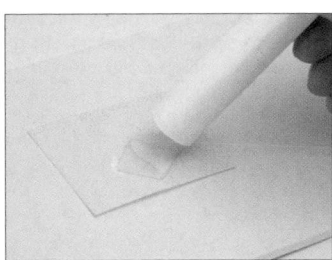

4 Breathe on to the gesso to create moisture, then quickly lay a sheet of loose leaf gold on it and apply pressure. If there are areas without gold, repeat this process.

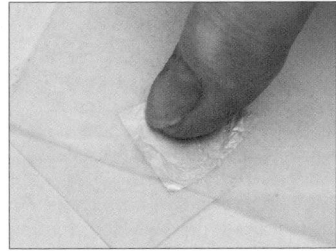

5 Leave for an hour or so before burnishing first with the burnisher through a piece of glassine paper and then directly with a finger through the glassine paper.

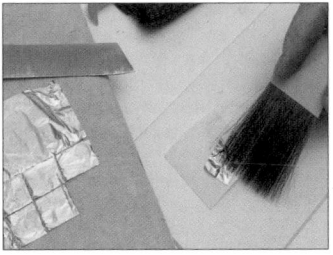

6 Applying additional layers of loose leaf gold will add even more brilliance. Brush away the excess gold with the soft brush, using short, light strokes to flick the gold away.

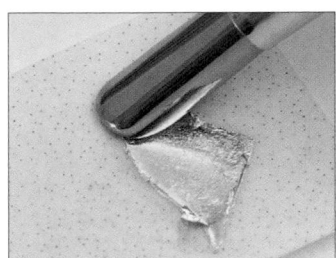

7 Burnish directly on to the gold, making sure that the gold has stuck at the edges.

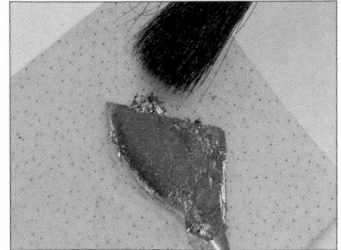

8 Brush away the loose gold at the edges. Continue brushing until all the surrounding gold leaf is removed. Burnish until smooth and polish with a clean cotton rag.

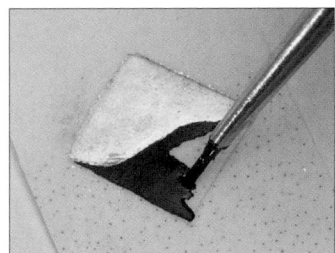

9 Complete the decoration. The gesso produces a raised gold finish to the piece.

Digital Calligraphy

Digital calligraphy is a very new art form that is now becoming increasingly common. Calligraphy is usually considered to be a creative hand-rendered skill. Unlike the use of so-called 'new technology' in many other art forms, digital calligraphy has been slow to catch on, in part because lettering traditions are firmly steeped in the past. This is also because there is a concern that traditional skills may be subsumed by mechanical and technological methods. These fears are entirely unfounded.

The definition of digital calligraphy

What do we mean by 'digital calligraphy'? This question is best answered by defining what digital calligraphy is not. Digital calligraphy is not typography. Type designers have been using computers for many years to design and manipulate fonts, many of which are calligraphic in character. However, using script typefaces such as Lucida Calligraphy or Vivaldi as a substitute for handwritten script is not calligraphy.

Digital calligraphy is calligraphy only when the artist, creator or scribe has contributed some original creative element to the lettering and its application. This could be by applying digital effects to lettering that has been scanned. Perhaps calligraphic forms could be used to build up a creative piece of work using digital techniques. In more advanced cases the calligraphic forms themselves are generated as 'virtual' calligraphy on screen without the need for any of the traditional writing instruments or materials such a pen and paper.

Equipment

Although the majority of designers use Macintosh computers, the more widely owned PC is equally adequate for digital calligraphy. The software used is available on both types of computer and is very similar. Almost any new computer available today will run the necessary software at an adequate speed and will usually have been supplied with a mouse. An alternative to the mouse for writing calligraphy directly on to the screen is the digital pen and tablet. With practice, this will feel more 'natural', and effects that are impossible with a mouse, such as line thickness changing with pen pressure, can be achieved. A scanner is useful for converting traditional calligraphy into a digital file. If you want to keep hard copy prints of your work a colour printer is essential.

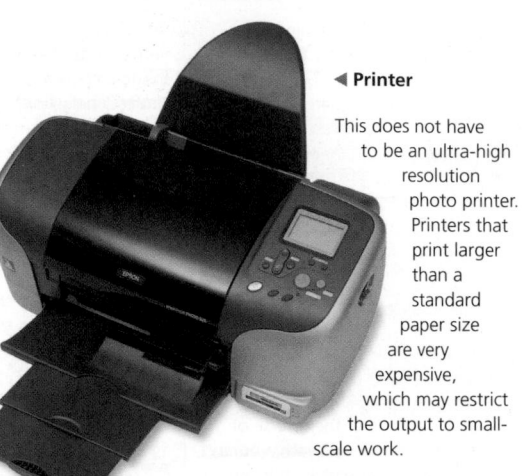

◄ Printer

This does not have to be an ultra-high resolution photo printer. Printers that print larger than a standard paper size are very expensive, which may restrict the output to small-scale work.

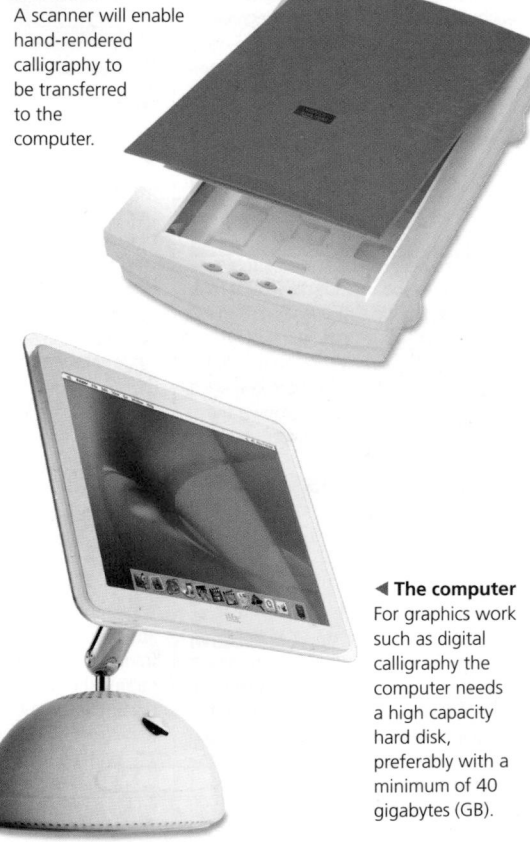

Scanner ►
A scanner will enable hand-rendered calligraphy to be transferred to the computer.

◄ The computer
For graphics work such as digital calligraphy the computer needs a high capacity hard disk, preferably with a minimum of 40 gigabytes (GB).

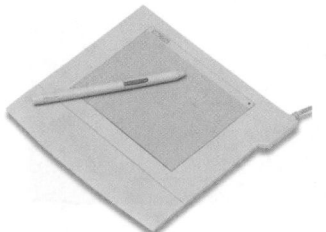

◄ Digital pen and tablet

The pressure sensitive nature of this tool makes it ideal for digital calligraphy.

Software

Professional level software is expensive. An ideal list would include Illustrator™ and Photoshop™, both available from Adobe as the Creative Suite® (CS), or CorelDRAW® that includes CorelDRAW itself and Corel PHOTO-PAINT®. Another version of Photoshop is available as Photoshop Elements®, a more compact version of the full Photoshop package. Other professional packages that can be used for digital calligraphy include Jasc's Paint Shop Pro®. Remember that software is being updated and refined all the time so it is worth keeping up to date with what is available.

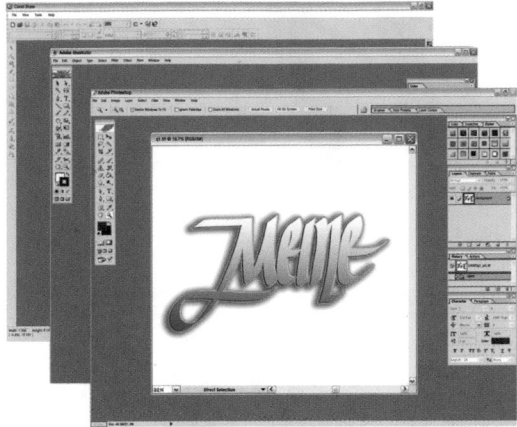

Software packages ▲
These are some of the software packages available for digital calligraphy. The menus of some professional software are wide ranging but even a limited number of options can produce sophisticated calligraphic effects.

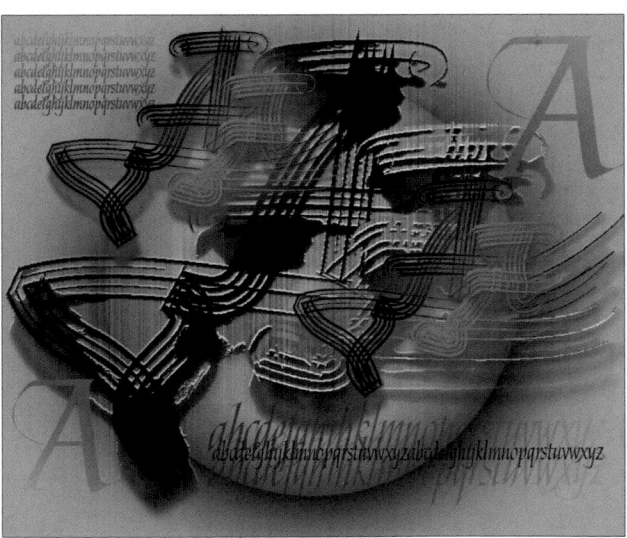

Digitally modified script ▲
An example of what can be achieved using digital calligraphy. The script produced on the computer is then modified using software filters and effects.

Tip: Some software packages are available to buy in 'cut-down' versions, which are less expensive. These versions have fewer features, but may be perfectly adequate for the needs of many digital calligraphers.

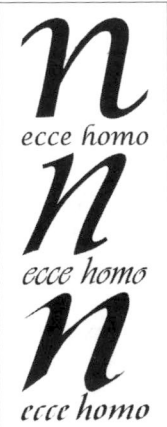

◀ Calligraphic typefaces and type
The top two illustrations (Lucida Calligraphy and Vivaldi) are calligraphic but are not calligraphy. The bottom example shows how calligraphy reflects the free movement of the broad-edged pen and produces a 'sharpness' absent in the typefaces.

n
ecce homo
n
ecce homo
n
ecce homo

'Virtual calligraphy' ▲
This complex image using calligraphy is designed to be viewed on a computer screen rather than in print.

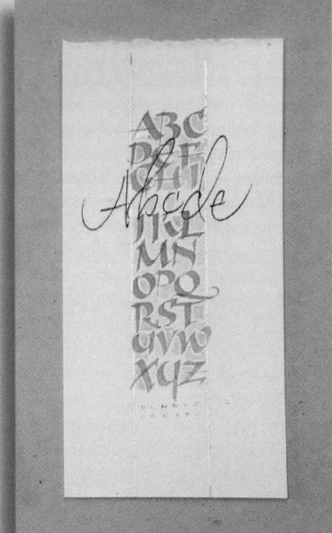
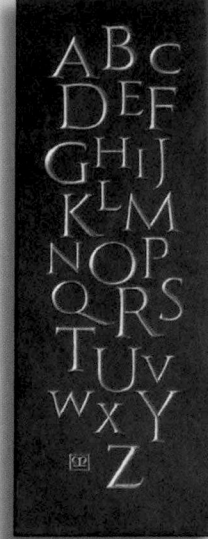

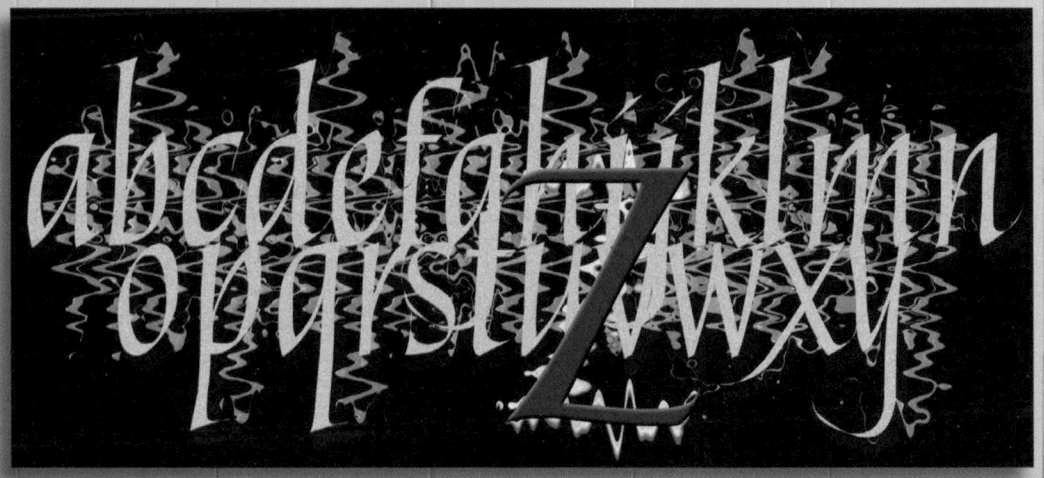
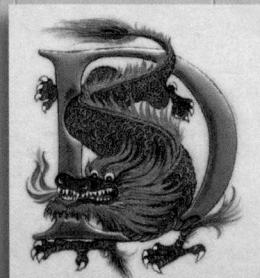
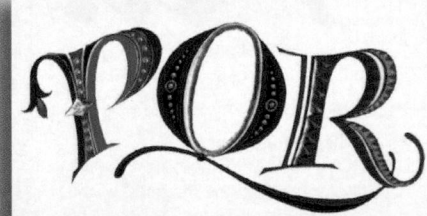
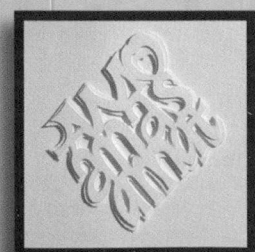

Gallery

This book would not be complete without a tribute to the many faces of calligraphy in today's world. The following pages showcase the different ways in which calligraphy has been put to use, stepping beyond conventional applications to incorporate less obvious techniques and materials such as slate and stone. The result is a stunning gallery of work from a range of contemporary artists that shows off calligraphic techniques in the most inspiring way.

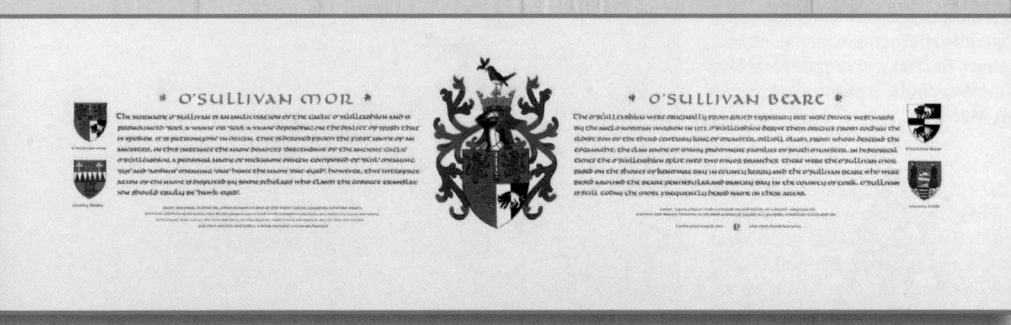

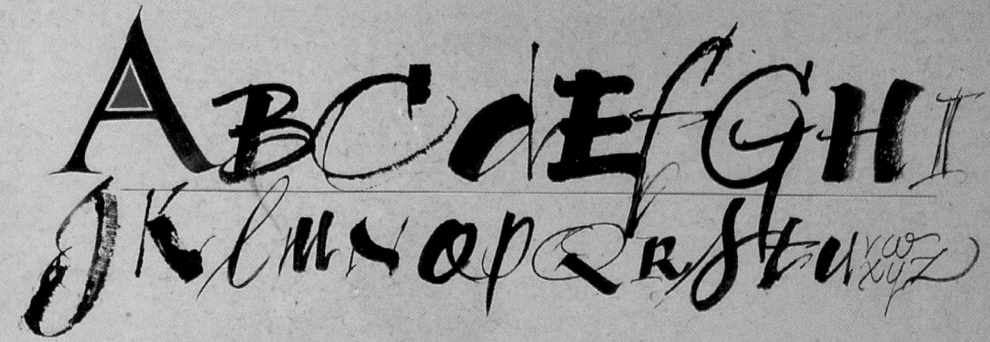

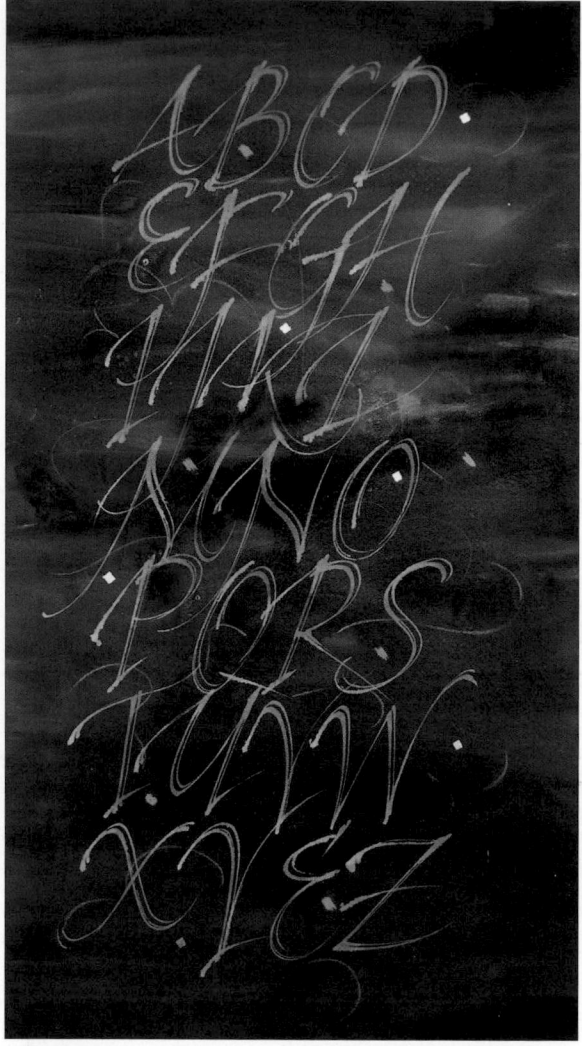

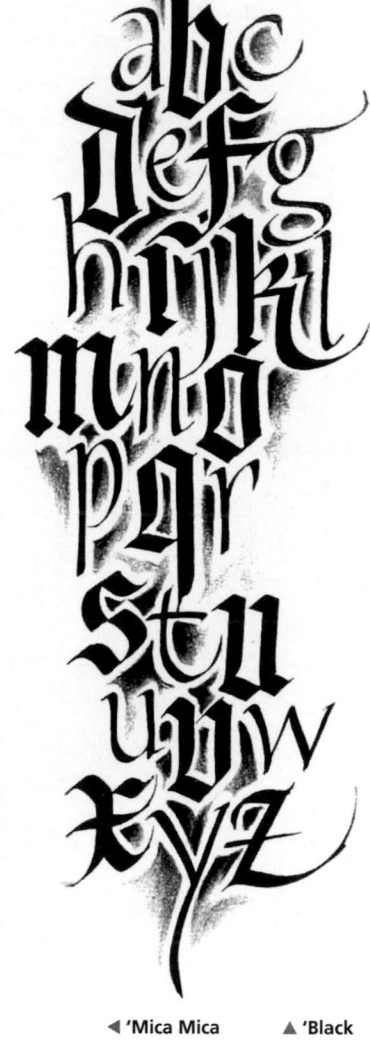

▲ **'Ocean's Reflection'**
Italic capitals making up an alphabet written in bleach on a blue ink background using coit pens.
Gaynor Goffe

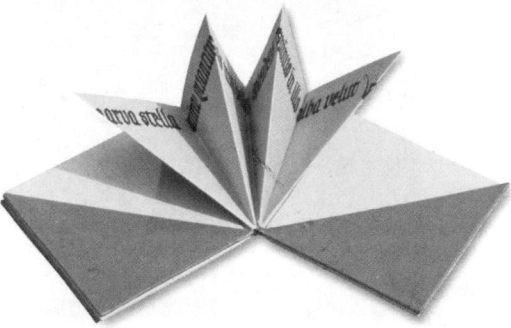

◀ **'Mica Mica Parva Stella'**
Written in the Gothic hand in black gouache on Ingres paper, the concertina pages enclosed fold out to reveal the nursery rhyme inside.
Viva Lloyd

▲ **'Black Shadow'**
A striking alphabet in a combination of Italic, Gothic and Foundational hand. Depth has been added by shading among the letters and in the counters.
Jan Pickett

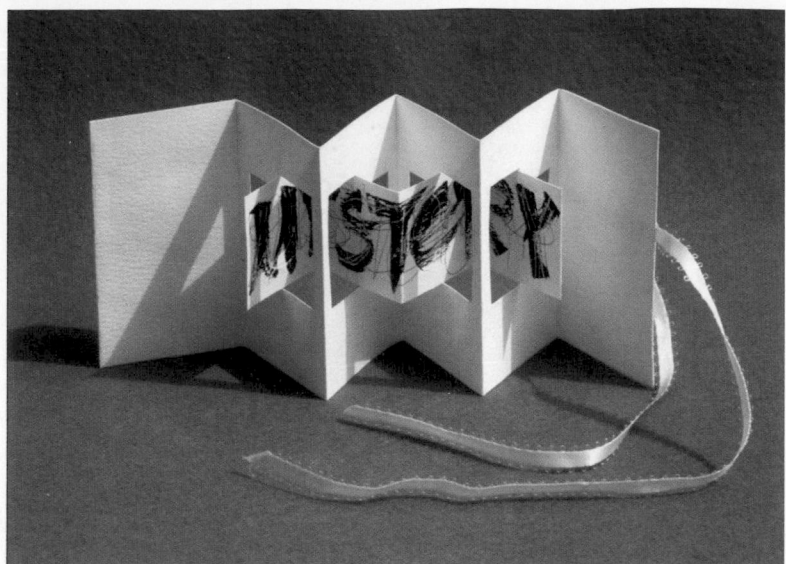

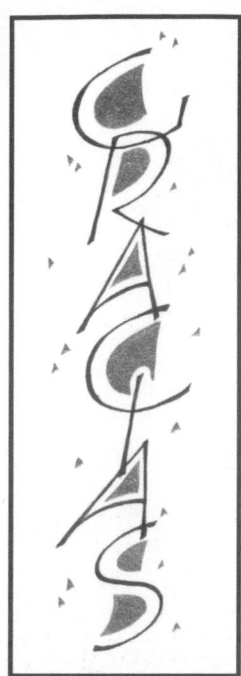

▲ **'Mystery Book'**
A concertina within a concertina, written with a pointed brush and various coloured inks on Bockingford paper.
Viva Lloyd

▲ **'Gracious'**
This tall card has been written in gouache paint on watercolour paper and embellished with gold.
Maureen Sullivan

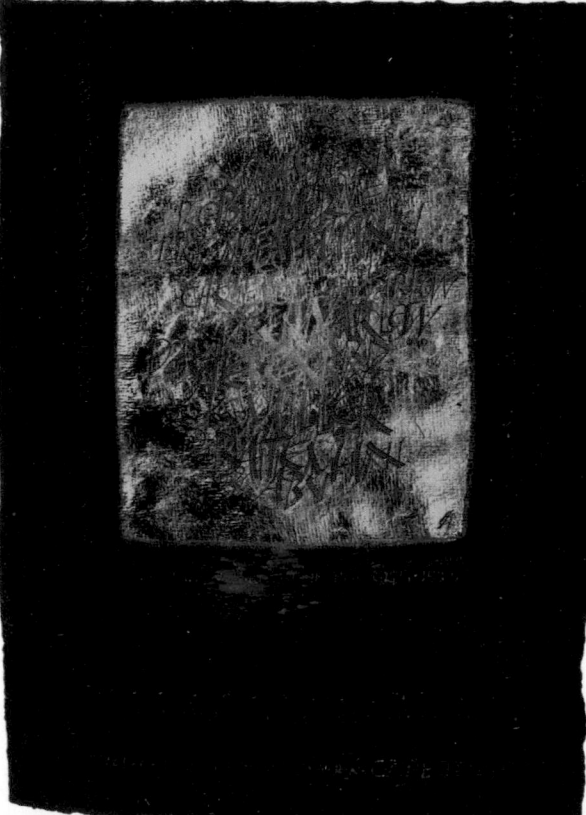

▶ **'Alpha and Omega'**
A striking but simple display of the words in blue and red brush lettering on calico.
Viva LLoyd

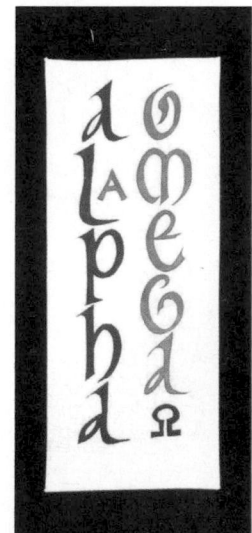

◀ **'Presentation Panel'**
A panel using gold leaf, oil pastel and coloured pencil on Indian paper.
Peter Halliday

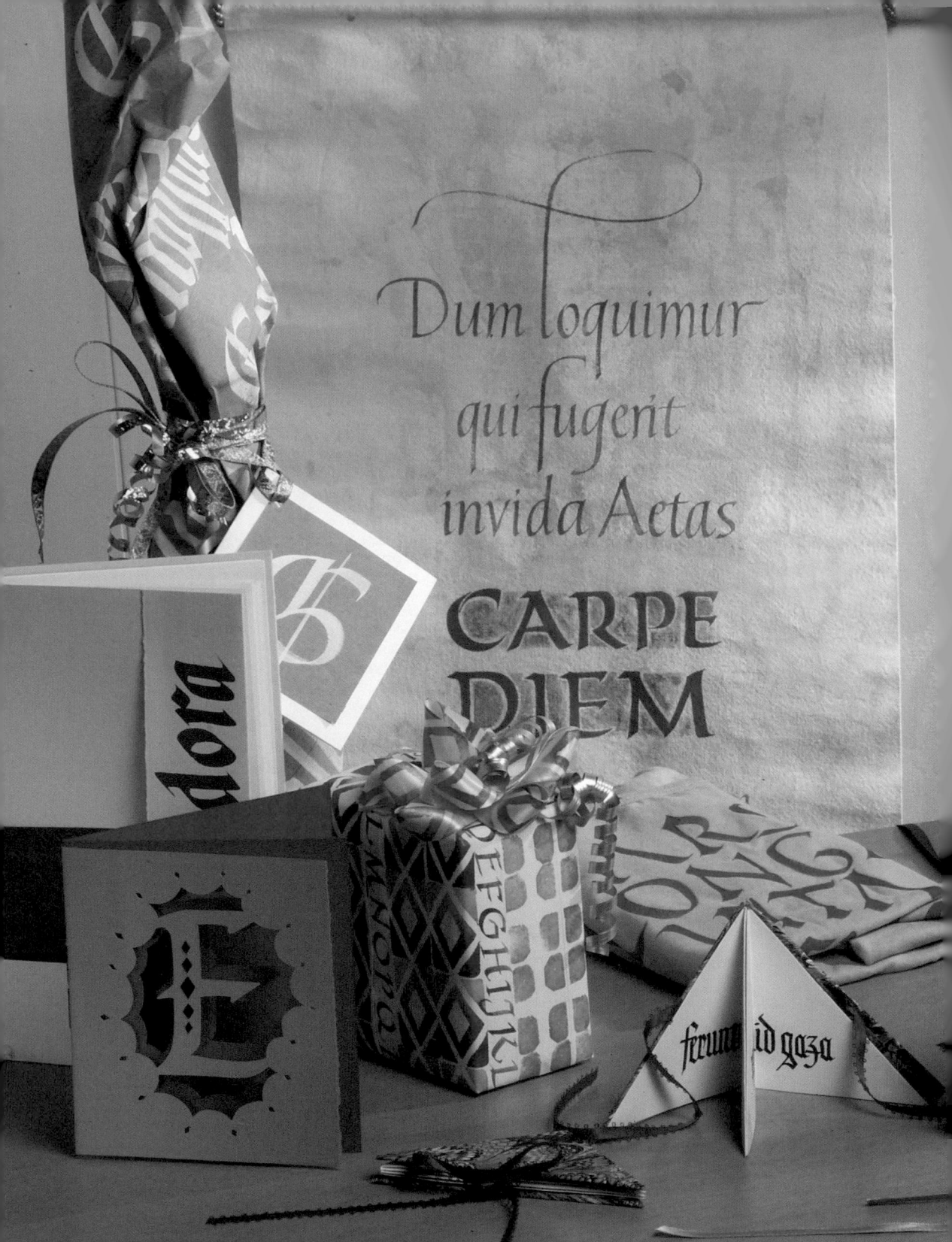

Dum loquimur
qui fugerit
invida Aetas

CARPE
DIEM

Calligraphic Projects

Having mastered the fundamental techniques of calligraphy, you can enjoy the rewarding process of putting calligraphic skills to creative use. This section contains 50 inspiring projects that enable you to practise calligraphy while creating a beautiful keepsake or gift. There is something for all occasions: from decorative boxes to handmade notebooks, from fridge magnets to scripted T-shirts – with each project allowing space for individual artistic expression and interpretation.

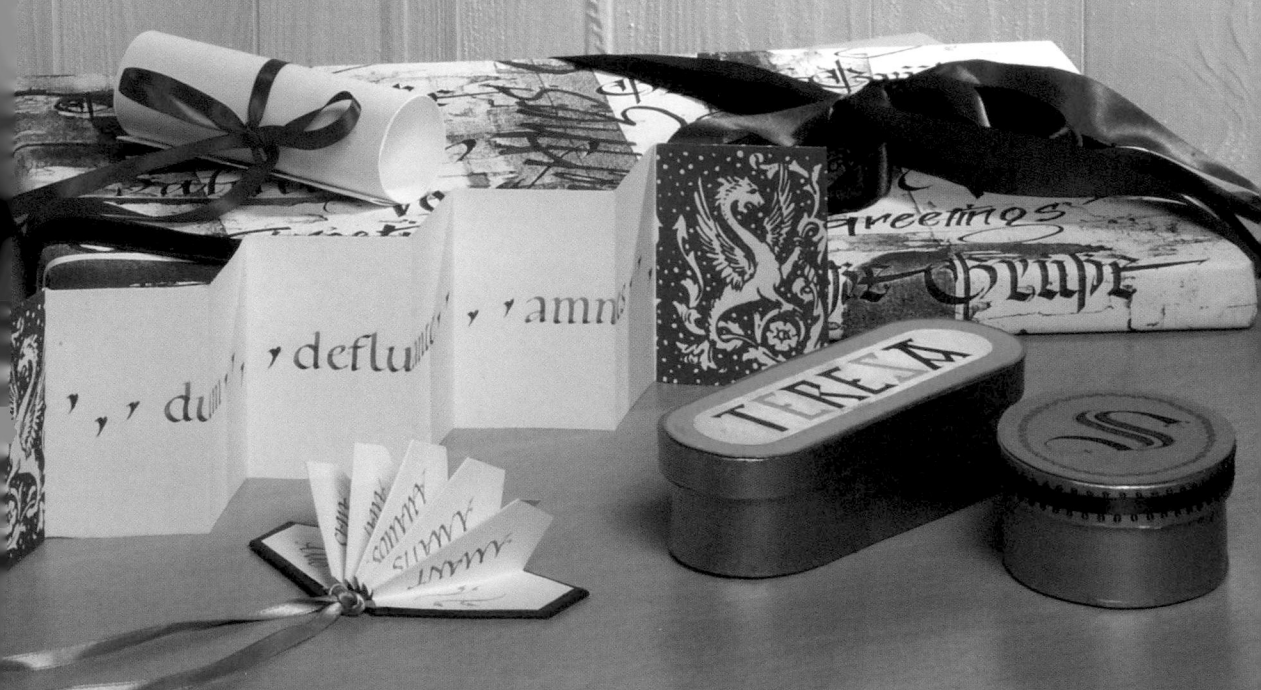

Brush lettering on ribbon

This is the calligraphic solution to making an attractively gift-wrapped present for those awkwardly shaped or oversized items – such as flowers or a plant – by wrapping it in wide florist's ribbon. Ribbon comes in a variety of colours and widths, and you can purchase it by the roll or length from any florist. Personalize some ribbons with your message – either repeated along the length of the ribbons or just close to the ends. Wrap them around your gift loosely or in an extravagant bow. By splitting the ribbons at the ends you can write smaller messages if you wish.

Use a broad-edged brush to write on the ribbon. For a good result, choose a brush that is nylon or acrylic because it will spring back into shape as you write – brushes containing sable are too absorbent and floppy to use on ribbon material. A small pointed brush is an optional extra to colour some counters for decorative effect. Write as much or as little as is effective on the ribbon – but remember that writing along the length of the ribbon may not be entirely satisfactory, as much of the writing becomes obscured once the ribbon is wrapped or tied.

The design

Here the message has been repeated all along the ribbon, and the name written again on the narrower strips with a smaller brush. Red and orange are chosen for the ribbon and paint to complement the colour of the gift it will decorate. Roman Capitals have been used at the equivalent of three or four nib widths to produce a pleasingly chunky script.

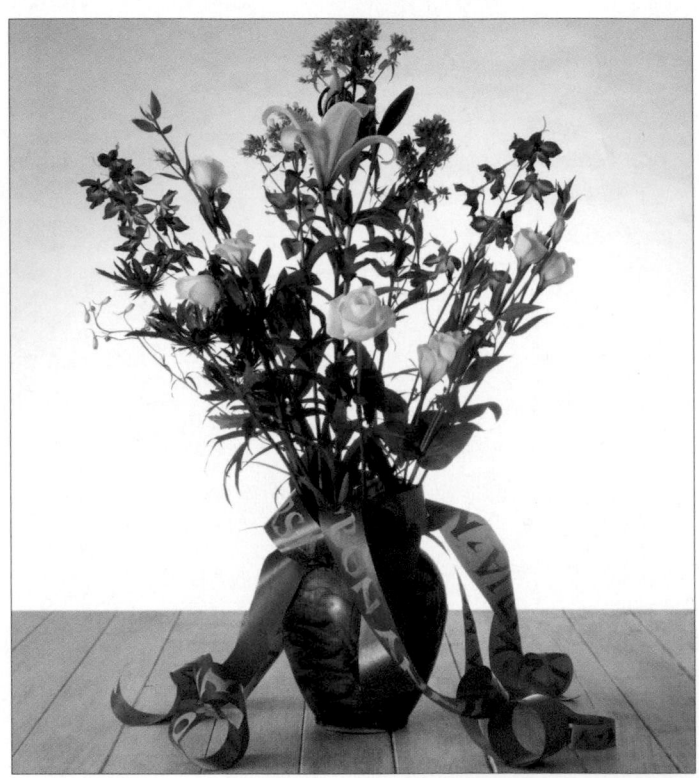

Materials
- *Household emulsion or Plaka casein-based paint: red and orange*
- *Saucer and water pot*
- *Two chisel-edged brushes: approx.1cm (1/2in) wide, and 5mm (1/4in) wide for optional smaller writing*
- *Layout or practice paper*
- *Wide florist's ribbon: red and orange*
- *Scissors*

> **Tip:** Do not overcharge the brush with paint. Hold the brush perpendicular to the paper in order to make both fine and thick lines.

1 Decant some paint on to a saucer. Fill your brush with paint and then wipe most of the paint off against the side of the saucer, to keep a sharp writing edge. Practise Roman Capitals at three or four nib widths on some layout paper, holding the brush perpendicular to the paper.

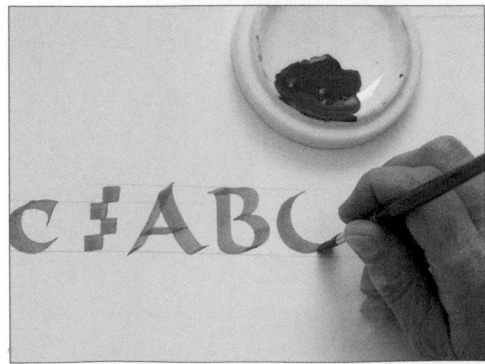

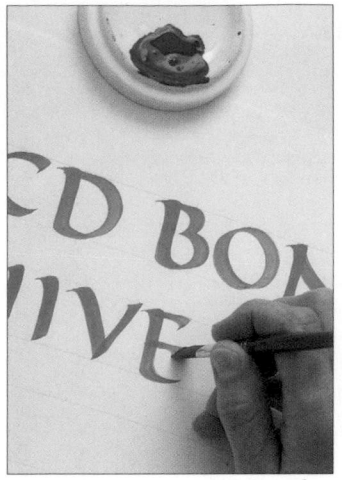
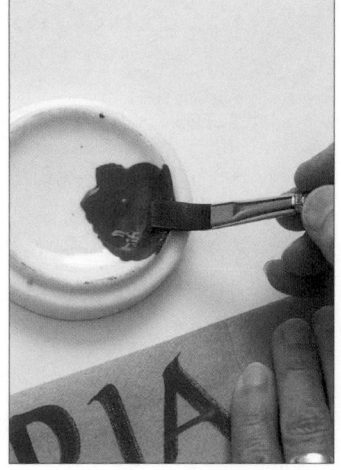
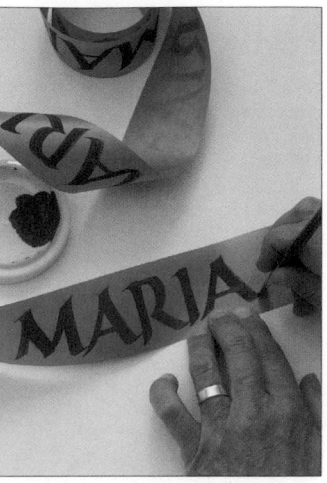

2 Practise the words you plan to use on the ribbon, keeping the message brief. Make adjustments to the letters to accommodate their being very chunky – for example make 'B' wide enough to allow good counter shapes.

Tip: If you prefer to write between lines, rule some heavily on practice paper and lay the ribbon over; it is translucent so lines should be just visible.

3 Try writing on the ribbon. It may feel slippery at first. Keep the paint undiluted if possible, as this will increase the 'drag factor' and enable you to write slowly, with more control. Remember to hold the brush perpendicular to the ribbon and keep reshaping the edge, by refilling then wiping off, to create sharp lettering – an over generously filled brush will produce blobby letters.

4 Repeat the message several times along the ribbon, or just at the ends. If you do a lot of repeats, consider placing a dot in a different colour between each for decorative effect, or using a smaller, pointed brush to colour in some counter shapes.

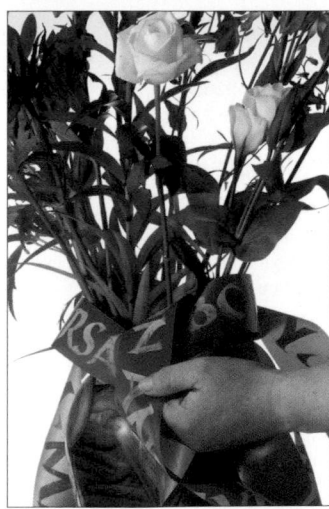

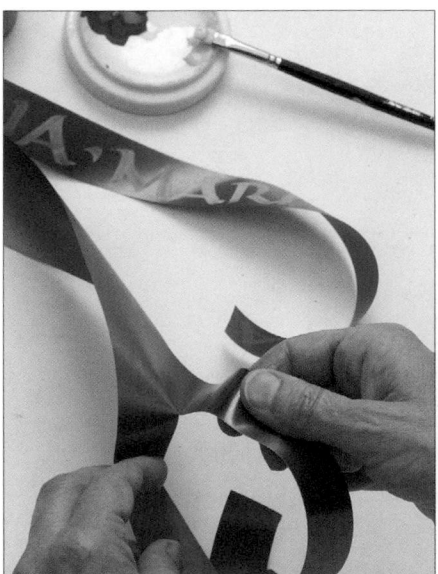

Tip: The best paint to use for ribbon is household emulsion or Plaka casein-based paint. These will wash out of your brush with water but will dry waterproof, which is important if there is any chance that the ribbon will get wet.

5 If you have a smaller chisel-edged brush, you can split some of the ribbon – florist's ribbon splits very easily – and write smaller messages on the separate strands to create a more interesting effect.

6 Tie the ribbon around the gift loosely or as a large bow, so as to show it off as much as possible. Split any spare strips of ribbon and run them against the sharp edge of a pair of scissors to make them curl, and tie these round the gift separately.

Quotation in graduated colour

Writing with coloured gouache paint or coloured ink is great fun, and will add extra interest to a piece of work. Creating a gradual change in the colour when writing the letters adds variation. All that is required is practise in loading the pen with different coloured paint from a brush, and in choosing colours that work well alongside each other. Learning to mix up each colour to achieve the best results is also important.

Gouache paint has been used for the writing as it has an opaque finish when dry, giving a good, even colour to the letters. Coloured inks are just as easy to use, but the calligraphy produced using inks is more transparent. Learning to blend colours together to create the best effect takes practice so it is worth having some trials first.

Begin by choosing only two colours from the three primary colours: red, blue and yellow. The two colours used in this project provide harmonious changes in colour – from red, through to orange and yellow.

Squeeze about 1cm (¹/₂in) primary red gouache into a mixing dish or palette and add water until the consistency resembles thin cream. Have your practice paper ready for writing. Load the brush with paint and feed the paint onto the dip pen by stroking it across the nib and reservoir. Practise the Foundational script in one colour first. Then try out the ideas on layout paper, before gradually mixing the colours as you write.

Materials
- *Mixing palette*
- *Gouache paints or coloured inks:*
  primary red and cadmium yellow
- *Two mixing brushes*
- *Two water pots*
- *Dip pen: William Mitchell 2¹/₂*
  (medium nib)
- *Layout or practice paper*
- *Kitchen paper*
- *Scalpel or craft (utility) knife*
- *Metal ruler*
- *Self-healing cutting mat*
- *Good quality white paper*
- *Card (stock) for mount, if required*

The design
This project combines primary red gouache and cadmium yellow. The quotation is written in Foundational script. The finished project is worked on good quality white paper but once you feel confident with the technique, you can start experimenting using coloured paper.

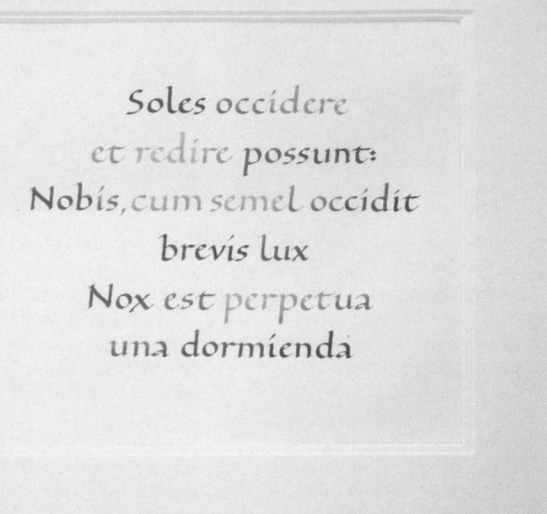

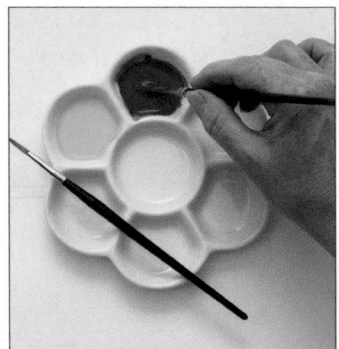

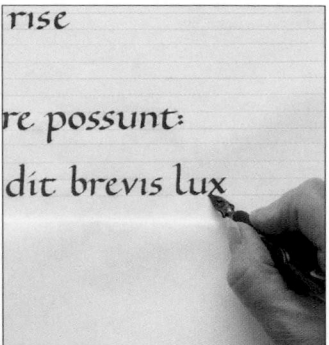

1 In separate sections of a palette or in separate mixing dishes combine primary red gouache and cadmium yellow gouache with water until each is of a thin, creamy consistency. Use a clean brush for each colour. Mix a generous amount of each so that you do not run out halfway through the writing.

2 Use the dip pen to write out the quotation on a practice sheet of layout paper or similar, using one colour only. Load the brush with red gouache and feed the colour into the pen by stroking the brush across the reservoir and nib.

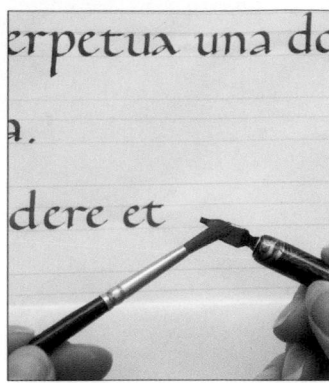 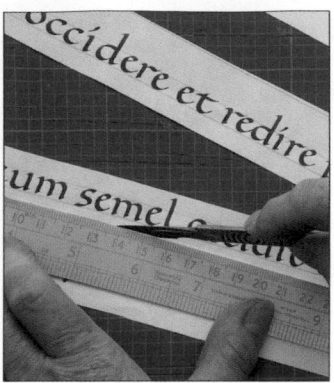 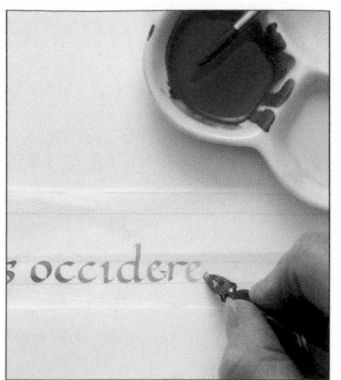

3 Write carefully and when required wipe the pen with the brush loaded with red paint, recharging to maintain the flow of colour.

4 Cut the text into sections and arrange these on another piece of layout paper to create a good layout or design. Once you have decided on the layout to use, paste the text into position.

5 Practise writing using two colours. First, place another piece of layout paper over the top of the pasted design and begin to rewrite the quotation, using the original underneath as a guide. Use a different brush for each colour, wiping the nib with the different colours as you proceed. Blend the second colour into the first colour by carefully adding the second colour to the top of the pen nib with the second loaded brush. The colour will mix gradually in the pen as the paint travels through the nib on to the paper.

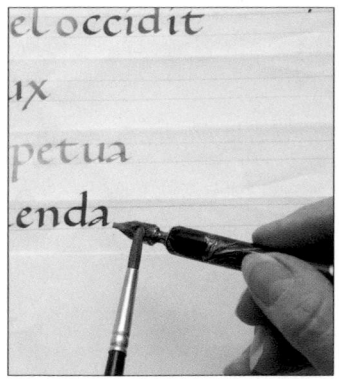 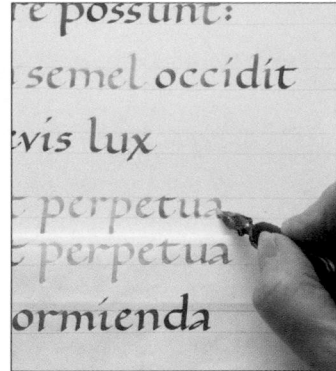

6 Change back to the first colour by loading the pen nib again from the top. The idea is to create gradual changes of colour throughout the writing. A subtle effect requires practice and your first attempts may not appear as gradual as you would like.

7 Change to good quality paper and prepare your guidelines for writing. Place a guard sheet underneath the section you are working on and, using the writing from your practice sheet as a guide, write out your quotation as the finished piece of work.

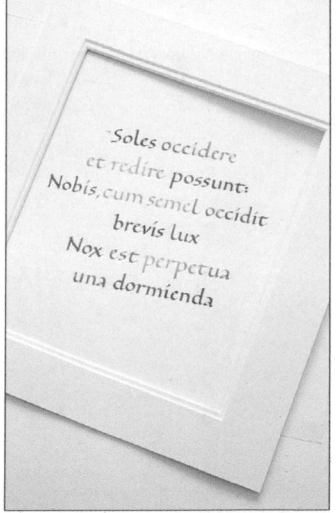

Tip: Sometimes it may be helpful to work with three colours especially if using a very dark colour such as dark blue and a very light colour such as a pale yellow. Mix the two colours that are being used to produce a mid-colour, in this case mid-green. You will then be working with three colours: dark blue, mid-green and pale yellow, using one pen but three brushes, one for each colour. This will give you a range of changes through your writing from yellow, yellow-green, mid-green, blue-green through to dark blue.

8 Cut or buy a small mount in a similar or contrasting colour to frame your quotation.

Flourished decorative letter

'Swash' or 'Flourished' Italic letters are based on Roman Capitals. The flourishes are the fluid extensions that make the letters appear decorative. Written at about seven nib widths with a slight forward slant, flourished Italics can be elegant and full of movement. They are also fun to do and can be used with added decoration on cards, at the beginning of a calligraphically written quotation, to spell out a child's name, or presented just as a single letter to be framed.

Every letter of the alphabet can be adapted in the same decorative way. You can use black ink, or write in colour and add detail within the shape of the letter itself, or you can decorate with gouache around the whole letter. If you are very ambitious, you can create a whole alphabet design using the same decorations for each letter, or instead create 26 individual patterns.

The main letter shape should be written with a large nib or an automatic pen. There are many different pens with large nibs you can use to create multiple strokes, including coit pens or even your own handmade reed and balsa wood pens. Try experimenting with different writing tools to expand your ideas and encourage creativity.

The more exuberant the writing the more thought needs to be given to the space allowed for layout and design; be careful not to over flourish the letters. Flourishing can become even more adventurous, innovative and exciting with experience.

The design
In this project a flourished letter is created (and decorated with white gouache) by mixing up two colours. It could be used as an initial of a child's name and placed in a frame or on a card.

Materials
* *Gouache paints: ultramarine blue, primary red, lemon yellow, primary blue, zinc white and permanent white*
* *Brush for mixing paint*
* *Palette or mixing dishes*
* *Automatic pen or dip pen with a large nib*
* *Layout or practice paper*
* *Dip pen such as William Mitchell 5 (small nib)*
* *Hot-pressed watercolour paper*
* *Fine paintbrush No.000*
* *Two water pots*

> **Tip:** Begin by writing in formal Italic. Lead into the chosen letters by extending the first serif – making it longer and more sweeping – before beginning the letter. Start with the letters you are most comfortable with.

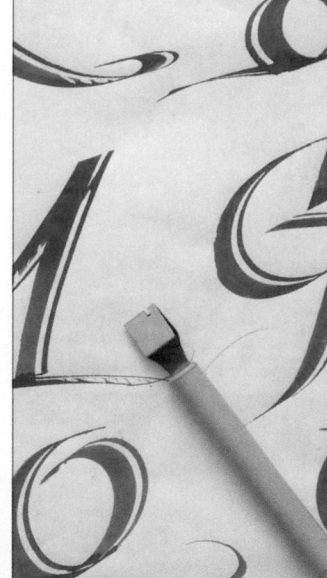

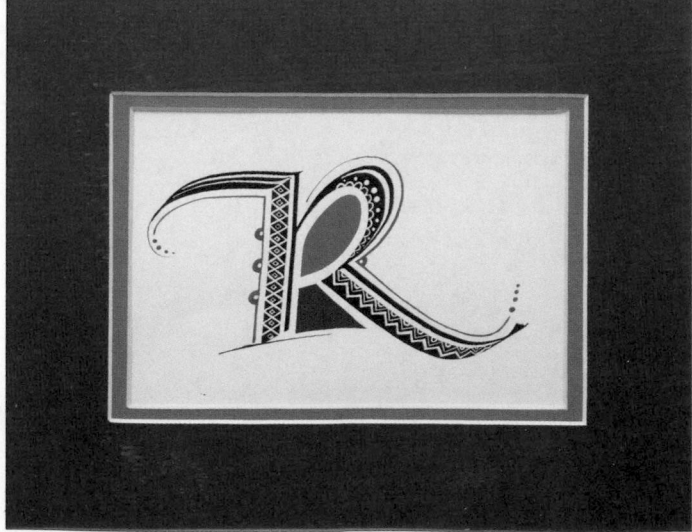

1 Mix some gouache paint in a palette or small container to the consistency of cream. Load your large pen with the paint and try creating some large, different flourished Italic capitals. Use layout paper to practise elongated serifs leading into and out of the letters. Do not be over ornate with your flourishes; try to keep them balanced and under control.

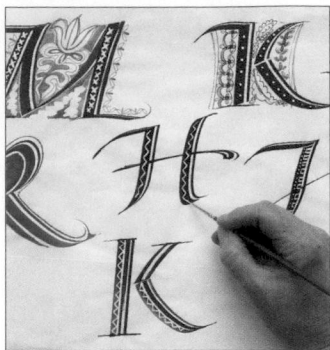 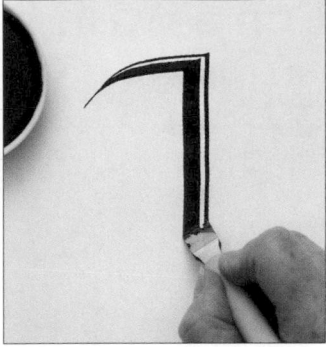 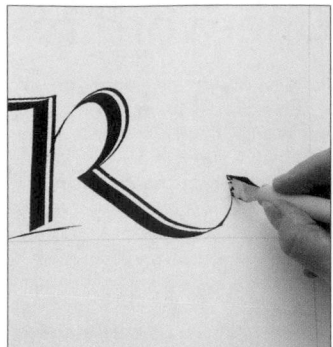

2 Try out some different decorative ideas, which you can add to the letter using the smaller nib and filigree lines and designs.

3 Choose a capital flourished Italic letter 'R' to develop and write it carefully on the watercolour paper with the large pen. Mix ultramarine blue and primary red gouache to make dark blue. Using a brush, load the nib with the colour. Do the stem first, twisting the pen to get the fine lines.

4 Add the fine lines to the flourishes with the edge of the pen nib for extra decoration.

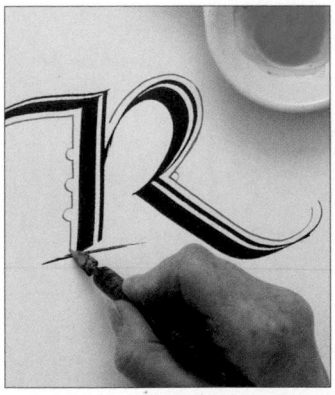

5 Add the fine lines around the letter in green – mix lemon yellow and primary blue gouache with a dip pen and a fine nib.

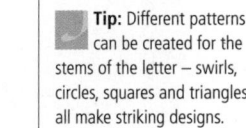

Tip: Different patterns can be created for the stems of the letter – swirls, circles, squares and triangles all make striking designs.

Tip: Various colour combinations can be used to write the letter and decorate the counters. Try out several ideas.

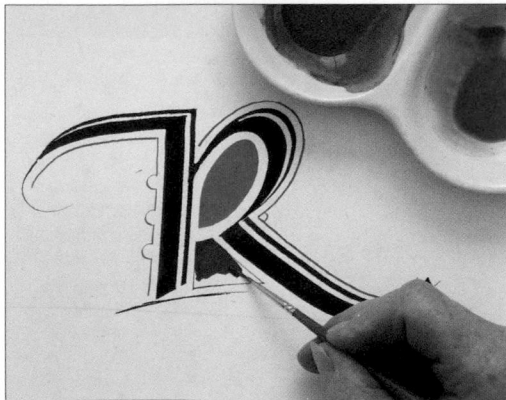

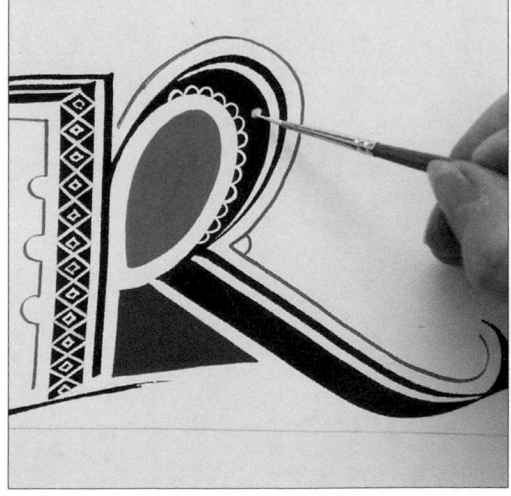

6 Add further embellishment to the letter by filling in the letter counter or centre with primary blue gouache and purple – a mix of primary blue and primary red.

7 Paint filigree designs and dots on the letter with a fine brush and permanent white gouache to finish the letter. If you wish, frame your final letter with a matching colour.

One-word resist on a wash background

This is an excellent opportunity to work spontaneously with water and paint effects and to experiment with colour and texture. There are easy ways to produce exciting visual background effects by using a brush alone, as this project clearly demonstrates.

In this design a variegated wash is created with acrylic inks or watercolour paint and the colours are left to dry. A one-word resist is then added by writing over the background with a dip pen that has been dipped in art masking fluid. This forms an area of resist, which further paint cannot penetrate. The intensity and texture of the piece can be built up with colour using brush and paint effects. A toothbrush can be used to randomly spatter paint or ink over an area on the surface of the paper adding further texture and colour to the overall design of the piece.

To spatter colour on the surface of the paper, mix up paint to the consistency of thin cream. Dip the toothbrush into the paint or ink and, with the bristles uppermost, run a ruler or a narrow strip of stiff card over the top of the bristles towards you. This will create spatter away from you, over the paper's surface. Point the toothbrush to direct the spatter to the areas that you wish to cover. Different colours can be used. Rinse the toothbrush when you change colour, or use several toothbrushes – one for each colour. Different sized toothbrushes or other stiff brushes will create larger or smaller spatter. Experiment with the different effects you can produce – fine baby toothbrushes will produce fine dots of paint; nail brushes will produce larger dots of spatter.

Stencils can be used to make individual areas of interesting colour and texture. Gold and silver metallic powders add interest and sparkle to a project and will stick to wet paint. Think creatively about how you can make your project individual and exciting – the process of inventing different techniques when using paint introduces interesting and varied results that can be applied to all sorts of different projects.

The design

This project is centred around the word *Fantasia,* which is Italian for 'fantasy'. The word is written in Batarde script surrounded by random spatter and variegated washes. A star shape is stencilled in the background.

Materials

- *Layout or practice paper*
- *Dip pen: William Mitchell 0 or 1 (large nib)*
- *Watercolour paper*
- *A large brush*
- *Acrylic inks or watercolour paints*
- *Masking fluid*
- *Old newspapers and old toothbrushes*
- *Stencil or transparent sheet to cut a stencil*
- *Gold and silver metallic powders*
- *Water pots*
- *Mixing brushes*
- *Gum arabic (optional)*
- *Eraser*

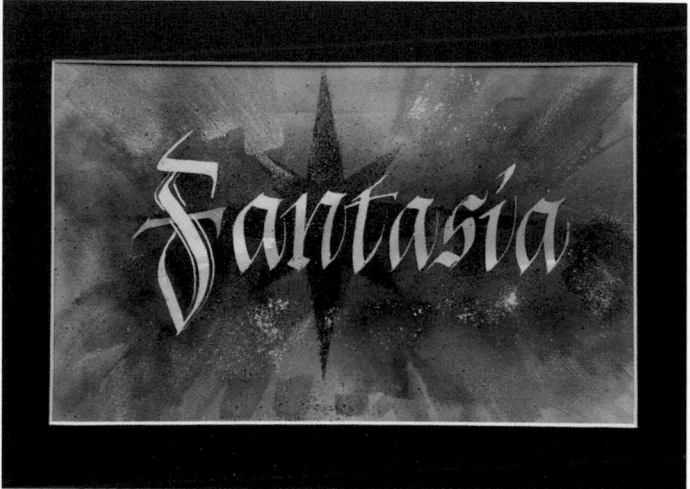

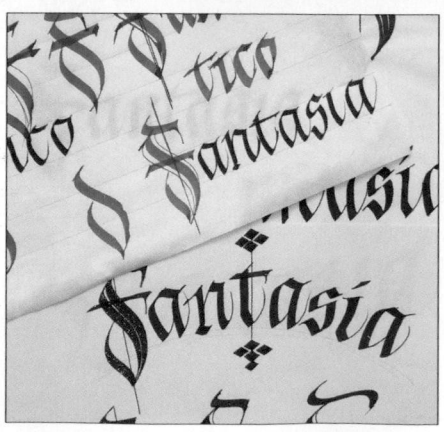

1 Practise writing the word *Fantasia* in Batarde script on your practice or layout paper. Decide on the size you wish your letters to be and the colours to be used in the design to convey the essence of the word you have chosen.

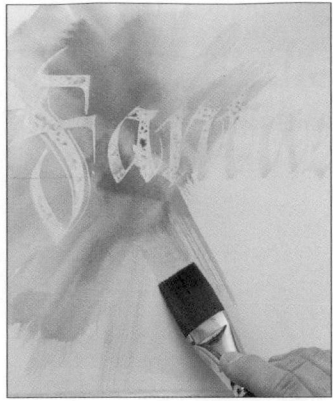

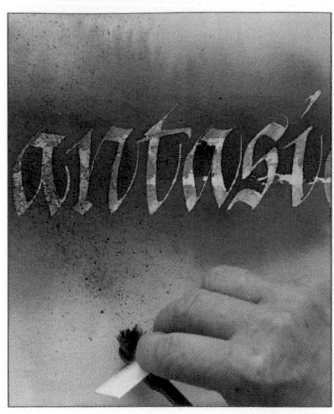

2 Using the watercolour paper, paint a variegated wash with acrylic inks. Leave to dry. Write in Batarde script the word *Fantasia* using a large pen, dipped in masking fluid. While the masking fluid is drying, prepare the area in which you are going to work by covering the surfaces with scrap paper or old sheets of newspaper.

3 Paint small areas of the watercolour paper with random washes, using acrylic inks or watercolour paint, building up the colour. Leave to dry.

4 Use a toothbrush dipped in ink or paint to spatter different areas of the paper with fine sprays of colour to build up layers of different colours.

Tip: Test your spattering on newspaper first to perfect your technique. Also test on the newspaper just before spattering on to the piece of work. Sometimes it is easy to overload your brush with the ink or paint and then it blobs everywhere.

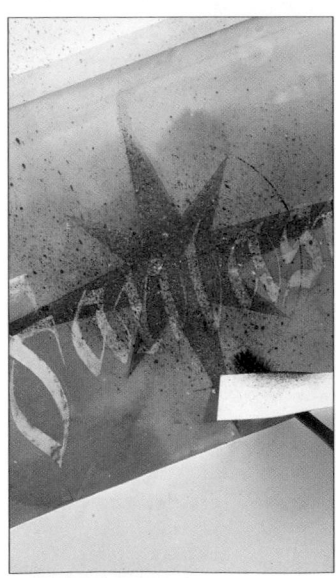

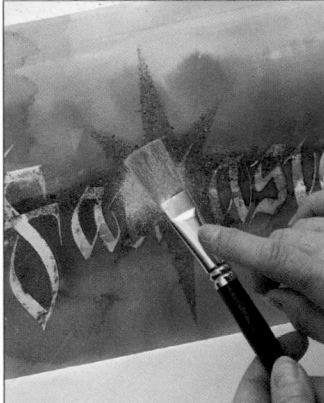

Tip: The spatter can be blended carefully with a large damp brush if it becomes too dotted. Carefully stroke the brush over the area to blend into the rest of the colour, and leave until dry.

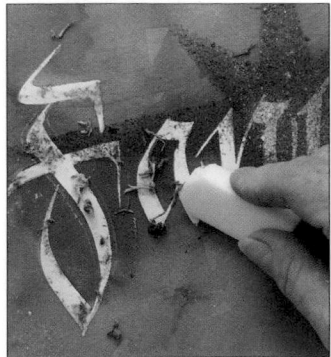

5 Choose a stencil shape, such as a star. Shield the rest of the work with paper. Spatter colour through the stencil to create a pattern.

6 Before the stencil shape has fully dried, shake some gold or silver metallic powder over the design. It will stick to the wet paint and make it sparkle. Dust away the excess when dry. Alternatively, mix the metallic powder with water and two drops of gum arabic, which makes it stick to the paper and spatter the resulting gold or silver paint into your work. This paint can also be used in the pen to add decoration.

7 Finally, remove the masking fluid by carefully rubbing with an eraser, to reveal the hidden word underneath the layers of paint. If you wish, frame your artwork with a harmonious colour.

A poem and leaf print design

Printing can form the basis of interesting design and alleviates the need to draw or paint. This can be quite appealing for some calligraphers who are less confident about their artistic skills, or who would like to combine printing and calligraphy together in a simple and effective way.

In this project leaf printing is combined with calligraphy. Leaf prints are made by dropping leaves into gouache paint and then using an ink roller or brush to cover the leaves with paint. The leaf is pressed onto watercolour or coloured paper to create a design that combines with prose or poetry. This may relate to trees or flowers. Each subsequent print made with a painted leaf becomes a little paler than the previous imprint. For bold prints the paint will need to be replenished on each printing. Gouache paint will give dense, thick colour. Printing with acrylic inks produces a finer image.

Natural materials are ideal to use for design work. Leaves, ferns and grasses can all be used to create effective, quick results by dipping them in paint and printing them as a well arranged design. This project features a small mounted panel in green, which would make a delightful gift for a gardener.

Materials
• *Layout or practice paper*
• *Metal ruler*
• *Pencil*
• *Gouache paints: oxide of chromium and forrest green, alizarin red and cadmium yellow, or acrylic inks*
• *Dip pens and various nibs, including William Mitchell 2¹/2 (medium nib)*
• *Scalpel or craft (utility) knife*
• *Self-healing cutting mat*
• *Glue*
• *Collection of small leaves*
• *Kitchen paper cut into squares*
• *Paint brush*
• *Mixing palette or small tray*
• *Ink roller (optional)*
• *Tweezers (optional)*
• *Watercolour or coloured paper*
• *Card stock for mount*

The design
This is a design to complement a Latin poem about trees. Carolingian hand has been chosen to create a soft, natural feel, echoing a gently undulating landscape. The writing is in soft green oxide of chromium gouache colour with a small amount of forrest green. These colours were also used to print the leaves with the addition of alizarin red and cadmium yellow to add a more realistic feel.

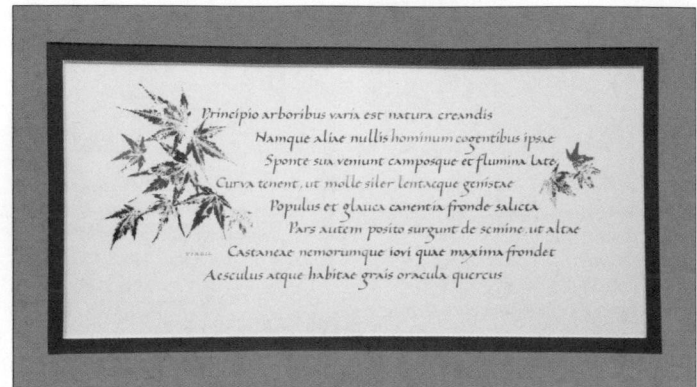

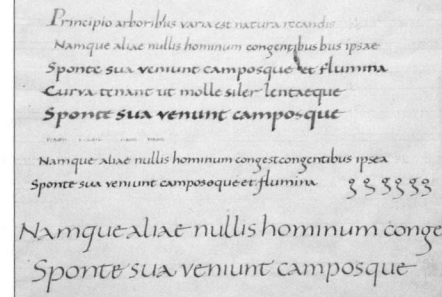

1 Rule up a piece of layout paper so you can practise the text. Write in colour using gouache paint or inks. Experiment with different letter weights and sizes of Carolingian script.

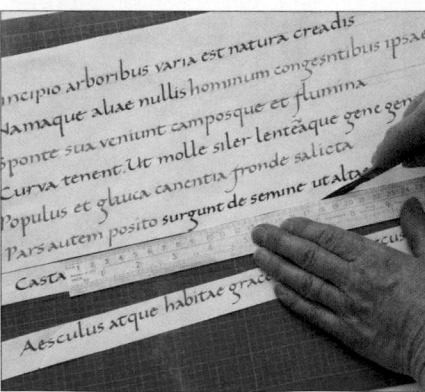

2 When the letterforms are correct and you have decided the size of the writing, write out the poem using the chosen nib. Try some different arrangements, remembering to include the leaves in each so that you can judge what your panel will look like when finished. Using a scalpel carefully cut out the writing in fine strips.

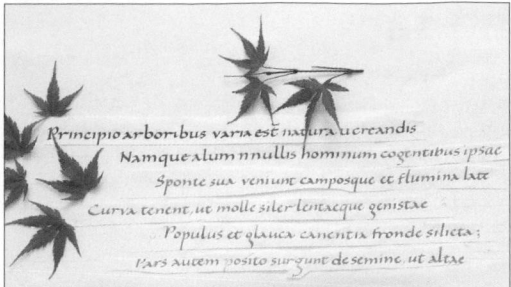
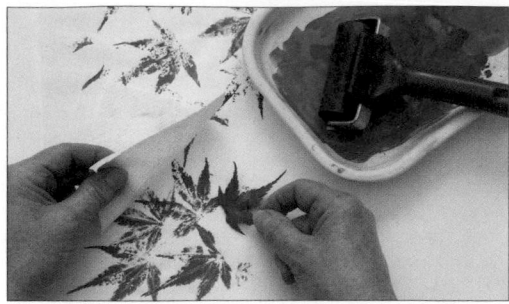

3 When you have decided on a design, paste the writing into position. Place the leaves on the paper, too, and quickly draw round each to give yourself a guide. You may wish to do some trial printings with the leaves.

Tip: The small squares of kitchen paper used to press the leaf patterns help to prevent smudging with the paint. Small pieces of paper can be used instead, which will give you reversed leaf patterns. These can be used in card making.

4 Squeeze the gouache colour, or acrylic ink, on to the small tray and mix them together with the ink roller or brush. Do not add water. Drop a leaf into the paint and press with the roller, or paint with the brush. The leaf will inevitably stick to the ink roller, but pick it off and lay it on to the paper in the position you have marked. Take a small piece of cut kitchen paper and press the leaf gently on to the paper. Remove it carefully with your fingers or tweezers. It may print a second time, though the impression will be much lighter. Discard the leaf when it becomes too wet.

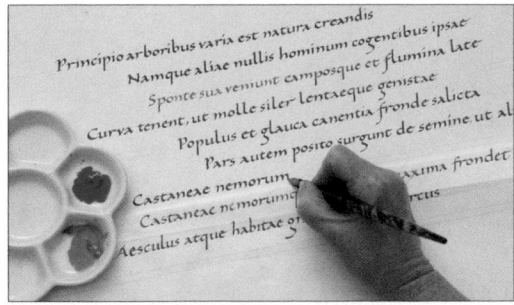

5 After practising leaf printing, rule up some good quality paper so you can begin on the project. Write the text first. When the text is dry, protect it against paint splashes by covering it with layout paper.

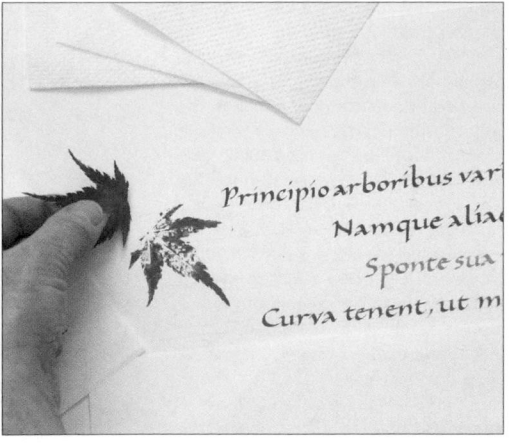

Tip: If you choose leaves with strong textures the prints will appear more structured and interesting than without. If the leaves are very smooth, the resulting colour will be flat and solid.

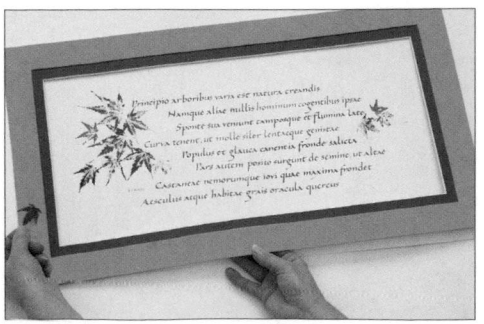

6 Print your leaf pattern, copying the design of your practice sheet. You may wish to enhance the leaf colours by adding small amounts of alizarin red and cadmium yellow to the colour in your palette, blending slightly with a roller or brush as before.

7 Mount your finished work in a suitable colour. You may find it effective to continue the leaf pattern on the mount.

Embellished gift box and tag

A hand-decorated box and tag gives a unique and personal touch to any gift. You can buy plain, undecorated cardboard boxes in a wide range of shapes and sizes from art and craft suppliers, or you may already have the perfect plain box at home, which you can use to decorate. If you wish, you can begin by painting a plain box with craft paint – and use this initial colour as the starting point of your design. A matching gift tag is easily created by reducing the tracing on a photocopier. This is then traced and transferred on to watercolour paper.

This project decorates the lid of a box with an initial letter to personalize it for a friend. The letter is outlined and then filled with gouache paint. Decorative detail is added and the letter finally embellished with silver paint. As a final touch, a ribbon is placed around the box and some ribbon attached to the matching gift tag.

There are many examples of initial letters in manuscripts from which you can take inspiration for your design. The letter in the project can be traced and then reduced or enlarged to fit your chosen box. You may prefer to transfer your chosen design directly on to the box lid, ready for decorating. However, if this is very small it will be quite difficult to work on. It is often easier to make a template by placing the lid of the box upside down on to some watercolour paper and drawing around the outside with a pencil. You will find it easier to work on a larger flat surface. When the design is completed, the template will be cut to shape and glued on to the lid of the box. Repeat the process for the gift tag by reducing the design on a photocopier by 30 per cent.

> **Tip:** Consider making a box with a simple monogram by choosing two initial letters that work well together.

The design

An oval box has been selected for this project as the chosen letter 'S' fits very well into this shape. The box is painted silver with craft acrylic paint. The lid of the box is used as a template for the design and once finished will be cut out and glued on to the lid. A Versal letter 'S' is painted with purple gouache and embellished with silver. A simple decorative pen-made pattern encompasses the letter. A smaller version is made for the gift tag.

Materials

- *Small plain cardboard box with lid*
- *Layout or practice paper*
- *2B and 2H pencils*
- *Tracing paper*
- *Hot-pressed watercolour paper*
- *Photocopier*
- *Craft acrylic paint: silver*
- *Paint brushes, including size 0 brush*
- *Gouache paint: purple*
- *Pen with pointed nib: Gillott 303*
- *Scissors*
- *Hole punch*
- *PVA (white) or craft glue and brush*
- *Ribbon*

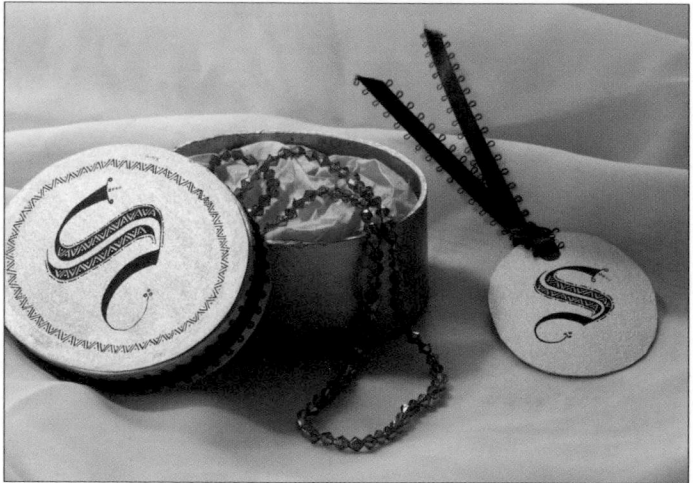

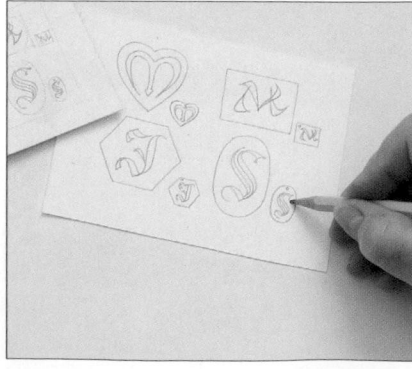

1 Consider the shape of your box and which kind of lettering would be most effective for it. A rounded letter is suitable for an oval box, while a small delicate letter might be suitable for a small heart-shaped box. For larger boxes a bolder letter would be more appropriate. Think whether the letter you have chosen may work well with a square, round or hexagonal box. Draw your design on to layout paper.

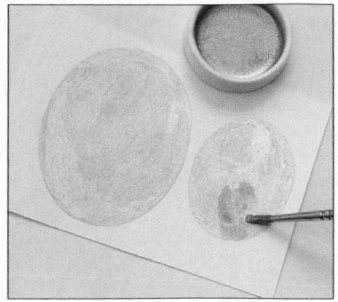

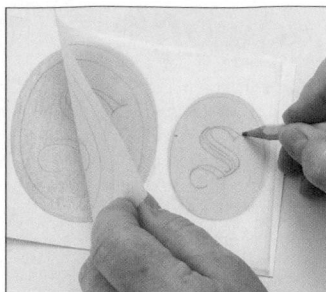

3 Trace down the Versal design on to the silver template and also trace the outline of the 80 per cent photocopy as a guideline for the decorative pattern. For the gift tag, trace and transfer the reduced design on to the smaller silver template.

2 Place the lid of your chosen box upside down onto a piece of watercolour paper. Draw around the lid with a pencil to create a template outline. Take two photocopies of this template, one at 80 per cent (a guideline for the decorative pattern that will be added later) and another copy reduced to 70 per cent for the outline of the tag. Trace the tag template and transfer it on to watercolour paper. Paint both of these watercolour templates with silver craft paint and put aside until completely dry. You then have an easier surface on which to work and do not have to paint on an uneven or raised box lid. This template will be glued to the box when finished.

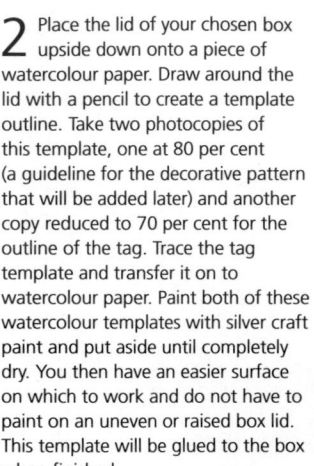

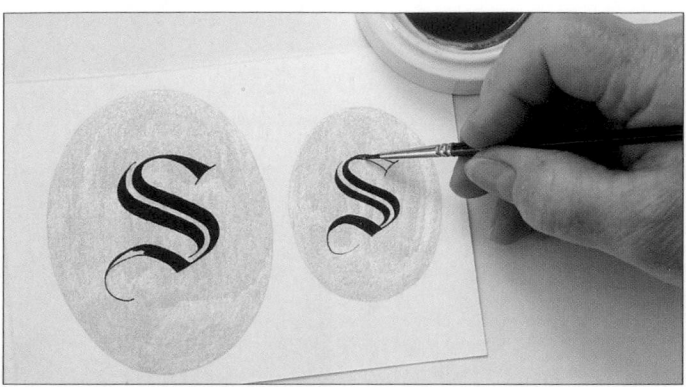

4 Outline the letter with some purple gouache paint using a pointed nib. Use a size 0 brush to paint the letter. Short, overlapping strokes will give you more control filling in the letter.

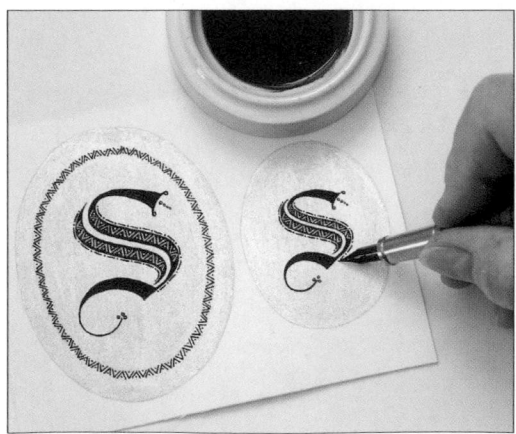

5 The lines and dots are now added using the pointed nib. The pen-made border is drawn and decorated with tiny dots. Once the paint has dried, slightly dilute some of the silver acrylic paint, or use silver gouache, and add the final embellishment to the letter. Then repeat the decorated initial to create the gift tag.

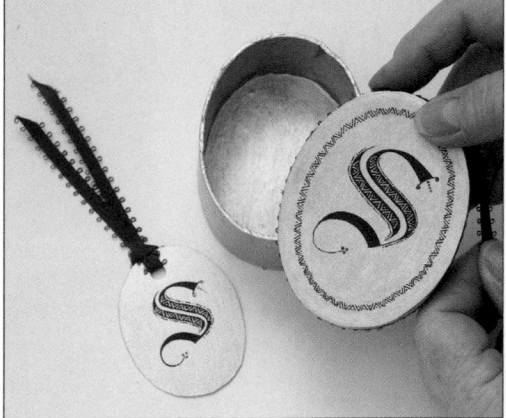

6 Carefully cut around each template. Make a hole in the top of the tag with a hole punch and thread some ribbon for a tie. Finally, glue your design on to the box lid with some craft glue or PVA glue, and place some ribbon around your completed box.

Decorated message on a pillow-box

This box is very easy to make and can be decorated in many different ways. You can use the template provided on this page to make a pillow-box of any size you like by reducing or enlarging it using a photocopier.

It is best to choose card that is 200gsm (90lb) or heavier. Generally, the larger the box, the thicker the card you need to use. The box in this project measures 10cm x 5cm (4in x 2in) at its narrowest point when folded. Use 250gsm (115lb) card if the size of the template is increased by 50 per cent or more.

A plain or textured card, in a colour of your choice, gives you an opportunity to create your own decoration. Adding a name or message will give the box a very personal touch.

Do not fold the card until you have finished your lettering, as it is far easier to work on a flat surface than on a curved area.

Experiment with ideas to decorate your box. A pleasing effect can be made by ruling chequered lines, painting every other square and writing an initial in the blank squares. For a special event such as a wedding, an appropriate decoration such as bells or horseshoes could be randomly placed with the name of the couple encircling each motif.

This project uses gouache paints and Gillot 404 pointed nib for ruling the lines and a William Mitchell 5 nib for the writing to create an interesting texture of lettering at angles using a variety of colours. Guidelines are ruled in pencil on the template measured 5mm (¼in) apart with a 1cm (½in) gap between each set of lines. This will effectively repeat the pattern on both sides when the box is finally folded. The lines are then ruled over with alternate colours of red, green and purple gouache paint using the pointed nib. The ends have been left blank but this space could be used to add a name or personal message. Complete your box by tying ribbons around it in complementary colours and finishing with a bow.

The design

By using a slightly compressed Cursive Italic hand for this project, there is enough space to allow words to be repeated across the box. Choose your own colour scheme, whether striking or subtle. Alternating the use of a size 4 and size 6 nib for each letter of a word produces an interesting thick and thin design.

Materials

- *Tracing paper*
- *2H pencil*
- *Card (stock) in a weight to suit the size of box*
- *Photocopier*
- *Layout or practice paper*
- *Mixing brush*
- *Gouache paints: red, green, purple*
- *Dip pens: pointed nib Gillott 404 and William Mitchell 5 (small nib)*
- *Ruler with bevelled edge*
- *Scoring implement*
- *Scissors*
- *PVA (white) glue or craft glue and brush*
- *Ribbon*

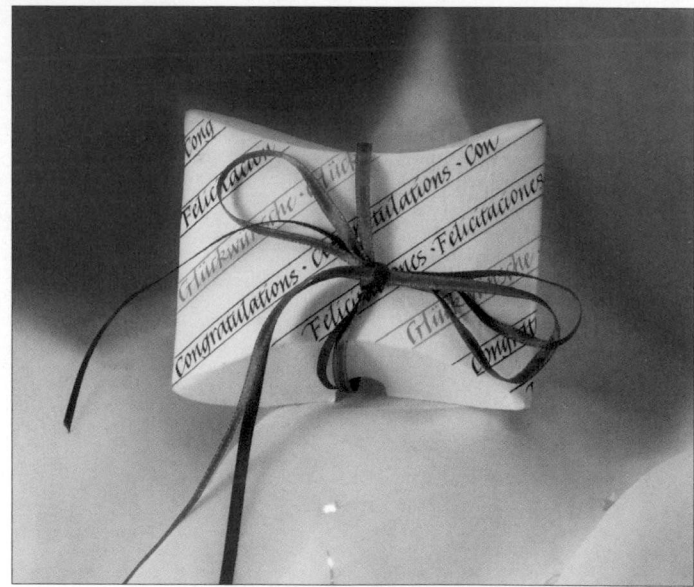

Template

enlarge by 200 per cent

——— Cut
——— Fold
- - - - Score

Tab

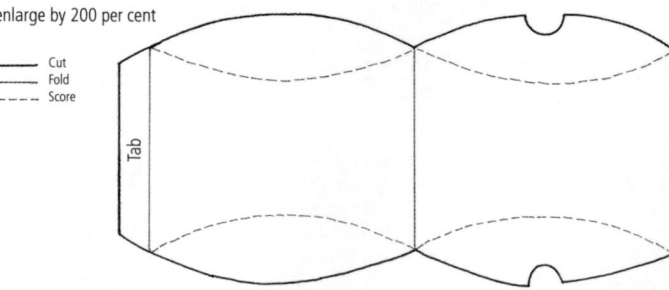

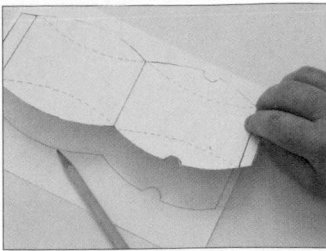

1 To make the box, first trace the template as shown here and transfer the design onto the card. Enlarge or reduce the template on a photocopier to a size that suits your purpose. Do not cut, score or fold the card at this stage.

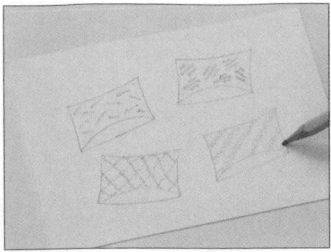

2 Try out some design ideas on layout paper. Experiment with random lettering, blocks or diagonal lines of text. Be bold and have fun with the colour scheme or else keep the colours subdued and elegant. Use a separate mixing brush for each colour and use a paint brush to fill the nib with gouache.

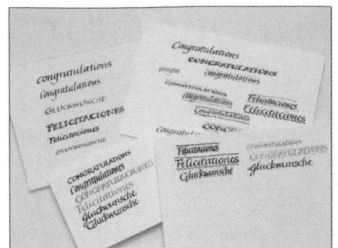

3 Write out the words in a range of sizes so that you can judge which will fit the box best. Try writing in different colours, too, to find the combination you prefer.

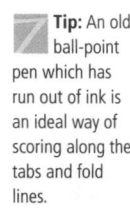
Tip: An old ball-point pen which has run out of ink is an ideal way of scoring along the tabs and fold lines.

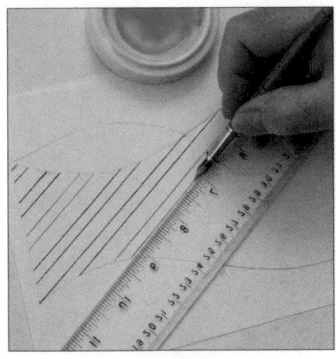

4 Use a pencil and ruler to draw some guidelines on to the card. The large dots indicate where to start. Now paint over the pencil lines by loading a pointed nib with a little gouache – too much will make a blob – and drawing the nib along the side of the ruler with the bevelled edge facing downwards. It will be easier to paint all the lines of one colour and wait until they have dried before proceeding with the next colour.

Tip: Draw guidelines very lightly so that the pencil does not leave an impression on the card.

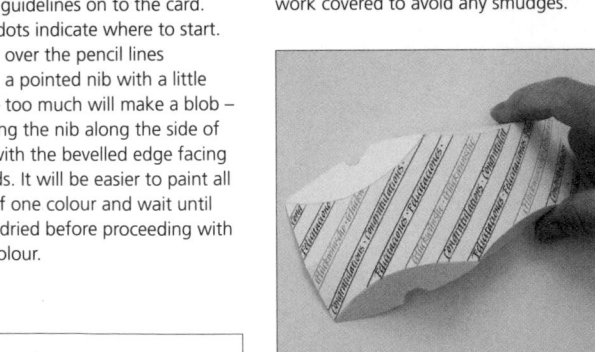

5 Write out the wording using a size 5 nib. Write out the lines with only one colour at a time and wait until the paint has dried before proceeding with the next colour. It helps to keep your work covered to avoid any smudges.

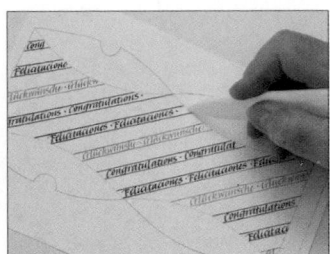

6 When the wording is dry, score along the lines indicated. Use a bone folder or other tool to score along the fold lines. Cut out the template.

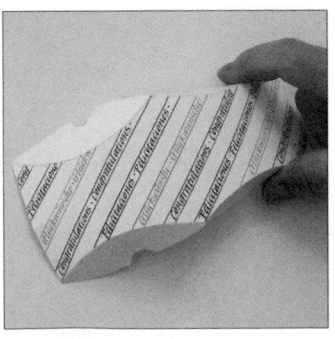

7 Carefully fold the card and press the box into shape. Glue the tab to seal the end of the box.

8 Add any final touches you may wish, such as ribbons in complementary colours.

Rubber-stamped wine label

This is a simple idea which can easily be adapted to all sorts of other labels for uses around the home. Making your own labels brings a warm and individual feel to any jar or bottle. This label is designed for use on a bottle of wine, but you can create all kinds of other labels for a variety of uses.

The label can be illustrated by using a variety of media. In this project a rubber stamp has been used to illustrate the label. You can create a rubber stamp from a craft block or plastic eraser by cutting out the shapes using a craft knife or a 'v'-groove linoleum tool to create the impression. The carving can be printed by using an ink pad or brushing on paint such as gouache or acrylic. While rubber stamping has been used as a simple and effective way of illustrating the wine label, other techniques could be used, such as watercolour painting or drawing with pen and ink or coloured pencils.

Adapt the label to suit your needs. It may be useful to create a generic design for your wine collection, or you may prefer to create individual labels. The description of the wine has been written clearly across the illustration using a bold colour as contrast.

Materials
- *Layout or practice paper*
- *HB and 2H pencils*
- *Coloured pencils*
- *Hot-pressed watercolour paper*
- *Ruler*
- *Pair of compasses*
- *Dip pens: William Mitchell 2, 3 and 4 (medium nibs)*
- *Scissors*
- *Glue stick*
- *Tracing paper*
- *Craft block or plastic square-edged eraser for the stamp*
- *Self-healing cutting mat*
- *Craft (utility) knife with curved blade or 'v'-groove linoleum-cut tool*
- *Ink pads (optional)*
- *Gouache paints: purple mixed with a little red, green and gold*
- *Paint brushes, including a size 0*
- *PVA (white) or craft glue and brush*

The design
This label for a bottle of wine features the 'house' name and the date of the wine written in Humanistic Cursive as a central feature, with a calligraphic border around the edge. The rubber stamp forms the decorative central motif.

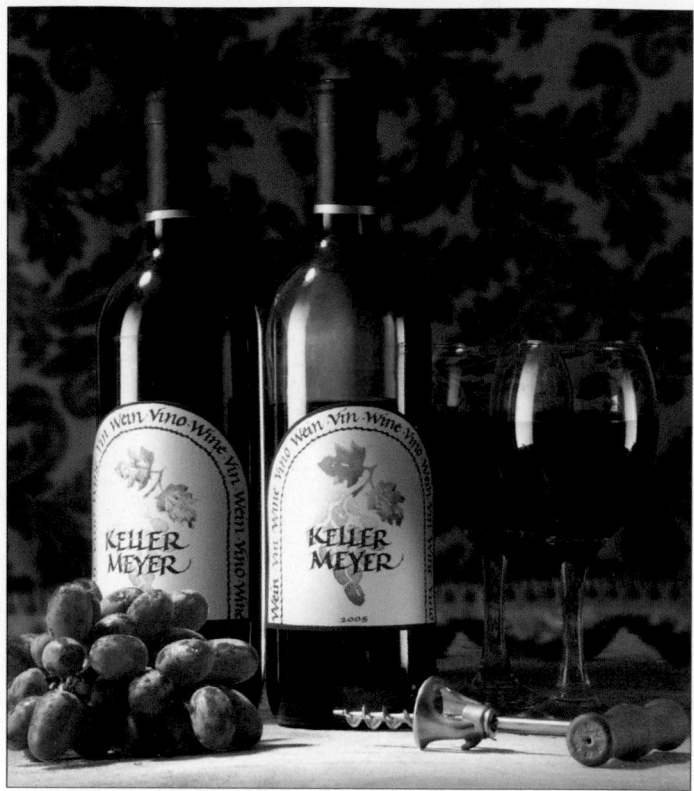

1 Begin by sketching out a few ideas on layout paper. Using coloured pencils will give you some idea of which colours work well together. Experiment with different shapes and sizes for labels.

Tip: Brush the glue from the centre outwards so that the glue does not seep underneath and spoil the label.

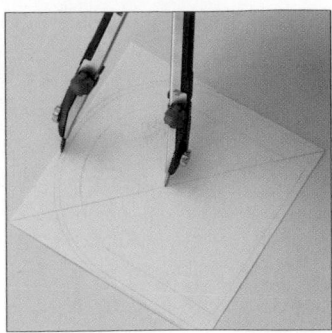

2 Once you have decided on the size of the label, you will have a clearer idea of how much space you have available for lettering and illustration. The label in this project is made by measuring 10cm x 10cm (4in x 4in) on to watercolour paper. Place a ruler diagonally from one corner to the other and mark the centre spot. Place the point of a ruling compass on this mark, open the compass to 5cm (2in) wide and draw an arc to form the top of the label. Repeat the arc 2mm (5/64in) smaller and again 1cm (1/2in) smaller for guidelines. Use a ruler to complete the side lines and base lines.

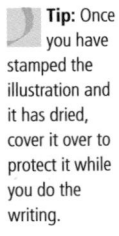 **Tip:** Once you have stamped the illustration and it has dried, cover it over to protect it while you do the writing.

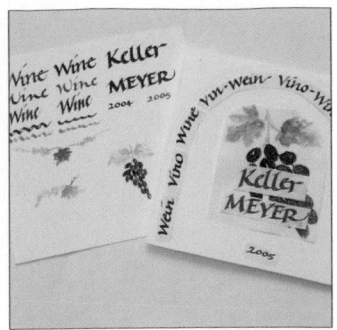

3 Try some writing trials, varying the styles, sizes and colours so as to emphasize the most important words on the label, and try out any ideas for illustration. Cut and paste the results to get the spacing right.

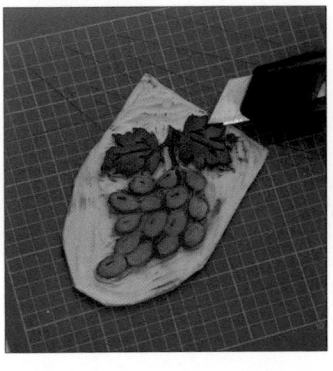

5 To carve the image, use a craft knife or 'v'-groove lino tool and cut away the parts of the image that you do not want printed, leaving the traced black lines. Carve unwanted areas away at an angle with short, shallow cuts.

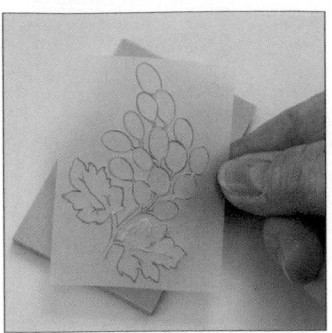

4 Trace your illustration onto tracing paper. Place the image face down on to the carving block or eraser and trace over the back of the tracing paper with a pencil to transfer the image.

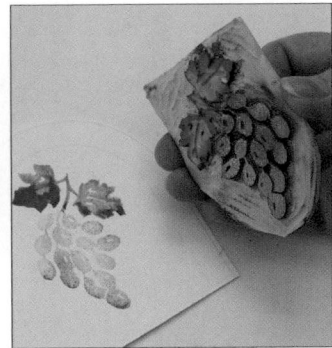

6 Mark some guidelines lightly with a pencil to show where the border will sit. Before using your stamp on the label, try practising on some spare paper until you are happy with the results. Cut out your label. Now stamp the illustration in the centre of the label.

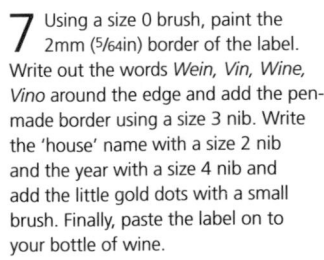

7 Using a size 0 brush, paint the 2mm (5/64in) border of the label. Write out the words *Wein, Vin, Wine, Vino* around the edge and add the pen-made border using a size 3 nib. Write the 'house' name with a size 2 nib and the year with a size 4 nib and add the little gold dots with a small brush. Finally, paste the label on to your bottle of wine.

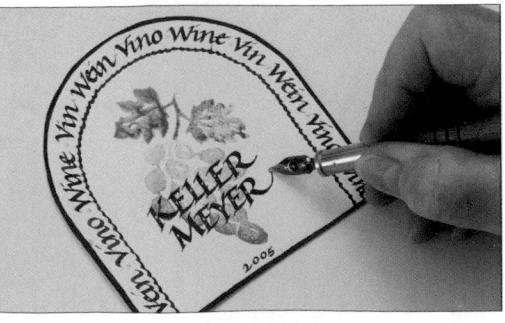

Large-lettered notebook

This little notebook makes a wonderful holiday journal, baby or wedding book, or everyday 'book of memories'. It uses eight sheets of handwriting paper folded to make a book of 32 pages. The notebook is covered with a heavier dove-coloured jacket made of a print-making paper that feels like felt and is extremely soft and thick.

Conventional three-hole stitching holds the book together. The outside pockets are created by folding the outsize cover piece at the tail and the fore-edges, and inserting a contrasting pocket strip.

In this example the inserted strip picks up the colour (Bengal rose), of the lettering. These pockets provide useful spaces in which to tuck in memorabilia and the name on the flap – the only piece of calligraphy to feaure on the notebook – clearly identifies the owner or subject of the book.

The design

Very little calligraphy is involved in this project – just one word. However, that single word defines the theme of the book. Here 'Theodora' is strongly lettered using a large automatic pen and an Italic hand, with the reduced x-height of four nib widths. Also adding to the impact is the variation in stitching, which takes the thread through to the outside of the book – a variation on the conventional sewing, which starts from the centre of the book and sews the spine in a less conspicuous way.

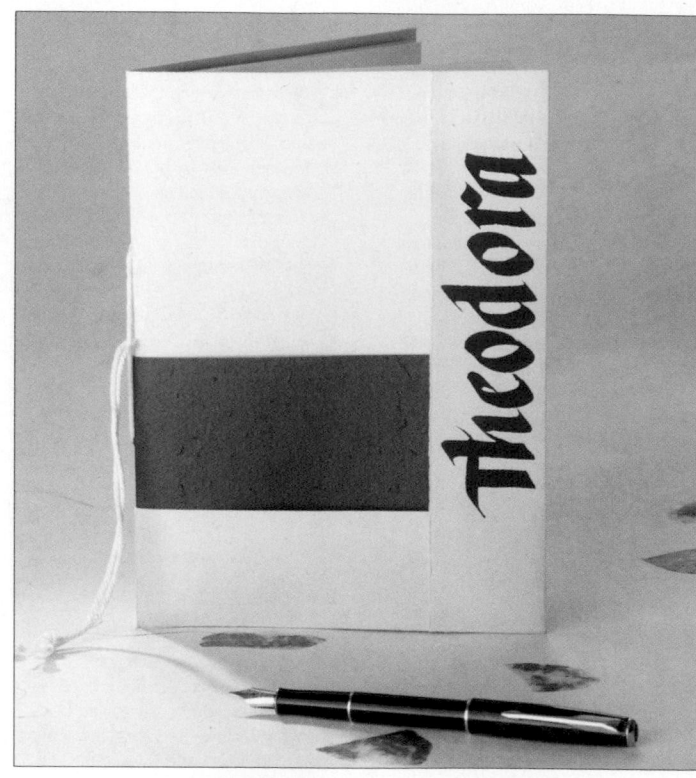

Materials

- *Eight pieces of handwriting-weight paper for the signature*
- *Bone folder*
- *Ruler or metal cutting edge*
- *2H pencil*
- *Rives BFK print-making paper or similar paper for the cover*
- *Craft (utility) knife or scalpel*
- *Self-healing cutting mat*
- *Contrasting paper for the inner pocket*
- *Gouache paint in one colour*
- *Palette*
- *Automatic pen, size 4*
- *Glue stick*
- *Bradawl or awl*
- *Large-eyed tapestry needle*
- *Thick thread or string*
- *Scissors*
- *Beads (optional)*

> **Tip:** Because the notebook is stitched with thick thread or string, it is possible to extend its life by replacing pages if required.

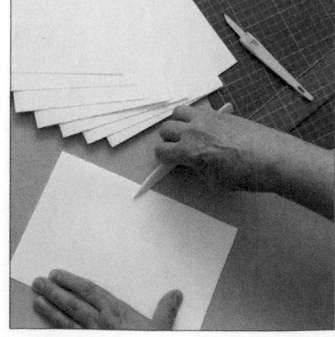

1 Check the grain of the eight sheets of paper. The grain should run parallel with the spine of the finished book. Use a bone folder to fold each sheet of paper in half, one at a time, then place the sheets neatly inside each other to form the signature. Note the measurements from head to tail (at the fore-edge and the spine) and from spine to fore-edge (at the head and the tail), then place your signature under a heavy book.

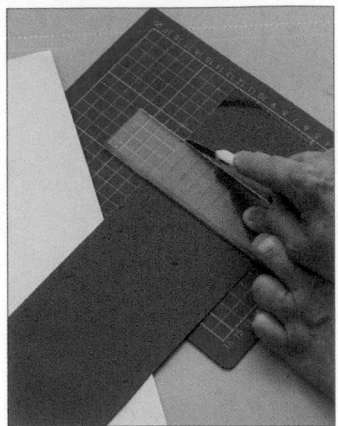

2 Cut the cover paper one-and-a-quarter times the height of the book – the head to tail measurement – and two-and-a-half times the width of the book – the spine to fore-edge measurement. Now cut a strip of contrasting paper half the height and twice the width of the book. This will be used for the pocket strip.

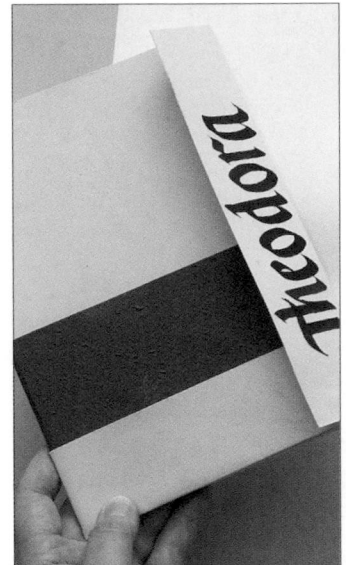

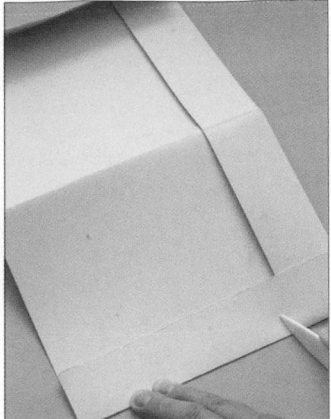

3 The cover and pocket strip should not be folded as crisply as the text block, so gently bring each piece together, short edge to short edge. Put the smaller piece – the pocket – to one side. Open out the larger piece – the cover – and, from the head, measure down the height of the signature plus 5mm (¼in). Do this at both the fore-edges and the spine. Score and fold. Unfold and, from the spine to each fore-edge, measure the width of the book plus 5mm (¼in). Score and fold. At the bottom corners of the cover will be overlapping creases. Trim these away.

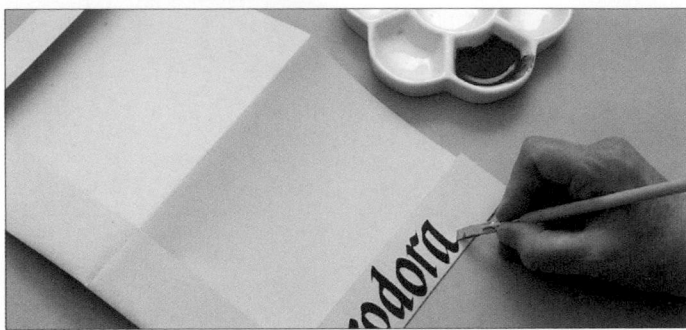

4 Use dilute gouache and a large pen such as an automatic size 4 to write your chosen word on the turn-back of the front flap.

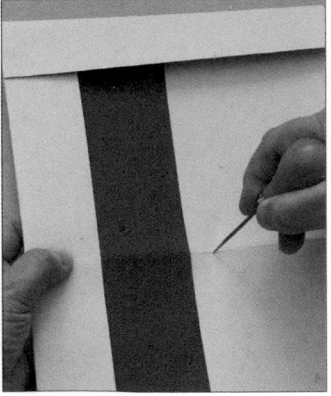

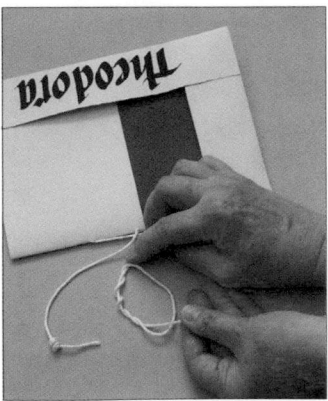

5 Fold up the flap at the tail of the cover and apply small dabs of glue to hold the fore-edge flaps back. Insert the pocket strip and wrap the cover evenly around the signature.

6 With the bradawl or awl, pierce three evenly spaced holes in the spine and, starting from the outside, sew the signature to the cover, finishing with a reef knot.

7 Tie a multi-wrapped overhand knot at each end of the thread, then trim and feather out the ends to make mock tassels. Alternatively, slip on some beads or charms.

Decorative concertina book

The concertina book was most likely to have been invented in China during the Heian period (794–1185). It was formed by folding a scroll backwards and forwards and adding covers to the front and back. It superseded the scroll which was difficult to store and awkward to use. Concertina books were often called *sempūyō*, or flutter books, because the concertina 'pages' were not attached to the spine so they could flutter out in the breeze. Books of this type were used traditionally for Buddhist *sutras* or for albums of painting or calligraphy.

This project creates a concertina book with eight identical sections. The text *dum defluante amnes* is Latin for 'until the rivers cease to flow'. The design has been used to make a Valentine's card, the theme being enforced by the decoration of pen-drawn hearts. After folding, the ends of the book are slipped into covers which, using origami techniques, complement the Chinese book construction. The outside covers are made from a piece of antique paper showing dragons. As dragons are a sign of good luck not only is the recipient assured of undying love but is also being sent good fortune.

The design

By using this folded form and the Foundational script, two simple but effective arts are united. The addition of small hearts, drawn with two easy pen strokes, turns this basic greetings card into a treasured keepsake.

Materials
- *Layout or practice paper*
- *Dip pens: such as William Mitchell 2½ and 3½ (medium nibs)*
- *Gouache paint in two*

diluted colours
- *Hot-pressed watercolour paper*
- *Ruler with cutting edge*
- *2H pencil*

- *Eraser*
- *Self-healing cutting mat*
- *Craft (utility) knife*
- *Bone folder*
- *Card (stock)*
- *Decorative paper*

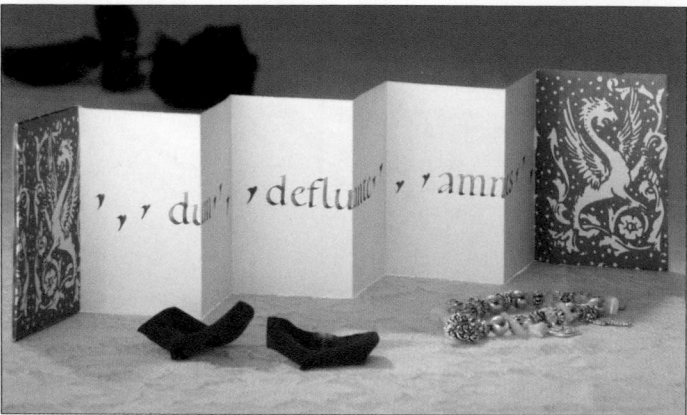

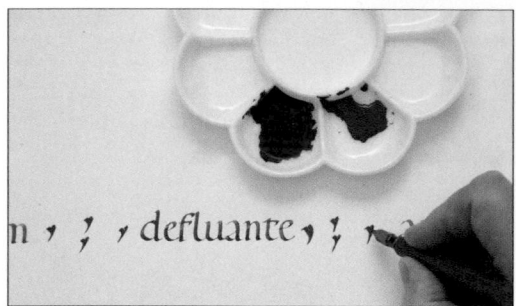

1 Practise the lettering and decoration on layout paper; this will help you choose what size nibs to use. When you are ready, start to work on the watercolour paper. It is best to write the final work on an oversize piece of paper. This means that you will be able to trim the paper and, if you have not quite centred the words, it will be possible to make allowances for this. Leaving a large space all around, rule up, write and decorate the text. The hearts look most effective if a nib two sizes smaller than the one you are using for the writing is used. When everything is thoroughly dry, erase your lines.

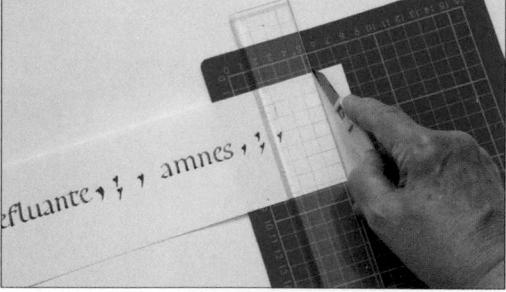

2 Measure the length of the line of writing. Divide this figure by 6 and multiply the answer by 8 to get measurement X. This is the length of paper needed for your concertina. To determine the width you need, divide X by 8 and multiply by 5 to get measurement Y. Cut the paper to measure X by Y, ensuring that the writing has an even amount of white space to the left and right, and lies slightly above the middle. This position is called the 'optical middle' and is more comfortably viewed by the human eye than the true middle.

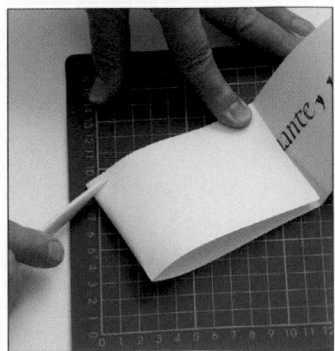

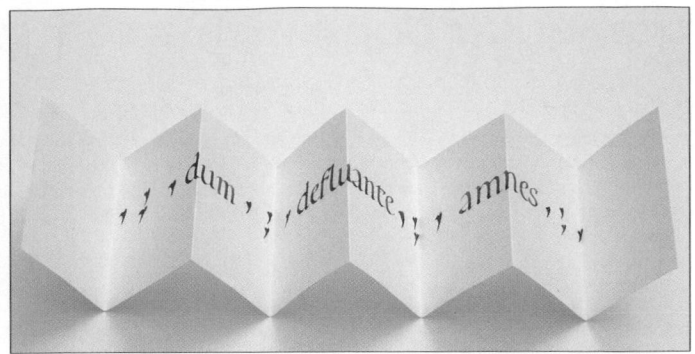

3 Using a bone folder to ensure a sharp crease, fold the paper in half, short edge to short edge and right side to right side. Using this fold as a 'gutter', fold one half in half again, written side to written side – so that the writing does not smudge or shine. Continue in this fashion until you have folded the strip into eight identical sections to form the concertina.

4 At this point the folds will not be in sequence. Change the directions of the folds to make sure you have a valley-mountain-valley-mountain sequence and that the concertina can be closed.

Tip: To fold a concertina, always start from the middle. The direction of the fold is easily changed from a mountain to a valley, or vice versa.

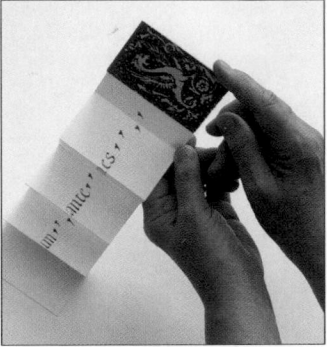

7 Slide these covers on to the front and back sections of the concertina, if necessary cutting a sliver of paper from the outside sections to allow them to slide in easily. The amount that is trimmed should be as little as possible, or the covers will slip.

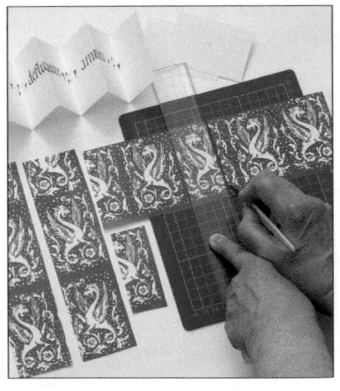

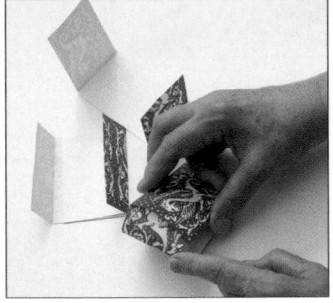

5 Measure the height and width of the folded concertina and cut two pieces of card to this exact measurement. Using decorative paper, cut two more pieces at twice the height of the concertina by the width of the concertina. Then cut two pieces twice the width of the concertina by the height. Finally, cut one piece three times the depth and once the height of the concertina.

6 Fold one of the double-sized vertical pieces around a centrally placed piece of the card. Remove the card and repeat this exercise using the remaining vertical double-sized pieces of paper. Repeat with the double-sized horizontal pieces of paper. Place one of the 'horizontal' pieces of paper around a piece of the card and, with the open ends facing you, fold over and slide the ends of a vertical piece of paper over the card but inside the first piece of paper. This will lock together to form one cover. Repeat for the other cover.

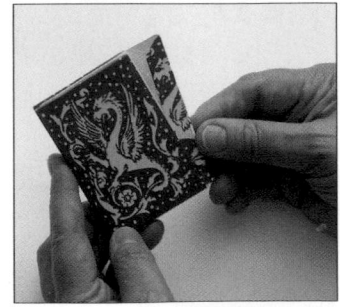

8 Measure the depth of the concertina and score the remaining strip of cover paper to provide a 'spine piece'. Crease firmly and slide into position to turn the concertina into a conventional book.

Triangular book with a centred script

The basic shape of this little book is formed by folding a square into eight equal triangles. The writing is centred on three sides of the square. It is an original and decorative vehicle for the Japanese verse form known as *haiku*, although of course it may be used to convey other messages.

Besides using the form as a *haiku* book, the triangular book makes a wonderful 'thank you', birthday, wedding or congratulations card, with a personalized message written inside. The attachment of the covered boards and ribbons turns a simple idea into a treasured object.

Materials

- *Hot-pressed watercolour paper*
- *2H pencil*
- *Ruler with cutting edge*
- *Eraser*
- *Gouache paint*
- *Dip pen (medium nib)*
- *Bone folder*
- *Self-healing cutting mat*
- *Craft (utility) knife*
- *or scalpel*
- *Card (stock) or small piece of mounting board*
- *Decorative paper for the cover*
- *Glue stick*
- *Ribbon*
- *Scrap paper, preferably shiny*
- *Weights*
- *Scissors*
- *Beads (optional)*

The design

Gothic, the script chosen for this project, is the easiest to space of all the calligraphic hands and its angularity, echoing the book's geometric design, ensures an overall harmony. Because it is so small only a scrap of decorative paper is needed for the cover, so any beautiful pieces you have hoarded because they 'might come in useful one day' are ideal for this project.

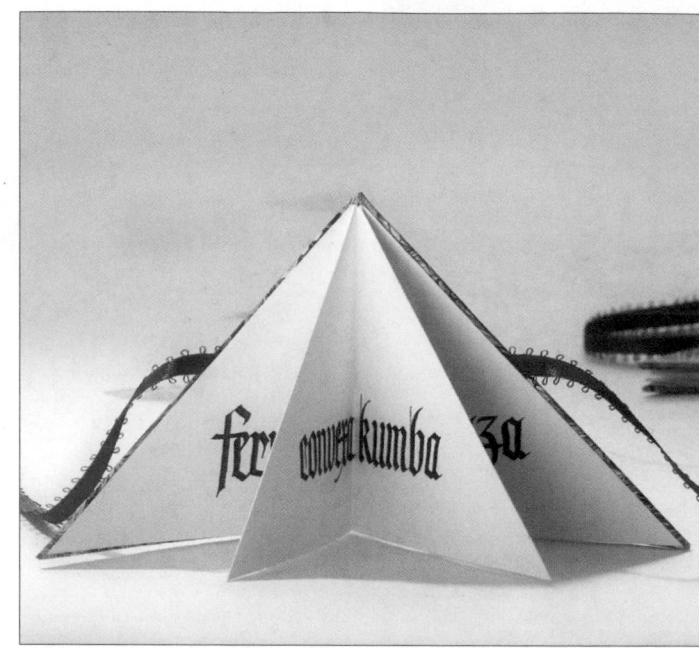

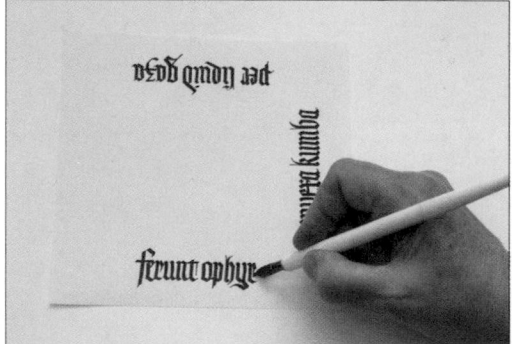

1 Rule up and write the *haiku*, or alternative text around three sides of the square cut to 20cm x 20cm (8in x 8in) making sure that each line of writing is centred within its own side. Erase any construction lines.

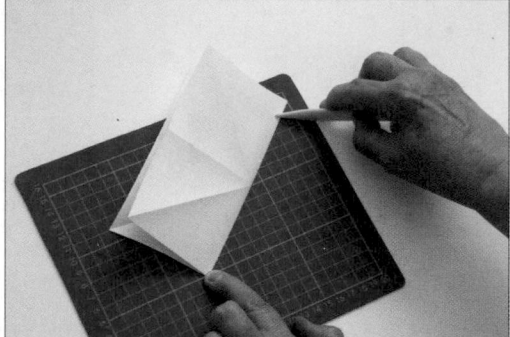

2 Using a bone folder to ensure crisp folds, fold the paper from side to side horizontally and vertically, then corner to corner bottom-left to top-right and top-left to bottom-right.

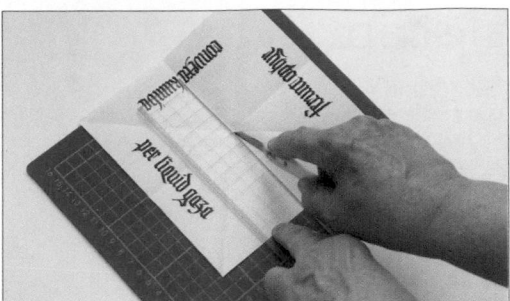

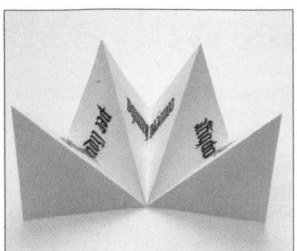

Tip: To centre work, write the words first on layout paper and place them above the writing line to help you space them correctly.

3 Cut through the paper along the fold from the centre to the middle of the unwritten section.

4 Change the direction of the folds, where necessary, so that they follow each other as a mountain or a valley to form a triangular concertina. Measure one of the resulting triangular sections.

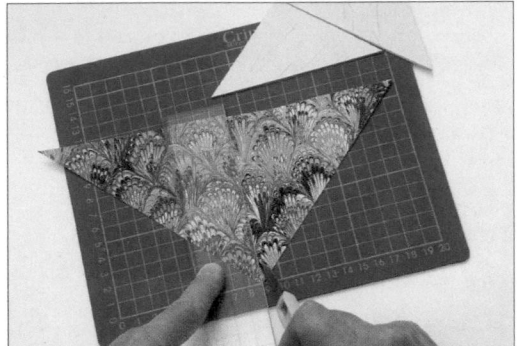

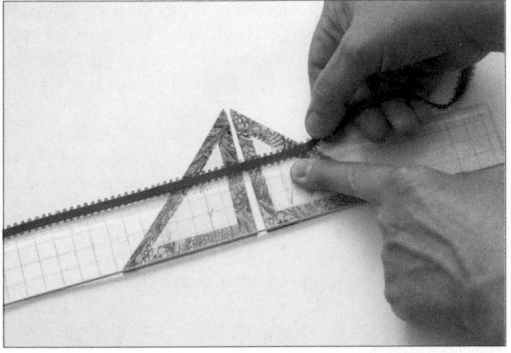

5 Referring to your measurements, cut two pieces of card (or board) to the size of a triangular section, and two pieces of cover paper, 1cm (1/2in) larger than the card all round, being careful to cut one piece of paper facing right and one piece facing left.

6 Carefully cover the card or board triangles with the decorative paper and glue. Lay the triangles face down, with the depth of the triangular concertina apart and the hypotenuses facing outwards. Place the ruler at the optical middle and draw a pencil line. Use this to help glue the ribbon to the cards. It need be only enough to make a hinge but can be longer if you prefer to use extravagant ties.

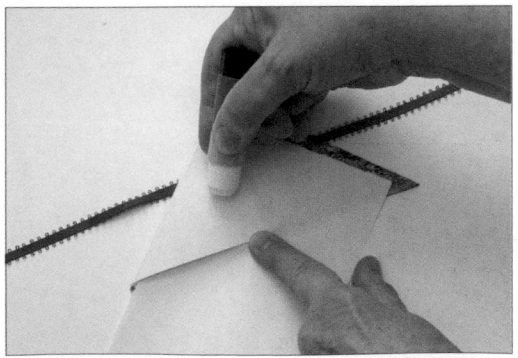

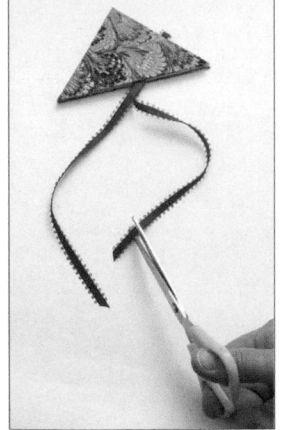

8 Finish the book by adding beads to the ribbon, or simply cut the ribbon ends diagonally, which will prevent fraying. Do not succumb to the temptation to cut 'fish tails' – they always fray.

Tip: To prevent 'show through' between the covers and the text, line the inside of the covers with decorative paper inserts.

7 Slide scrap paper between the folds of the triangular concertina to protect it and glue the front section. Throw away the messy waste paper and attach the section to the reverse of the front board. Repeat these steps for the back section and board. Leave the book to dry under weights.

Lotus book with a spiral script

The lotus fold is an ancient origami fold. In this book only one square of paper is folded and used to make the book. However, books may be made with several leaves, each created from individual squares of paper. It is thought that two leaves glued together resemble the flower of the lotus. A lotus may be folded using a circular piece of paper but, as that would emphasize the asymmetrical shape of the finished calligraphic spiral, the traditional square shape has been chosen. Writing around a spiral is much easier than you would think, and is very flattering to any standard of calligraphy. When closed, the square book gives no hint of the complex mysteries it encloses.

Make sure that there is plenty of ribbon available to make an extravagant tie in satin, velvet or silk as people often hang lotus books by their ribbons. If the paper or ribbon is very thick, or the text paper has 'show through', two smaller squares of decorative paper can be cut to line the inside of the cards. You can also cover the ribbon that is attached to each board with a small strip of masking tape.

The lotus fold takes a square and 'collapses' it into a square a quarter of its original size. In this project only one lotus is used, but you can join several of these folds together, openings outward, to make a more complex book. A lotus book is also an admirable vehicle to contain calligraphy that is written in straight lines. However, the shape of the lotus requires that the writing should run diagonally across the square of paper.

The design

Uncial is the ideal choice for this project – not only because it is a beautiful and round script, but also because its ascenders and descenders are relatively short and neat. By presenting the end result as a lotus book this exercise creates a charming gift, while enabling you to practise the art of producing calligraphy in the form of a spiral.

Materials

- *Layout or practice paper*
- *2H pencil*
- *Ruler with cutting edge*
- *Pair of compasses*
- *Hot-pressed watercolour paper*
- *Dip pen: William Mitchell 2¹/₂ (medium nib)*
- *Gouache paint or ink in one colour*
- *Eraser*
- *Craft (utility) knife or scalpel*
- *Scissors*
- *Four strips of black paper*
- *Bone folder*
- *Card (stock)*
- *Decorative paper for cover*
- *Glue stick*
- *Scrap paper, preferably shiny*
- *Satin, velvet or silk ribbon, not florist's ribbon*

> **Tip:** When writing in Uncials, it may be more comfortable to use a right-handed oblique nib.

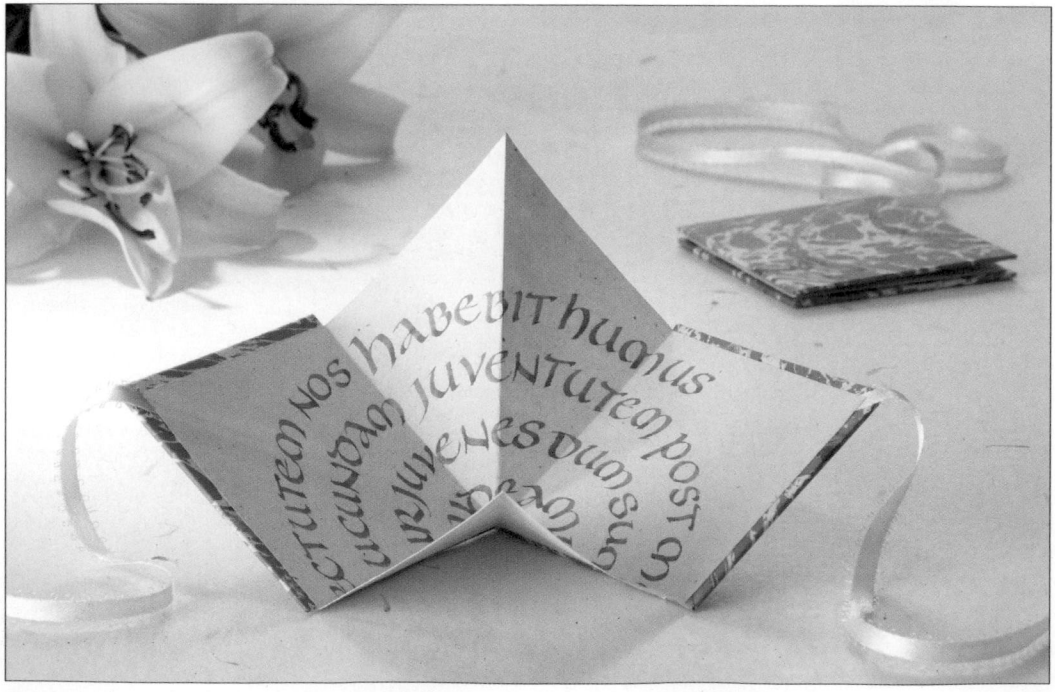

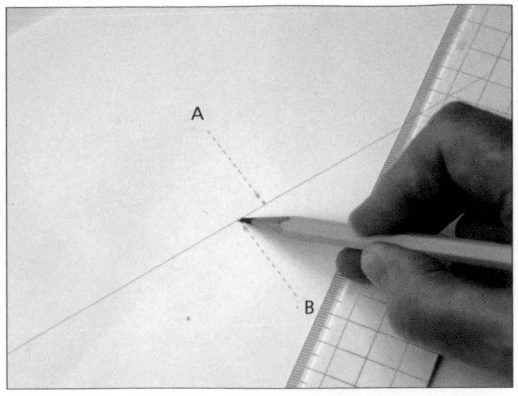

1 Using layout paper, practise drawing the spiral shape that will be the guide for your calligraphy. Draw a horizontal line and make two marks on it: 'A' and 'B'. Working from left to right, 'B' precedes 'A' and is on the underside of the line; 'A' is behind 'B' and sits on the top of the line. For the spiral to be compact, these two marks need to be close together.

Tip: If you are writing in a language that reads from right to left, your spiral needs to turn anti-clockwise. To ensure this, 'A' should precede 'B' on the horizontal line, sitting on the top. 'B' should follow 'A', on the underside of the line.

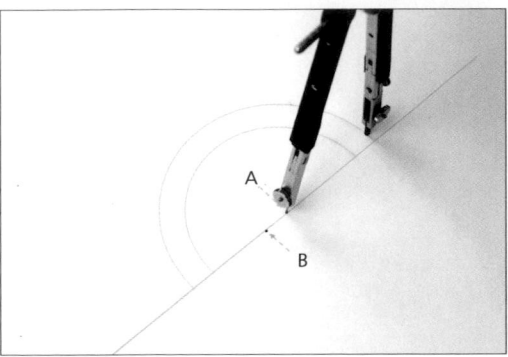

2 Using a pair of compasses, and point 'A' as the centre, draw two concentric semicircles. These need to be separated by the x-height of your chosen script.

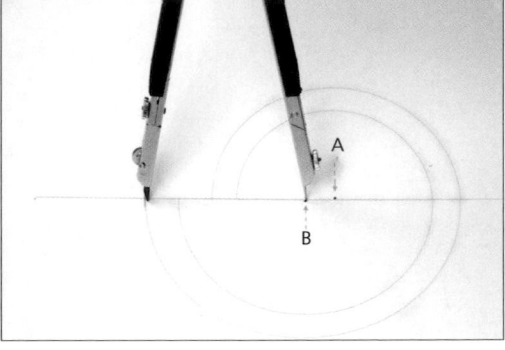

3 Using 'B' as the centre, draw another two concentric semicircles, adjusting the radii to touch the right-hand finishing points of the two semicircles you have already drawn.

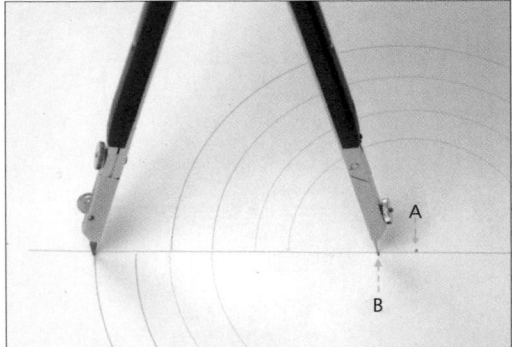

4 Return the compass to point 'A'. Draw another two concentric semicircles, touching the finishing points of the 'B'-centered semicircles. Continue moving between points 'A' and 'B' until the spiral is large enough to hold what you propose to write.

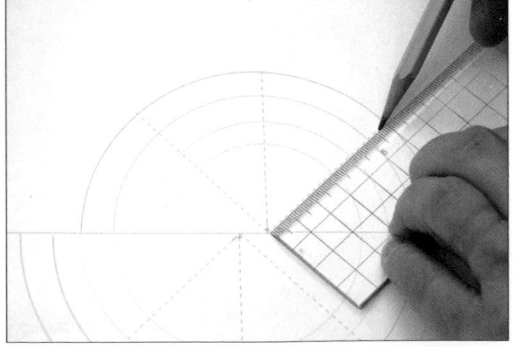

5 The axis of every letter needs to be parallel with its associated radius of the semicircle in which it is situated. To make this easier, pencil in radii for both semicircles. Note that these only share alignment along the original horizontal line. Having practised on layout paper, redraw the spiral on watercolour paper in exactly the same way.

▶

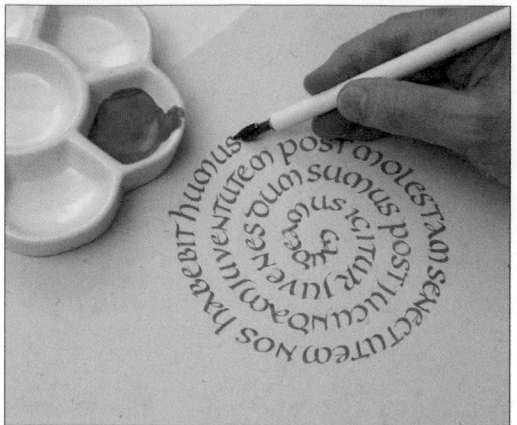

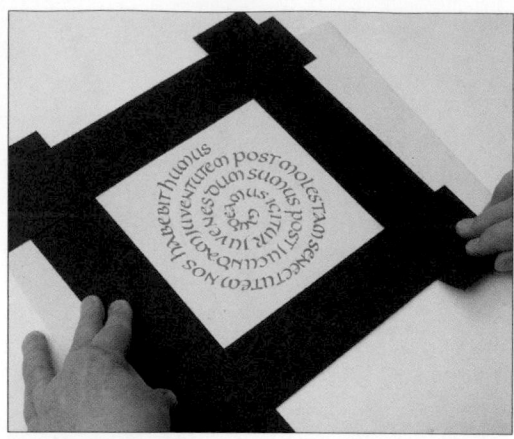

6 Write around the spiral using your chosen colour. Remember to keep turning your paper as you write. To prevent smudging, wait for the paint to dry at some points before continuing.

Tip: Black strips are used to work out the size and layout of the finished piece of calligraphy. If you have a large, unwanted picture mount, it is easier to cut this into two 'L' shapes and use these instead.

7 When the writing is complete, all the construction lines can be erased. At this stage, the spiral may look a little lopsided but this is easily put right. Take four strips of black paper or card and lay them around the work. Keep trying different orientations until you achieve one that you are happy with. Make careful pencil marks in the corners before removing the black strips and cutting the piece to the required shape. (Note: for this project the piece needs to be perfectly square. If you wanted to present your spiral as a finished broad sheet, you could choose a rectangular shape.)

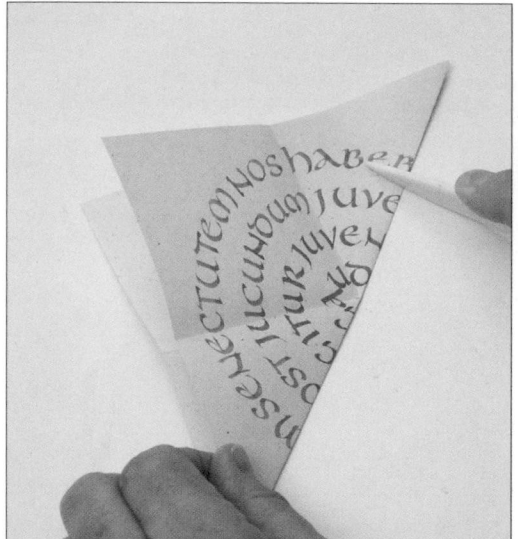

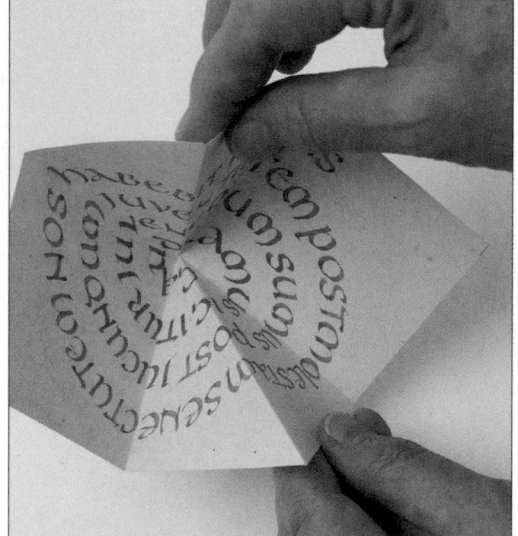

8 Fold the resulting square from side to side both horizontally and vertically. The calligraphy should be facing inwards. Turn the square over and fold once diagonally. Use a bone folder to ensure crisp folds.

9 Pick up the square of paper and gently ease the diagonal crease together. The square will fold down into a square shape, which will be a quarter of its original size. This is the lotus fold.

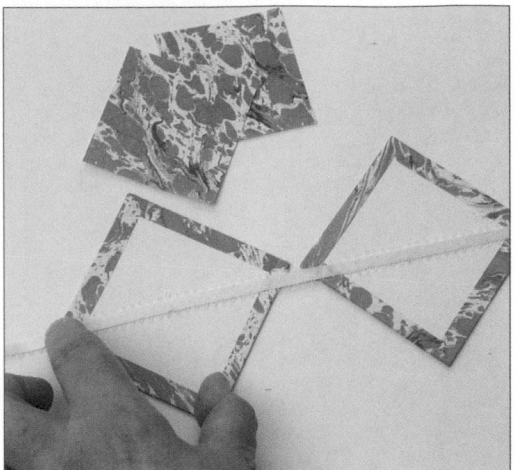

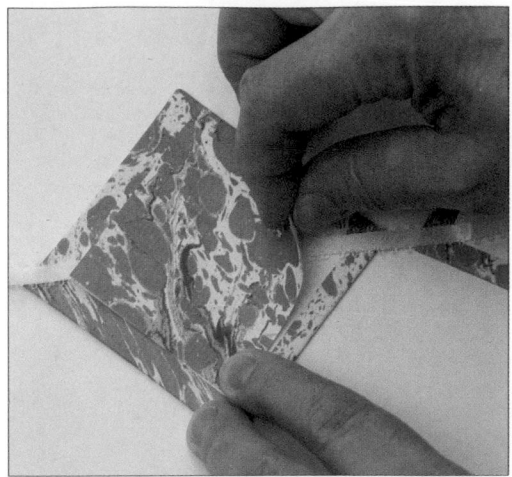

10 Measure this new, smaller square. You should be able to calculate its size from your original dimensions, but it is always safer to check. Cut two pieces of card to the same size, and two squares of decorative paper with an extra outside margin of 2.5cm (1in).

11 Lay the covered cards or boards face down, point to point and the depth of the lotus apart. If the space is too small the lotus will not open without damaging the covers. Glue straight across both cards horizontally. Fold the ribbon in half as a guide and lay it down on the glue. You may wish to line the insides of the covers to prevent 'show through'. Slide scrap paper between the folds of the lotus to protect it and glue the front section.

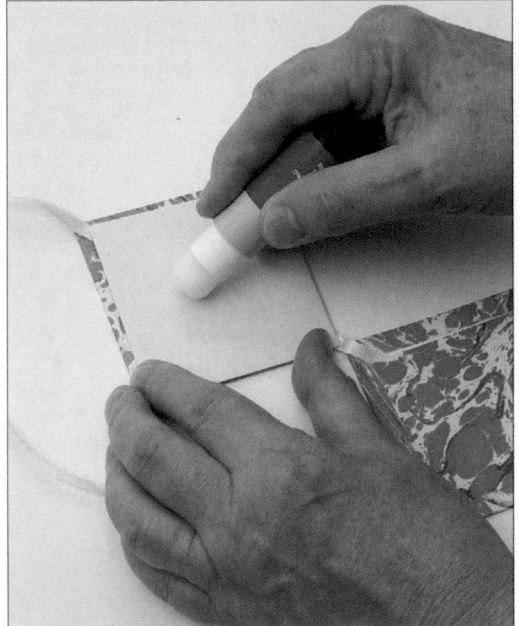

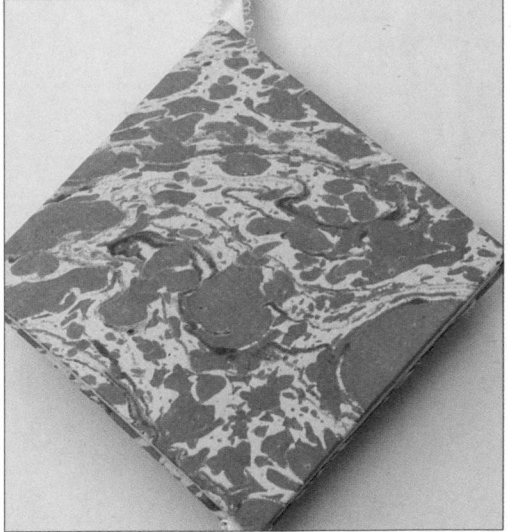

12 Throw away the messy waste paper and attach the front of the lotus to the reverse of the front board. Repeat these steps for the back of the lotus and board. Leave the book to dry under weights.

13 The finished book. These little books are so decorative that they can be displayed open or hanging up.

Rubber stamp patterns for place cards

This project is an excellent opportunity to bring something personal to a special occasion, such as a birthday dinner or wedding banquet. Once you have learnt the art of cutting your own designs for a rubber stamp this becomes an easy and effective way to create attractive single images, or repeat patterns for borders and larger areas.

A selection of place cards are created, which are then folded in order to stand up on a table. They have the individual name of each guest written on one side of the card, and are decorated around the edge by a rubber-stamped border. The guest's name can either be added to the card before you start stamping or can be written in afterwards – depending on the design you wish to create. You can attempt letters with the rubber stamp, but remember to cut them in reverse.

An infinite number of designs can be produced simply by overprinting with different colours or reversing the direction of a non-symmetrical stamp. Stamping can also be used to produce larger, more complex designs that combine several intricately cut stamps. The key to this project is to keep your stamping designs

to basic geometric shapes as they are easy and quick to cut and make stunning patterns, especially if non-symmetrical. The designs can be turned through different angles for variety.

> **Tip:** Have a damp cloth handy to clean stamps between colour changes, so stamping pads are not contaminated by different colours.

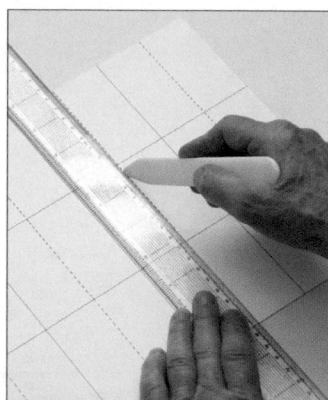

The design

The lettering in Italic is written before the 'v'-shaped cuts have been made in the stamps to produce an interesting border. Dots or tiny diamonds may be added once the cards have dried.

Materials

- *White card (stock)*
- *Bone folder*
- *Ruler and pencil*
- *Self-healing cutting mat*
- *Scalpel or craft (utility) knife*
- *Dip pen: various sizes*
- *Inks: various colours*
- *'Plastic' square-edged erasers*
- *Coloured stamping pads or foam*
- *Gouache paints and gel pens*

1 On a large sheet of card, rule up the place cards. A 7.5cm (3in) square is a recommended size to use. Divide this square in half lengthways to allow for the fold. Using a bone folder score all fold lines against a ruler to create a sharp indent in the card surface, ready for folding. Cut out the individual cards, but leave them unfolded.

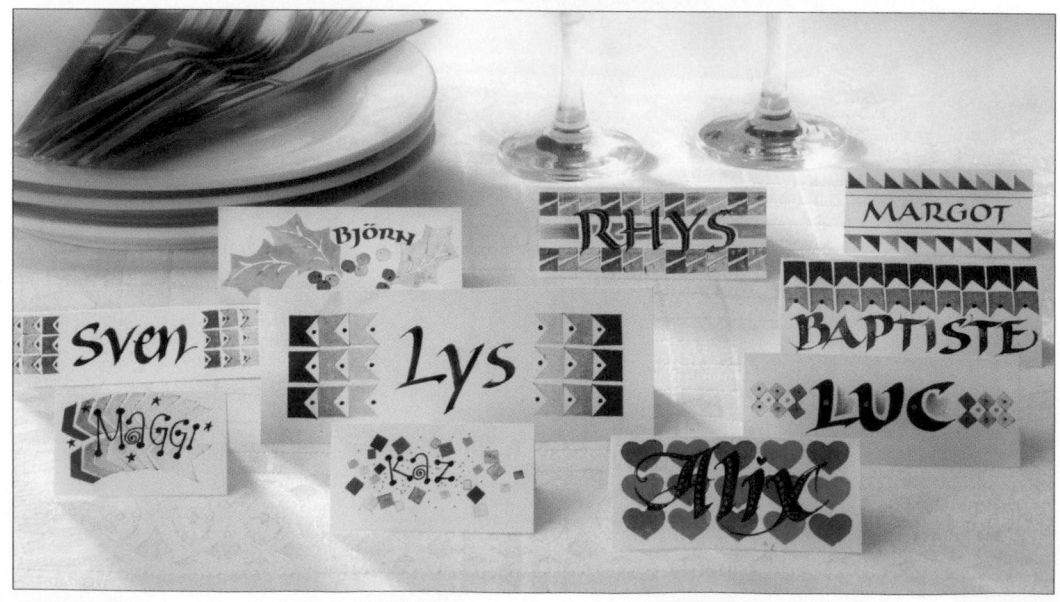

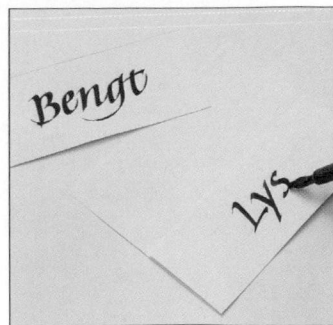

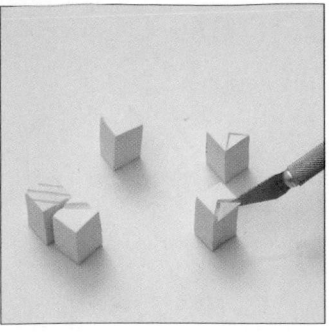

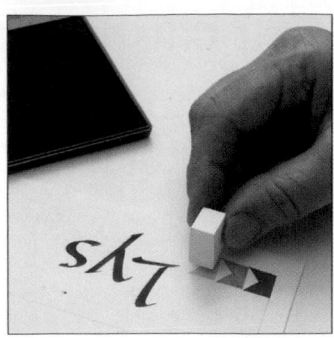

2 Write out the names of the guests in Italic lettering in your chosen colour on one side of the unfolded card. Allow to dry thoroughly. If you plan to stamp the whole surface of the card, you can write the name later, on top of the stamped design.

3 To prepare your rubber stamps, cut a small portion of an eraser, with the uncut edge at approximately 1cm (½in) square. This is the printing surface on which the design should be cut. If you attempt letters, they must be cut in reverse. Cut 'v'-shaped slivers from the printing surface of the stamp, with the blade entering at 45 degrees each time for clean cuts.

4 Whatever is cut away will show as a gap in the printing. Many varied designs may be achieved by simple cuts. A row of randomly placed 'v'-shaped cuts along the long edge of an eraser will create a terrific border pattern.

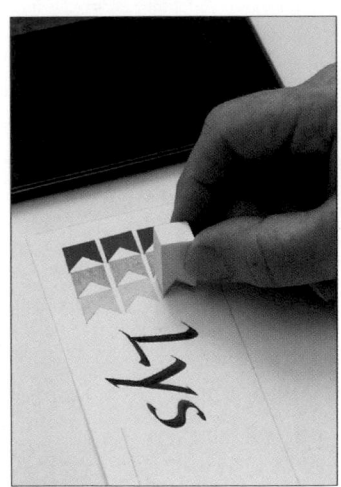

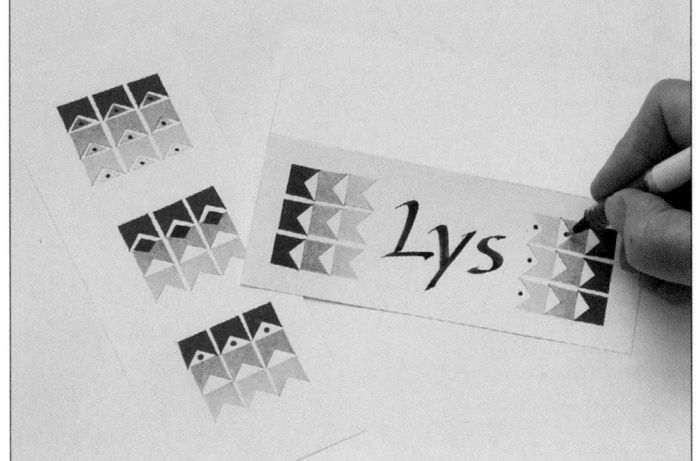

5 If this is your first attempt at printing, you will find it easier to use a purpose-made stamping pad, but you may also want to try making your own, with a little gouache spread on to a dampened foam pad. This adds texture to the prints. Practise stamping in rows, only re-inking every three or four prints. A pattern of repeated shapes, giving a graded tonal effect, makes a very attractive design, before and after the name.

6 Once your cards are dry, you can fold them. You may want to add dots in black, gold or silver with gel pens. Alternatively the designs could be overstamped with further stamps of tiny diamonds or other shapes. Try out some ideas on a separate sheet. If you are writing over stamped designs, wait until the paint is fully dry before writing on top of it.

Tip: Stamp carefully and firmly, placing stamps in close proximity for the best results, in order to build up an effective pattern.

Tip: Keep the stamped designs simple, avoiding circular shapes as they are more difficult to cut. Keep your fingers away from the cutting direction.

Embellished magnets or badges

This project is one that all the family can enjoy. Choose your favourite sayings, write them on to white or coloured paper, and decorate with crayons, paints, fibre and water gels. Embellish the lettering with a pattern or shapes. Think about the edge of the paper and perhaps make a torn edge to expose the fibre. Add a colour to make it more individual or interesting by rubbing pastel into the torn fibre, or by running a brush loaded with colour around the outer edging.

For durability, the finished designs could be encapsulated in plastic, and then cut to shape. Adding magnetic strips or badge pins to the back can make gifts that are ideal stocking fillers.

This project can easily be adapted to create more ambitious designs for drinks coasters and placemats, using the same simple method, by preparing suitable, larger designs on paper, encapsulating them in plastic and adding a thin cork backing to stop them slipping when placed on a tablecloth.

Materials

- White or coloured paper
- Pencil and ruler
- Dip pen: William Mitchell 1 (large nib)
- Black ink
- Felt-tipped pens
- Coloured crayons
- Eraser
- Watercolour paints
- Plastic (for laminate), optional
- Scissors
- Self-adhesive magnetic strip
  or magnetic buttons
- Badge pins

> **Tip:** To infill a letter counter, colour a small portion only, rather than the whole area, leaving a gap between the colour and the letter. Graduate from full-strength colour to a very pale outer edge, as you approach the opposite side of the letter counter.

The design

This project uses bold Uncials for the message, but these can also be combined with another type of lettering such as a Monoline style.

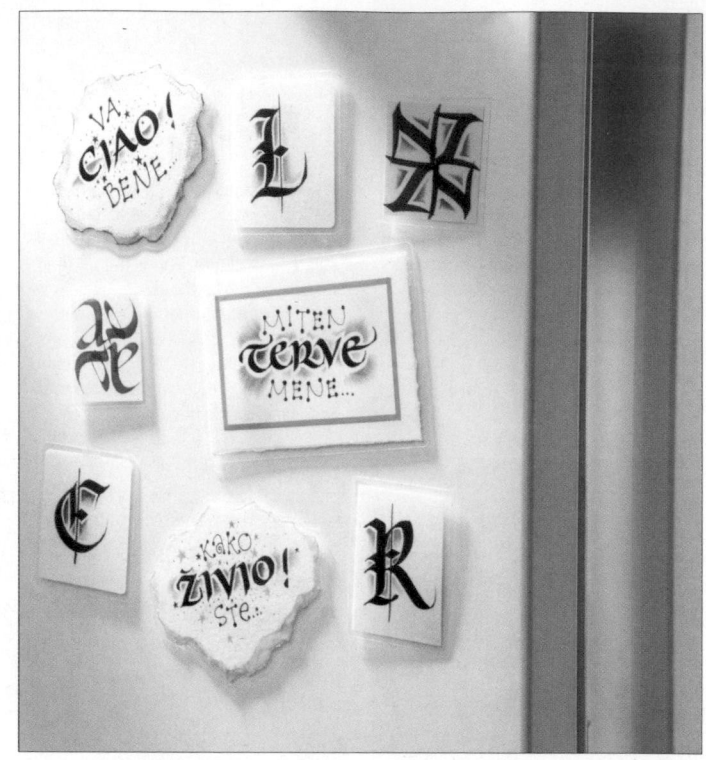

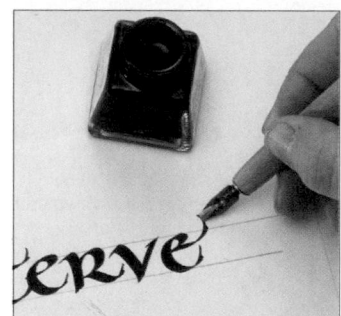

1 Prepare your layout and start the design of the piece. Begin with some bold calligraphic letters, such as modern Uncials, writing out the first part of your phrase or saying.

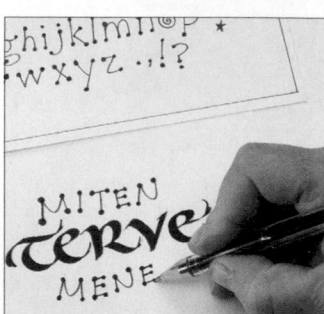

2 Consider combining the Uncial letters with a contrasting lettering, such as the Monoline alphabet.

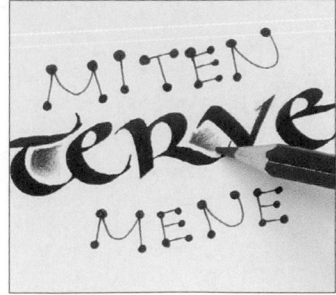 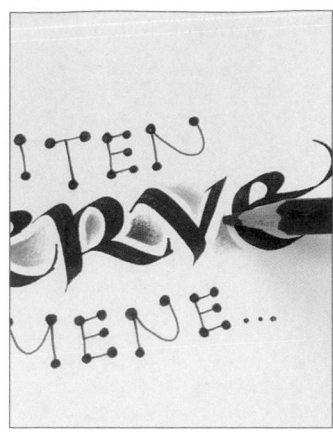 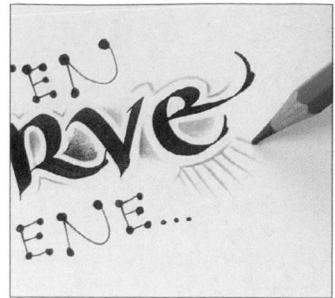

3 Choose two or three coloured crayons to fill the letter counters, varying the pressure as you work. Practise some bigger letters first. Start by paralleling the inside letter shape, taking care to leave a gap between the letter and crayon line at all times.

4 Fill the gaps between the letters with a second and third colour.

5 Start the profile colouring, using pressure on a sharpened crayon tip to give a crisp line. Continue to blend colour away from this line, gradually reducing pressure so the colour tails off to a soft, barely noticeable edge.

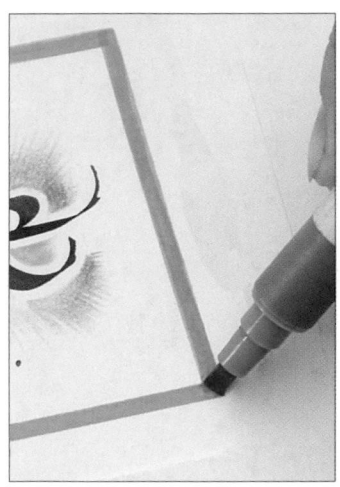 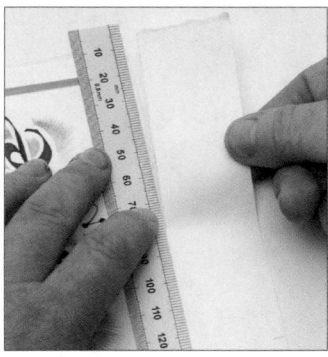 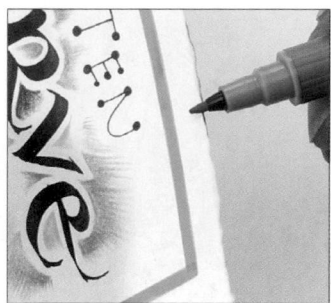

8 To add colour, run a felt-tipped pen or brush lightly along the edge of the torn surface.

6 Draw around the design using a thick felt-tipped pen or brush to create a colourful border.

7 The borders can be 'deckled' or torn to expose the fibres of the paper. Lightly mark the edges of your work and place a ruler along the inside of the line, so it covers the work – this way, the attractive torn edge will remain on the work and not on the piece being discarded. Put pressure on the ruler, tearing the paper against it and slightly moving the paper strip from side to side, creating a wavy edge.

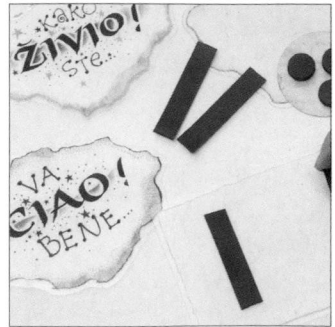

9 The finished designs can be laminated in plastic and then cut to the required shapes. Add a small piece of magnetic strip or a pin to complete the fridge magnet or badge.

Tip: The deckled edge does not have to be a straight edge. Another idea is to tear the paper around a curve to create different shaped fridge magnets. Try rubbing pastel dust on the deckled edges to create a delightful effect.

Tip: For a curved random effect, hold the work in your left hand (or right hand if you are left-handed) and tear in a wavy fashion, slightly waving the paper back and forth during tearing and moving slowly around the edge.

3-D shadow cards

Colour can be used to give shape and form, creating informal, decorative graphic and calligraphic letters that can be used in many situations. However, letters can also be given an extra dimension. By imagining the direction of a light source, you can draw in 'shadows', which should always fall directly opposite the direction the 'light' comes from.

Once you have practised this technique, several different types of shadow effect can be created, which will make your letters appear almost to lift off the page. One method is to add single lines that are slightly removed from the letter. Another is to extend shading away from each shadow to give a 'brush' look, then erase the original letter. This kind of lettering is ideal when the object is to catch attention or to make an impact, as with a poster.

The design
Shadows are most effective when bold letters are used. This project uses chunky Neuland letters.

Materials
- *Sharp pencils*
- *Tracing paper*
- *Paper or card (stock)*
- *Watercolour paints*
- *Pen*
- *Coloured crayons*
- *Black fine liner*
- *Gel pens*
- *Scissors*

Tip: Practise finding out where shadows fall on a word or a letter by shining a torch on to chunky cut-out cardboard letters. Draw its direction on the page to allow easier positioning of the shadow.

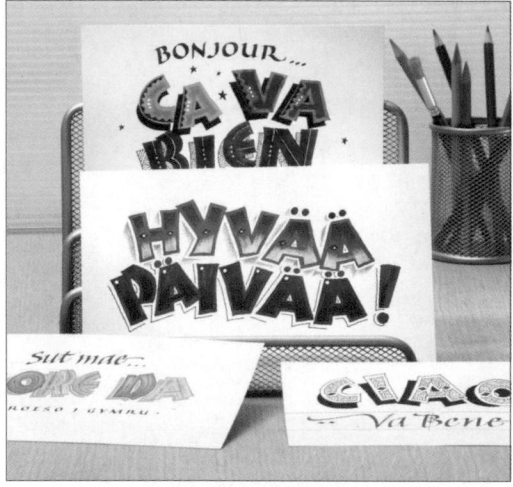

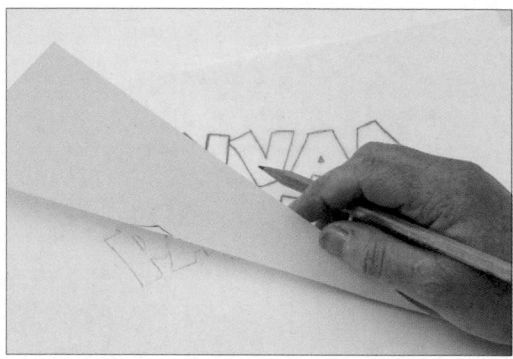

1 Trace your chosen word or letters and transfer them on to card or paper. Alternatively, cut out a letter shape to use as a template and draw around it, then reposition it slightly to draw the shadow. Remember that the shadow should always lie opposite the imaginary source of light.

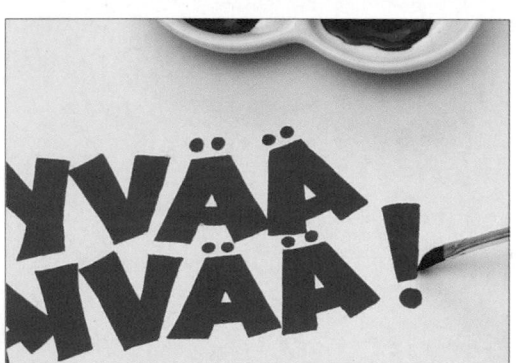

2 Using the watercolour paints, colour the letters of your chosen message. Wait until the paints are completely dry before adding the shadow.

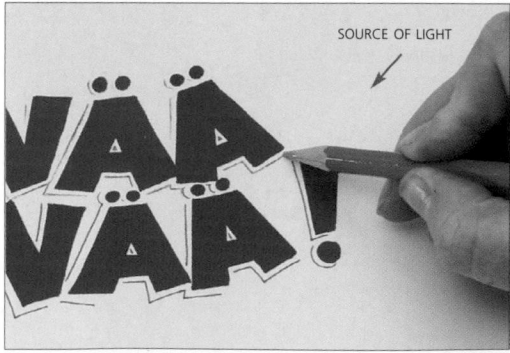

SOURCE OF LIGHT

3 Draw an outline in pen and crayon next to your letters as appropriate. The shadow can be placed anywhere around each letter, dependent on the direction of the light source.

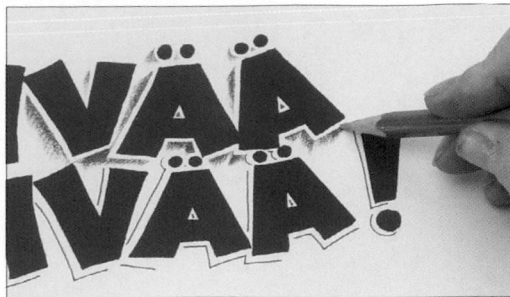

4 To increase the 3-D effect extend shading away from each shadow line to give a 'brush' look. This contrasts with the black lines on the lower line of lettering.

Tip: You can create this brush shadow effect around a lightly drawn pencil letter and then erase the drawn letter, leaving only the elongated shadow look. When you add an elongated brush shadow, be careful not to draw over your invisible letter.

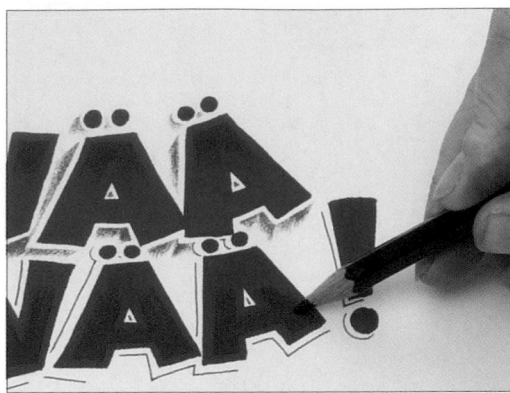

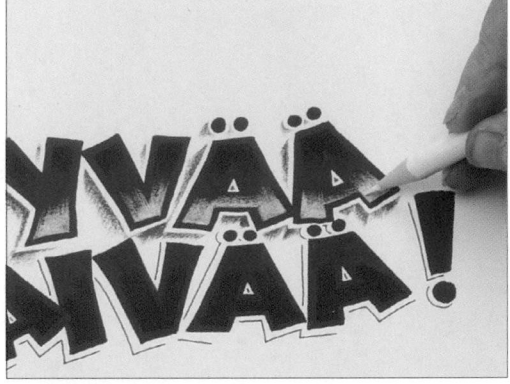

5 Add an inner shape of further colour using crayon, leaving a gap around the perimeter to show the watercolour. Vary the pressure, graduating from the solid outline and tailing off towards the middle of the letter to create a contrast.

6 To heighten contrast, highlight the letters with a white crayon, again graduating from the solid outline towards the centre of the letter.

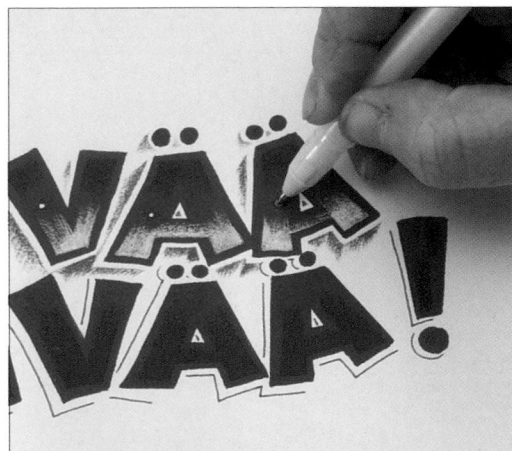

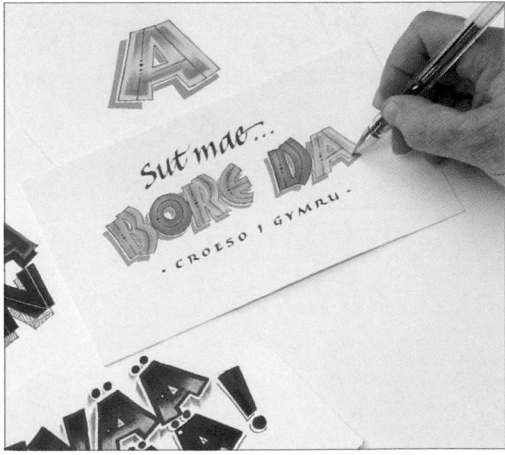

7 Draw patterns on the coloured surface with shapes or embellish with dots, for a more delicate effect. White pen on dark colours can be extremely effective.

8 Try some other ideas for decoration and shadow. The shadow style of lettering can be effectively applied to a wide range of materials, such as cards and posters.

Mouse mat using digital calligraphy

This personalized mouse mat is created by combining scanned lettering with a graduated coloured background. The project involves turning handwritten calligraphy into a pattern on the computer by using some fairly simple graphics procedures. The project can be undertaken using any graphics software to achieve the same effects. Although the illustrated mouse mat is rectangular, a different shape such as a circle could also be used.

Materials

- *Dip pen, such as William Mitchell 2 (medium nib)*
- *Black ink*
- *Layout or practice paper*
- *Scanner*
- *Graphics software (e.g. Adobe Photoshop or CorelDRAW)*
- *Mousemat or thick card (stock) cut to size*
- *Inkjet printer*
- *Craft (utility) knife*
- *Glue*
- *Self-healing cutting mat*
- *Adhesive laminate sheet (recommended)*

The design

This project uses Italic as the font for a mouse mat with a name or message of your choice, with a repeating patterned effect.

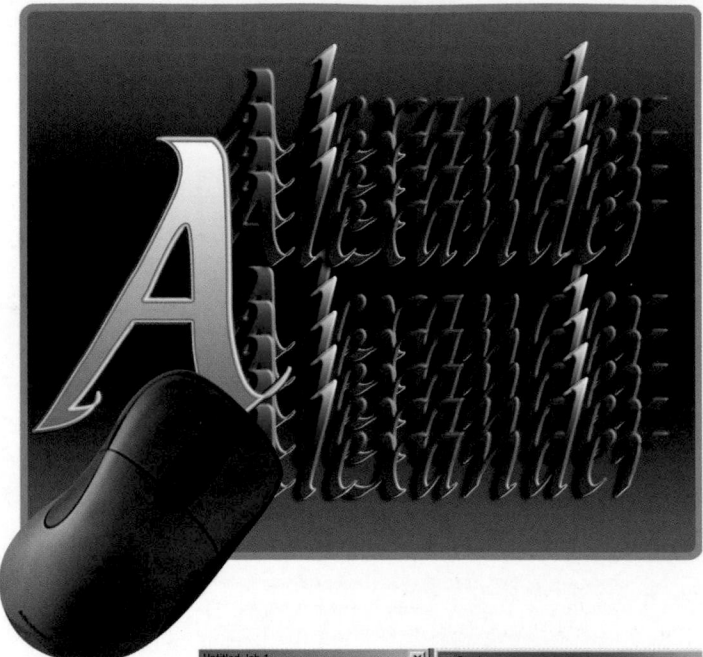

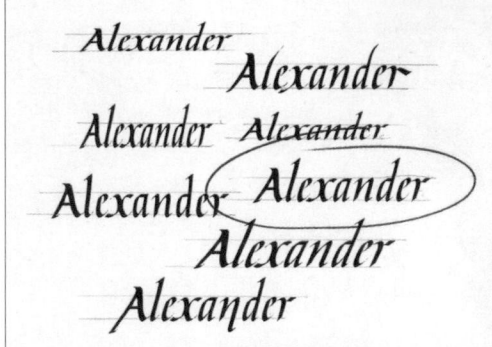

1 Decide on a word or words that you would like to use as the basic element of your calligraphic design. Using black ink on white paper, write this several times until you are happy with it. The lettering can be treated as freely or as formally as you wish. In this project, the name *Alexander* has been chosen, but you can choose your own name or any other words you prefer.

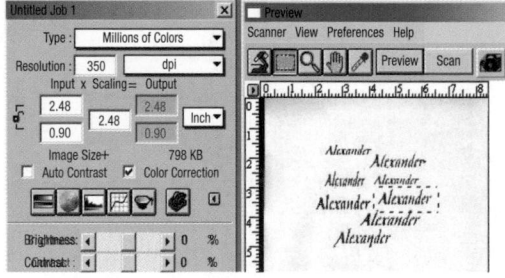

2 Scan your selected word or words. Here a very basic Italic has been used to demonstrate how even the simplest lettering can be made much more interesting by using computer graphics. Your scanner software may look different on screen from the illustration but it should work equally well.

Tip: Be careful with inkjet prints. If you use a water-based adhesive be careful that it does not get onto the printed surface. Use a thick paper so that the moisture from the adhesive does not bleed through.

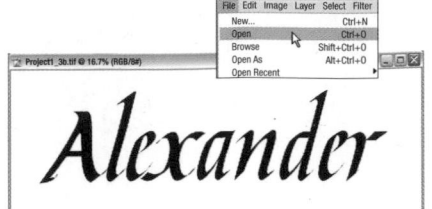

3 Import the scanned lettering into your graphics software. The screengrabs show Photoshop but you can use other software for the project. If the scanner is set to colour or greyscale convert the image to black and white line art and then back to colour. This should remove any unwanted background, leaving just the text.

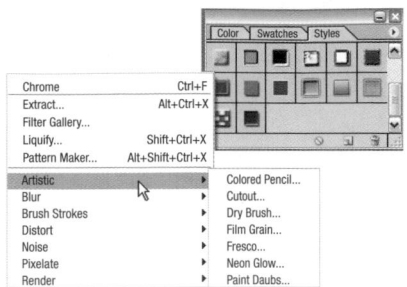

4 Experiment with different effects using filters or styles in Photoshop. These can be found as different menu items, depending on the software you are using. Whatever graphics software you are using you should be able to try out a wide range of effects.

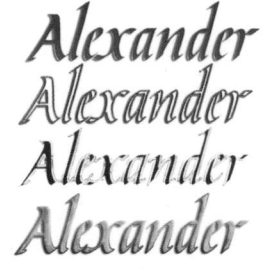

Select the one you prefer. As this will be used as a repeat design, make sure that your filter does not create a background colour or texture. For example, embossing and some of Photoshop's Artistic filters affect the background.

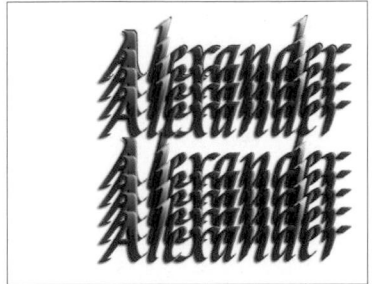

5 Draw a rectangle the size of your mat. Using 'cut' and 'paste', repeat the name several times to form an overall pattern. Each time you paste the image it can be located above or below the previous one. If necessary, make final adjustments to the design.

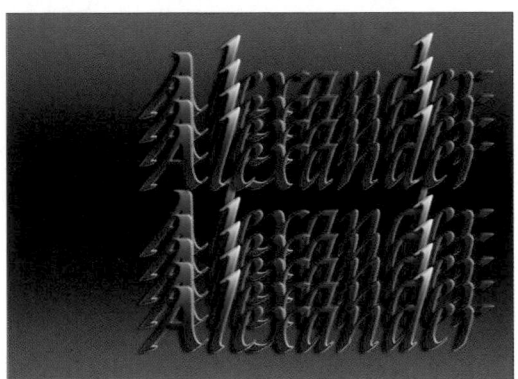

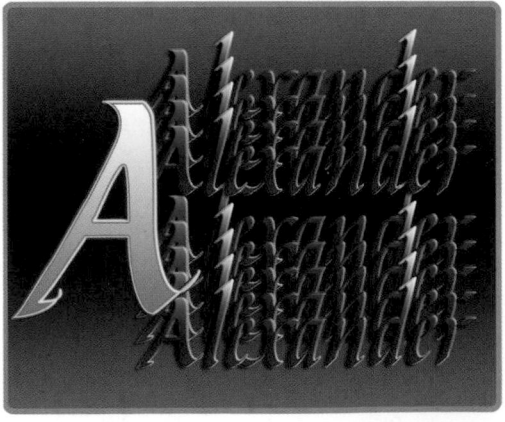

6 Apply a background to the design. This can be a single colour, a gradient colour or even an image. If you use an image, be careful that it does not detract from the effect of the repeat lettering design.

7 Experiment with different embellishments to finalize the design. Print the mat design on a thick paper or thin card. Choose the thickest material that will safely feed through your printer. Carefully cut out the shape on a cutting mat using a craft knife rather than scissors. Glue this to the mat. If possible, cover the image surface with laminate.

Carolingian scroll

The scroll is an ancient invention, which predates the book by thousands of years. It usually consists of a parchment, papyrus, or paper roll adorned with writing and ornamentation. Some of the most beautiful scrolls are on display in museums, where they serve as a record in words and pictures of important historical events. The tradition continues today, as scrolls are used to commemorate important ceremonial occasions – such as the military tradition of granting 'Freedom of the City'. Scrolls are also often seen beautifully decorated with heraldry.

The scroll that is created in this project takes a more lighthearted approach, and could be made to celebrate a birthday or congratulate someone for passing an examination. The layout for this design is landscape rather than portrait, simply to minimize the number of lines you need to rule up. The name of the person being congratulated is written large in the centre, with smaller, flowing script arranged above and below to frame it, so you need to use two sizes of dip pens.

Traditionally, a ribbon was threaded through the top of a scroll in a complex arrangement to keep it closed, but the ribbon here is attached very simply to tie up the scroll and hold it in place. It is a good idea to select your ribbon first, if not choosing gold or silver, and mix your ink to match, as ribbon colours are limited.

The design

Use a sturdy paper such as cartridge or watercolour paper so that your scroll will roll up successfully and keep its shape. Carolingian script has been used for this scroll because it is wider than many hands but with elegant lengthy ascenders, giving a graceful effect even with few words.

Materials

- Sheet of sturdy white cartridge or watercolour paper
- Pencil
- Ruler
- Layout or practice paper
- Pens in contrasting sizes: such as Speedball C-1 and C-3
- Gouache paints: orange, red and gold
- Mixing palettes and water pot
- Paintbrushes
- Craft (utility) knife
- Ribbon

> **Tip:** All machine-made papers have grain direction: the paper will feel stiff if it is rolled against the grain, but will roll more easily at right angles to it.

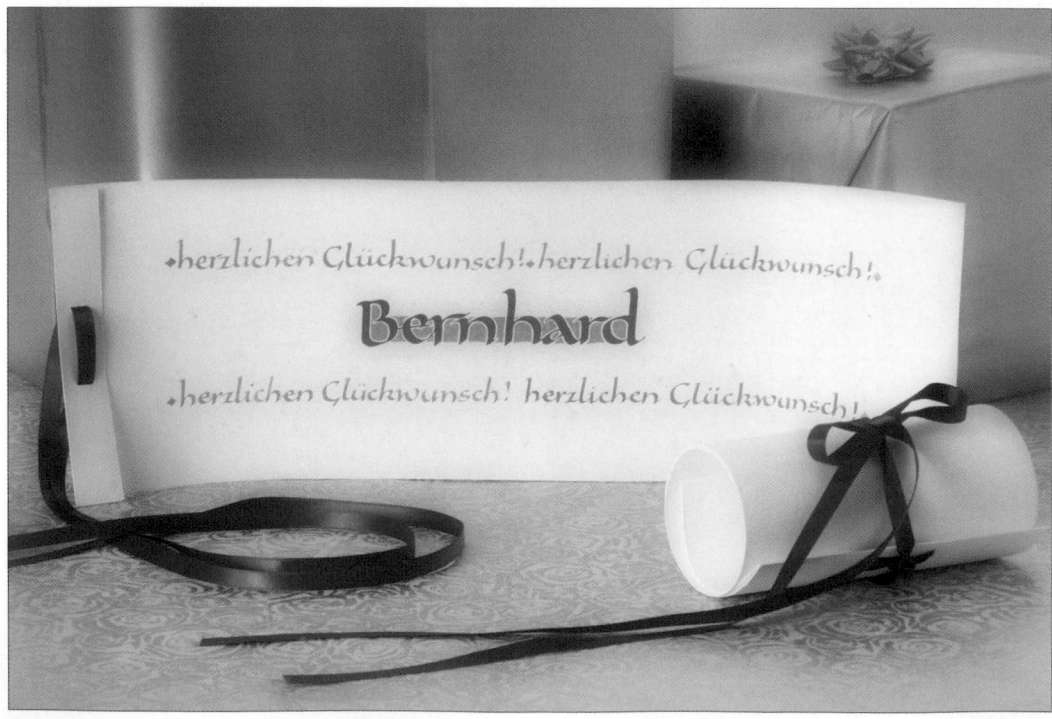

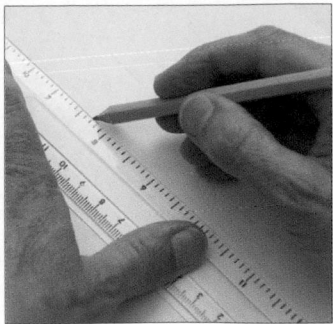

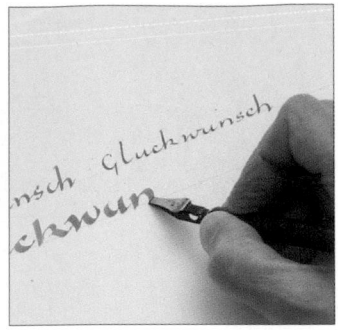

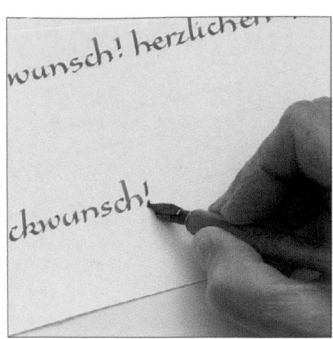

1 Select a sturdy paper, check the grain direction for ease of rolling, and trim to size – approximately 40cm (16in) long and 13cm (5in) wide. Rule lines working out from the centre, for the name, and a line of message above and below.

2 On a separate piece of layout paper, practise writing your chosen phrase in Carolingian; try it out in several sizes of pen. Create contrast by selecting a much larger pen to write the name.

3 Mix the gouache and write the top and bottom lines of small text on the scroll, taking care not to allow ascenders or descenders to intrude into the centre space.

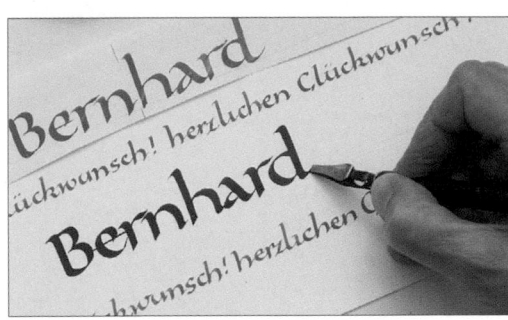

4 Wait until you are sure the first writing is dry, then carefully write the name in the central space in another colour, with the larger pen. Some pre-planning is necessary to ensure it sits in the middle; write it on another sheet first and lay this above your work as a guide.

Tip: When you fold over the left-hand edge of paper, score it lightly with the craft knife against a ruler to allow it to fold more sharply or use a bone folder.

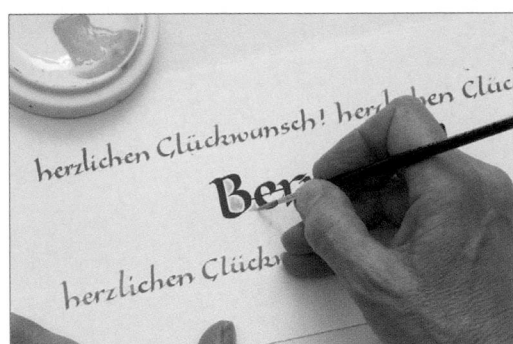

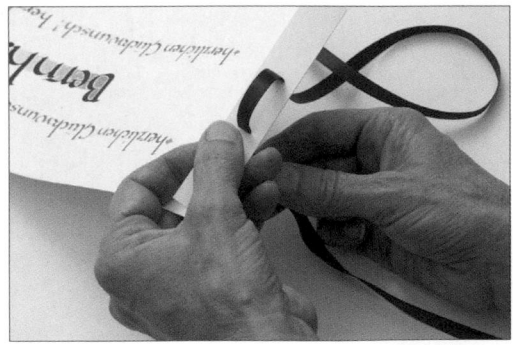

5 Mix the gold gouache to a fairly thick consistency, to fill in the counter spaces in some of the letters. Do not colour right up to the edge; leave a white line to separate the colours, to avoid runs and to allow the colours to stand out against each other.

6 Fold over 2cm (³⁄₄in) of the left-hand edge, cut two slots with a craft knife through both layers, and thread through the ribbon. Roll up the scroll from the other end, so the ribbon's end is outermost. Tie up your finished scroll in a decorative bow. Scrolls are more commonly 'portrait' in layout; try this next time, with a more ambitious quantity of text, ruling more lines.

Calligraphic word with type

The advent of desktop publishing and the ease with which posters or leaflets can be produced on screen may appear to have made traditional calligraphy less important. In reality, a combination of methods whereby a single name or phrase in calligraphy is inserted into a sea of computer-generated type, can be very effective.

The degree of lettering perfection required will depend upon the use to which it will be put. If it is for a one-off occasion, perhaps saying 'Sale' or 'Exhibition', what is needed is legibility coupled with lively writing. If it is likely to be used many times, such as commercially in a business letterhead, or on packaging, then it will require much more refining, as small inconsistencies seen frequently will irritate and will spoil the effect. Graphic designers therefore have to spend a lot of time attending to fine details of shapes and spaces for company names or initials that are put together as logos, as these are intended to become immediately recognizable, and must be without any imperfections.

This project falls into the first category, but the refining process that is required for more ambitious logos, or artworks for business letterheads, is also touched upon. Logo design generally requires pages of trials, and the meticulous process of cutting and pasting the best letters together. However, this project concentrates on the fun of simply rendering a single calligraphic word, and incorporates colour using gouache paints for added vibrancy. Its destination is for scanning into a computer to be linked with a block of text, but if you lack the computer skills you can add the word freehand on to a previously typed page.

The design

Here, a Latin version of the Lord's Prayer appears in capitals, with the focal point being the final calligraphic 'Amen' – which signals at a glance that this is a prayer. Uncials have particularly interesting forms for those four letters, and this script is historically appropriate as it was used to write bibles from the 4th century AD as Christianity spread in western Europe.

Materials

- Felt-tipped pens
- Automatic pen or wide dip pen such as William Mitchell O
- Layout or practice paper
- Pencil
- Ruler
- Watercolour paper
- Gouache paints: ultramarine and magenta
- Mixing palette
- Paintbrushes
- Craft (utility) knife or scalpel
- Self-healing cutting mat
- Glue stick

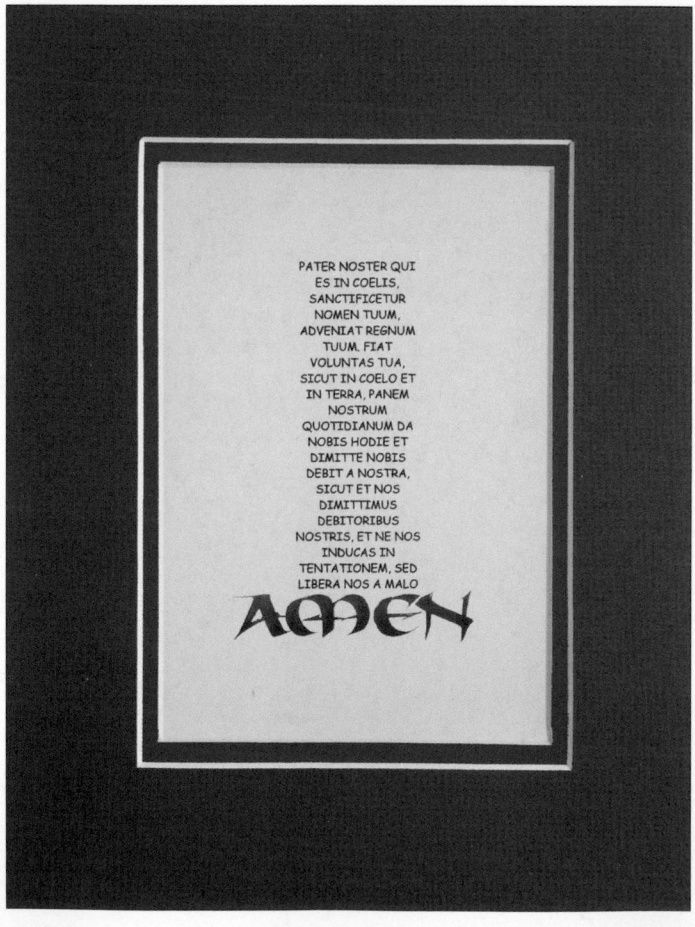

> **Tip:** When using a brush for lettering, remember to twist your fingers and not your wrist.

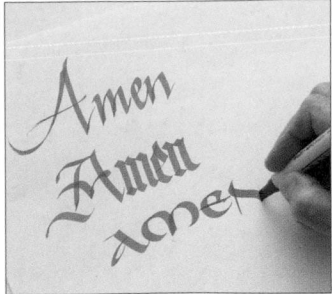 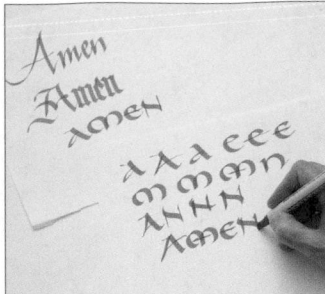 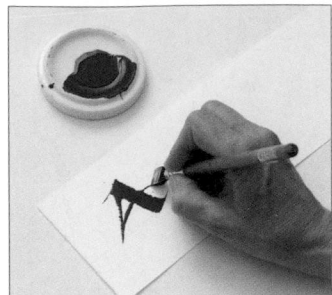

1 Explore your chosen word in various calligraphic formats to decide how to express the meaning. Gothic has a splendid 'A', but the narrowness of the complete word may not suit the layout. The letters have no ascenders or descenders and so will not easily lend themselves to flourishing, but the choice here of Uncial will allow plenty of lettering area in which to add colour.

2 Once the script has been decided, the letters should be examined for any awkward combinations, and to check for inconsistencies of style. If this was a business logo, much more time would be spent at this stage in refining the details and improving the design.

3 Mix two colours in the palette that will blend well together and check that they do not turn muddy when combined. Do not choose colours that oppose each other on the colour wheel, such as red and green. Write a letter in colour on the watercolour paper.

4 While the letter is still wet, charge a paintbrush with another colour and touch it on to the wet areas in the letter; watch the colour spread. Move the paper about to increase the spread if necessary. Continue this process for the rest of the word.

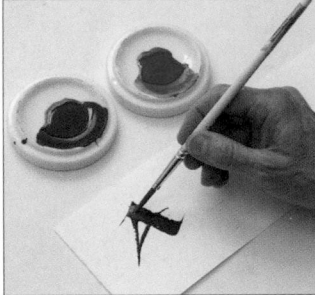

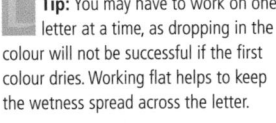 **Tip:** You may have to work on one letter at a time, as dropping in the colour will not be successful if the first colour dries. Working flat helps to keep the wetness spread across the letter.

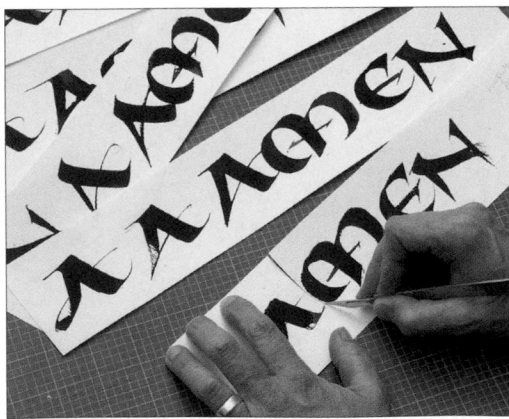

5 Select the best parts of the lettering. Often a word is successful except for one letter or the spacing needs adjusting. Make any changes by cutting and pasting the best letters or groups of letters to form the final word.

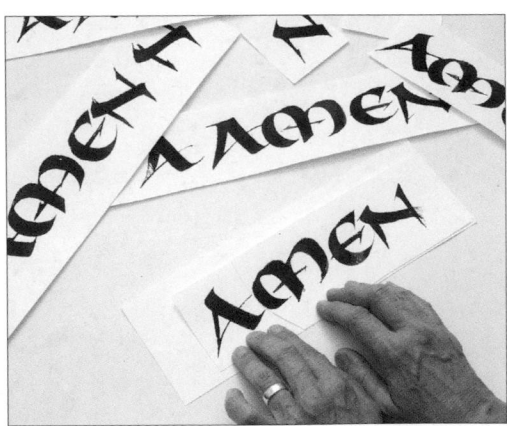

6 The completed title or logo has now been refined and is ready to be scanned into the computer. If you have the necessary skills, the paste-up exercise can be done on computer, but you may still find it quicker to physically cut and paste.

Personalizing gift wrap with gouache

Brown paper is strong and works well as gift wrap, but is often underused in this capacity because of its utilitarian appearance compared to attractively designed printed papers. However, it is a very economical paper and can be purchased in big rolls. This makes it good for covering a wide surface area – and also means you can make mistakes without worrying too much about wasting expensive materials.

Brown Kraft paper takes gouache paints very well, and being a mid-tone colour it will accept both white and black writing. In this project white gouache paint is used for personalizing Kraft paper as gift wrap. The paint should be applied as thickly as possible. This is to preserve its opacity and provide clear edges and sharp lettering. Kraft paper has a shiny side and a matt side. The matt side is best for brush writing, as it provides the resistance needed for the brush to travel slowly across the paper. A chisel-edged brush gives excellent results in this project, but you can achieve a similar effect using a large automatic pen, if you water down the paint to allow it to flow through the nib.

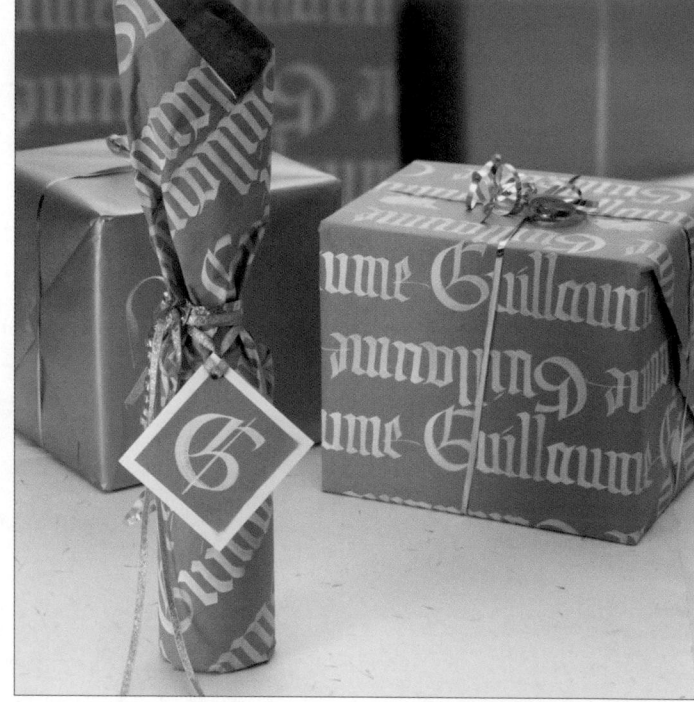

The design
Bold names in Gothic are used here to utilize the contrast of white on brown. Writing alternate rows upside down allows for the paper to be used and read either way up. If you are wrapping a bottle, it makes sense to do it from a corner, so that the writing is displayed diagonally, making a more dynamic effect.

Materials
- *Gouache paint: red and white*
- *Layout or practice paper*
- *Saucer and water pot*
- *Broad-edged brush, approx. 1cm (1/2in) wide or more*
- *Brown Kraft paper*
- *Pencil or chalk*
- *Ruler*
- *Gold gift tie*

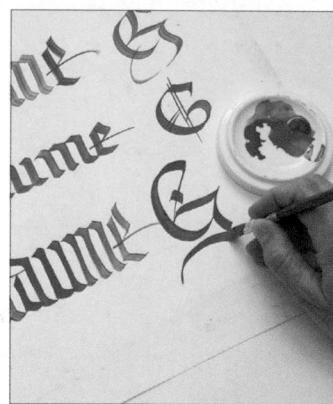

1 Mix red gouache paint and do some trials on spare paper to ensure opacity; if the paint is too watery it will dry too thin. Keep the paint thick for opacity and to keep the lettering sharp. Fill the brush then wipe most of it away to preserve the chisel edge.

2 Try out your chosen name as a trial in white on the Kraft paper. Explore the possibilities of a Gothic initial letter, to see if this can be varied decoratively. Retain the compactness of the lower case Gothic lettering, to contrast with the rounded capital.

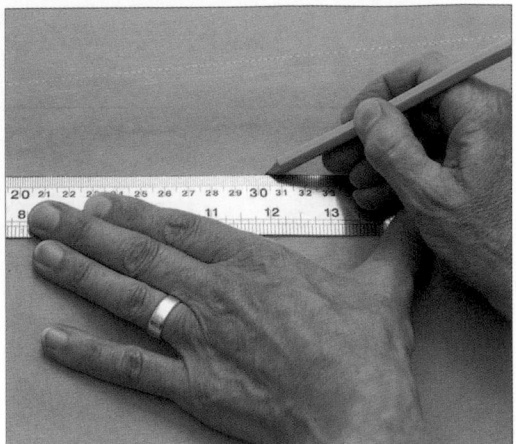

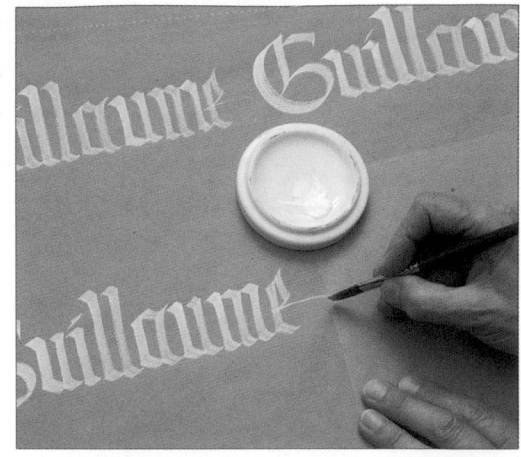

3 Rule lines lightly on the brown paper; if pencil is difficult to see, try using a piece of chalk. Kraft paper already has faint lines, which will help you keep yours straight; rule up a square of paper large enough to wrap a bottle or box.

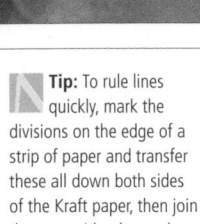 **Tip:** To rule lines quickly, mark the divisions on the edge of a strip of paper and transfer these all down both sides of the Kraft paper, then join them up with a long ruler.

4 Write the name repeatedly along one line, leave three gaps and repeat again, aligning your lettering with the names above. Continue until the sheet is completed.

Tip: It would create an interesting design to alternate black and white writing for variety and contrast.

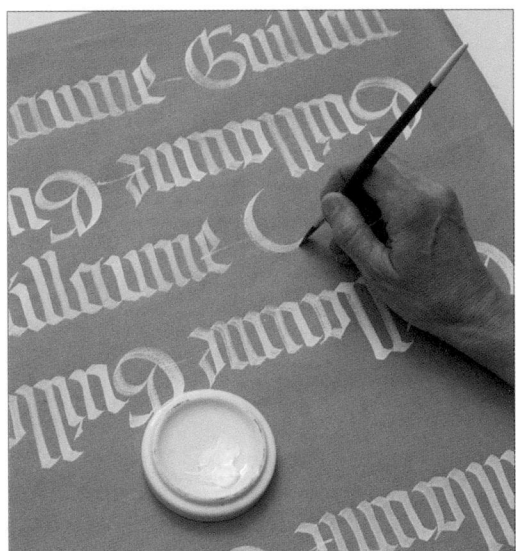

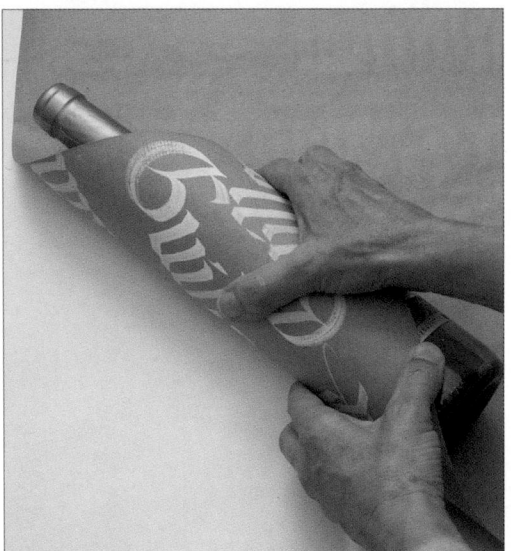

5 When dry, turn the sheet upside down and repeat the process in the gaps between; start the capital so that it occurs staggered between those above and below.

6 To wrap the bottle start from the corner, so that the writing runs diagonally across the finished parcel. Complete the presentation with a festive ribbon and perhaps a label from a spare practice name pasted on to a piece of card, with your message on the reverse.

Brush lettering on cloth

It is possible to write on many more materials than paper, provided you are willing to experiment with the versatility of brushes. This project employs a fine pointed brush and uses a letterform that was traditionally drawn as decorative initials. In this project this initial design or monogram is used to decorate one corner of fine cloth.

It is advisable to keep the design simple if you plan to make a series of the same or a similar design. Initialled table napkins or handkerchiefs make excellent gifts. Choose a fabric that is thin enough to see through, as you need to be able to see the letters through the fabric in order to paint them accurately. If you cannot see the letters easily, use a lightbox or tape the fabric to a window. Fine cotton handkerchiefs are perfect, especially as they are already cut to size and finished. Alternatively, you could cut some fine lawn or muslin (cheesecloth) fabric. Fray the edges by pulling out several threads, then stitch along the solid edges to prevent further fraying.

In this project cotton handkerchiefs are painted with a single repeated letter 'R' in different colours, and are moved around to make a lettering square. You can choose your own initials, provided they combine and work well with each other; extra planning will be necessary if the letters are different widths.

Use fabric paints to work the lettering on to cloth, which can be bought from artists' suppliers. Do not use silk dyes, which are too watery and designed to spread – these letters need sharp edges. Add as little water as possible, while maintaining some flow of colour. Controlling the brush and the wetness of the paint will take some practice.

Materials
- *Alphabet exemplar*
- *Tracing paper*
- *Sharp pencil*
- *Squares of fine fabric*
- *Masking tape*
- *Mixing saucer or palette*
- *Water pot*
- *Fabric paints*
- *Narrow pointed brush*

The design
The Versal letterform, built up with several pen strokes, lends itself to fine pointed brush painting. Its geometric shapes also combine well when juxtaposed to make a pleasing pattern. Using two colours adds interest to the motif.

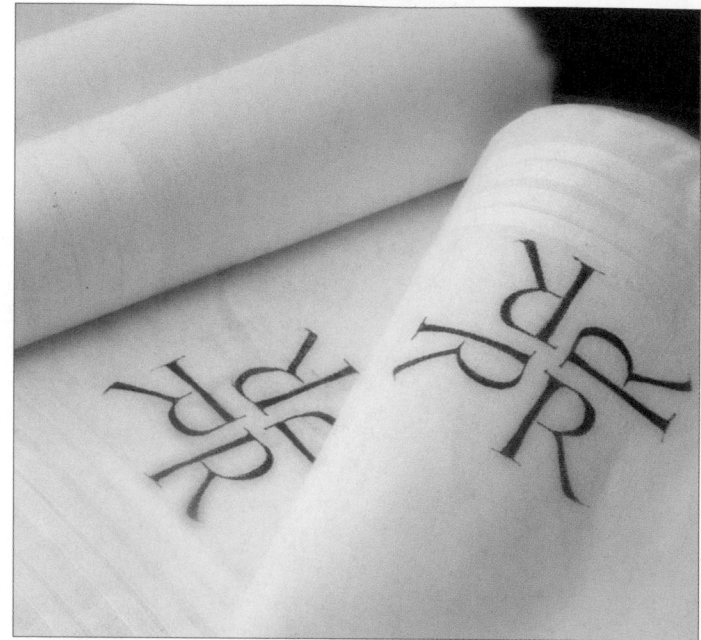

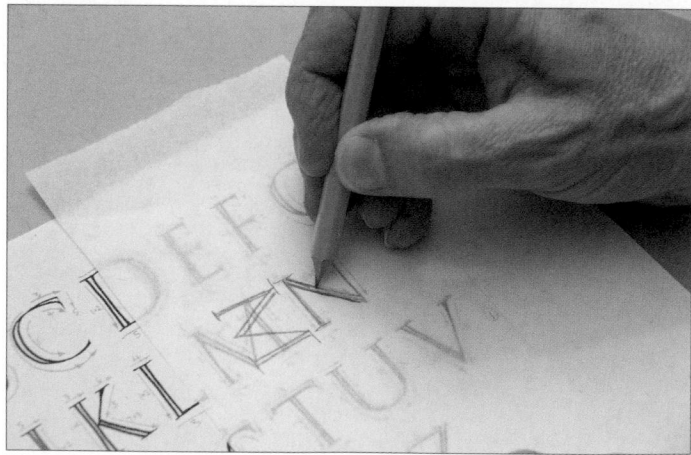

1 First select your letters and try out designs to see how they will combine by tracing one letter from the alphabet exemplar with a pencil then moving at right angles to fit another letter alongside.

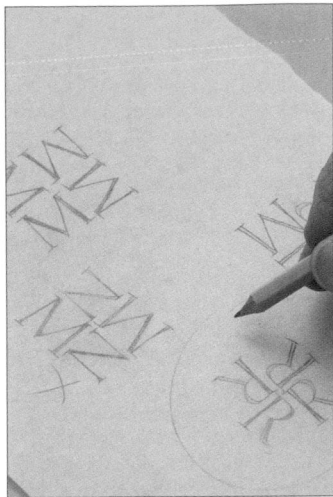

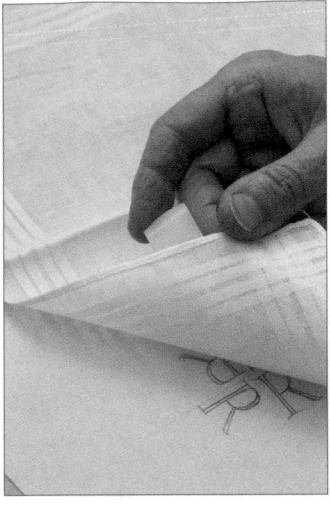

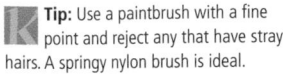

Tip: Use a paintbrush with a fine point and reject any that have stray hairs. A springy nylon brush is ideal.

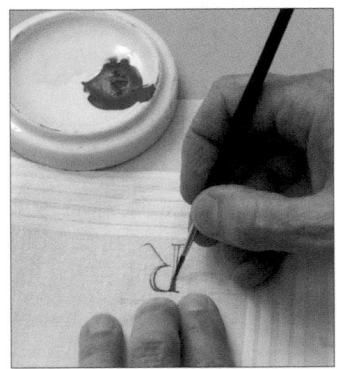

2 Here 'M' and 'N', and two 'M's together have been tried as combinations. If using two different letters, fit them together by keeping them closely spaced at the centre. The final choice here is a repeated 'R'.

3 Attach thin fabric, or the corner of a handkerchief over the drawing with masking tape. Put some fabric paint in a saucer and add as little water as possible, so that the paint can flow without bleeding on the fabric.

4 Carefully and accurately paint in your first letter, paying particular attention to the serifs; these must be rendered as fine lines and need a steady hand.

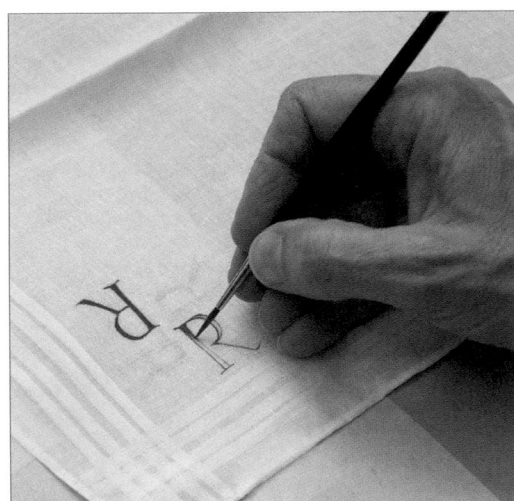

5 Repeat the opposite letter in the same colour. Try to ensure you see clearly your design underneath, for accuracy; outline a stem before filling it in.

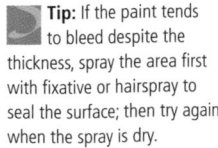

Tip: If the paint tends to bleed despite the thickness, spray the area first with fixative or hairspray to seal the surface; then try again when the spray is dry.

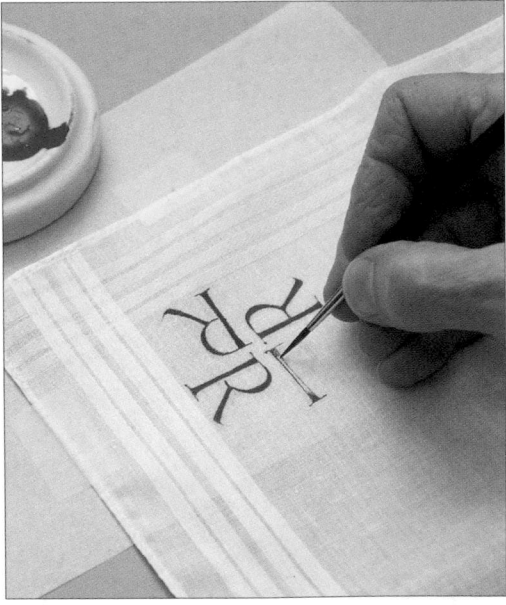

6 Use another colour for the second letter, here a darker red, again taking care to be accurate. Keep the fabric over or attached to the tracing at all times. Follow the paint label instructions for fixing the colour – usually by ironing.

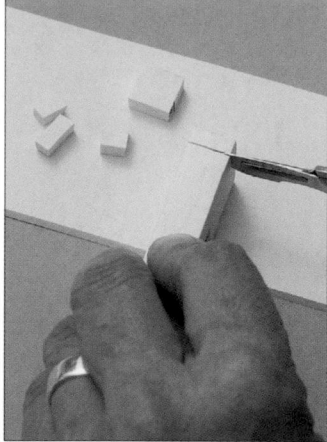

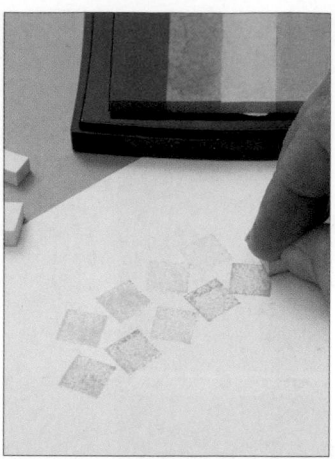

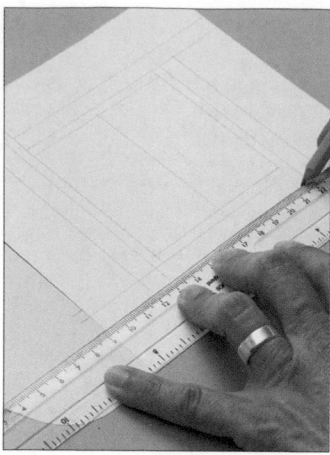

6 Cut simple rubber stamps for the pattern-making. Cut squares in three sizes from a plastic eraser, using a craft knife. More complex designs can also be cut, requiring more dexterity, or you could use ready-made stamps.

7 Use a small pad of absorbent soft cloth as a stamping pad, filled with paint mixed to an ink consistency, with a series of mixed colours that blend well together, or find a commercially produced multicoloured stamp pad.

8 As there are 12 pages to rule up, it is worth preparing a template to save time. Mark all the measurements clearly on the edge of a strip of paper, and transfer them with a pencil on to the four edges of the square, then lightly rule across.

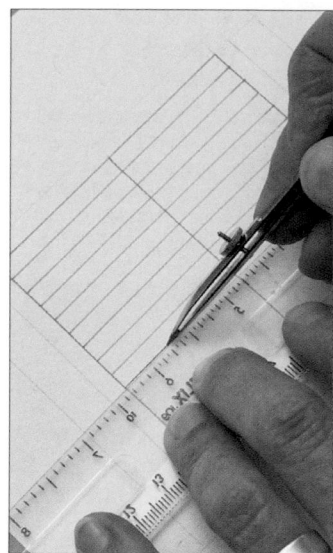

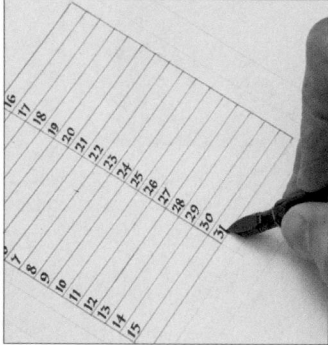

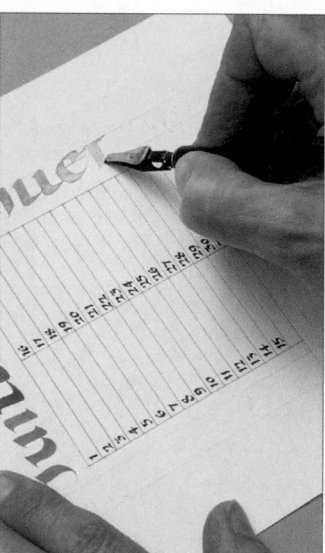

9 For the numerals box, rule all the lines in your chosen colour with the ruling pen. Make sure the ruler has its bevel edge up to prevent ink running underneath.

10 Write all the numerals first, noting which months have 31, 30 and 29, and reject any pages with mistakes.

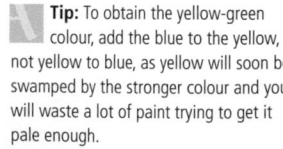

Tip: To obtain the yellow-green colour, add the blue to the yellow, not yellow to blue, as yellow will soon be swamped by the stronger colour and you will waste a lot of paint trying to get it pale enough.

11 Then add the months, in a strong colour, here mixed with phthalo blue with a touch of lemon yellow. Write the second word in a more watery, yellower mix, so that it is less dominant than the first.

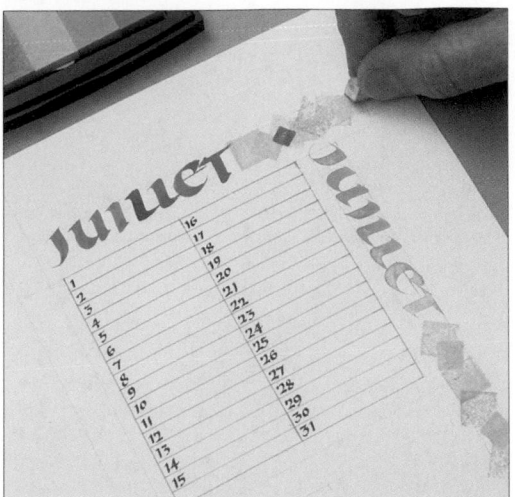

12 Do the stamping last, following the lines to bleed off the edges; experiment with colours and overlapping shapes and sizes. Make the stamping random, with lightest colours first.

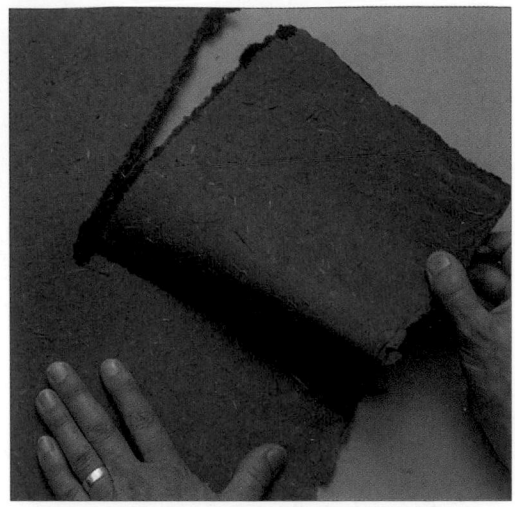

13 Assess the required size of a cover. Make it a little larger than the pages, to protect them. If using hand-made paper as here, you can trim the sides to mimic the deckle edge by running water from a paintbrush along a ruler, then pulling apart when the water has soaked in.

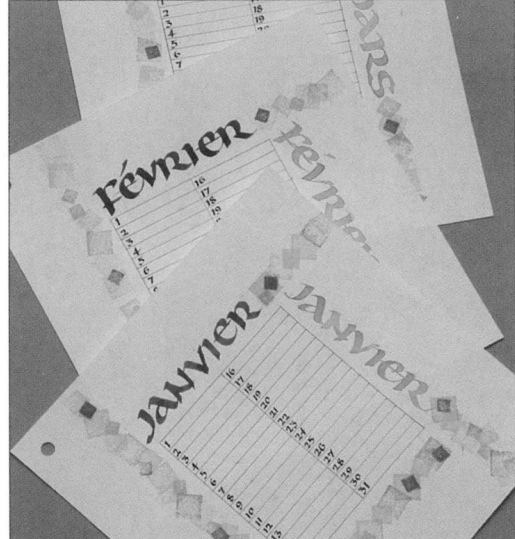

14 Assemble the pages in the right order, and use a hole puncher to make a hole in the corner. You will need to try this out on spare paper first, and when successfully positioned, mark how far in to push the paper by taping a piece of card to the machine.

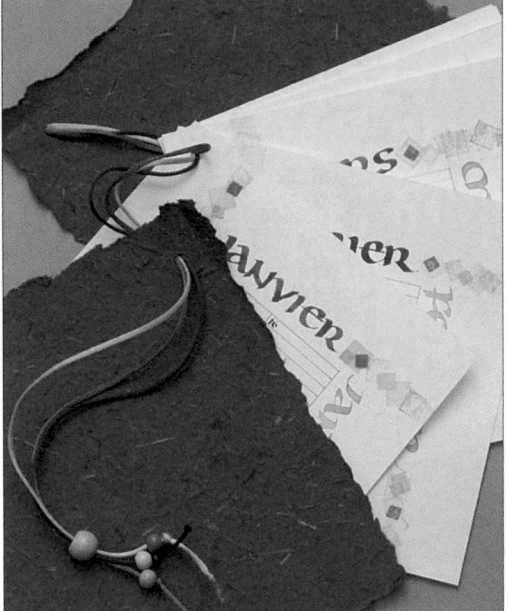

15 Fix all together with a ribbon and beads, choosing colours that repeat those used inside. Include a hanging thread to allow the calendar to be displayed on a wall for easy reference.

Curved lines on chalk pastels

Once you are confident in writing calligraphy along straight lines, you may want to try something more challenging. Many poems and quotations are expressive in nature and ask to be interpreted in a less rigid way than suggested by straight lines. Gentle, wavy lines may be the solution. However, they should not be overdone. Be aware that it is easy to overdo the curve of the waves. The curves should have gentle undulations, and parallel curves will help them blend into a design. Plan to vary the start and end point of each line of writing, in order to maintain the illusion of movement; wavy lines that all start ranged left are not usually so successful.

This project uses chalk pastels as a background. They can be purchased in many subtle colours and can usually be bought individually. The advantage of pastels is that you can choose to build up either a very subtle colour or a strong, powerful one, and they allow the beginner more control than watercolour paints. Chalk pastels are a dry medium, so will not make the paper cockle (wrinkle).

The design

The chosen text is a Celtic blessing about coming home safely. It is written in Uncial, and is arranged to fit offset on three lines, to give a feeling of movement. The background is laid first, using layers of pastel colours rubbed into the surface. The wavy lines are drawn in pastel so that they can be blended into the background after completing the writing in gouache.

Materials

- Pencil
- Thin card (stock)
- Self-healing cutting mat
- Craft (utility) knife
- Chalk pastels: conte red, orange and ochre
- Cotton wool (balls)
- Smooth watercolour paper
- or cartridge paper
- Mixing palette
- Gouache paints: purple lake and ultramarine
- Dip pens, such as William Mitchell 1 1/2 and 2 1/2 (small nibs)

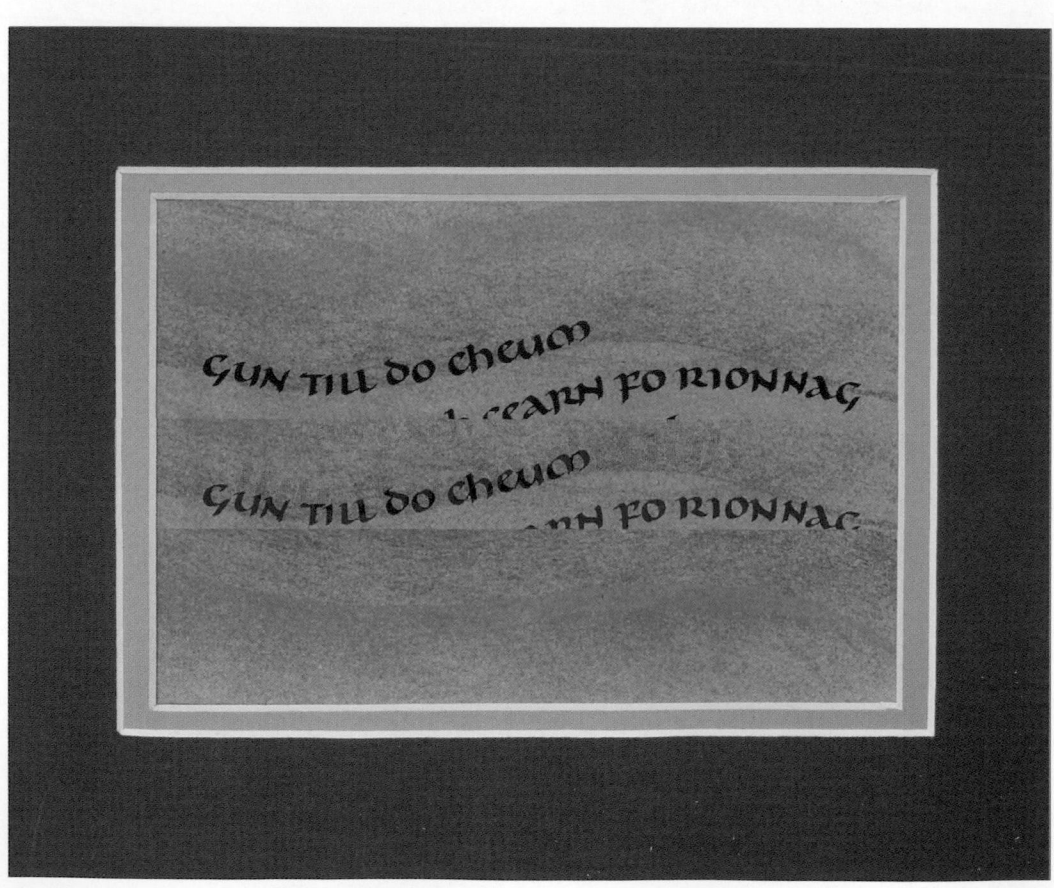

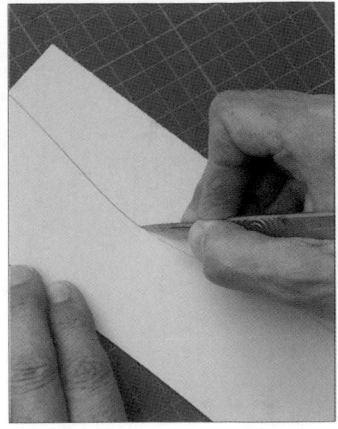

1 Pencil freehand a gentle curve on a piece of thin card. When you are satisfied with its profile, lay it on a cutting mat to protect your work surface and cut smoothly along the line with a craft knife to make a template.

Tip: You can spray with fixative or hairspray if you are concerned about the pastel smudging.

Tip: The harder you rub the pastel into the paper, the better the writing surface will be for sharp writing – loose chalk will clog the pen.

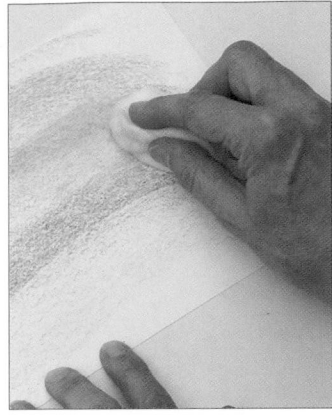

2 Select three pastel colours that work well together when mixed – red, orange and ochre are used here – rub them over the paper in wavy movements and press them firmly into the surface using a wad of cotton wool.

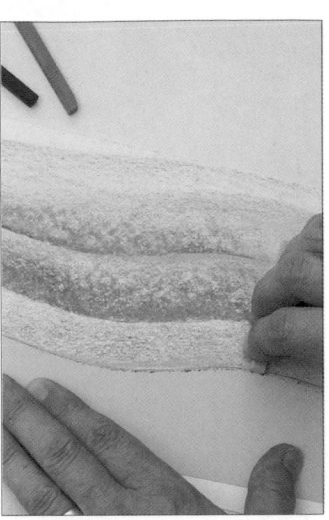

3 Lay the template over the colour background and use the pastel on its side to make a sweeping stroke along the curve of the template. Move the template down for the next line and repeat using another pastel colour, and so on for the third line. This should give sufficient mark for writing on – but you will have to manage without a top line.

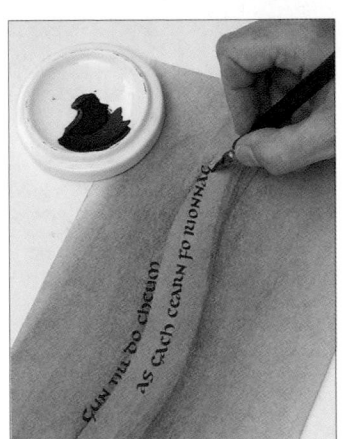

4 Mix the purple gouache paint to writing consistency and write the first line of text, moving the paper regularly so that the writing stays perpendicular to its line. You may have to press quite hard to make the paint stay on the pastel, but it will provide very sharp lettering.

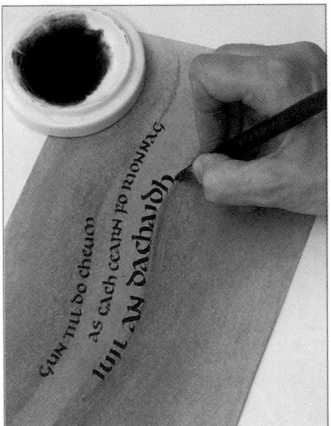

5 Use a bigger pen to write the last line, in ultramarine gouache, for emphasis. Leave it for some time to make sure it has dried before blending in the lines.

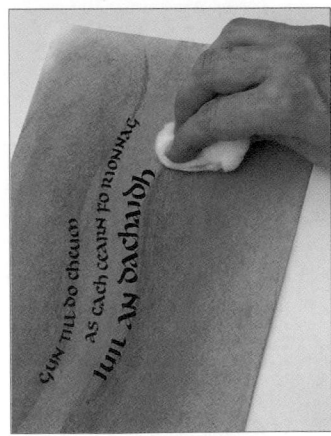

6 Erase the lines by rubbing in the pastel so that it blends into the background; this rubbing may slightly affect the paint in the writing, so take care not to write in too pale a colour. At this stage, you can touch up the background with extra depth of colour if needed.

Brush lettering on a T-shirt

Writing on T-shirt fabric can be very successful if you use a broad-edged brush rather than a pen. Choose a fabric paint if the T-shirt is likely to be washed frequently. Alternatively, if you are using a cheap T-shirt for a one-off occasion, use household emulsion paint which is available in sample pots – this dries as a waterproof paint but will eventually wear off in the wash. The positional area for the wording on an adult sized T-shirt is generally accepted to be a maximum 200mm (8in) wide, placed centrally. If the wording goes much wider, it will be lost in creases when the T-shirt is worn, although this will vary according to the size of the wearer. The choice of paint colour will be influenced by the colour of the T-shirt. If you find a bargain batch of navy blue T-shirts, choosing white paint will ensure your writing has dramatic impact. Pastel coloured T-shirts can cope with soft coloured paints, but when in doubt, choose black paint as it will always show up. A dramatic wording is a pleasing result.

Materials
- *Practice paper or brown Kraft paper*
- *Broad-edged brush, nylon, approx.1cm (¹/₂in) wide*
- *Fabric paint or household emulsion (latex) paint: red*
- *Scissors*
- *Tape*
- *Ruler*
- *White chalk*
- *Plain cotton T-shirt*

The design
Rustic letterforms, with their tall, slender shape, lend themselves to a vertical arrangement, which suits the four short words of the quotation. To hold together as a design, the words need to be laid out close together with minimal space between the lines. One colour has been used here, but when you get more ambitious, you can consider including more colours. Keep the message brief. The Latin quotation chosen here translates as 'the art is long and life is short' (Hippocrates, c.460–375BC).

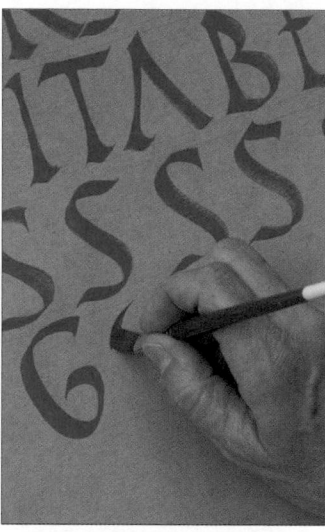

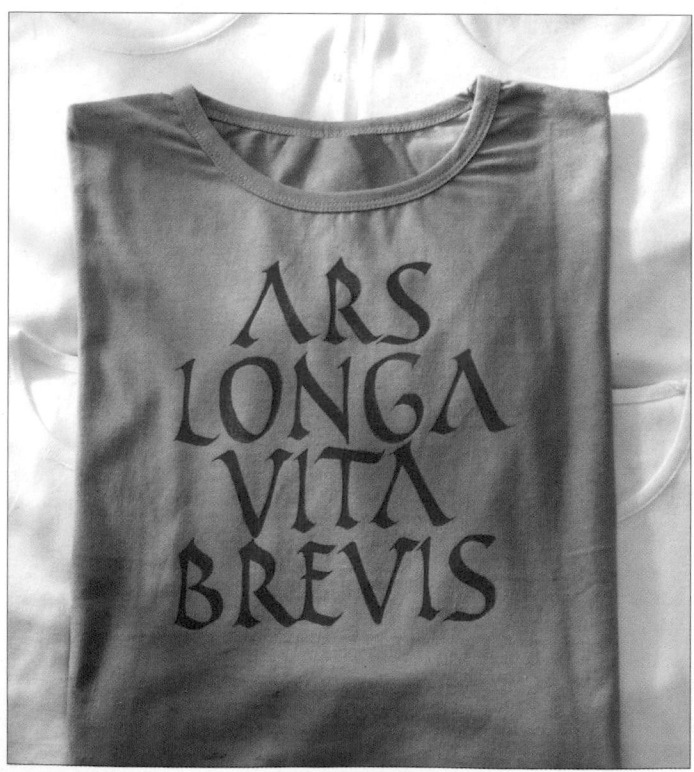

1 Practise the letterform, focusing on those letters needed for the quotation. If the broad-edged brush is a new tool for you, take time to adjust to its feel. If you can practise on the rough side of Kraft paper, this will give a resistance that is similar to the surface of fabric. For a 1cm (¹/₂in) brush, try letters that are 5cm (2in) high.

Tip: Light colours on dark T-shirts may need extra brushstrokes to obtain dense coverage of the paint and help it to read clearly.

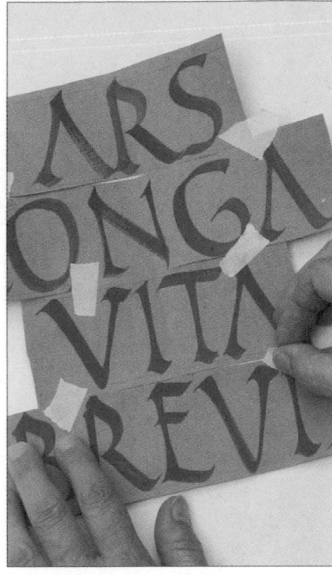

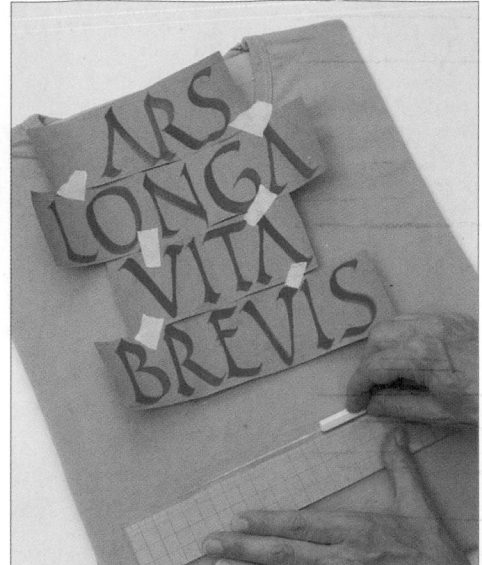

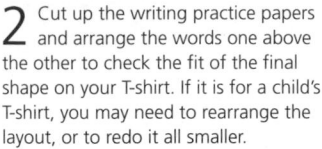

Tip: Rule the chalked lines only where the writing should go — if you extend them too far it will take a long time to remove them. Also, any remaining lines will be much less noticeable where the writing is. If rubbing the chalk off with your fingers is unsuccessful, try using a putty eraser.

2 Cut up the writing practice papers and arrange the words one above the other to check the fit of the final shape on your T-shirt. If it is for a child's T-shirt, you may need to rearrange the layout, or to redo it all smaller.

3 Wrap your T-shirt around something flat, such as a large piece of card (stock) and tape it steady, or simply tape it to a worksurface. Take measurements from your taped-up practice writing and lightly rule lines with chalk – trim the chalk to an edge if necessary.

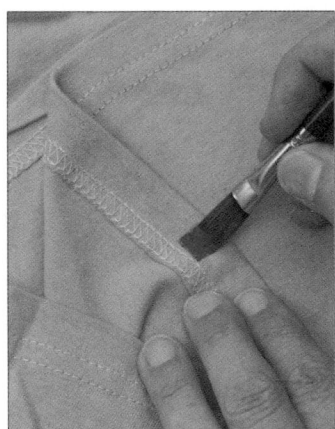

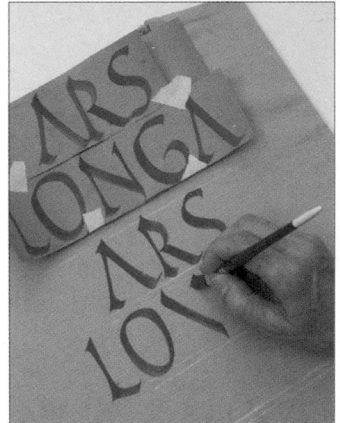

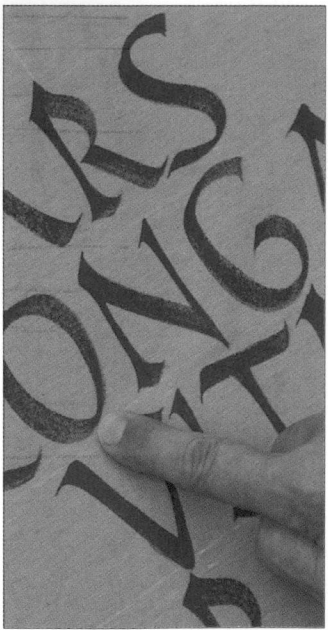

4 Test your paint on a non-visible area of the T-shirt first – an inside seam perhaps – to check it will show up and not bleed; add as little water as possible, and keep the brush wiped to a sharp chisel edge at all times.

5 Position the practice sheet directly above or below, for reference, and start painting. Recharge the brush frequently but wipe most of it off to maintain the chisel edge; too much paint on the brush will cause blobby marks.

6 When the writing is complete, leave it to dry then rub the chalk lines away with your finger. Remove the tape and iron it on the reverse to fix the paint or follow the directions on the fabric paint bottle.

Congratulations card with resist

Handmade cards are always a pleasure to receive, especially if the message is a joyous one. Decide on your greeting or message before you begin as this will help you choose the right colours for the finished card. If the message is bright and cheerful then the colour of the card can be bright and bold. A congratulatory card should be exuberant and vivid. Acrylic inks or luminous inks will give you this brilliance and are easy to write upon when dry as the paper surface becomes waterproof.

When making your card, plan your designs on layout paper first and practise your writing. This project uses a Carolingian script. Choose the colours and the media you wish to use. Pour some acrylic ink into the palette and mix with water. Paint the individual colours on to the paper allowing them to blend: this keeps them bright and fresh.

When the ink has dried write the message with a dip pen and art masking fluid. This forms an area of resist which paint cannot cover. The colour and texture of the card is created by brush and paint effects using a toothbrush spattered over the surface of the paper.

To spatter effectively, dip the brush into the ink and turn bristles uppermost. Draw a thin strip of card across the bristles toward you and the brush will spatter the design with ink. Make sure that you have shielded the area where you are working with old newspaper to stop the paint from sticking to everything.

The design
The idea of the project is to produce a colourful card with a congratulations message in several languages that will fold well and fit a standard envelope. You can make an envelope for an individual card but if you wish to produce many of the same cards the cards will need to be folded to fit commercially sized envelopes. You can design the card using standard sized paper to ensure that when folded it fits into a standard envelope.

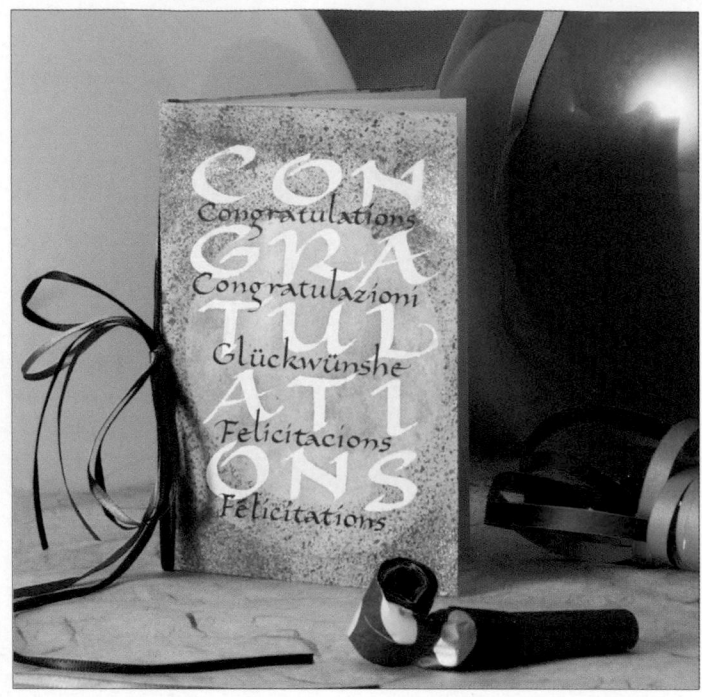

Materials
- *Photocopy paper or layout paper*
- *Dip pens: Speedball C-0 or William Mitchell 00 (large nib) and William Mitchell 3 (medium nib)*
- *Black ink*
- *Pencil*
- *Scissors*
- *Glue*
- *Hot-pressed watercolour paper*
- *Large paint brush for ink washes*
- *Acrylic inks: red and yellow*
- *Gouache paints: scarlet lake and alizarin red*
- *Masking fluid*
- *Old toothbrush*
- *Stencil*
- *Eraser*
- *Matching envelope*
- *Ribbons*

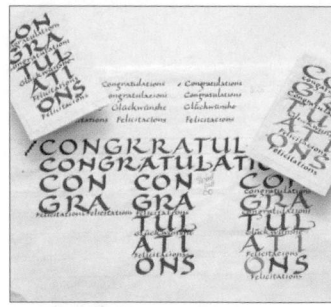

1 Practise your writing trying different sizes for the messages. Record the nib size used on the different trials. Create the design for your card and paste into a 'mock-up' of the card. This can be achieved by folding a sheet of photocopy paper in half then in half again and attaching the strips of your writing to the resulting card shape. Now you have an idea of what the finished card will look like.

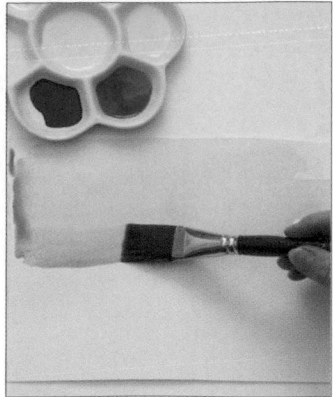

2 Draw and cut the card size from the watercolour paper. Use the large brush and paint a bright background colour on your paper in the red and yellow acrylic ink. Mix the two colours to produce an orange, but also add both the red and yellow colours as you work allowing them to blend on the paper with the orange. This will keep the ink fresh and bright.

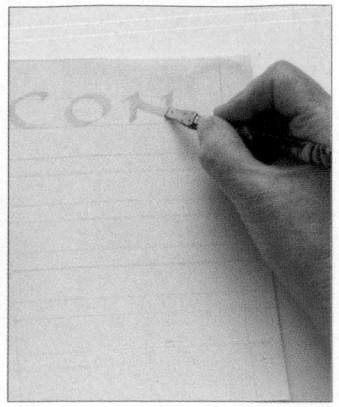

3 Wait until the paint dries then draw some faint writing lines on which to write using your mock up card as reference. Write your chosen word in masking fluid on the paper. Make the word look bright and happy.

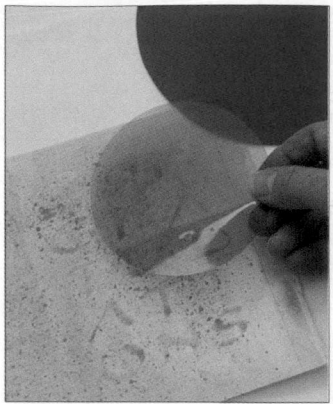

4 Once the masking fluid has dried, spatter the surface with acrylic ink using an old toothbrush. You could add further colour interest by spattering through a stencil shape.

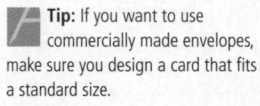
Tip: If you want to use commercially made envelopes, make sure you design a card that fits a standard size.

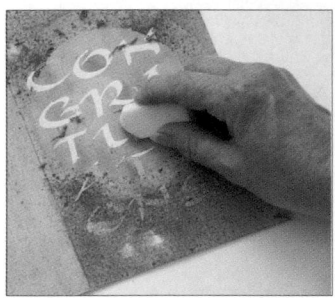

5 When all the colour has dried, remove the masking fluid from the paper by rubbing gently with your finger or using an eraser. The word will be revealed in the orange of the background colour.

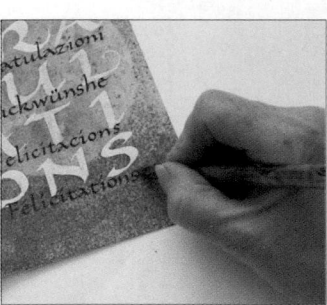

6 Mix up some scarlet lake and alizarin red gouache paint and, using a smaller pen nib size, write some smaller 'congratulations' messages on the card. Fold the card and trim it to the correct shape.

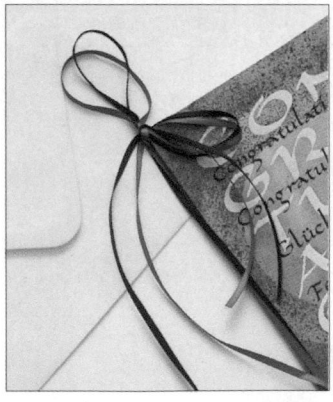

8 Finally, tie colourful ribbons round the spine of the card and match with an envelope.

7 Fold a sheet of standard sized copy paper for the inside, to enable you to write your personal message. Put the white paper with your personal message inside the card and carefully stick with a thin line of glue.

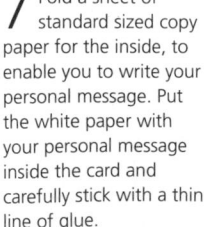
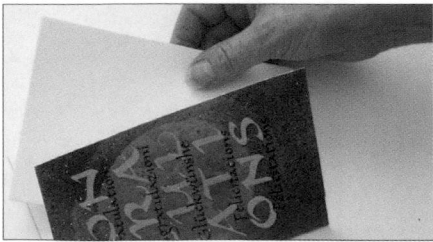

Tip: Stencils can be bought ready made or you can cut you own designs with a craft knife or stencil cutter.

Gift wrap with painted background

This project involves rolling ink on to a quality lightweight paper to create a striking monochromatic background for gift wrap. Watery black ink is used which gives the paper an interesting textured effect. When the background is dry a message is written on the gift wrap using different sizes of pen nibs – which makes the same message appear different depending on the nib that has been chosen. Black ink or gouache is used for the first layer of writing. The paper is then given a quarter-turn before the message is written again, this time in a different, contrasting colour.

This project provides a good opportunity to use different types of pen. There are many to choose from besides the usual dip pen – coit pens, automatic pens, ruling pens, plus the pens that you can make yourself, such as quills, reed pens or cut balsawood pens. Each will produce a different mark.

To add to the fun of using a variety of writing tools, experiment with the interesting letter weights that can be produced by altering the letter nib width height. Using less than the standard x-height of a chosen script will make the letterform appear not only smaller but heavier and denser. Letters given a greater nib width height than the standard x-height of its letter style will appear lighter and more elegant.

The wrapped gift can be completed by the addition of a personalized tag.

Materials
- Layout or practice paper
- Dip pens: in various sizes
- Ruling pen
- Automatic pen
- Scissors
- Glue
- One or two sheets of lightweight cartridge paper, white or coloured
- Transparent overlay or similar
- Old newspapers
- Printing ink roller or similar
- String
- Acrylic inks: black and red
- Gouache paints: black and red
- Ribbon

The design
A complete alphabet script written in altered weights and sizes and with different pens can have great impact. This project features flourished Italic and Gothic.

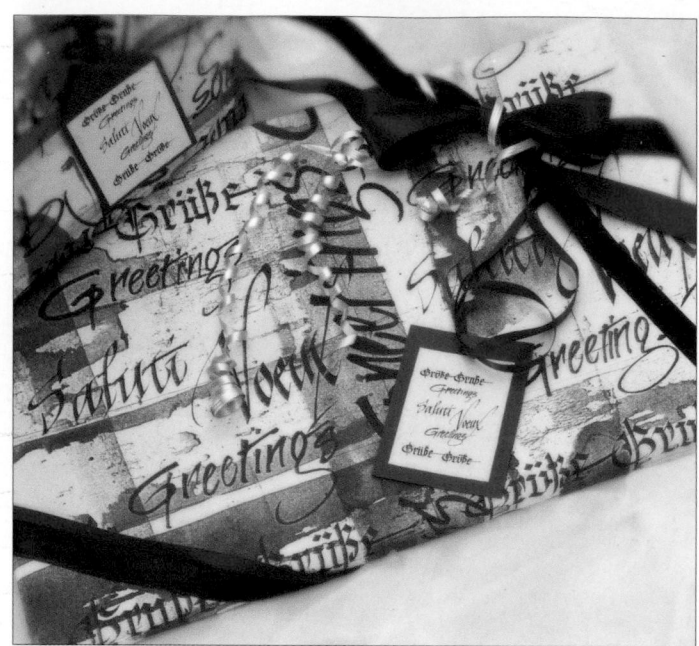

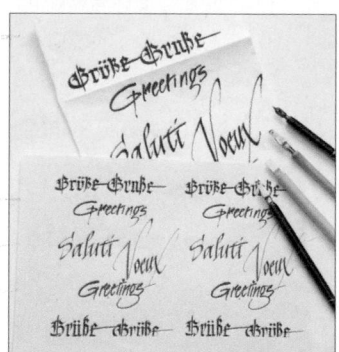

1 Using the layout paper, write some 'greetings' in Gothic and flourished Italics. Try different sizes of pens and nibs; changing to an automatic pen or larger nib size will create heavier writing. Practise with further pen sizes within the same lines.

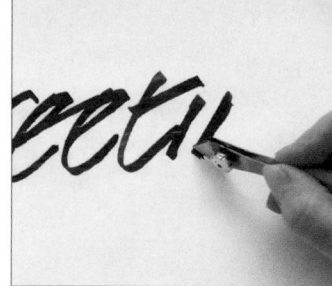

2 Try writing with the ruling pen, which will make the words appear particularly vibrant. Notice the differences in the weights of all your experimental writing examples. Remember to record the nib sized used each time.

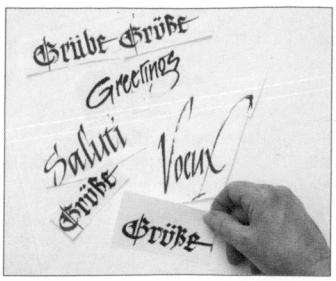 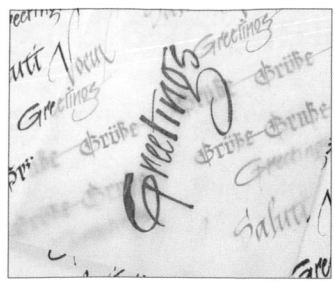 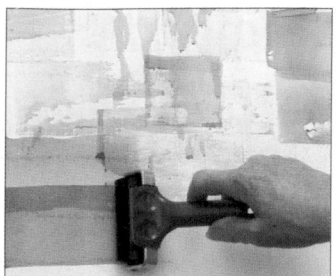

3 Cut and paste the various texts into different positions to create a design you like. The design will be repeated over the large sheet of cartridge paper so that the actual writing area will need to be no more than about 30cm x 20cm (12in x 8in). This will be repeated to cover all the paper.

4 Either photocopy some of the words on to a transparent overlay or write on a piece of drafting film or tracing paper and lay over your writing at different angles. This will make the design look busy, but exciting. Move the overlay around to view the effects.

5 Lay some old newspapers on the table to protect it from the roller carrying acrylic ink. Use a good quality piece of paper on which to lay a background colour. Pour some black acrylic ink into a tray and add water. Run the print roller through the ink and roll on to the paper, first one way, then the other, making random strokes of pattern.

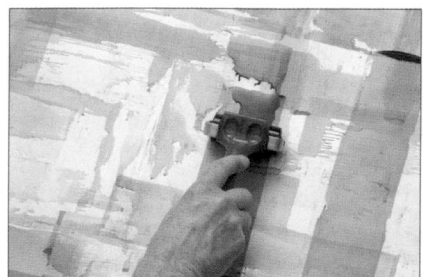

Tip: You can use coloured or textured paper instead of colouring your own. Black paper decorated with white and red writing always looks stunning.

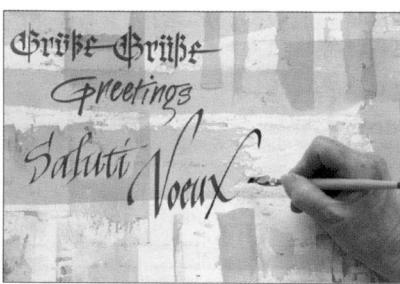

6 Create an all over lightweight patterned background that will appear textured. The ink roller does not print the pattern the same all the time. By tying string around the roller other patterns can be produced. Do not use the ink too black, keep it watery and grey in colour. Let it dry thoroughly.

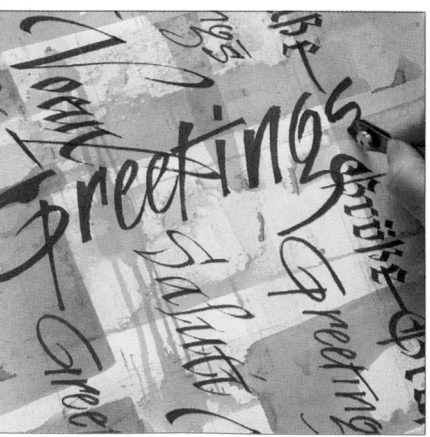

7 Write over the background with gouache paint or black ink. Draw in the guidelines using double pencils to help you place the writing correctly, then write your personal greetings.

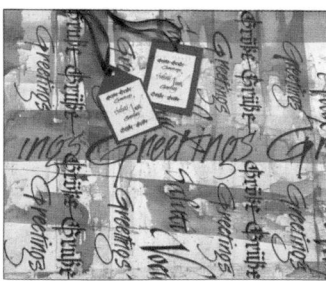

Tip: A completely different type of pattern can be produced by using a domestic roller that is used for house painting.

8 When your work is dry, turn the paper at 90 degrees. Mix up some gouache in the second, contrasting colour and write the greetings with a ruling pen according to your planned design.

9 The finished paper can be wrapped around a box and tied with ribbon. The gift tags can be made by repeating the pattern in smaller pens or by photocopying the original design.

Copperplate address on an envelope

There is something very special about receiving a decorative, handwritten envelope and, in the age of computers, it makes it all the more individual. You could try this project for a one-off envelope, or make several for celebratory cards. You could even take it to a grander scale for that special occasion.

The hand chosen here is Copperplate, which is elegant and lends itself easily to flourishes and decoration, and will look good in several colours. If you do not have much experience in writing Copperplate, begin with fairly large writing. This will allow more space to cope with the thick and thin strokes of the script. To accommodate working at a larger size, a fairly large envelope should be used. You will be surprised how much space is needed for a handwritten address. With practice, you will know instinctively what size of envelope will suit your needs.

The design

This decorative envelope has been designed to incorporate various sizes of lettering and two colours. The large lettering is approximately 1cm (1/2in) high and the smaller approximately 7mm (3/8in) high. The Copperplate has been written with gouache using a pointed nib. If an envelope is to be posted it needs to be easily legible so it is good to bear this in mind when adding any decorative elements.

Materials

- *Dip pen with script nib, such as a Gillott 303 or 404, or Manuscript nib*
- *Black ink*
- *Layout or practice paper*
- *Envelopes*
- *Gouache paints: magenta and ultramarine; or coloured inks*
- *Pencil*
- *Ruler*
- *Protractor*
- *Mixing brushes*
- *Eraser*

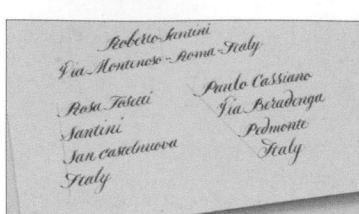

1 Jot down the name and address you are working with in a variety of ways – left aligned, offset or centred. The length of the lines in the address will have some bearing on which design you choose and also on the shape and size of envelope.

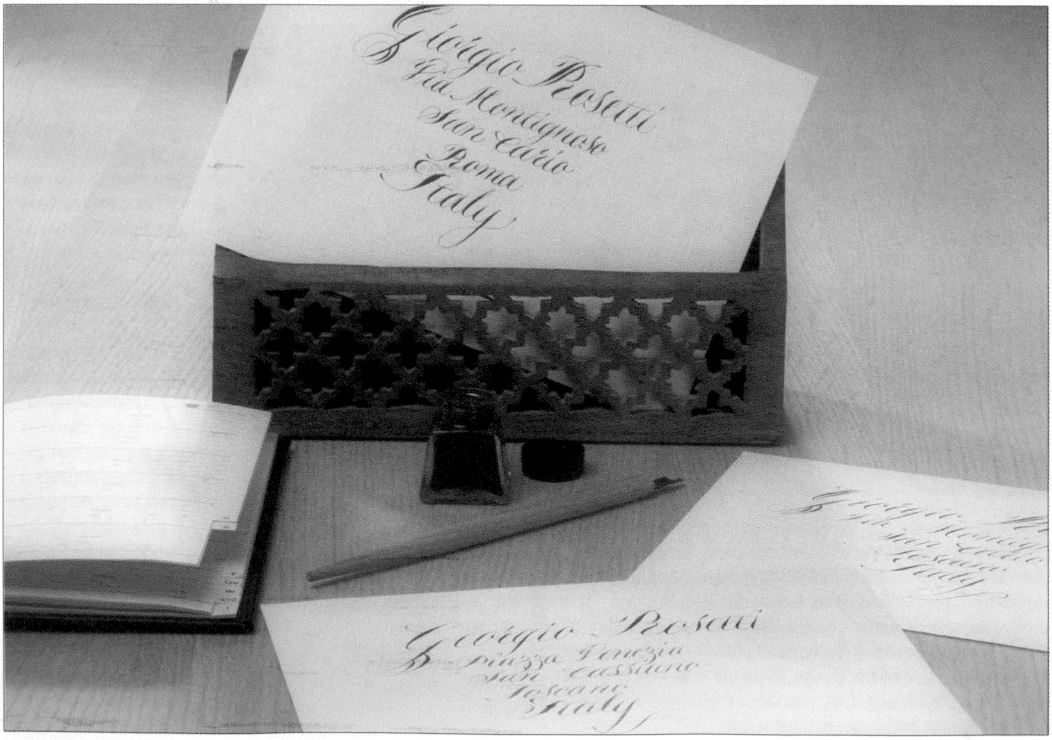

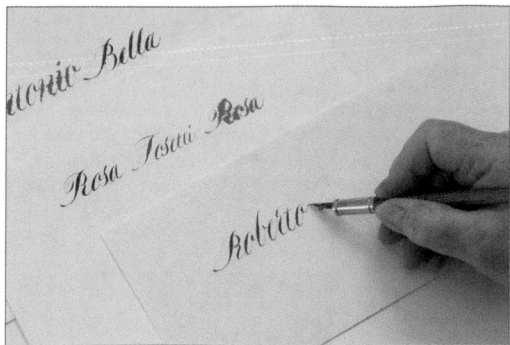
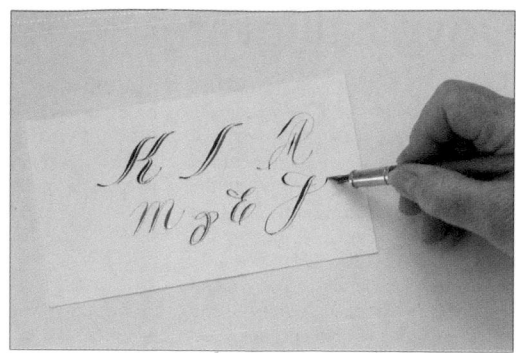

2 Do some writing trials on the type of envelope you intend to use. Sometimes the ink 'bleeds' on the envelope, spoiling the appearance of the lettering, so it is worthwhile doing some tests on a variety of envelopes to find a type that works well with the inks you are using.

3 Try experimenting with colours. It is helpful to try out several colour combinations until you find one that is most suitable.

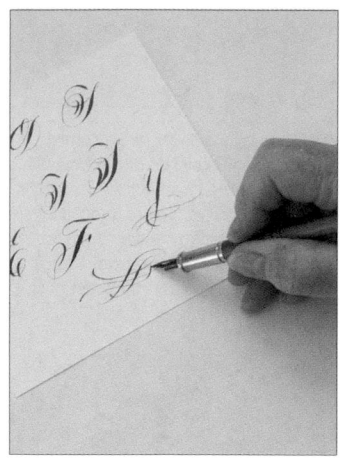

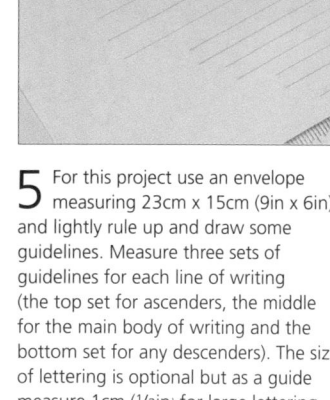

4 It can add interest to 'flourish' a letter. It is a good idea to practise on layout paper first. If necessary, the flourish can be drawn with a pencil to 'plan' the route.

Tip: Keep your surface flat when writing Copperplate and dip the pen into the paint or inkpot until it completely covers the whole of the nib, which will ensure it is nicely loaded.

5 For this project use an envelope measuring 23cm x 15cm (9in x 6in) and lightly rule up and draw some guidelines. Measure three sets of guidelines for each line of writing (the top set for ascenders, the middle for the main body of writing and the bottom set for any descenders). The size of lettering is optional but as a guide measure 1cm (1/2in) for large lettering and 7mm (3/8in) for a smaller size. The slope of Copperplate writing is 54 degrees so if it helps, you could mark some guidelines using a protractor.

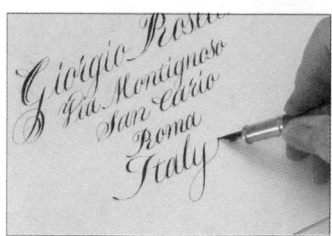

6 Mix up your chosen colours of gouache paints to the consistency of thin cream. If you are alternating colours it might be easier to use two different pens so that you do not need to keep rinsing the nib. Write out the envelope and when the writing has thoroughly dried carefully rub out the lines.

Painted monogram

A monogram is a character or figure made up of two or more letters – often the two initials of a name. A monogram may vary from the simple and understated to a more elaborate or complex design. Some letters work well together but others are more difficult to arrange into a satisfactory design.

Whichever style of monogram you choose, there is the satisfaction of creating something truly exclusive. Try experimenting with colour. Coloured pencils are quick and easy to use for initial trials, then, when you have some idea of a design, try it with a pen. Simply changing the nib size or the height of the letters will alter the look of your monogram, so it is worth spending some time doing this. As a rough guide, the size of the monogram will probably need to be between 2.5cm to 4.5cm (1in to 1¾in).

A single colour scheme can look very elegant and a combination of two or even three colours can be exciting. Simple pen drawn patterns and motifs can be used to embellish the initials. Letters can be adorned with flourishes but it is probably better to limit them to the first or last letter, depending on which lends itself most naturally.

The finished monogram can be applied to a range of uses. The design can be scanned and saved on a computer so that it can be printed when it is needed. The scale of the monogram can also be adjusted to complement the size of the item you are printing.

The design

In this project, the monogram is designed by using drawn and painted Versal letters on watercolour paper and painted in gouache. The initials are painted in two colours and a little decorative detail adorns the largest letter. The finished monogram will be used on stationery such as letterheads, invoices, notelets, labels and calling cards.

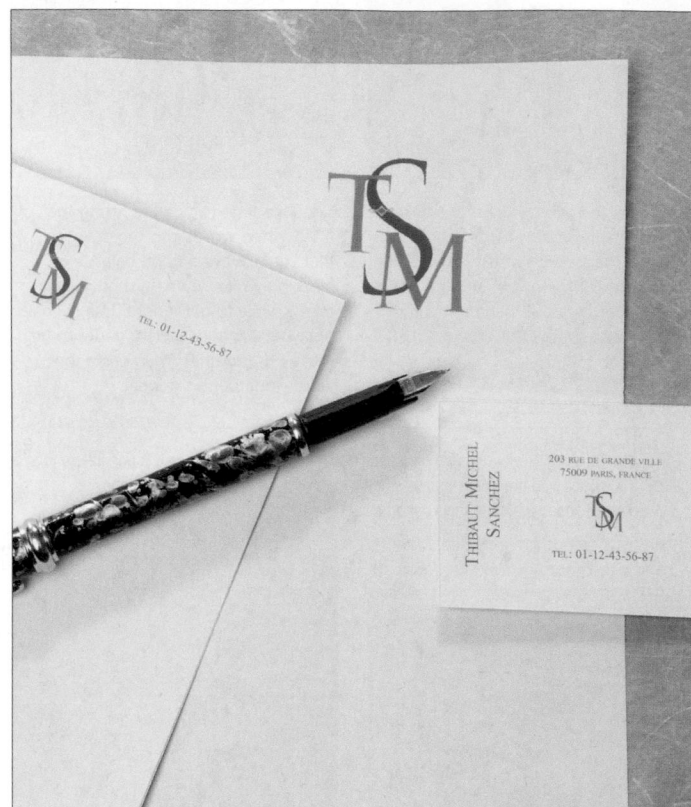

Materials

- *Layout or practice paper*
- *Pilot pens*
- *Dip pens in various sizes*
- *Watercolour ink or gouache*
- *Pencil*
- *Tracing paper*
- *Hot-pressed watercolour paper*
- *Tape*
- *Kitchen paper*
- *Scissors*
- *Paintbrush: size 00 or 1*
- *Gouache paint: cereulean, indigo, gold*
- *Writing paper, notelets etc. (optional)*

1 Spend some time drawing out different permutations of your chosen initials. It takes some letter juggling to find a design that is attractive and legible. Firstly, try two letters that sit together but are separate.

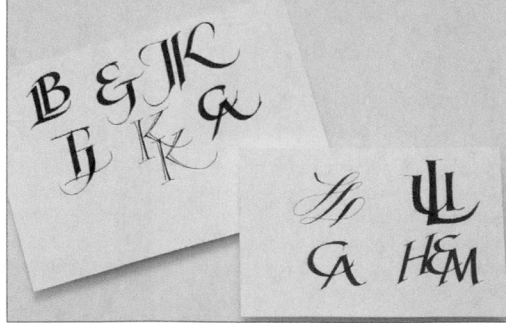

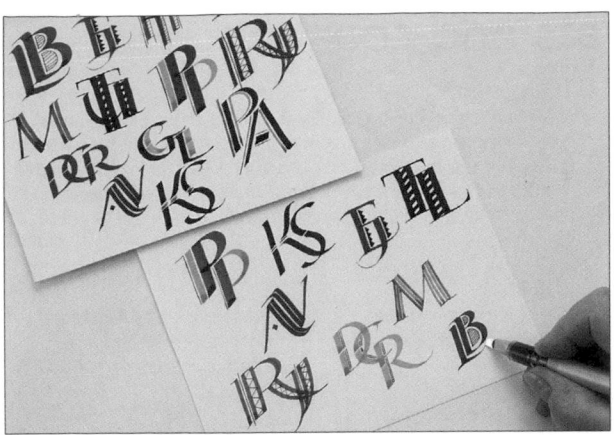

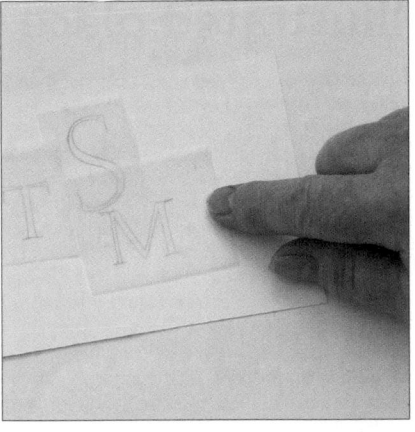

2 Now try some possible ways of linking two or three letters together. Letters could overlap, interlink or fit in to one another. There are many variations on styles of letterform, but remember that the design should not be over-complicated or too fussy as legibility is a main consideration. Introduce some colourways and add any decorative detail.

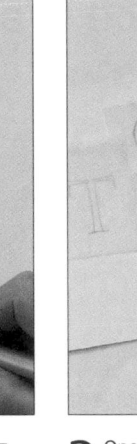

Tip: Keep your pencils sharpened to a good point when preparing tracings so the result is clean and clear.

3 Once you have some idea of a design, pencil your letters separately on to some tracing paper and cut them into squares. Overlap the initials and try moving the tracing squares around until you are satisfied that the initials sit well together. Draw any additional ligatures, or joins that may be necessary to link the initials, or leave them separated if you prefer. If you wish to add any flourishes, draw them on to a separate piece of tracing paper, lay the tracing on the design and move it around until the position looks good.

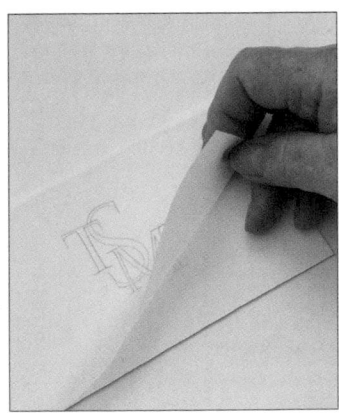

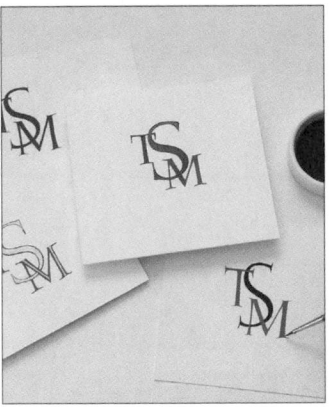

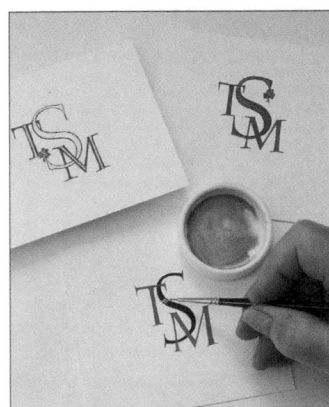

4 Trace down your design on to watercolour paper. Make your own carbon paper by scribbling over some tracing paper with an HB pencil until the piece is covered with graphite. Rub some kitchen paper over it to remove excessive graphite. Tape down the tracing into position and carefully slide the carbon paper underneath. Trace the design using a 2H pencil.

5 Mix up your gouache colours. Using a size 00 or 1 brush, paint one colour and leave to dry thoroughly before proceeding with the next colour. You can then try out some different colour combinations.

6 Add any decorative elements using either a pen or brush. If you have access to a computer, scan the monogram and save on file then print it on to your chosen article.

Reversed-out bookplate

A bookplate is a label that indicates a book's ownership. Adorn a cherished volume with a bookplate and anyone you lend it to will have no chance of forgetting whose it is. The practice probably originated in Germany, where the earliest known example of a bookplate dates from the 15th century.

The bookplate created here has *Ex Libris,* Latin for 'from the books of', written across it, and you can personalize it with your own name. An elegant decorative effect is achieved by writing around the edges and by drawing simple pen patterns in the corners, made up of small oval loops forming butterflies.

You can easily create many bookplates to personalize a full collection of titles by using a photocopier to obtain multiple copies. Alternatively, you can scan the design into a computer using a scanner and the accompanying software. Choose a high number of pixels to ensure sharp definition. Take the resulting scan into a photo-manipulating package on your computer. By choosing 'invert' or 'negative' a black on white bookplate will show as white on black, which is much more eye-catching. By saving the bookplate design on the computer copies can be printed when needed.

The design

For this bookplate two weights of Modern Gothic script and pen patterns have been chosen as they will reproduce on a computer or photocopier very successfully. If you do not want any of the writing around the words *Ex Libris* in the centre to appear upside down, begin the writing at the bottom left-hand corner and continue to the top right across the top of the design. Then start at the bottom left-hand corner and once again travel to the top right, but this time traversing the bottom of the design.

Materials

- *Layout or practice paper*
- *Dip pens: in various sizes*
- *Gouache paint or ink: black*
- *Craft (utility) knife*
- *Self-healing cutting mat*
- *Ruler with cutting edge*
- *2H pencil*
- *Hot-pressed watercolour paper*
- *Deckle-edge scissors (optional)*

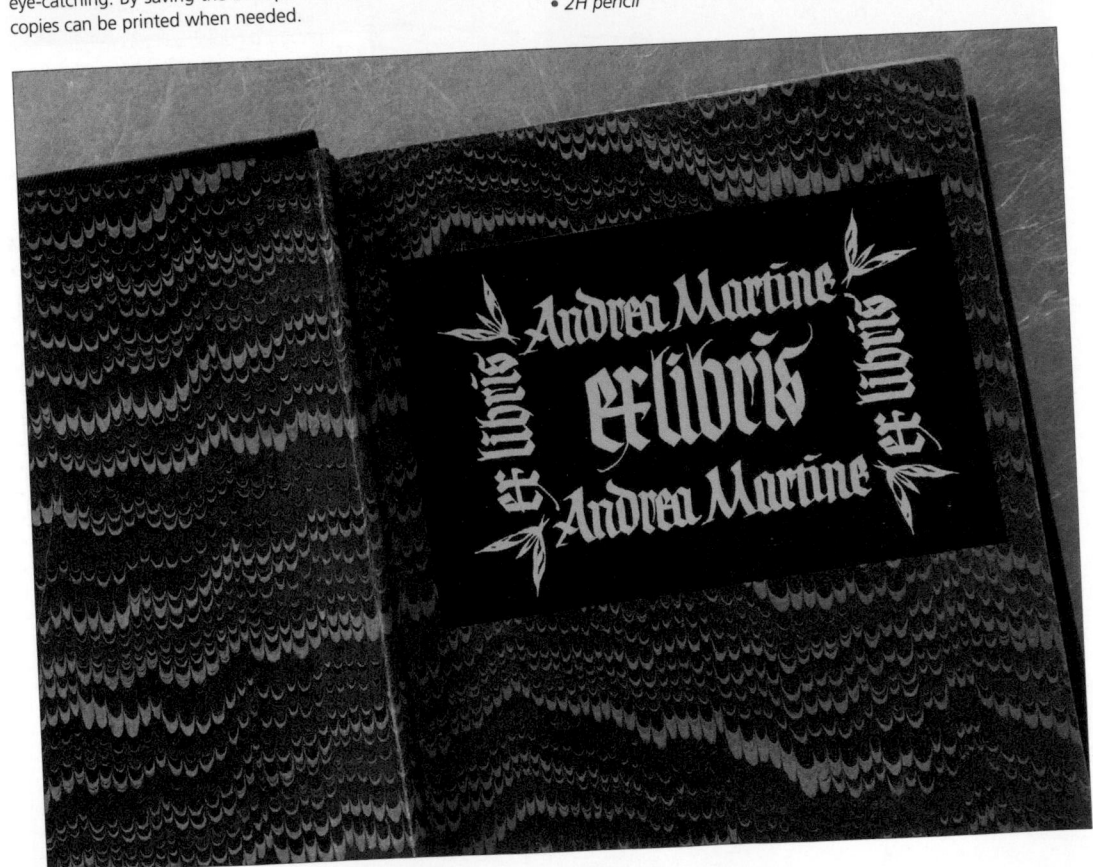

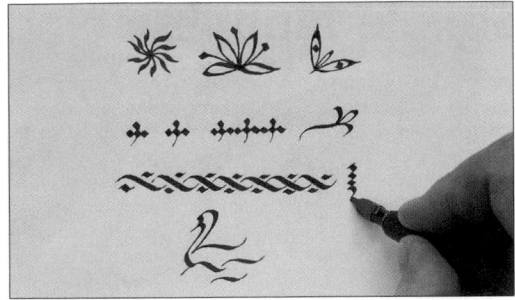

1 Experiment with various nib sizes. A strong contrast between *Ex Libris* and the name is desirable so a difference of at least two nib sizes is recommended. It may be useful to use large nibs and reduce the size on a photocopier.

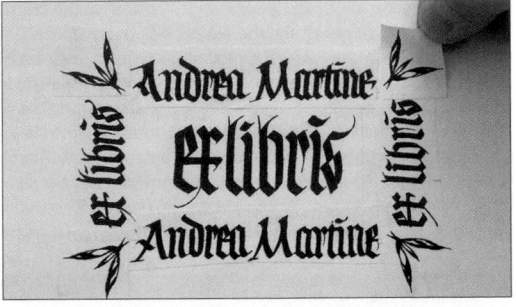

2 Practise making some simple pen patterns, again using different sized nibs. Your preferred pattern will be used to decorate the corners of your plate.

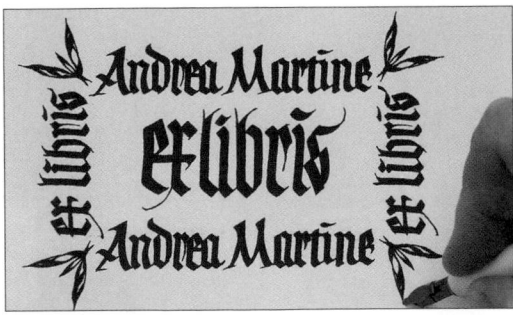

3 Once you have decided on the nibs, write the name several times on a strip of paper.

> **Tip:** Use the nicest paper you can find for your bookplate, as this will reflect the quality of your personal library.

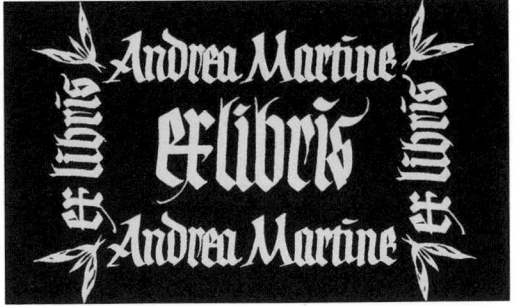

4 Try out various paste-ups. For this design the large lettered *Ex Libris* is being framed by smaller *Ex Libris* at the sides and the owner's name repeated top and bottom.

5 Once the layout has been decided, rule up and write on the watercolour paper. Any spaces in the corners can be filled with simple pen patterns. The pattern chosen here starts at the left-hand edge with a small oval loop, followed by a larger oval loop and a small oval loop to finish. Larger loops have been drawn around the outer ovals and, with the addition of antennae, the pattern has become a butterfly. This has been repeated in the other three corners.

6 Scan and print out your bookplates – most photo-manipulating packages allow you to print multiple images on a single page and change or reverse the colours if you wish. You could choose a handmade paper, or one that appears handmade, to make the bookplate look as though it has history. Most photocopier machines and computer printers will accept lightweight hand-made paper though they may need to be hand-fed. You can cut out the bookplates using deckled-edge scissors to emphasize the effect.

Embossed designs for a letterhead

This project combines lettering skills for a letterhead with the art of embossing – shaping letters and patterns so that they are raised above the surface of the surrounding paper.

Embossing requires the use of a template and involves carefully and accurately cutting shapes out of a piece of thin card. Working from the reverse side, the surface of the paper is then gently pushed down into the cut shape. This creates a raised image on the front surface, casting shadows and giving an appearance of quality, which is suitable for both personal and business use.

Once you have cut your template it can be used many times, and the actual embossing is quick and easy to do. With practice you will acquire the necessary skills to be able to do crisp accurate cutting, making an infinite number of designs possible. Many papers emboss well and you might find it useful to keep a paper sample file of experiments and results. Best papers to use have a soft surface.

Materials
- *Dip pens: in various sizes*
- *Coloured inks*
- *Glue stick*
- *Layout or practice paper*
- *Watercolour paper or soft surface paper such as BFK Rives*
- *2H pencils*
- *Craft (utility) knife*
- *Tracing paper*
- *Thin card (stock)*
- *Masking tape*
- *Embossing tool, or cable knitting needle*
- *Pastels*
- *Cotton bud (swab) or soft brush*
- *Crayon*

> **Tip:** Always use a sharp blade for cutting stencils. For complex projects, you may have to replace the blades several times.

The design
This letterhead is made up of a personal name and address with an embossed initial letter, which can be subtly decorated with colour. The calligraphy is written using Foundational Hand and Roman Capitals in blue and black.

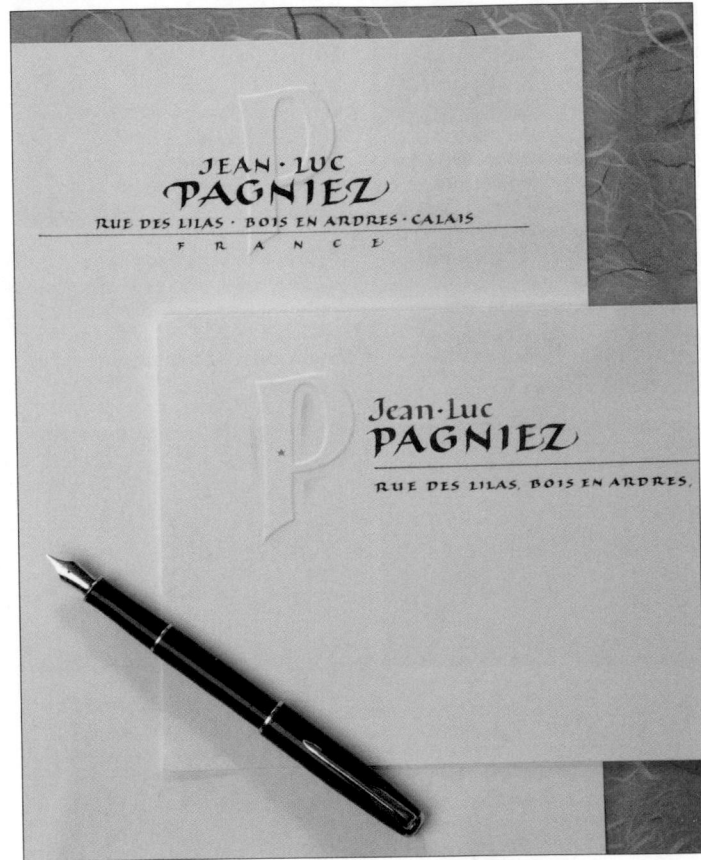

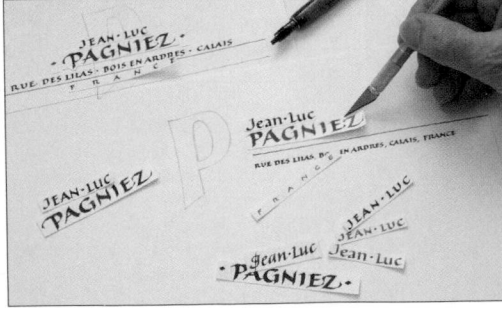

1 Design the lettering, using layout paper. Paste up your name and address strips leaving a space for the embossed image. Finalize the writing on the design and write out on a paper of your choice.

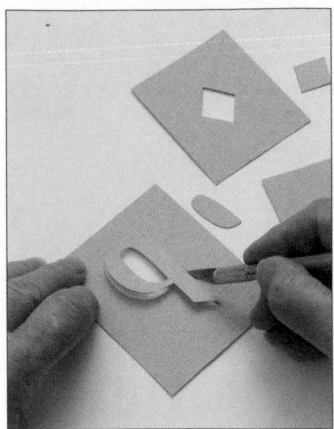

2 Draw or trace and transfer the image on to thin card. Cut out the shape, keeping your fingers clear of the cutting direction.

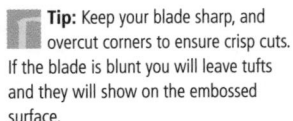

Tip: Keep your blade sharp, and overcut corners to ensure crisp cuts. If the blade is blunt you will leave tufts and they will show on the embossed surface.

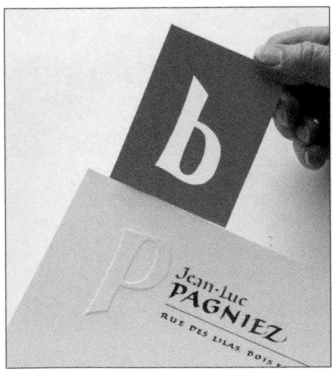

5 Use the hinge to check the quality of the embossing. If it is not crisp enough replace the hinged template, turn over and further emboss. Crisp edges and sharp points on corners are vital, so run the embossing tool firmly into the corners, to ensure good results.

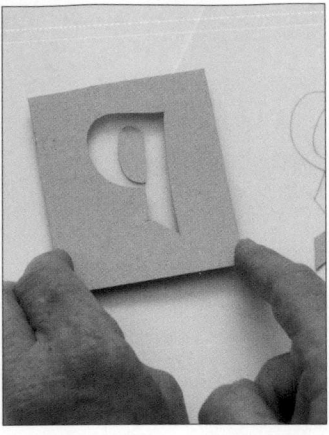

3 For letters with 'island' counters, stick the reverse image card template on to tracing paper. This backing allows you to stick the counter safely in place.

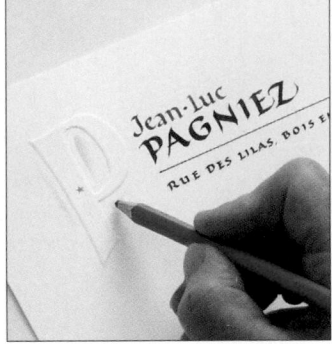

6 To add a blush of colour, scrape some dry pastel dust, using a cotton bud or soft brush, rubbing well in with a circular motion. Keep colour away from the embossed edge, or the subtle shadow effect will be lost. Use colour very sparingly. Alternatively, use a crayon to add final touches to the embossing.

Tip: When embossing, place the template down first, reverse face towards you if it is a letter, and position paper over, right side face down, and work from the reverse.

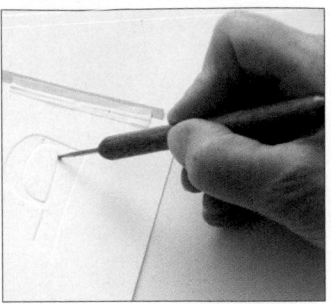

4 Once the lettering is complete, position the work face down on to the template and tape securely along one edge so that it acts as a hinge. To do this, place the template (reverse side up) against a window, to allow you to position it before taping it securely. Working on the reverse, gently run a fingernail into the depression, pushing the paper into the cut shape. Using the embossing tool, gently but firmly run it along the already depressed shape, working all around the perimeter, taking care to push well into the corners, to make crisp edges and points.

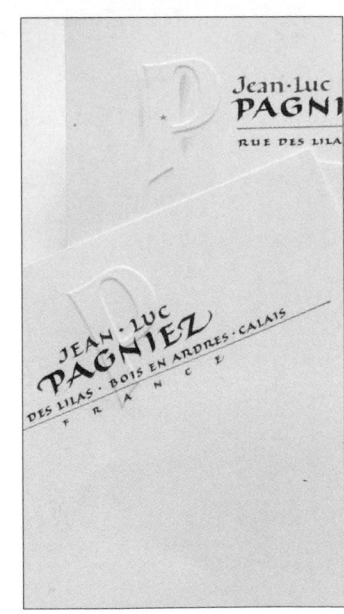

7 Prepare a variety of embossed images, some single and others with multiple embossings.

Alphabet on woven paper

Historically, the most important legal and other formal documents often had a wax seal affixed. Occasionally, when the cost of a vellum or parchment scroll was too high and paper was available, a paper design was woven and either applied to the document or woven directly into it.

This idea can be used to create an unusual textured effect for a design. Although the cutting and weaving in this project appears complex, the calligraphy itself is not. This means that you can spend some time and effort on the individual letters of the alphabet to make them as interesting or decorative as possible. Take the opportunity to try out variations on your usual calligraphic scripts or to develop new alphabets that you can use in other designs.

It is possible to create an even more intriguing piece of work by making several woven alphabets in different sizes and arranging them on a plain or coloured background. To do this mark up a much larger single sheet of paper with grids of different sizes and weave the strips into this, rather than making separate pieces of work and mounting them afterwards.

Another variation of this project is to cut the slits horizontally and weave the strips from top to bottom.

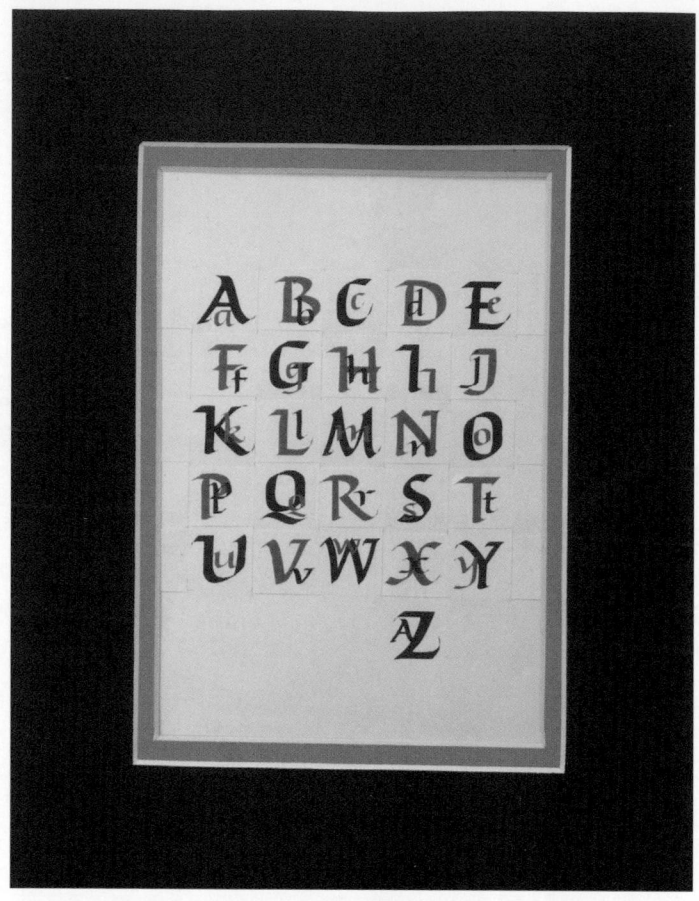

The design
Twelve of the letters are written in Italic on the grid and all the other letters, excluding 'Z', are written on the strips that are woven to form the alphabet.

Materials
- *Layout or practice paper*
- *Black and coloured writing ink*
- *Dip pens, such as William Mitchell 1 and 2*
- *Good quality paper*
- *Pencil*
- *Metal ruler, T-square or set square*
- *Scalpel or craft (utility) knife*
- *Eraser*
- *Tweezers (optional)*
- *Frame (optional)*

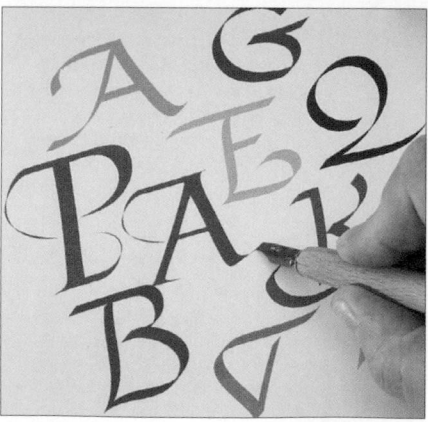

1 Write some letters of the alphabet in a range of styles on layout paper and choose one you want to use in the design. You can write capitals or lower case and mix them if you wish. Decide on a size for the final design without making it too large or too small. A basic module of 2cm (³⁄₄in) square is a good size. Choose a good, strong paper. This can be white or coloured.

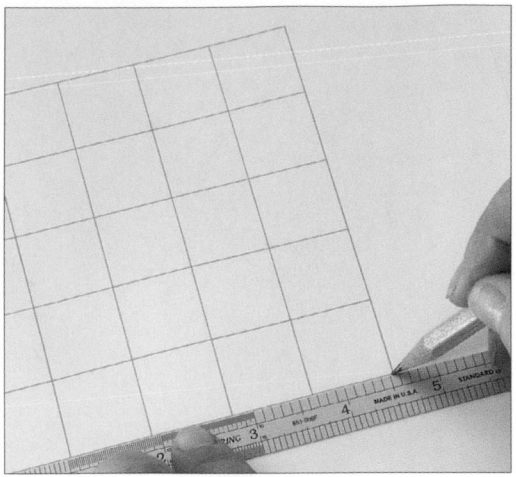

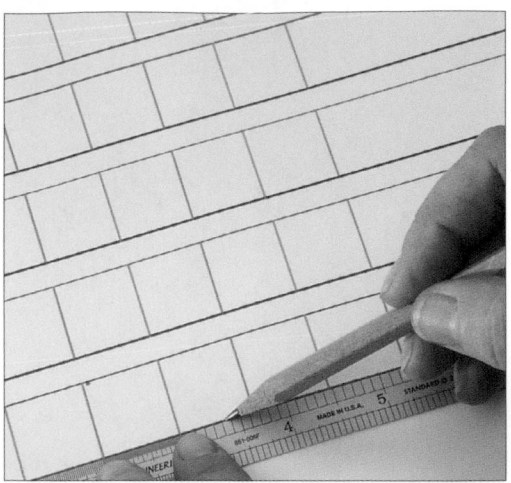

2 Mark up the paper lightly and accurately in pencil with a 5cm x 5cm (2in x 2in) square grid with a ruler. To be even more accurate use a T-square, set square or some other method that ensures that the grid lines are exactly at right angles to each other. Leave a margin of at least 10cm (4in) all around the grid. The surplus can be trimmed off afterwards.

3 Measure and draw up paper strips to the width of the grid squares. Make them about 20cm (8in) longer than the width and height of your grid. These can be of the same or different paper from that on which you drew the initial grid. To make the weaving a little bit easier, make the width of the strips a tiny bit less than the grid squares.

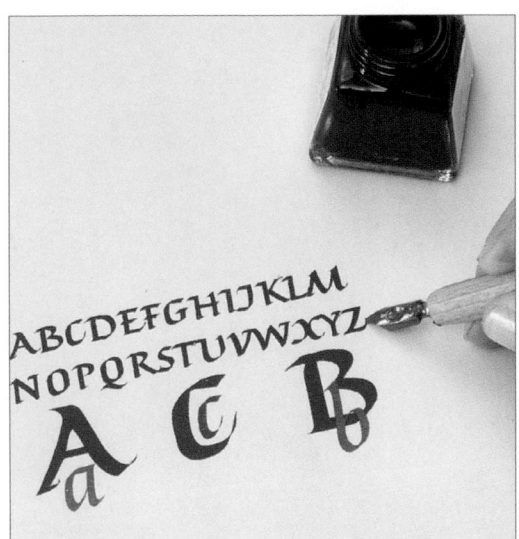

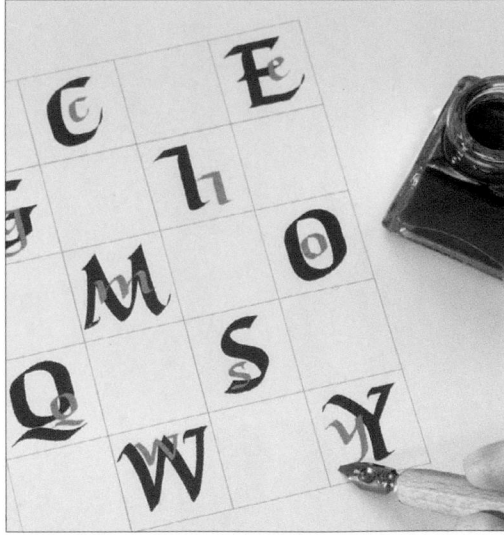

4 Plan out the letters for the whole alphabet. Experiment with variations on the letterform that has been selected. Try combining capitals and lower-case letters. Experiment with colour combinations. Remember that each letter or group of letters must fit with the squares of the grid.

5 Write every second letter of the alphabet within the squares of the grid on the marked-up paper. This grid has capital letters in black and lower-case letters in orange. If two colours overlap, ensure that the first colour is dry before writing the second. Also, make sure that the medium of the second colour will not mix with that of the first letter.

▶

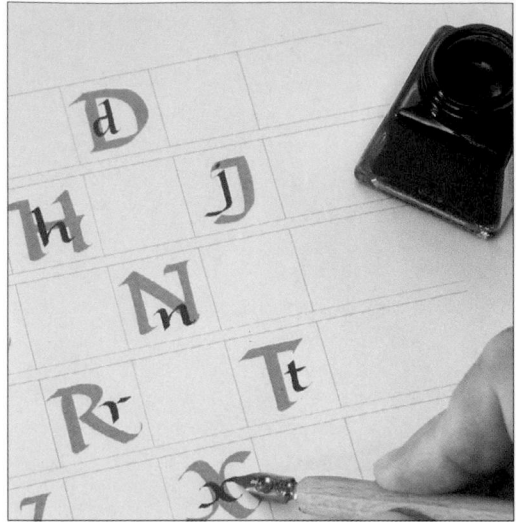

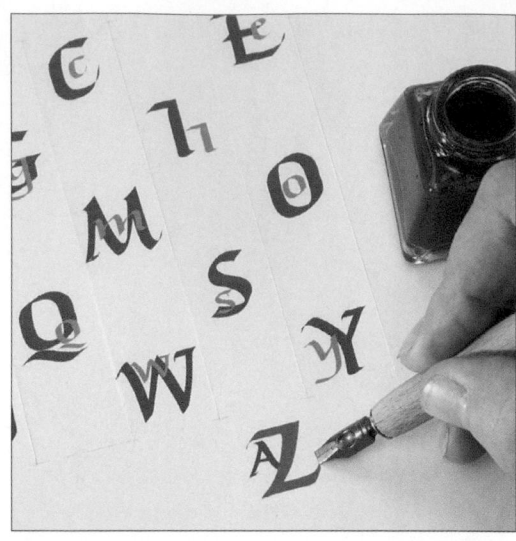

6 Write the remaining letters on every second square of the marked up sheet. The grid comprises 25 squares so this will leave the letter 'Z'. The colours of the capitals and lower-case letters have been reversed for the strips – the capitals are now orange and the lower-case letters black.

7 Decide on the position of the last letter 'Z' either on one of the strips or on the paper. This letter does not have to be the same as the others. In this example a small 'a' has been placed beside the 'Z' to suggest the whole alphabet. Red is used to contrast with the other letters.

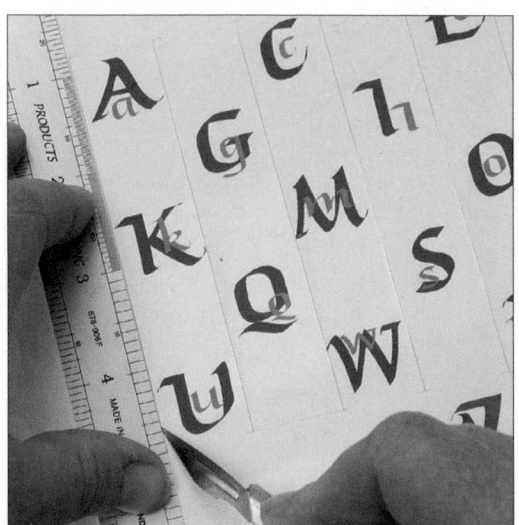

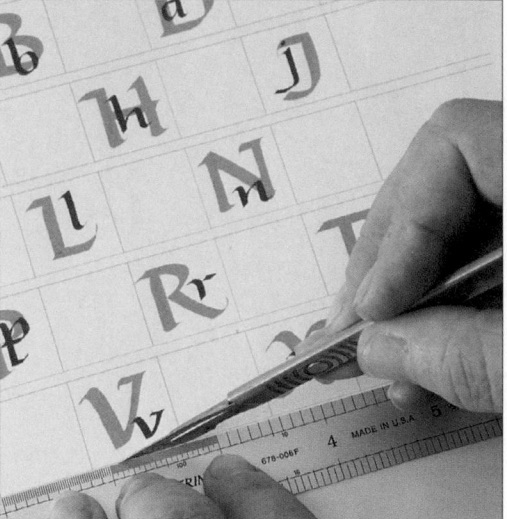

8 Cut six vertical slits on the paper within the grid to allow the strips of paper to be inserted and woven. Use a very sharp blade as any roughness will make weaving the strips of paper a little more difficult. Avoid extending cuts beyond the grid. If you cut the slits too long it will be hard to keep the paper strips in the correct position.

9 Cut the paper strips horizontally, using a scalpel and a metal ruler. When the lines have been cut, rub off the vertical lines that have been drawn between the letters using an eraser.

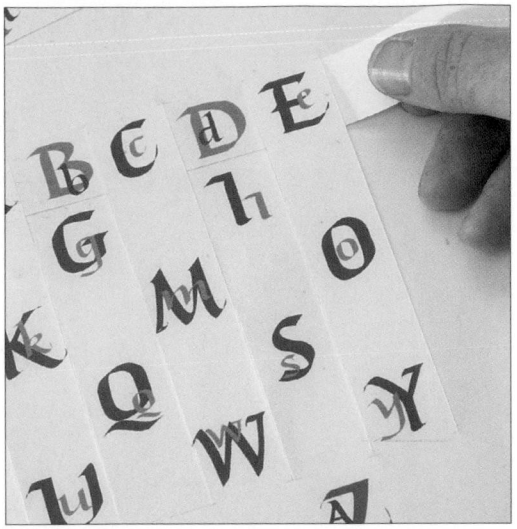

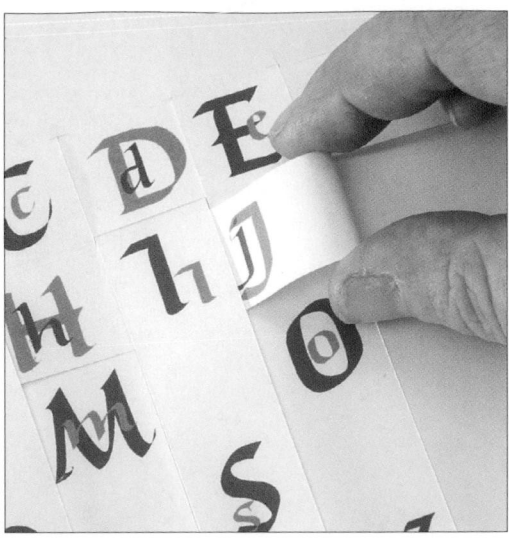

10 Feed the first paper strip (with the letters 'B' and 'D') through the slits, one at a time, from right to left. Feed it below the 'E', 'C' and 'A' and pull it through until the correct letters are positioned centrally with the squares. Push the strip upward until it butts up against the top of the slits.

11 Similarly, feed the second strip (with the letters 'F', 'H' and 'J') through the slits from the right to the left. This time, feed it from below through the first slit under the 'I' and 'G' and downwards through the last (left) slit.

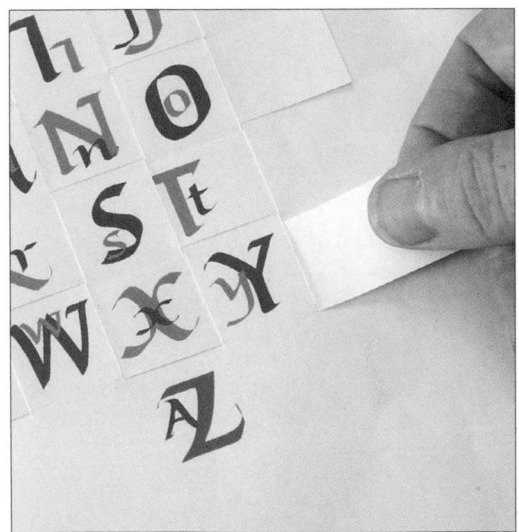

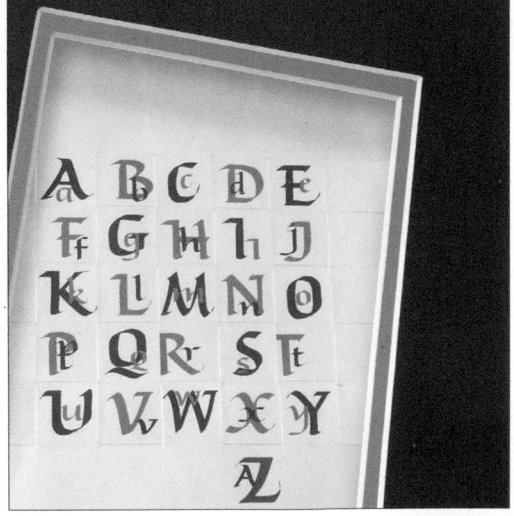

12 Continue feeding the other three strips alternately. The last strip will be the most difficult as the fit will be very tight. Make sure that the upper four strips are pushed hard up against each other. It may be helpful to use tweezers or some other method of gripping the leading edge of the strip. Cutting the leading edge to a point can also help.

13 Trim the surplus paper from the strips leaving them the same length. Trim the calligraphy to its final size. Frame the calligraphy if desired with a matching frame.

Desktop using digital calligraphy

One of the things that helps to make computers more user-friendly and individual is to be able to design your own desktop. If you decide not to use one of the designs supplied with the Operating Systems (Windows or Macintosh) the chances are that you will be using imported personal photographs or a selection of other images that have meaning for you. The desktop that is designed in this project uses calligraphy, either on its own or combined with an image. As the desktop is seen only on the computer screen it is a 'virtual' design.

Materials
- *Graphics software (e.g. Adobe Photoshop, Illustrator, CorelDRAW, or Corel PHOTO-PAINT)*
- *Graphics tablet and digital pen (optional)*

The design
The chosen lettering is drawn on to the computer using an Italic script. Filters are then applied to the design to create an interesting embossed effect.

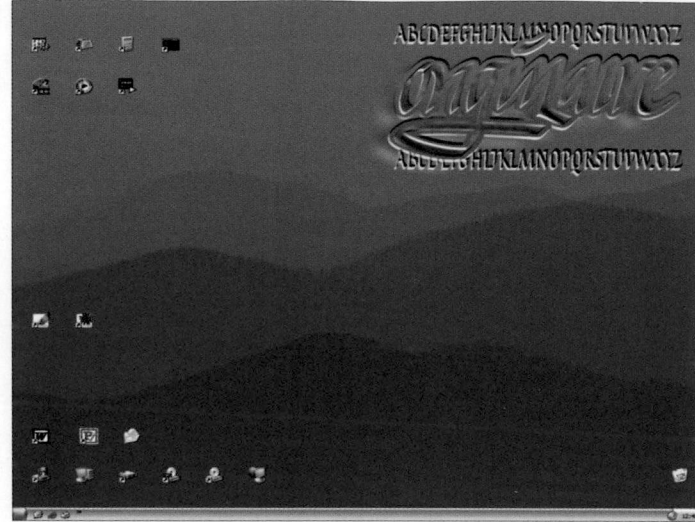

Tip: Use the mouse or digital pen very freely so that the calligraphy flows smoothly. Remember that you can try writing the words or even individual letters over and over again as it takes only a short time to undo.

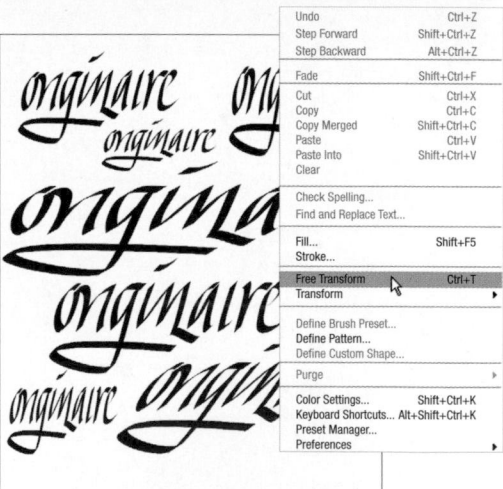

1 Write some words freely using your mouse or, if you have one, your digital pen. You can use bitmap software such as Photoshop or Coral Photopaint or vector-based software such as Illustrator or CorelDRAW. If you use vector-based software you can make extensive adjustments to the letterforms. With bitmap software you can only retouch the calligraphy.

2 Apply a range of transformations to the calligraphy. Try changing the height, width and scale of the lettering. Depending on the software you are using, you may have to use a command such as Image>Transform>Scale and then type in the new dimensions. Alternatively, you may have the facility to free 'transform' and drag the lettering to any size and shape.

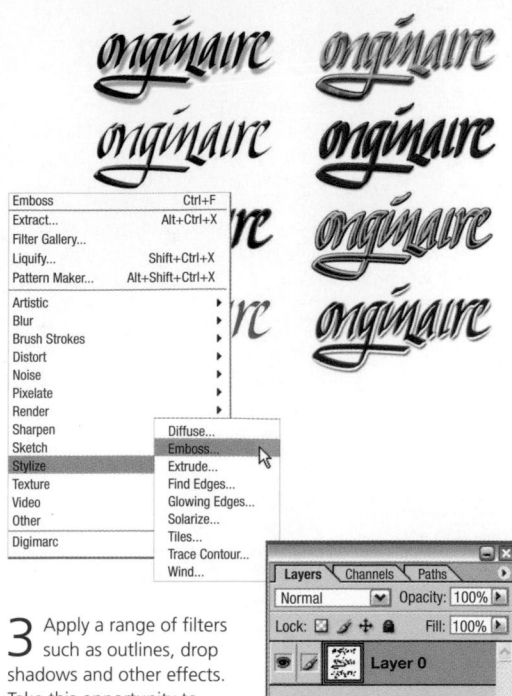

3 Apply a range of filters such as outlines, drop shadows and other effects. Take this opportunity to discover what your software can do to enhance calligraphic forms.

4 Similarly, apply a range of fills. Experiment with simple colour fills, textured fills, pattern fills and gradient fills. Try mixing the different effects until you get something you are satisfied with.

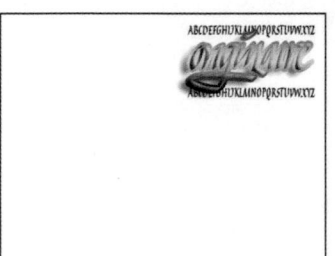

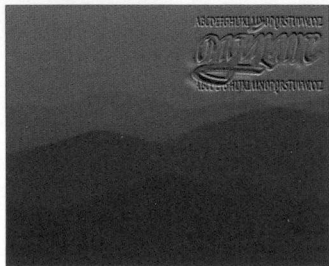

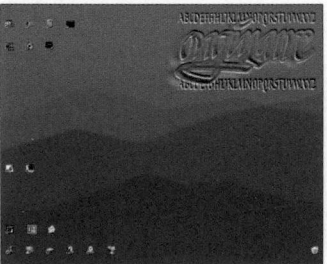

5 Experiment with a layout. Make allowances for the desktop icons so that they can be placed in your preferred locations. To make the design more interesting, consider adding additional calligraphic elements or repeats of the main design in the same size or smaller. In this project a calligraphic alphabet in capitals is placed above and below *originaire*.

6 Choose a background colour, pattern or image. If you use anything other than a single colour you will probably have to change the transparency, contrast or intensity of the fill or the image so that it does not obscure the calligraphy. On this desktop, the emboss was applied before the image was added.

7 Make any necessary adjustments or additions to the design as you wish and save the file in a format that can be used as a desktop image. For example, Windows requires the image to be in .bmp, .gif, .jpg, .dib or .png format. In desktop settings (Control panel>Display>Desktop in Windows) select the desktop design file that you have saved and reposition your icons as necessary in the same way as you probably have done with your current desktop.

Wall hanging using a broad-edged brush

This is an opportunity to exhibit your calligraphic skills on a grander scale by creating an elegant wall hanging. Getting the best results requires a skilful use of the broad-edged brush. To produce beautiful marks, the trick is to remember the edged brush is not a pen and so should not be used like one. Keep the paint as thick as possible, fill the brush and wipe most of it away, to preserve the chisel edge. Do this for every stroke, and the lettering will remain sharp. The calico will also accept large pens, providing it is prepared in the way shown here.

Unbleached calico can be bought from dressmaking or curtain-making stores. Writing on it directly is quite hard work as the surface of untreated calico is slightly water-resistant. For this project, household emulsion is first painted on to the calico, mixed with some glue to help flexibility and give a good writing surface. This also thickens the fabric and makes it sufficiently flat to work on without any need for stretching or extra preparation. If the paint has penetrated the surface, the edges will not fray when trimmed, so there is no need to neaten them by folding them over.

The design

This hanging is tall rather than wide, to give it more chance of fitting on a narrow wall. This practical shape does, however, mean there are more lines to rule, and quotations with long words can be awkward to accommodate. The Latin quotation, written using Roman Capitals and Flourished Italic, comes from Horace, and translates as 'While we talk, time is flying; seize the day, put no trust in the future'.

Materials

- Dip pen, such as William Mitchell 3, (medium nib) and ink, or felt-tipped pen, for roughs
- Broad-edged brushes, 1cm (1/2in) wide and 5mm (1/4in) wide or automatic pens of approximately these sizes
- Layout paper or brown Kraft paper
- Craft (utility) knife, metal ruler, self-healing cutting mat
- Calico
- Household emulsion paint: white or cream, and PVA (white) glue
- Household paintbrush
- Old newspaper
- Fine abrasive paper
- Two equal lengths of dowel
- Mixing palette
- Gouache paints: oxide of chromium (green) and Chinese red
- Art roller and roller tray
- Water pot
- HB pencil
- Ruler
- Set square (optional)
- Sheet transfer gold leaf (optional)
- Oil pastels (optional)
- Coloured rope for hanging

> **Tip:** Practise all the writing on brown Kraft paper, or lining paper, obtainable from wallpaper stores; these have a slightly rough surface that will simulate the 'drag' of writing on calico, and give good sharp marks. Warming up first in this way can make all the difference to the finished result.

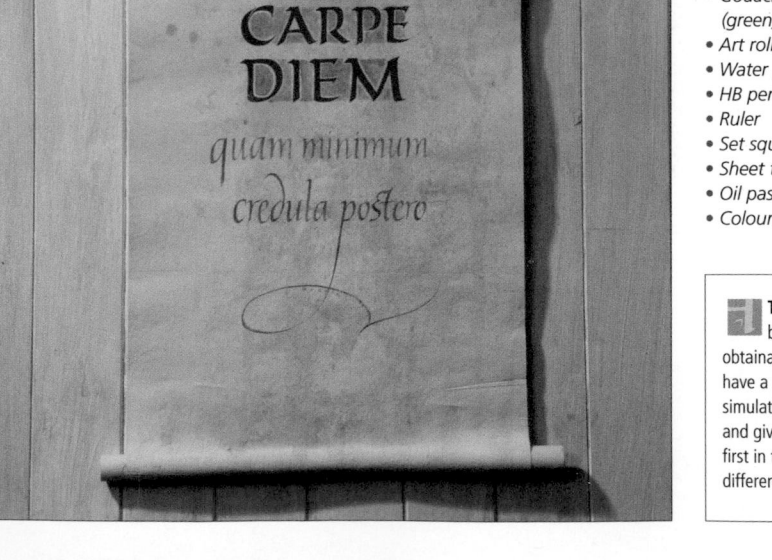

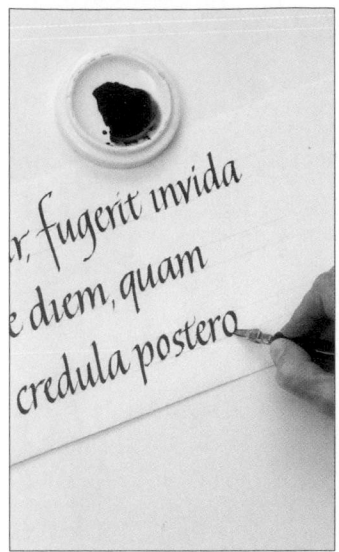

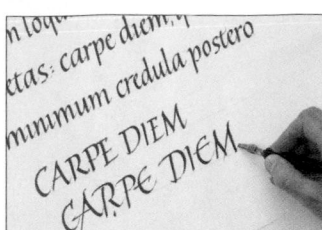

2 Pick a suitable phrase or word from your quotation to emphasize. This lettering can be written in a larger size, using Roman Capitals. *Carpe Diem* is a well-known phrase that will draw the reader's attention.

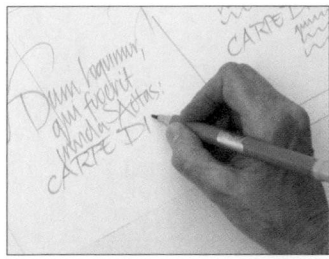

3 Do some trials so that you can practise the layout.

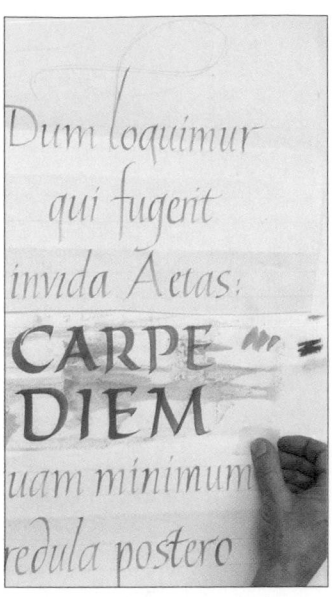

1 Try out the chosen quotation in Italic, with a dip pen or a felt-tipped pen. If you are using brushes, Kraft paper has a textured surface that will give the necessary 'drag' for good lettering. Use ordinary layout paper if pens are being used.

4 Write it all out in the sizes and tools you plan to use for the final work. Cut and paste it together into a design. If there is only one word per line, keep the interline spacing tight to bring the quotation together.

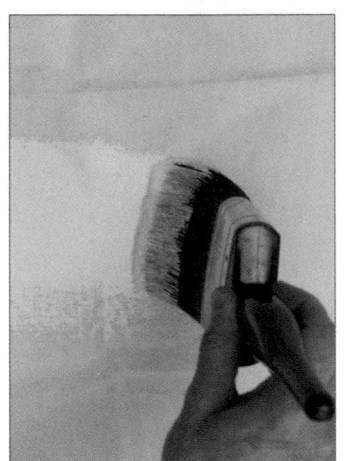

5 Prepare the calico by mixing household emulsion paint with PVA glue – approximately four parts paint to one part glue. Cover your work surface with old newspaper and then apply a layer of paint to the calico.

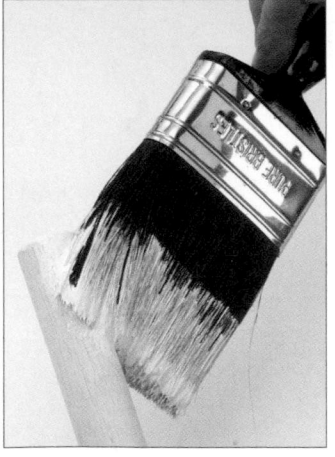

6 While the calico is drying, sand the ends of the lengths of dowel, and use emulsion to paint the parts that will show, unless you prefer to leave the wood bare.

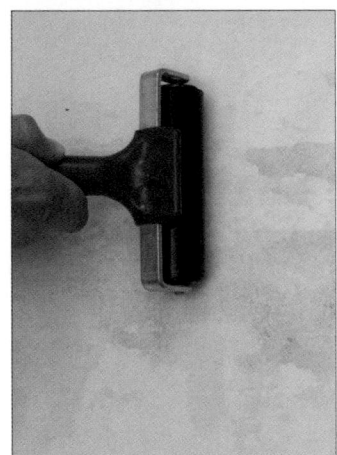

7 Mix up some of the red and green paint, but make it very watery, and apply it all over the surface in a vertical direction with the roller; apply one colour at a time but allow them to blend on the surface, providing a pale textured background. Leave to dry.

▶

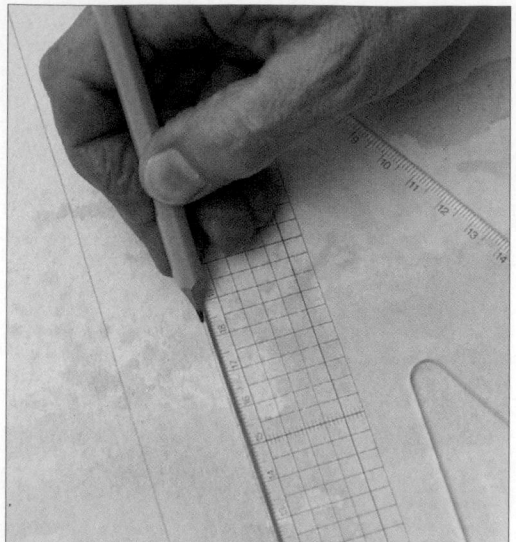

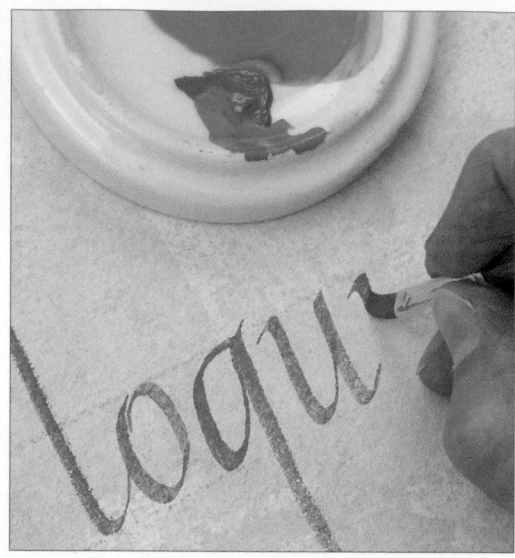

8 Allowing some space at the top and bottom of the calico length for rolling round the dowel, rule up the calico with fine lines using a pencil. Check first in a corner that the pencil can be erased without leaving a trace. To rule up, either measure down both sides of the calico and rule across, or if the calico edge is straight, use a set square as shown.

9 With the paste-up close at hand for reference, begin the lettering, using the oxide of chromium gouache. Keep the gouache as thick as will still come off the brush, to maintain drag. To preserve the chisel edge, fill the brush and wipe most of it away before every stroke.

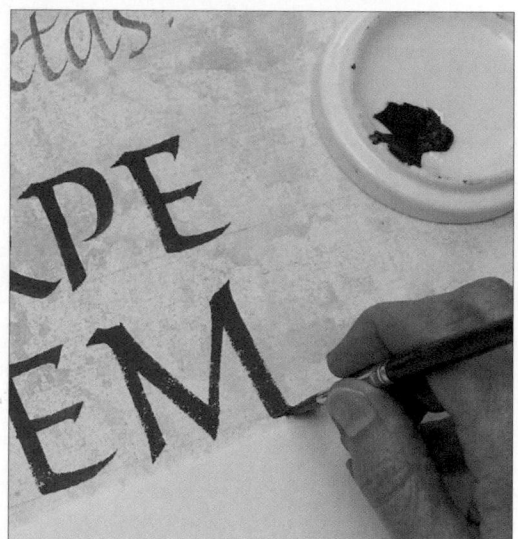

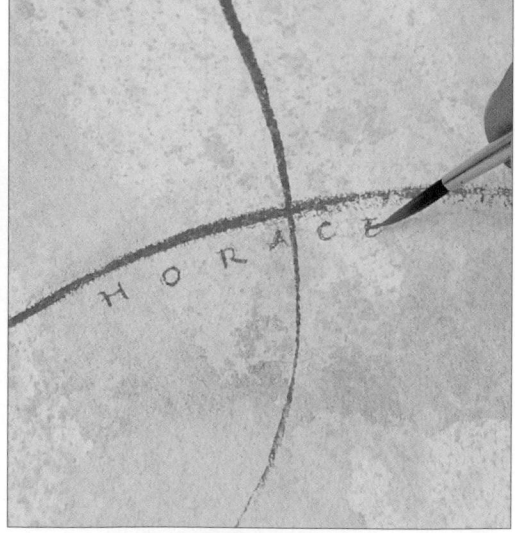

10 Write out *Carpe Diem* using a larger brush or pen, using the red gouache. These are heavyweight Roman Capitals, giving solid contrast to the wispier lower-case Italic.

11 Complete the rest of the quotation in Italic, taking special care (by practising many times first) with the flourish. Use a very fine, pointed paintbrush to add the credit 'Horace' in small capitals, spread out along the curve of the flourish or alternatively in a line below.

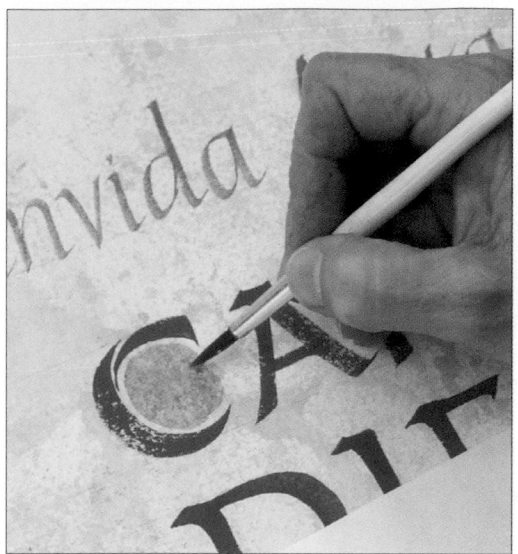

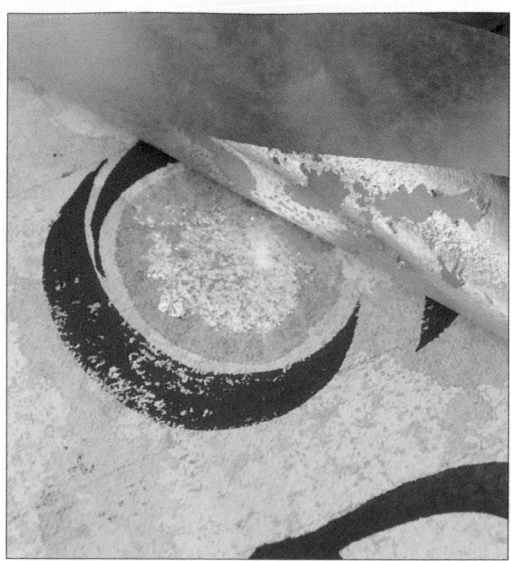

12 Add some delicate colour to the counters in the capitals by using very watery versions of the main colours, this time blending them into each other in each shape. Do not colour right up to the letter for fear of smudging. To make the chosen phrase really stand out, the colour can be applied in the spaces between the letters as well as in the counters.

13 The final touch is to add some gold leaf. For a 'distressed' look with gold, rub an oil pastel over the area to be gilded and press the transfer gold lightly on to it. If more gold is required, press harder.

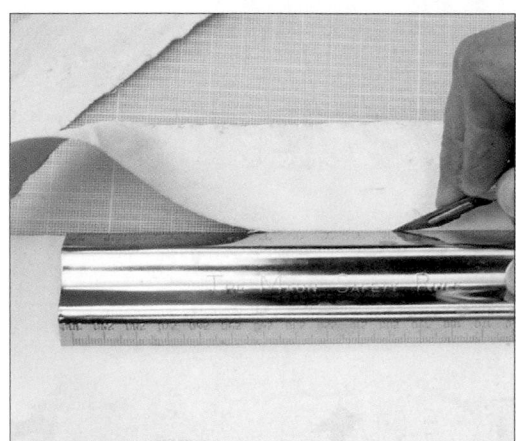

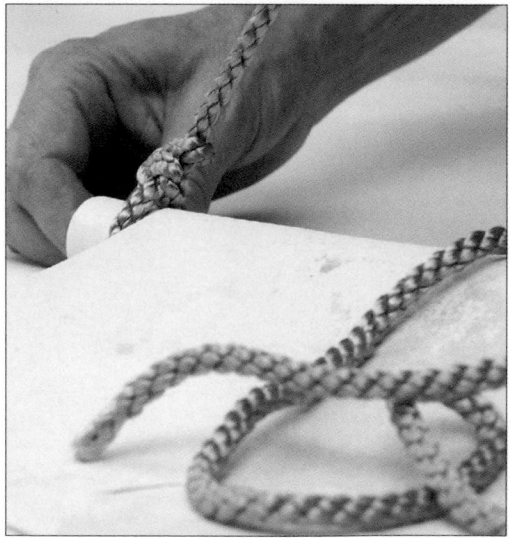

14 Working on a cutting mat or card, trim any uneven edges of the hanging with a craft knife, and attach the calico top and bottom to the prepared dowel. The simplest way to do this is to roll the calico round the dowel and fix it in place with PVA glue.

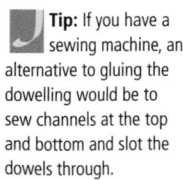 **Tip:** If you have a sewing machine, an alternative to gluing the dowelling would be to sew channels at the top and bottom and slot the dowels through.

15 Attach the coloured rope along the top dowel and tie a decorative knot at each end, or loop the rope across the back to tie the ends together. Your wall hanging is now ready to display.

Experimental lettering

Calligraphers like to experiment with different tools and letterforms. The former influences the latter. Some tools work best when used to make slow, careful movements, because they hold on to the ink. The tools that excite calligraphers who prefer gestural work are the ones that allow free-flowing expression, such as ruling pens, pointed brushes, and 'automatic' poster pens. Much effort has been expended in developing the potential of these tools for more expressive calligraphy.

The best experimental forms grow from informed practice. The freedom displayed in a professional ballet dancer's performance comes from years of rehearsal, and the same applies to these free forms of calligraphy. The gestural marks employed carry an underlying awareness of balance and form, based on a thorough acquaintance with whichever letterform you choose as your springboard. Italic, lower case and capitals are very adaptable letterforms and allow for great creativity.

The brush, ruling pen and automatic pen have very different characteristics, and the best results come from using them for what they do best. As a developing calligrapher, it is important to take time to discover the advantages and special features of each. This project uses automatic pens, but the principles of the design would apply equally if the brush or ruling pen had been chosen.

The design

The final result is an alphabet of letters based on Italic Capitals, which is portrait in orientation, and executed with automatic pens. The 'A' and 'Z' burst out, giving dynamism to the piece, and contrast with the block of remaining alphabet which is further held together by the gold lines and the random colouring-in of spaces.

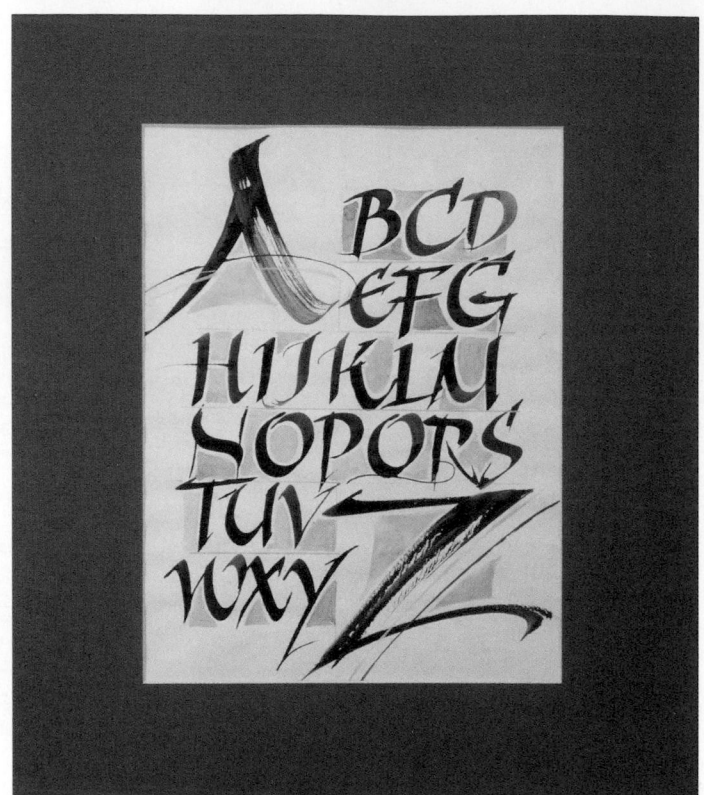

Materials

- *Layout or practice paper*
- *Dip pens: in various sizes*
- *Black or coloured inks*
- *Technical drawing ruling pen*
- *Gouache paint: ultramarine, purple lake, imitation gold*
- *Automatic pens, such as size 4 and 6*
- *Pointed brush: size 7 nylon or other springy hairs, not sable*
- *Watercolour paper*
- *Frame, if required*

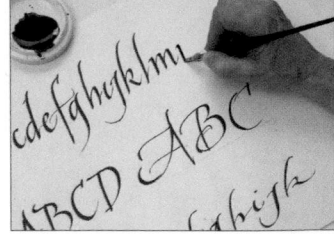

1 'Warm up' with standard Italic writing on layout paper before moving on to flourished Italic, using a standard dip pen and exploring inks that flow freely.

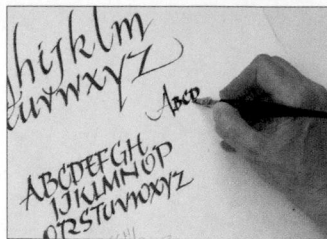

2 Try some landscape layouts, working out how many letters will fit per line to avoid awkward lengths. Explore both lower case and capitals.

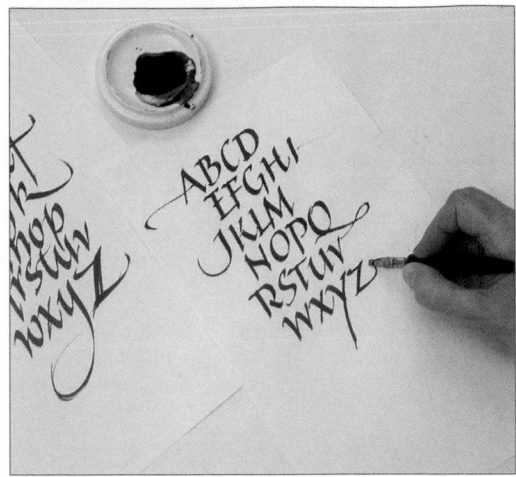

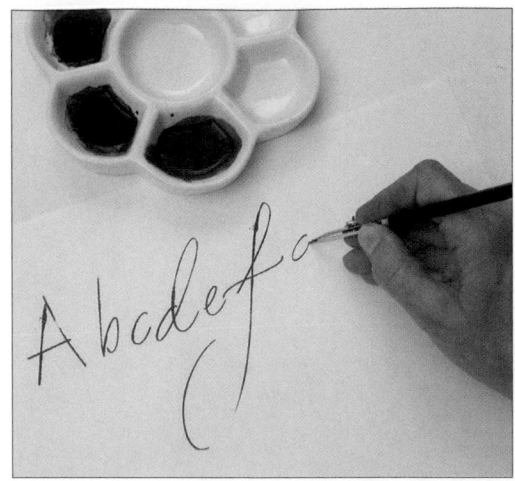

3 Experiment with portrait layouts. Again, several trials will be needed to gain an even number of letters on each line. If you already have a frame that you plan to use, consider the proportions at this stage.

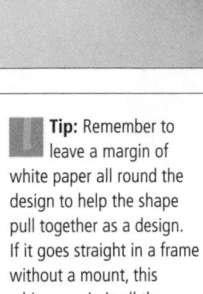

Tip: Remember to leave a margin of white paper all round the design to help the shape pull together as a design. If it goes straight in a frame without a mount, this white margin is all the more important.

4 'Loosen up' your writing by trying different tools. Investigate the properties of the ruling pen. Keep it screwed closed, and dip it generously into the ink; it will make free-flowing fine lines if held and used like a pencil.

Tip: Clean your ruling pen by unscrewing it a little and scrubbing the inside of the pen with an old toothbrush.

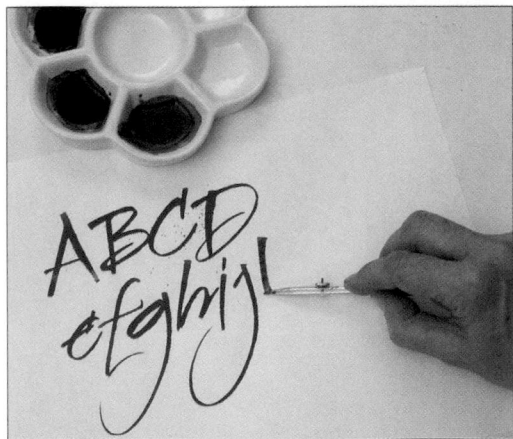

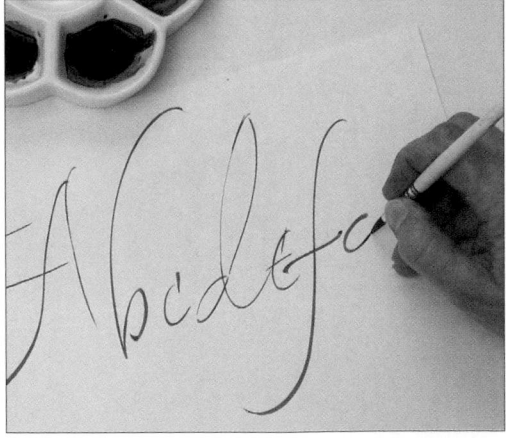

5 For bolder effects, the ruling pen needs to be held in an unconventional position, flatter to the paper, allowing more ink to escape from the side. Keep refilling and writing quickly. Creating a consistent alphabet this way will involve plenty of trial and error, and the ink or paint must be free-flowing.

6 Compare the results with the pointed brush. The brush needs to be filled, then wiped to preserve the pointed end. Hold it vertically to create fine lines; flourished lower case works well with this.

▶

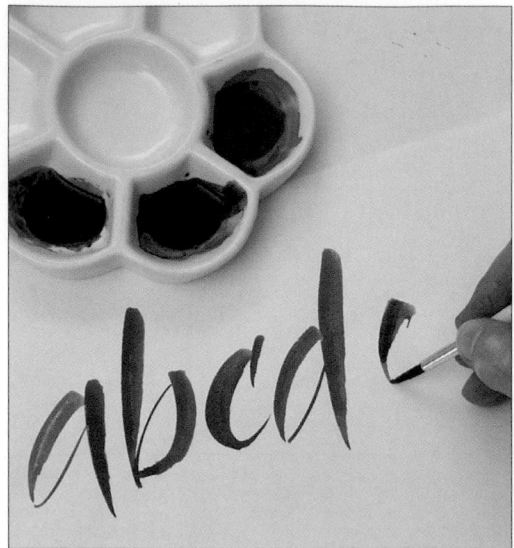

7 Hold the brush more on its side, or press more heavily, for thicker marks; this will produce a much bolder design, still with lower-case lettering. Subtlety can be obtained by combining thick lines with thin ones – in this case thick downstrokes and thin upward strokes.

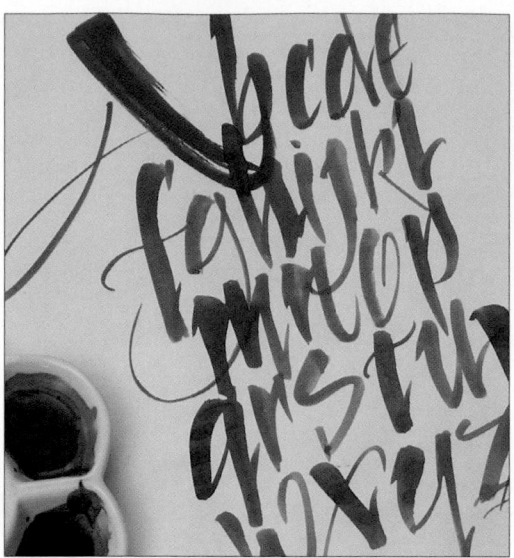

8 Try for a final design, combining a capital 'A' and lower case for the remainder. Think about the overall shape of the design, and try to keep all the letters compactly held together without gaps within the block of writing.

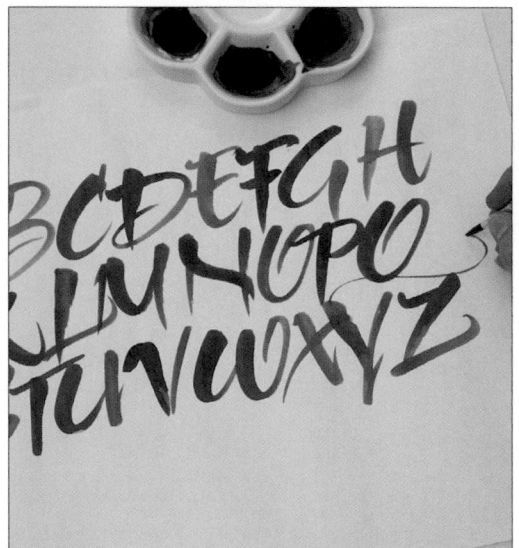

9 Develop more ideas for lettering, this time exploring how capitals can be made with this brush; try a 'landscape' design. Investigate thicks and thins with the pointed brush, trying to balance the weights as they occur, so there is an evenness of texture overall.

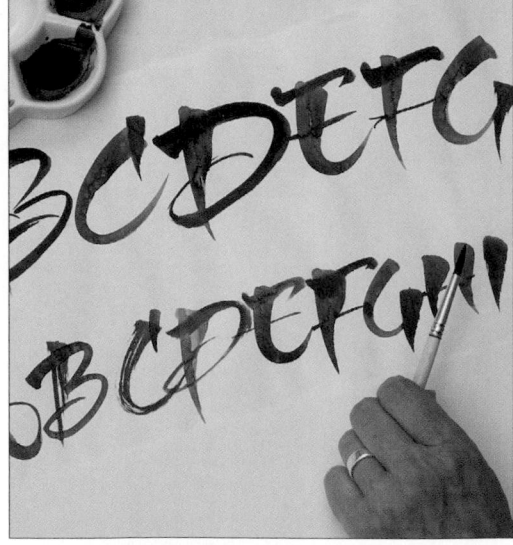

10 Try out some of the same lettering but using two colours of paint. Mix them to the same free-flowing consistency, and switch from one colour to the other for each stroke. For cleaner colours, use two brushes and alternate strokes with each brush charged with a separate colour.

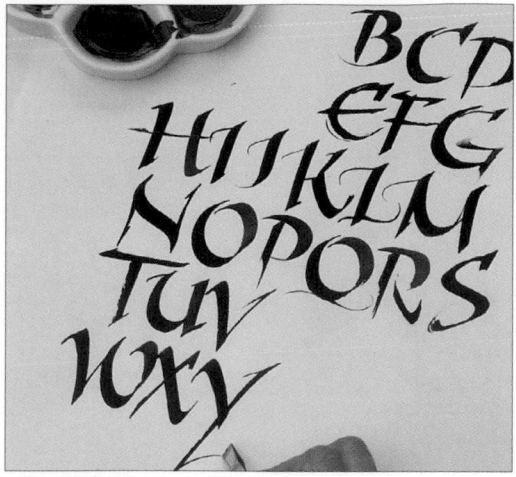

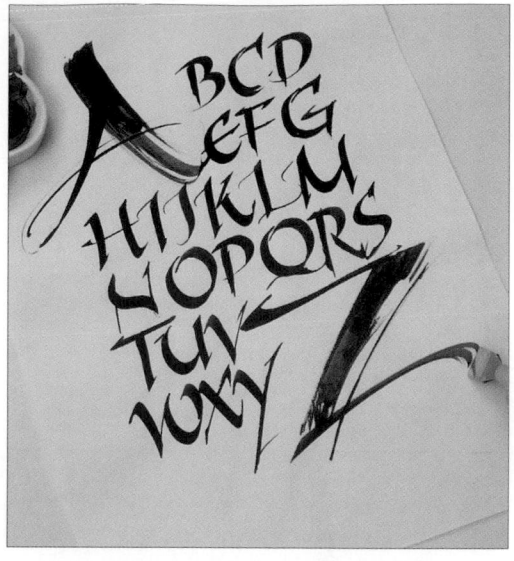

11 If you find you are not yet ready for the full freedom of the brush or ruling pen, explore large automatic pens instead; automatic pens are extremely broad pens that hold a lot of paint and flow very freely. Go back to a 'portrait' layout, and provide variety by using two sizes for contrast. Using the watercolour paper, prepare the final lettering. Roughly pencil the writing area, and write the main block of letters in blue and purple.

12 With the larger automatic pen, when the first writing is dry, add the 'A' and 'Z' (after practising on another sheet). Keep these two letters as freely written as you can, based on your trials with the brush.

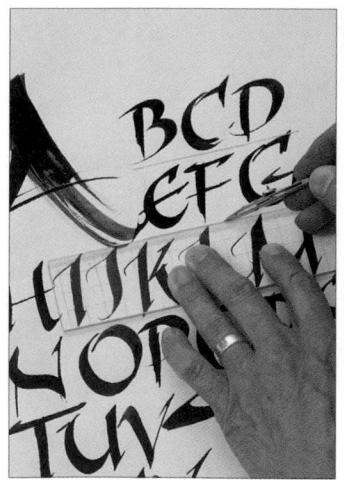

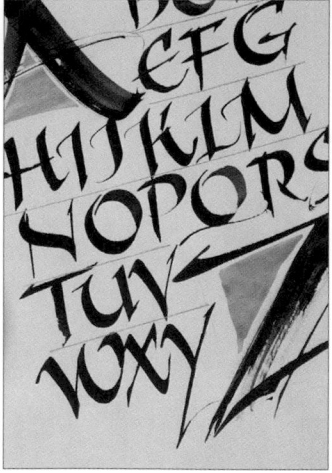

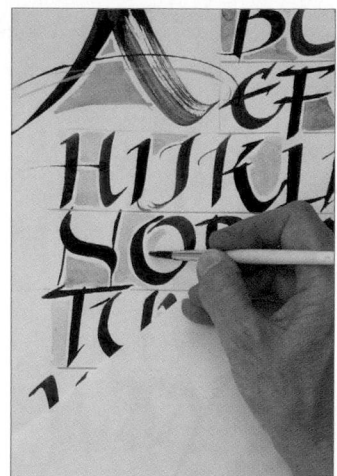

13 Use the ruling pen for its original purpose, and rule lines in gold gouache between the rows, for decorative effect.

14 Paint in the large counter spaces of the 'A' and 'Z' also with the gouache paint, using the pointed brush in the conventional way.

15 Fill in some of the counter spaces with very watery blue or purple paint, for extra decorative effect. Take care to leave a fine gap of white between the letter and the painting to prevent smudging of the writing. If you wish to display your lettering, place in a harmonious frame.

Gilded letter

The gilded lettering of medieval manuscripts is a rich visual treat. The gold appears so heavy and thick that it imbues the letters – usually stylized Versals or Lombardic letters – with an opulence that is truly remarkable. Even after hundreds of years hidden between heavy vellum pages the gleam remains, suggesting a text of importance.

The artists of today are no different from the artists of medieval times in their desire to design beautiful books and create precious artwork. The good news is that the materials are readily available and are not expensive. Decorating pages or panels of writing by adding real gold and other precious metals is immensely satisfying, and achieving stunning results need not be difficult.

A gilded calligraphic letter can be presented as a miniature work of art in its own right, as shown here, or placed as an initial to enhance a chosen word, or a paragraph of chosen text. Several letters grouped together will bring something extra special to a complete page of work. Further wonderful effects can be achieved with the addition of patterns and motifs within the design, painted with bright gouache paint.

Materials
- *Layout or practice paper*
- *Felt-tipped pens*
- *Tracing paper*
- *Hot-pressed watercolour paper*
- *HB and 2H pencils*
- *PVA (white) glue or craft glue*
- *Synthetic brushes, of various sizes*
- *Transfer gold leaf*
- *Glassine paper*
- *Agate burnisher or similar*
- *Square of silk*
- *Piece of glass*
- *Gesso (optional)*
- *Large brush*
- *Gouache paint: ultramarine, zinc white, scarlet lake, gold and permanent white*
- *Technical, fine dip or ruling pen*
- *Mount, if required*

The design
The letter that is used here is a modern Uncial 'H', which has been gilded and then decorated with gold and coloured diamonds. The letter has been painted in PVA as the medium on which to stick the gold. However, gesso can be used if you prefer. Once the gum has been laid the method of attaching the gold is the same. When the gold is polished both methods will produce a good bright shine but the gesso ground produces a slightly brighter, smoother brilliance on completion.

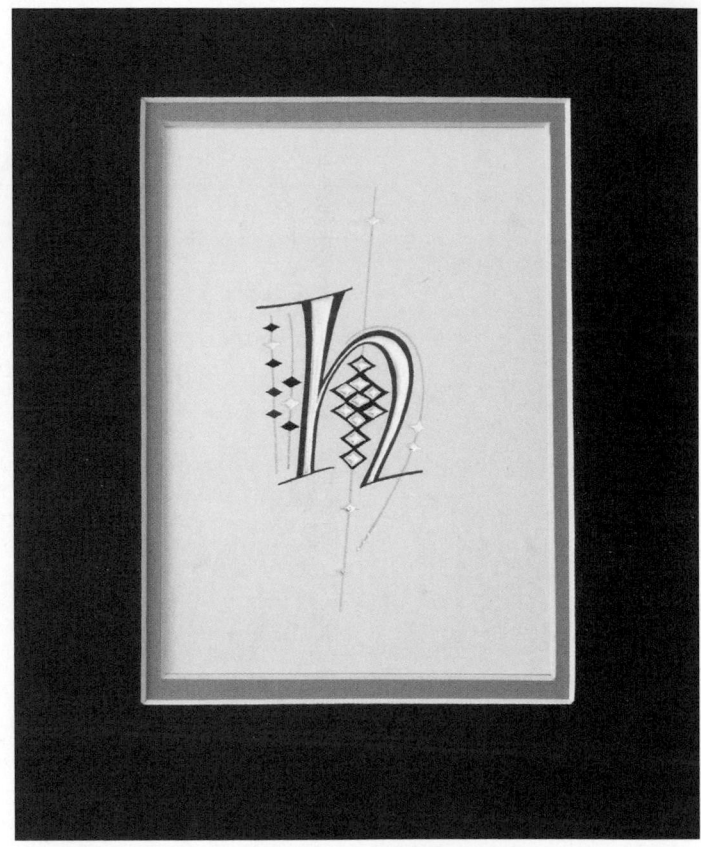

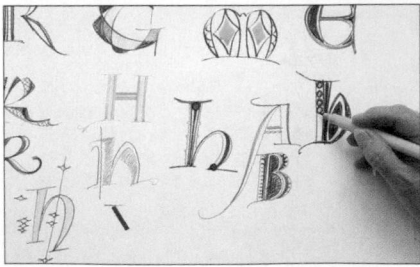

1 Design and sketch some letter shapes, adapted from Versals, Uncials or the Roman Capitals, with a felt-tipped pen or pencil. Add some simple decoration or change some of the shapes to enhance their effect. Add colour with felt-tipped pens as an aid to visualizing the finished project.

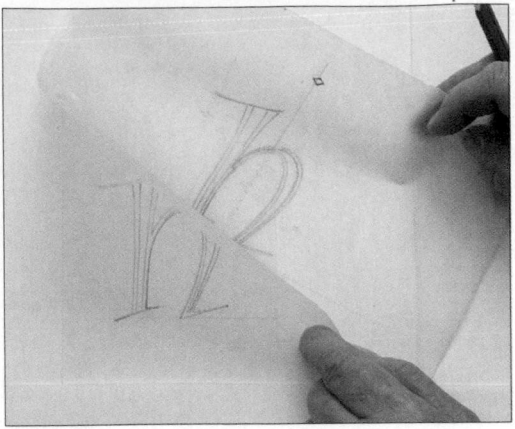

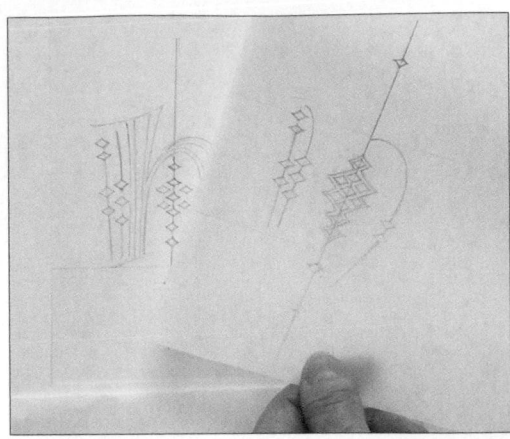

2 Choose a single letter and draw the shape onto tracing paper. Transfer the traced letter onto the watercolour paper and draw over the design with a sharp 2H pencil. The letter chosen for this project is a modern Uncial 'H'.

3 Draw some diamonds on to a separate piece of tracing paper and try the design over the letter. Add the diamond shapes around and inside the letter in a decorative way. Some of the diamonds will be painted in gold, and some in colour. Do not overdo the effect by drawing too many.

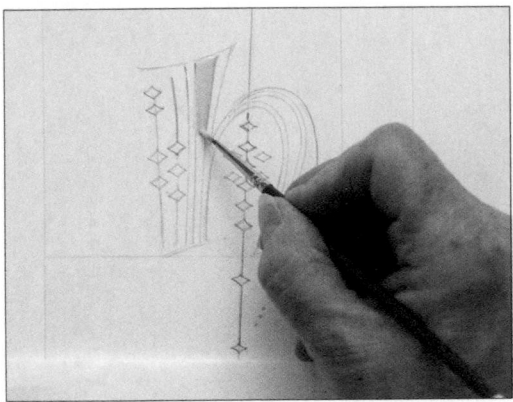

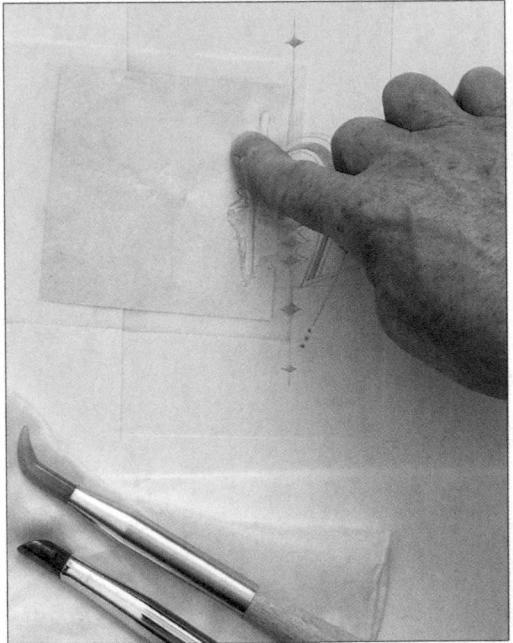

4 Paint the centre of the letter stem with PVA glue that has been coloured pink, using a synthetic 000 brush. Paint the diamonds that you plan to gild in glue, too. Leave the glue to dry, which will take 20–30 minutes, and arrange your gold leaf, glassine paper, burnisher, and a silk square close to hand. Protect your work with a paper shield, leaving only the design exposed.

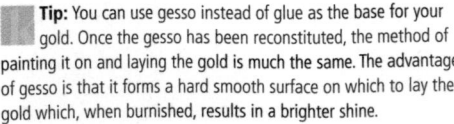
Tip: You can use gesso instead of glue as the base for your gold. Once the gesso has been reconstituted, the method of painting it on and laying the gold is much the same. The advantage of gesso is that it forms a hard smooth surface on which to lay the gold which, when burnished, results in a brighter shine.

5 Place your work on to a cold surface, ideally a piece of glass. Roll a small paper tube, about 7.5cm (3in) long. Place the tube against your mouth and breathe deeply on to the gum twice. Your warm breath will reactivate the glue and make it sticky. Quickly press the gold leaf, gold face down, on to the letter and rub it gently but firmly with your fingers.

▶

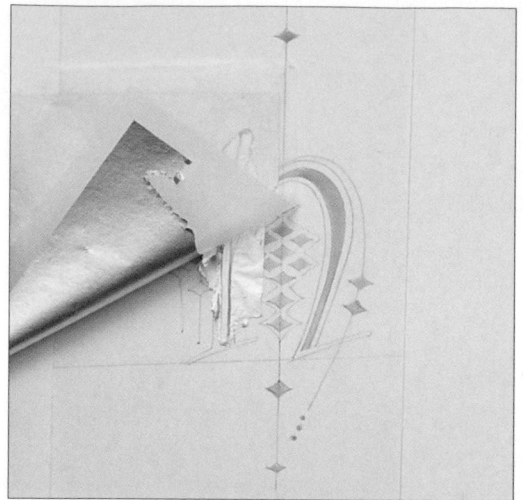

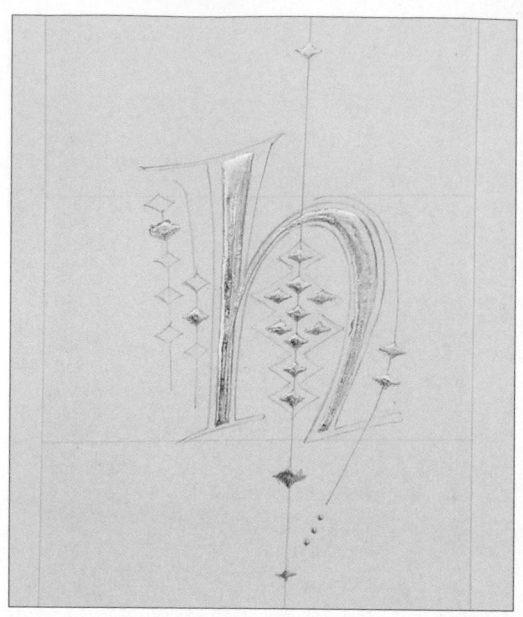

6 Lift the transfer and see how much gold has been deposited. To fill any gaps, breathe again through the tube and press the gold down firmly once more with your fingers. Repeat this process until the letter accepts the gold. When the letter is completely covered, still continue to press the transfer gold on to the letter. You no longer need to breathe on the letter beforehand, as the gold will now stick to itself.

7 The more gold that is deposited the shinier the letter will appear when burnished. Once you are satisfied with the letter, gild the diamonds in the centre of the letter and most of the diamonds around the letter.

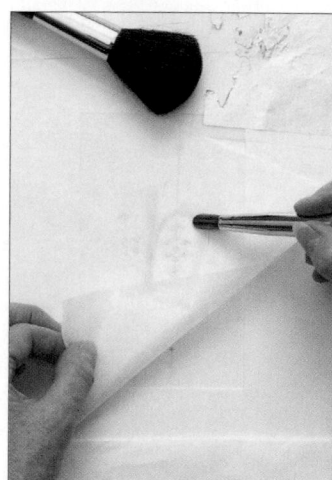

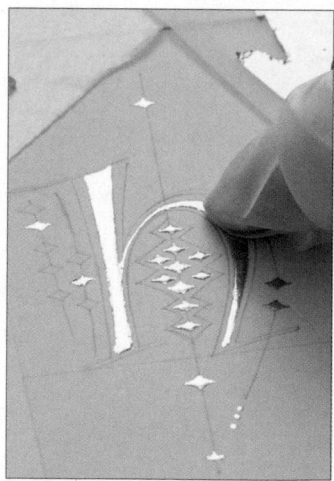

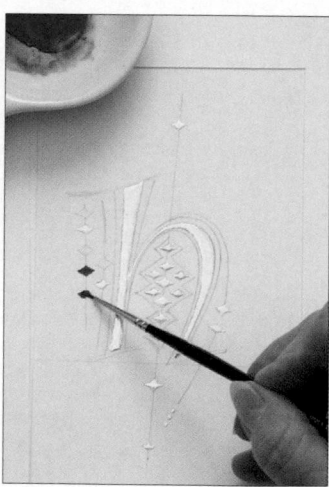

8 Brush away any excess gold with a large soft brush then use the burnisher to burnish the gold leaf through glassine paper. This will protect the gold surface. Try not to rub too hard as the gum may still be damp and the pressure will damage the gold surface.

9 Finish by burnishing direct with the burnisher. Or it can be polished gently with a piece of silk.

10 The letter is now ready to paint. Mix up some ultramarine plus a small amount of zinc white gouache paint, and paint two of the diamonds on the left of the letter in the blue.

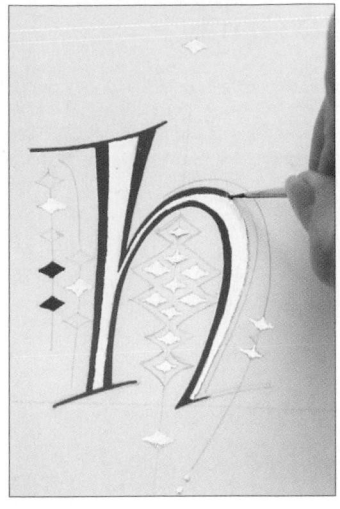

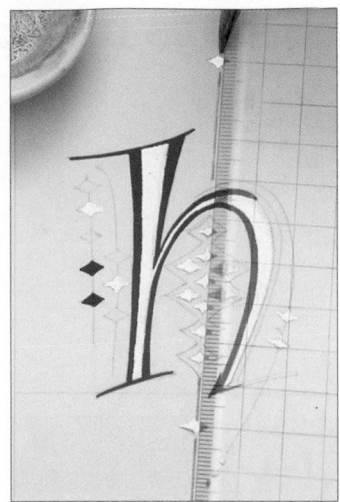

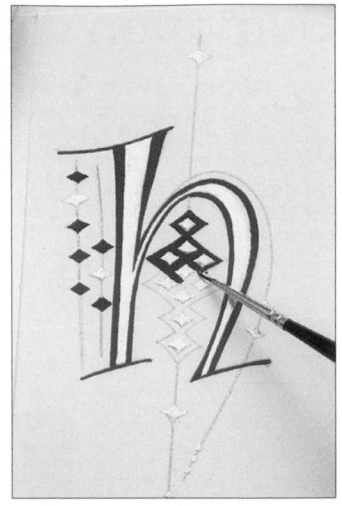

11 With the a fine brush, carefully paint a delicate blue line of colour around the letter stem.

12 Add the fine lines to the design with a ruling pen, a coloured technical pen or a fine dip pen filled with gold gouache paint.

13 Mix scarlet lake red gouache with a touch of zinc white and paint diamonds on the side of the letter and around the gold diamonds in the centre of the letter.

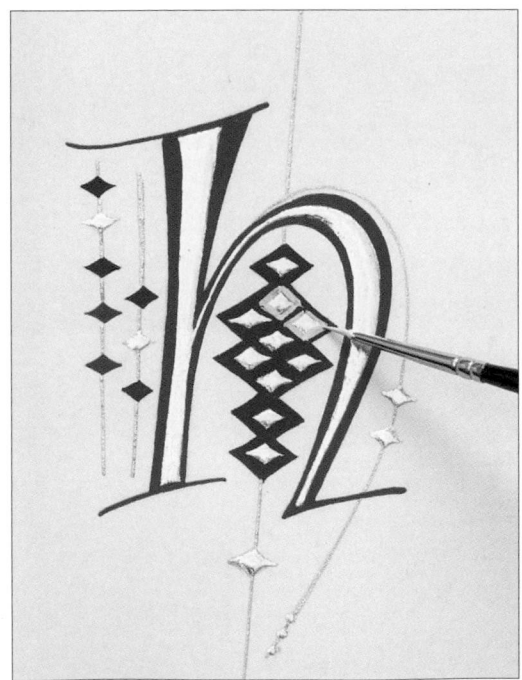

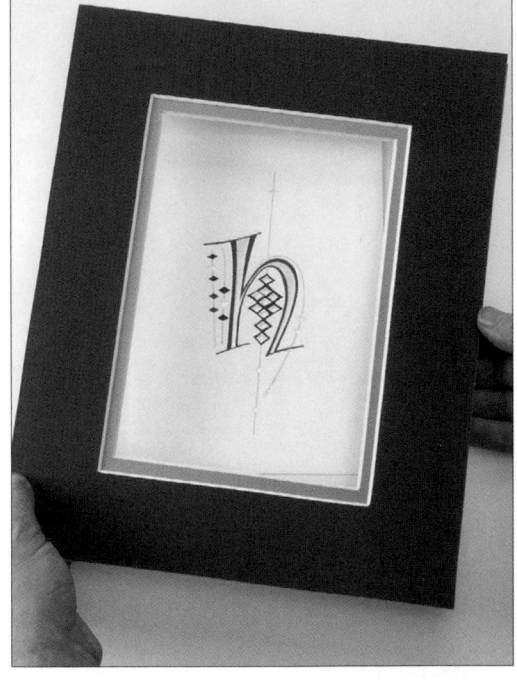

14 Finally, paint a border around the central gold diamonds in permanent white gouache.

15 Mount the finished letter. Use a complementary colour for the mount so that the whole project is harmonious.

Quotation with bronze background

Gold has always held a fascination for calligraphers and painters and it never fails to add ornamental extravagance when used in a design. In this project the background of a quotation is coloured with gold metal leaves, or schlag, which is cheaper than real gold leaf and fun to use. Schlag cannot be burnished but stays shiny, in much the same way as the gold foiling used in the card industry.

Metal leaves can be difficult to apply in small areas and you will need to use PVA glue or an acrylic medium to make them adhere to the surface. Only one layer can be used because, unlike real gold, the metal leaves will not stick to themselves. Shlag is also available in silver and copper, which you may prefer to use in place of gold. Real gold leaf is also used in small amounts in this project to give the image a slightly raised effect, adding further interest.

The design

The popular saying *'Tempus Fugit'* – 'time flies' – is the chosen quotation for this project. The design includes some coloured squares, which can be painted with a fine brush or drawn with a pen loaded with gouache paint. You may wish to add your own motifs or shapes to the project, or even extra colours. The finished piece of work can be mounted and framed, and makes a pretty gift.

Materials

- *Layout or practice paper*
- *Automatic pen or dip pen, such as William Mitchell 0 or 1 (large nib)*
- *Black ink*
- *HB and 2H pencils*
- *Hot-pressed watercolour paper*
- *Ruler*
- *PVA (white) glue or craft glue*
- *Large flat brush: 2.5cm (1in)*
- *Schlag or Dutch metal leaves in gold or bronze*
- *Glassine paper*
- *Fine-grade abrasive paper or pumice powder and cotton wool (balls)*
- *Piece of glass*
- *Transfer gold leaf*
- *Agate burnisher or similar*
- *Square of silk*
- *Gouache paints: cobalt blue, zinc white, scarlet lake and lemon yellow*
- *Synthetic brushes*
- *Mount, if required*

Tip: Before you finalize your illustration, find ways to use the gold, or other precious metals, to best effect.

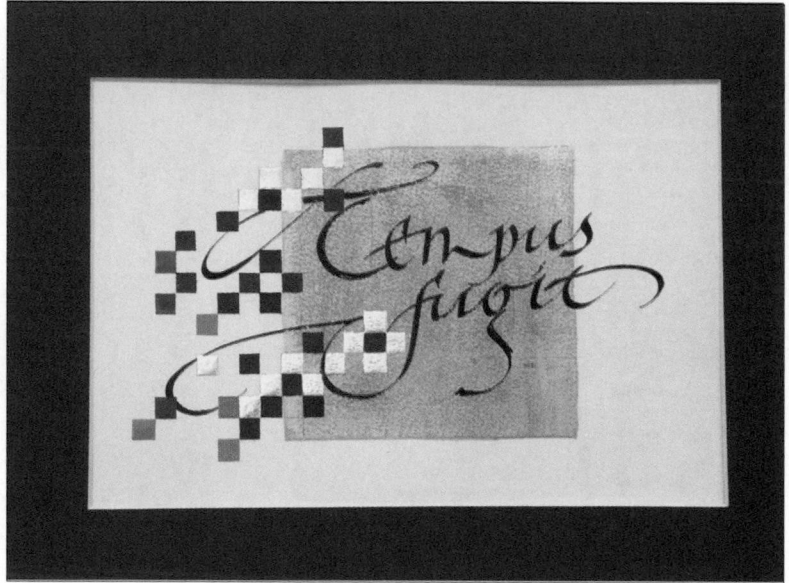

1 Create some pen design sketches on layout paper. Think about the meaning of the words you have chosen and adjust your writing style accordingly. Consider adding to your ideas with illustration, and experiment with layout and colour.

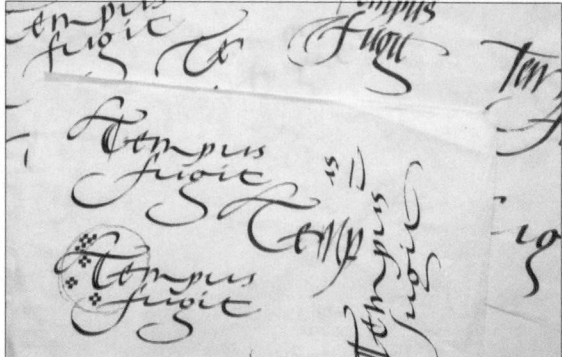

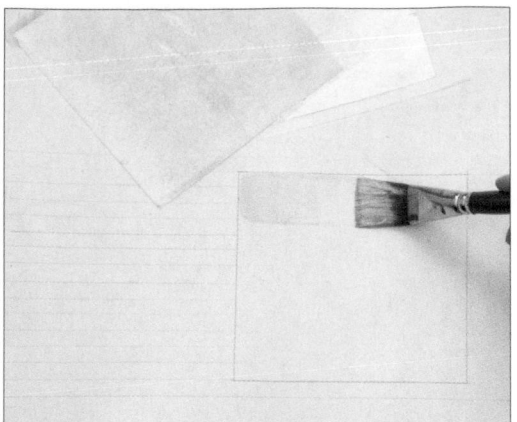

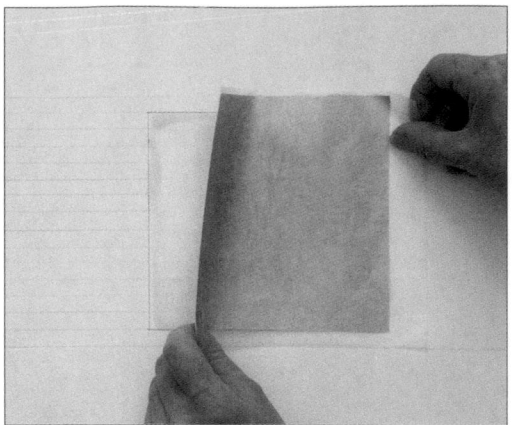

2 In pencil, draw the lines for your design on to the watercolour paper and mark a square for the PVA glue. To apply the schlag, first use a large flat brush to paint a layer of PVA glue in a square shape. Rinse the brush well in cold water after using the glue.

> **Tip:** Add a touch of red watercolour paint to the PVA glue. The addition of colour will make the glue easier to manipulate when wet and easier to see when dry. PVA glue can also be thinned with distilled water to allow finer work using a brush, or to be used in a pen.

3 Leave the glue for a few minutes, then, while still sticky, carefully place a sheet of schlag bronze or gold metal on top. Cover with glassine paper and press the metal carefully and evenly down on to the glue. Leave the bronze metal so that it can dry thoroughly. Remove the paper backing when dry.

> **Tip:** Instead of using abrasive paper you can use pumice powder or pounce. Sprinkle pumice powder on to the schlag square and, with cotton wool, lightly rub the shine away where you intend to write. This is a less abrasive way of creating a 'tooth' for the pen.

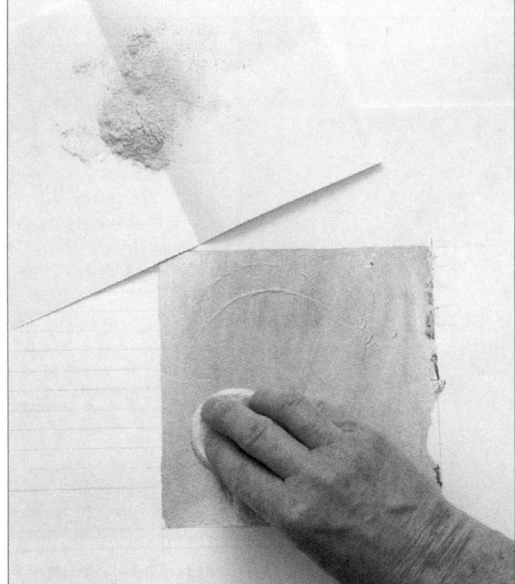

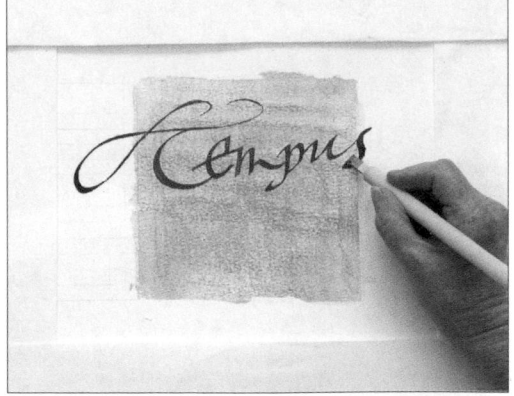

4 To create a surface with a tooth on which to write with paint or ink, slightly roughen the gold. Use fine-grade abrasive powder or pumice powder and lightly rub over the surface to lessen the shine.

5 Write out your quotation using black gouache or black calligraphy ink.

▶

Gilded zodiac sign miniature

Examine the manuscripts and scrolls of ancient times and you will find constant reference to ancient calendars and astrological charts, deriving from the widespread belief in the link between the movement and position of heavenly bodies with human activities and fortunes. These beliefs permeated to Western scholars from Egypt and Mesopotamia, and form the basis of astrology as it is practised today.

Even with limited knowledge of astrology, most people today know their 'star sign' – the Sun's apparent position on the celestial zodiac at the time of our birth. Each of the 12 signs is rich with symbolism, association and myth, which can be researched and distilled in a fascinating, gilded miniature. The illuminated illustration you create can be presented as a work in its own right, or as part of a larger project.

The design

The letter chosen for this project is modern, but based on the classical Roman Capital, which looks elegant and strong when well executed. This uncomplicated design uses a simple border of convolvulus flowers and the crab, attributed to the sign of Cancer, plus the approximate yearly dates. However, many other motifs and general characteristics attributed to this sign of the zodiac could be incorporated into your own design ideas including written calligraphic descriptions.

Materials

- *HB and 2H pencils*
- *Tracing paper and tape*
- *Layout or practice paper*
- *Hot-pressed watercolour paper*
- *Dip pens: William Mitchell 2 and 3*
- *Gouache paints or watercolour paints including: permanent white, lemon yellow, permanent green, permanent rose, cobalt deep blue, orange, caput mortuum violet*
- *Technical pen*
- *Gesso and a small jar*
- *Transfer and loose-leaf gold*
- *Glassine paper*
- *Agate burnisher or similar*
- *Small square of silk*
- *Piece of glass*
- *Large soft brush: 2.5cm (1in)*
- *Tweezers (optional)*
- *Synthetic brushes nos.1, 000, 0000*
- *Mount, if required*

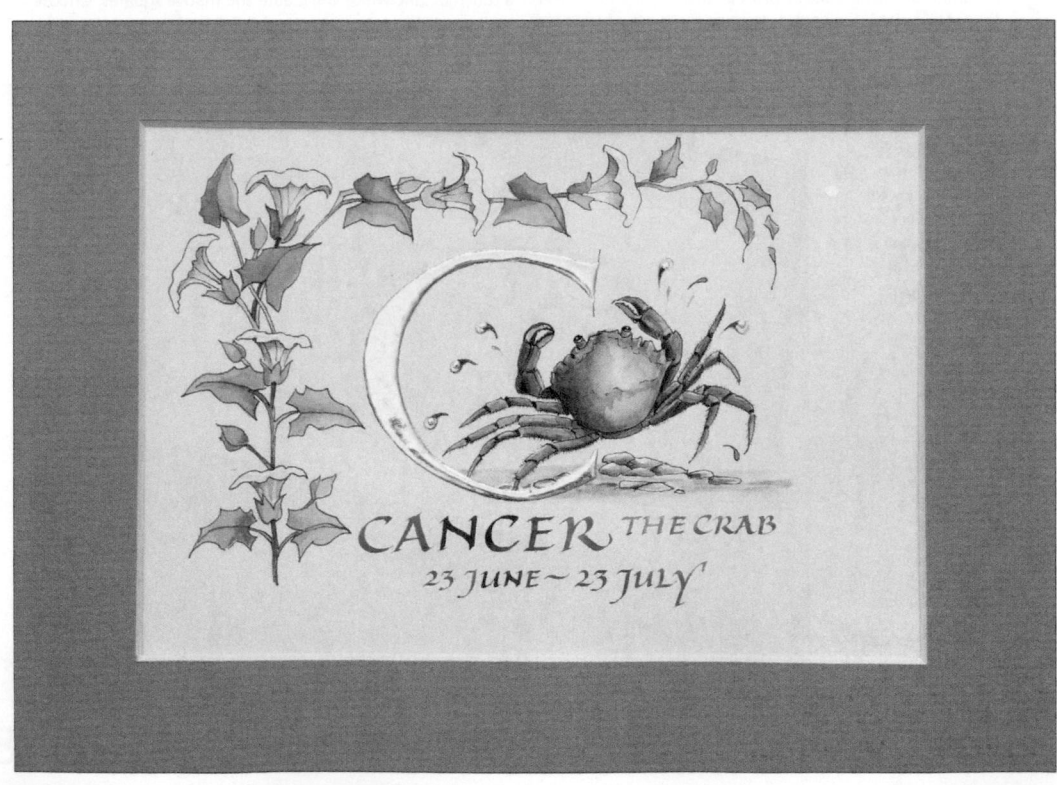

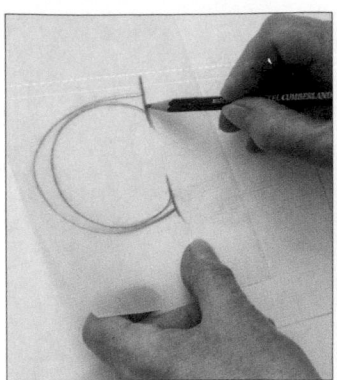

1 Draw the letter that you intend to illuminate, or gild, and paint. The letter 'C' has been chosen here. Make the letter about 5cm (2in) tall. This will allow space to illustrate inside the letter. Trace the letter.

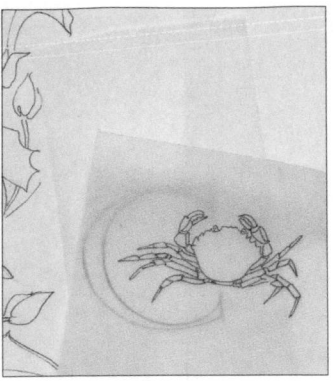

2 Do some thumbnail sketches of your designs for the illustration on layout paper. Make a tracing of the elements that you will be using in your design. Manoeuvre your chosen image – in this case, a crab – over the letter shape to see where it will look best. Trace the image and tape it into position on top of the letter.

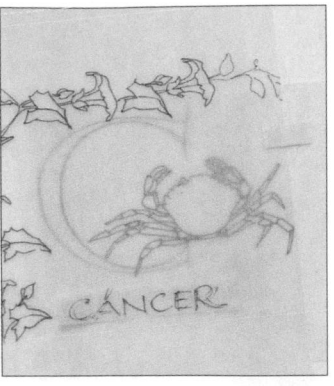

3 Trace a border design and add that to the tracing of the letter and the crab image by taping it on top. Trace the whole design on to a single sheet of tracing paper.

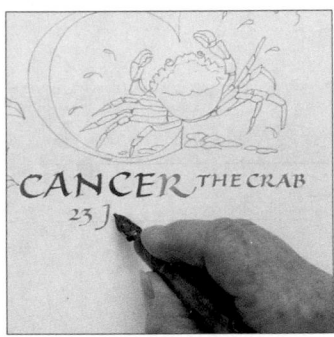

4 Trace the whole design on to watercolour paper. With a William Mitchell 3 dip pen and gouache colour mixed with water to a creamy consistency, write the zodiac sign and the dates. Use separate colours and blend them together as you write.

Tip: Leave the gesso to dry overnight. If the gesso is not completely regular, gently scrape it with a craft (utility) knife.

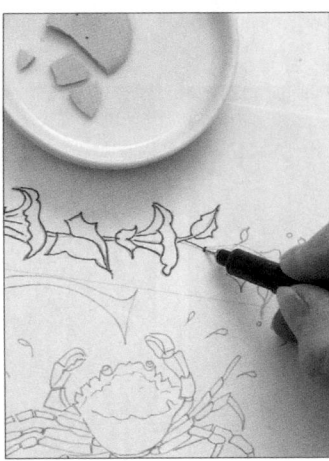

5 Draw an outline of the illustration with a black technical pen. Reconstitute the gesso by crumbling a small amount into a dish and covering it with distilled water. Cover and leave to soften to the consistency of cream.

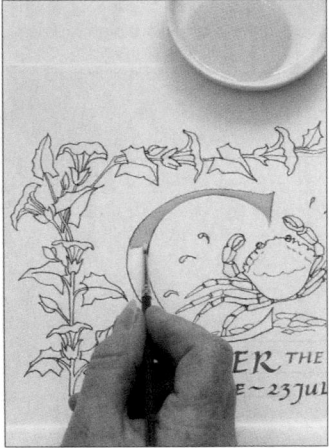

6 Apply the gesso to the letter with a synthetic no.000 brush. Load the brush with gesso and place the 'blob' on to the letter. Carefully, but quickly drag the blob along the letter stem rather than painting it as this will create grooves. Manoeuvre the gesso into the corners and avoid retouching completed areas. The surface of gesso dries quickly. Allow the gesso a few hours to dry, preferably 12 hours.

Illuminated letter

There is something magical about the richness of gold and most calligraphers will wish to try their hand at some form of gilding. The traditional method of laying gesso as a ground for gilding the letter 'Z' is used in this project. Furthermore diapering, a method often used in medieval manuscripts, is used to ornament the background of the illuminated letter. Diaper usually consists of geometric, floral or repeat motif patterns. These can range from very simple to quite complex patterns, producing very effective results.

To help locate the central point of each motif, a grid is drawn on tracing paper, and a square is then pencilled in. Dots are placed along each side of the box. Diagonal lines are used as a guide to join the dots and complete the grid.

Materials
- *Pencil*
- *Layout or practice paper*
- *Tracing paper*
- *Hot-pressed watercolour paper*
- *Ruler*
- *Gesso or PVA (white) glue*
- *Small vessel*
- *Distilled water and dropper*
- *Synthetic brushes*
- *Craft (utility) knife or scalpel*
- *Blotting paper*
- *Gold leaf (transfer, loose leaf optional)*
- *Glassine paper*
- *Burnisher*
- *Brush to remove loose gold*
- *Powdered gold or gold gouache*
- *Gouache paints: indigo blue mixed with a little ultramarine, gold*
- *Paintbrushes*
- *Pair of compasses*
- *Mount, if required*

> **Tip:** If using PVA glue instead of gesso for the gilding technique, the glue can be applied in layers, allowing 30 minutes to dry between applications. The first application will be absorbed into the paper so one or two more layers will be needed to build up the ground.

The design
An elegant letter 'Z' adapted from Roman Capitals is used in this project. It is enclosed in a gold-edged painted border with a dark blue background. On this background the medieval method of diapering creates little motifs painted in gold.

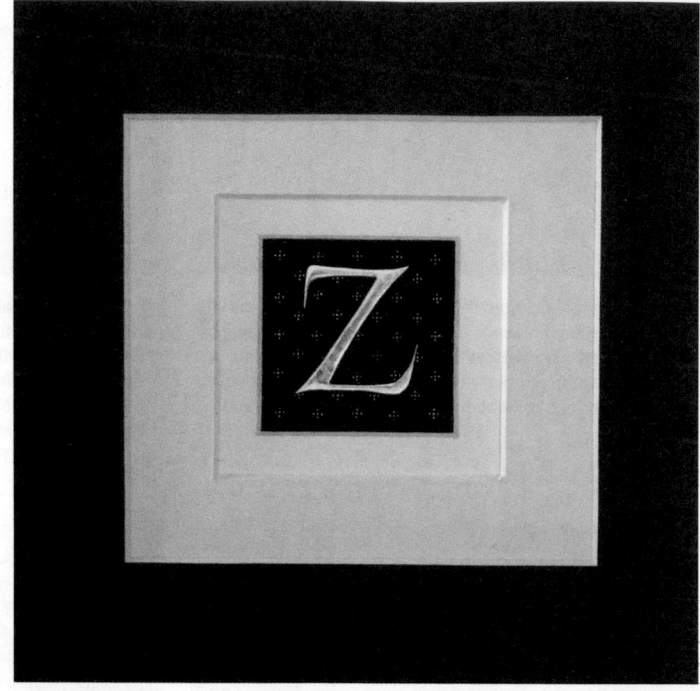

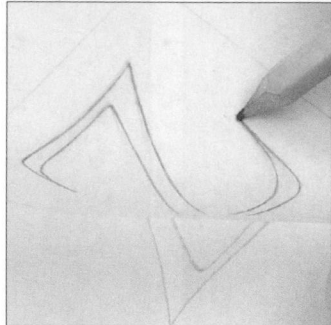

1 Sketch your letter on some layout paper. Versals or Roman Capitals are a good basis from which you can adapt your letter. Trace down the letter design on to watercolour paper.

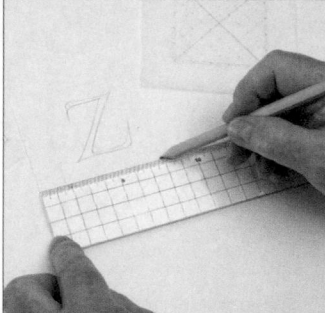

2 Draw a traced grid and mark up the dots that will create a decoration later. Draw an inner box 6cm x 6cm (2¹/₂in x 2¹/₂in) around the letter. Draw an outer box 1.5mm (¹/₁₆in) from the inner box to make a 'frame'.

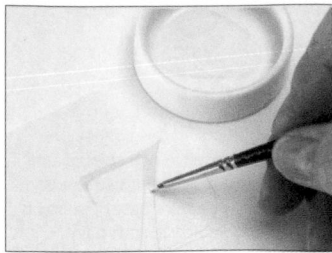

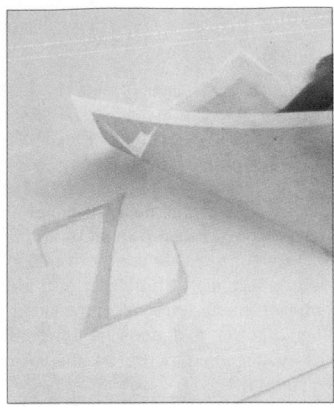

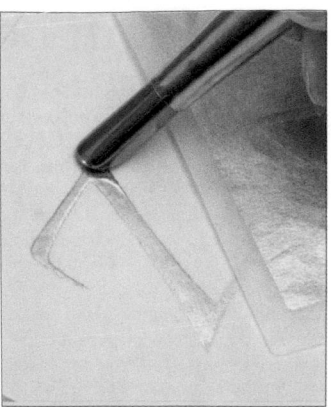

3 Reconstitute the gesso by breaking a cake of gesso into tiny pieces. Use a dropper and cover the gesso with two drops of distilled water and leave to soak for an hour. Stir very gently, avoiding creating any air bubbles, and if necessary add one or two more drops of distilled water until it is the consistency of thin cream. Apply the gesso by loading the brush and teasing the gesso into place with the tip of the brush, creating a nicely domed shape. Once the gesso has dried, any irregularities can be gently scraped away with a curved blade and burnished to a smooth surface.

4 Make a paper tube out of blotting paper and breathe on to the gesso to reactivate the glue and make the gesso sticky. Apply the transfer gold and press down firmly. Repeat the process until all the area is covered with gold. Leave the gesso to re-harden.

5 Burnish the gold leaf first through glassine paper and then directly on to the gold. For extra brilliance, a layer of loose-leaf gold can be applied and burnished.

> **Tip:** To remove air bubbles from liquid gesso, add one drop of water but do not stir. The bubbles will disperse to the side of the vessel and can be gently removed with blotting paper.

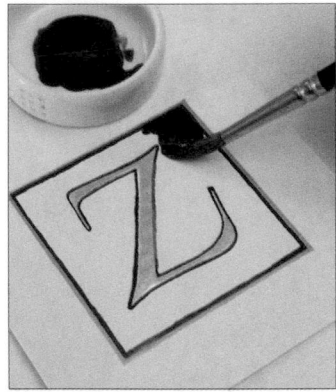

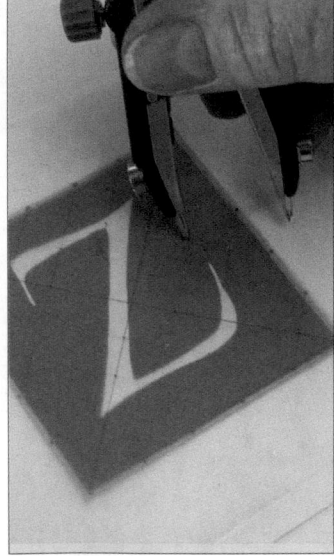

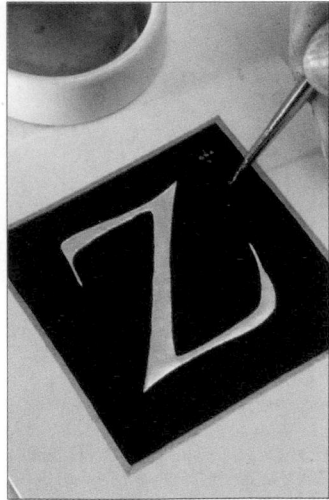

6 Paint the 'frame' with powdered gold or gold gouache. Mix up some indigo blue gouache and add a little ultramarine. Outline the letter, taking care not to get any paint over the gold, and also paint an outline inside the gold frame. Now load the brush with paint and fill in the background. Do not let any edges dry but keep adding more 'wet-into-wet' until the background is completed. The paint will then dry flat and even in colour.

7 When the blue paint has completely dried, place the tracing grid over the work aligning the sides of the box. Use the point of a compass to mark each intersection.

8 To diaper the background, place a little dot of gold on to each of the prick marks and encircle each dot with four little dots. If necessary, tidy up the gold frame with another layer of gold. The letter can be framed if required.

Fan book

Books can take many forms and in this example the shape of a fan has been chosen to send a message of love. During the 18th century, young people would convey messages to each other just by the way they held their fans so the shape seems a very suitable choice for this project and is stunning to look at. Making the fan requires accurate measuring, folding and cutting. The fan book was originally designed to stand next to a wedding cake but can, of course, be used to mark many other celebratory occasions. The ribbons flowing from its base should be velvet, satin, or silk, and form an integral part of this calligraphic *tour de force*.

This is a complicated book. Before attempting a finished fan, experiment first with layout paper until you are comfortable with the construction.

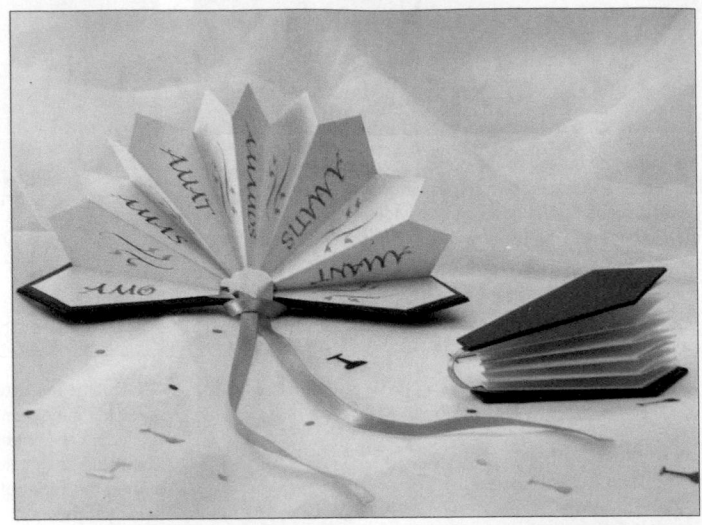

The design

The basic shape is a circle with lines of blue writing and flourishing radiating out like the spokes of a wheel. If used for a wedding the colour can echo that chosen for the wedding theme. The text – *amo, amas, amat, amamus, amatis, amant* – is the Latin verb 'to love', and is written in Italic based Free Capitals. The words are separated by flourishes embellished with gold.

Materials

- *Pair of compasses*
- *Hot-pressed watercolour paper*
- *Pencil*
- *Ruler with cutting edge*
- *Pens*
- *Gouache paints: ultramarine and gold*
- *Dip pen, such as William Mitchell 5 (fine nib)*
- *Eraser*
- *Bone folder*
- *Self-healing cutting mat*
- *Craft (utility) knife*
- *Scissors*
- *Card (stock) or mounting (mat) board*
- *Decorative paper*
- *Scrap paper (preferably shiny)*
- *Glue stick*
- *Ribbons: at least 1m (1yd)*

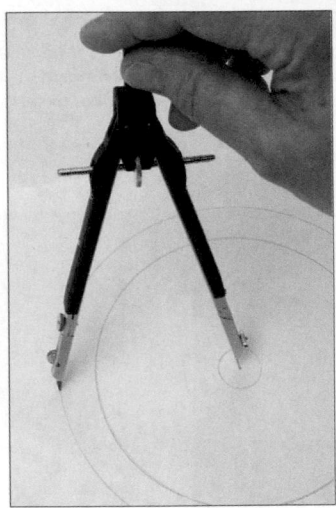

1 Using a pair of compasses, draw three concentric circles on the watercolour paper – the first one quite small, the second the diameter of the fan, and the third just a little larger, which will be cut away during the book's construction.

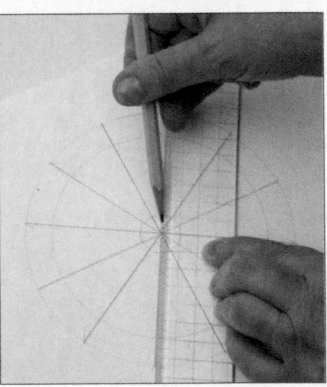

2 Divide the circles into 12. To do this, apply the rule that the radius of a circle can be stepped around its circumference six times. First draw two lines of diameter across the circles at right angles to each other. Open out the pair of compasses to the radius of the largest circle. Place the point at the end of one diameter, swing in a semi-circle, marking off where the pencil intersects the circumference. Do the same at the other end of this diameter and at the two ends of the other diameter. Draw radii from these marks to the centre of the circles. You should now have 12 segments.

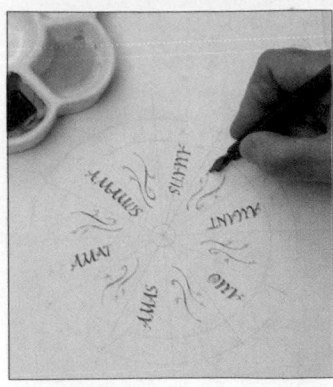

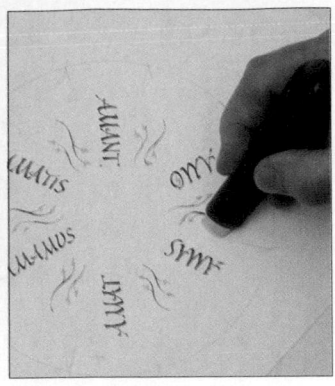

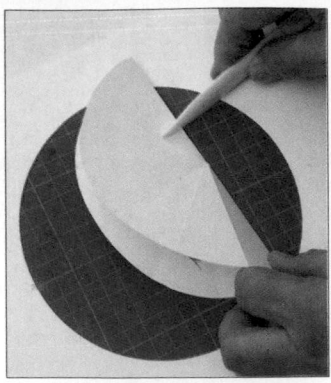

3 Rule up alternative segments and write out the Latin verb *amo*. With a finer pen, draw a flourish in the adjacent sections and decorate with pen-drawn hearts.

4 Erase the ruling up and the construction lines between the inner and outer circles. If these are erased later the fan may be damaged. Cut around the outer circle.

5 Using a bone folder, fold the circle into the 12 segments. Each time you fold the circle in half, the segments on the outer circles must meet.

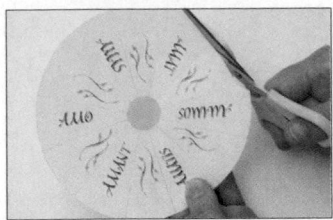

6 Cut away both the inner and outer circles (the latter was needed only to aid the folding process).

Tip: Avoid erasing over metallic gouache. The mica filaments can easily be dislodged. Cut your eraser into small pieces so that you can get between the writing and design without going across the top.

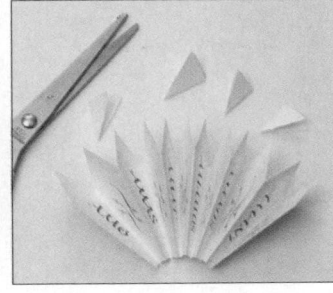

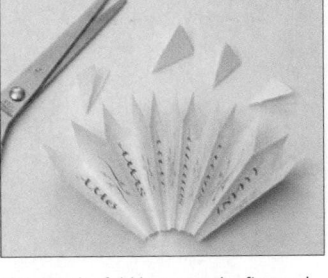

7 Cut the fold between the first and last segments and fold the fan accordian-style, in a valley–mountain–valley sequence. Use a sharp pair of scissors to cut off the pointed tops.

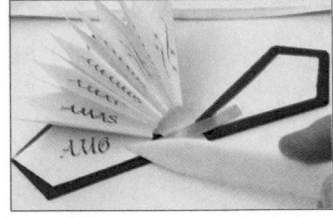

10 Apply glue to the reverse of the first section of the fan. Throw away the messy waste paper and attach the section to the reverse of the front board. Repeat these steps for the back section and board. Leave to dry under weights. Attach long ribbons to the ribbon loop – the longer and more extravagant the ribbons, the better.

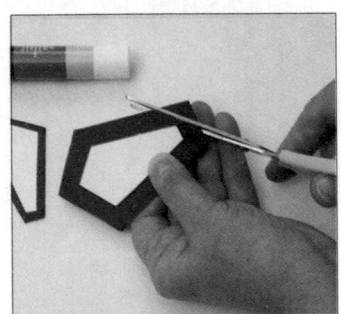

8 Measure an outside segment and cut two pieces of mounting board into the same shape but slightly larger all round. Then cut two pieces of the decorative paper the same shape but 1.5cm (3/4in) larger than the board all round. Cover the boards by gluing on the decorative paper.

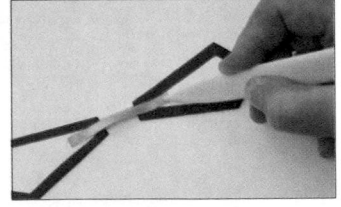

9 Cut a short length of ribbon and attach this to the 'wrong' side and lower ends of the board. Press down with the bone folder. If the decorative paper is very thick, or the fan paper very thin, line the inside of the board.

Tip: Slide scrap paper between the folds of your text block to protect it and glue the front section.

Simple gallery book

Gallery books are a new type of book used by artists to display their work. By the action of folding and cutting the book appears to be a miniature art gallery with separate wings to display each illustration.

While gallery books are undoubtedly beautiful they involve making a 16-section accordian-style design and require an very long piece of paper. The variation shown here allows for fewer display panels but is simpler to construct, while retaining the impact of the original gallery book design.

This project involves an eight-section book. Cutting and gluing four specific sections together and cutting two other sections into horizontal thirds produces a simplified but still stunning gallery book that reflects a medieval diptych – the double-folding panels used as an altar or to carry a pair of religious pictures.

Even though this is meant to be a 'simple' gallery book, it is still complicated. Try a mock-up first using layout paper. Do not worry about the writing at this stage; just make pencil marks to show where the calligraphy or decoration will be.

Materials
- *Hot-pressed watercolour paper*
- *Pencil*
- *Gouache*
- *Ruler*
- *Two pens of contrasting sizes, such as Brause 2mm (5/64in) and Brause 1mm (3/64in)*
- *Scissors or craft (utility) knife*
- *Scrap paper (preferably shiny)*
- *Glue stick*
- *Weights*

The design
Gallery books are intended to be eye-catching and this version is enhanced by the use of elegant small Roman Capitals for the body text, contrasting with large Uncial display letters. Two sizes of pen are needed to achieve the desired effect. In this project Brause 2mm (5/64in) and 1mm (3/64in) nibs are used.

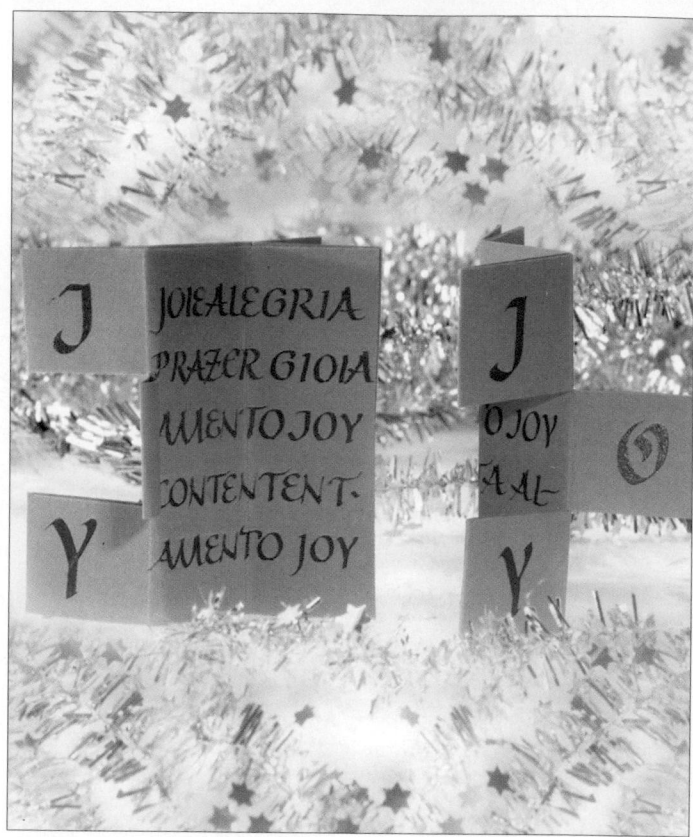

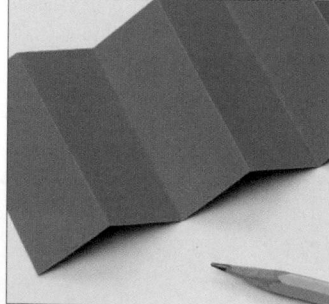

1 Using the watercolour paper prepare a long rectangular shape. Fold eight equally sized sections into an accordian-style concertina. Using a pencil, number the sections 1 to 8 on the front and 8 to 1 on the reverse.

> **Tip:** A soapstone pencil is ideal for numbering and ruling up on dark backgrounds.

> **Tip:** This example uses three display panels, but the design works well with four panels or more.

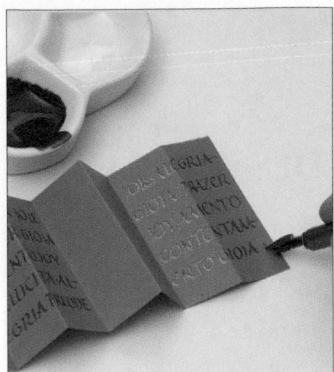

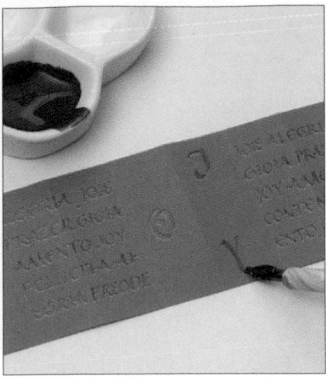

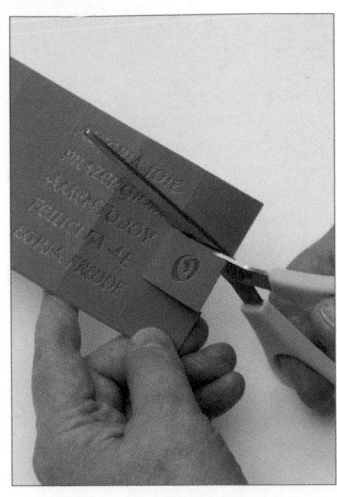

2 With the front facing you, rule up and write on sections 3 and 4 and 7 and 8 all the words you can find, in every language you can find, for 'Joy'. If you cannot find many, just keep repeating the ones you have, or use a quotation with the word 'joy' prominent within it. The writing can be vertical or horizontal. Leave it to dry before erasing your ruling lines.

3 Measuring down from the head to the tail of the concertina, divide sections 5 and 6 into thirds and write the individual letters that form your words for 'joy' using the larger pen, on alternating panels. You will achieve a better contrast if your chosen script differs from the one used for the smaller writing.

4 Carefully cut panels 5 and 6 into thirds horizontally using scissors or a craft knife.

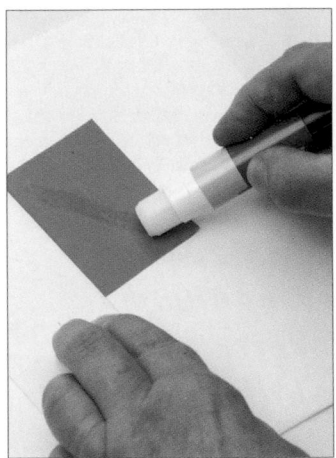

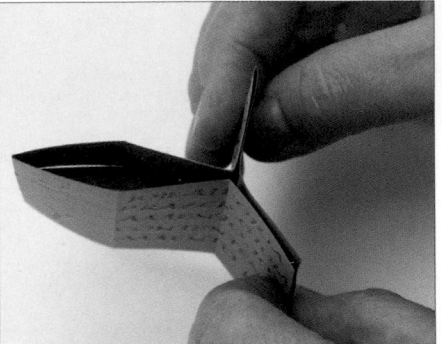

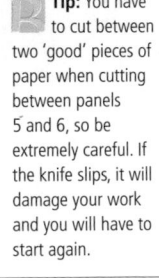

Tip: You have to cut between two 'good' pieces of paper when cutting between panels 5 and 6, so be extremely careful. If the knife slips, it will damage your work and you will have to start again.

5 Turn the book over and lay it face down on to a piece of scrap paper. Carefully glue sections 1 and 2, having first covered the other sections with scrap paper for protection. Throw away the scrap paper.

6 It is easier to complete the next step with the book held in your hands, rather than lying it flat. With the reverse side facing you, pinch together sections 2 and 3, gluing them together. Then bring the reverse of section 8 to the reverse of section 1 and glue these together. Sections 4 to 7 should now be touching back to back. Carefully bone down the two glued sections and leave to dry overnight. Put separate weights – books are ideal – on each of these sections, with the unglued 'tongue' standing up between them.

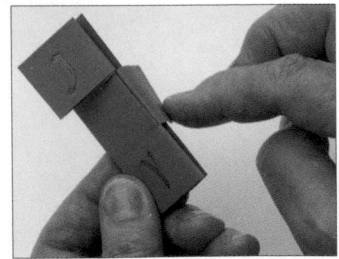

7 When the glue is completely dry, fold the resulting covers around the text, allowing the three display panels to enfold the whole book.

Certificate using digital calligraphy

Many calligraphers who are recognizing the potential of computer graphics are investigating the possibility of converting their hand-rendered script into a digital alphabet that can be used in the same way as a font in word processing, page makeup or graphics applications. This project demonstrates the possibilities through a relatively simple task of adding names of recipients to pre-printed certificates. This is one of the most frequent jobs that calligraphers are asked to undertake but it can also be one of the most tedious when a large number is involved. Imagine how simple it could be if the names were simply typed and then appeared as calligraphy on the documents.

Ideally this project requires the use of specialist font design software such as Fontographer™ or FontLab™. There is an alternative, although more cumbersome way, of adding names using your own digitized calligraphy. This project covers both approaches in the steps using a unique one-off presentation certificate as as an example. However, the method could equally apply to the addition of names to several documents.

Materials
- Dip pen in various sizes
- Black ink
- Practice or layout paper
- Good quality thin card (stock)
- Font design software such as Macromedia Fontographer or FontLab (recommended)
- Word processing or graphics software (e.g. Adobe Photoshop or CorelDRAW)
- Scanner
- Inkjet or laser printer

Tip: You will need a good working knowledge of the software used before attempting this project.

L'ASSOCIATION DES ARTISANS

Présenté à
Jean-Baptiste Boileau
à l'occasion de
son quatre-vingtième anniversaire
en reconnaissance de
sa contribution à
L'Association des Artisans
22 Avril 2005

L'ASSOCIATION DES ARTISANS

Présenté à

à l'occasion de
son quatre-vingtième anniversaire
en reconnaissance de
sa contribution à
L'Association des Artisans

---

1 Take note of the size of the certificate to which the names are to be added and the typeface or lettering used on it. This example is a small landscape format and the typeface is formal and elegant. Decide on a script form that will complement or contrast with it. In this case it would be best to use a contrasting letterform.

2 Using the largest size nib that you have, write the letters of the alphabet, capitals and lower-case, numerals and punctuation in black ink on good, smooth paper. They can be written in any order and you may wish to write each letter several times so that you can choose the best ones.

oqoonnnmmau
dgcccebbpp
hillfjkkrrs
tvwxyzz
AABCDEEFGH
IIIJKKLMMNOP
QQRSTUU
VWWXXYZL..
0123456789O

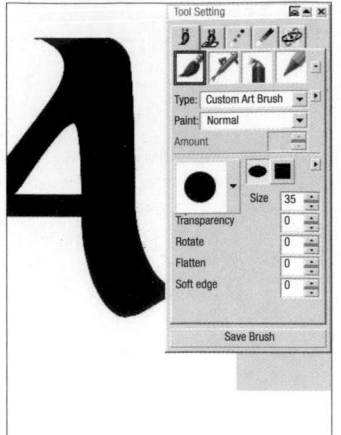

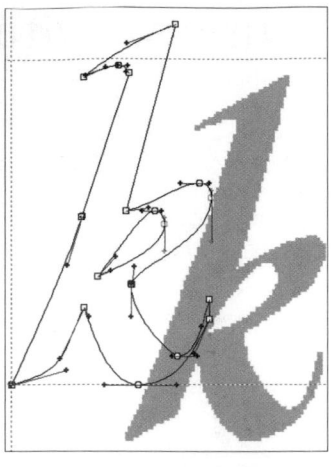

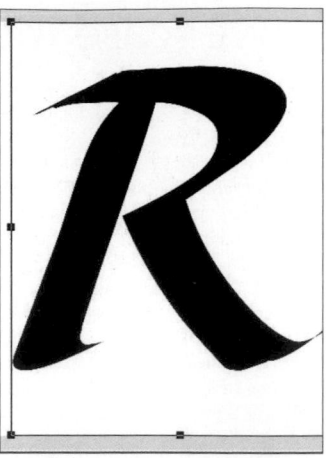

3 Scan the lettering at high resolution (at least 600dpi). Transfer it to your graphics software. Select the best examples of the letters, numerals and punctuation and make any corrections or modifications to them that you think are necessary. Make sure that the background is pure white. Save each letter as a separate file.

4 Option 1: If you are using font design software, import the first letter into your font design software. Your software will have a tracing facility that creates a vector outline of the letter. Trace the letters and make any further modifications to the form that you think are necessary. Import all the other characters in turn. Adjust the spacing parameters, known as tracking, and save the full set as a font.

5 Option 2: If you are using graphics software, import each lettering in turn and crop the 'paper size' or 'canvas' so that there is little or no margin on the right or left of the letter. This is so that the letters that need it can be placed physically close to each other when you are adjusting the letter spacing. Save the modified images of the letters.

> **Tip:** If you want to retain a true calligraphic look and keep the individuality of your own script, do not make too many changes to your scanned letters whichever way they were formed.

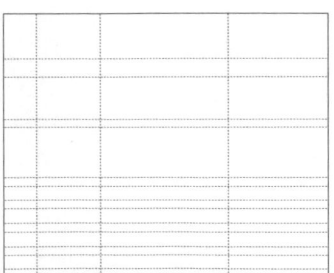

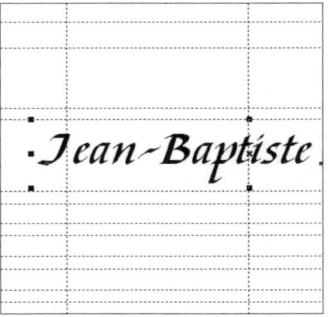

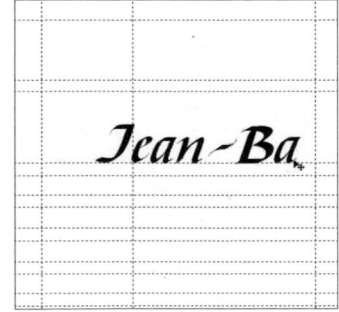

6 Measure the positions of the typography on the printed certificate. Measure both the vertical locations and the margins of each text line. Use the graphics software to set the page dimensions to the same size as the certificate. Drag or draw guides to the positions of the text and margins.

7 Option 1: If you used font design software to create a font from the script, type the name to be added to the certificate. Adjust the size either by changing the font size or by resizing the lettering if your software permits. Drag the name into the position on the certificate where you want it to print. Repeat the same procedure for the date, if needed. Feed the pre-printed certificate into the printer and print the name.

8 Option 2: If you did not use font design software, drag guides to the location on the certificate where you want the name to be. Open a copy of each letter required and place it in the correct position. Adjust the letter spacing and the size. Make any final adjustments to the position of the name by dragging the group of letters. Repeat the same procedure for the date, if needed. Feed the pre-printed certificate into the printer and print the name.

Jewel case insert using digital calligraphy

The use of digital calligraphy with type opens up all sorts of possibilities for creative work. Designers use computer graphics to design logos based on modified typefaces that are then used with typeset text. This project has only a short amount of text – but you can extend this, if you wish, or use a more complex layout. The project involves designing a jewel case for a CD or DVD. You will need to select a typeface that either complements or contrasts with the free lettering. The project also utilizes vector graphics to create a flourish or flourishes in the title words.

Materials

- CD or DVD jewel case
- Layout or practice paper
- Graphics software with vector drawing facilities (especially Adobe Illustrator and CorelDRAW)
- Graphics tablet and digital pen (optional)
- Inkjet paper
- Scalpel or craft (utility) knife
- Metal ruler and cutting mat

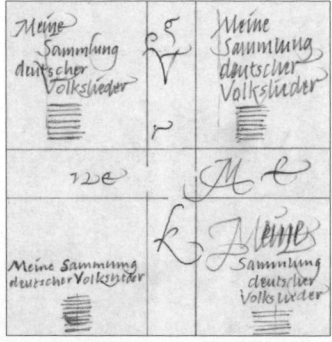

1 Choose one of your CDs or DVDs to make a jewel case insert for. If it is one of your own collections of images, music or videos decide on an appropriate title for the insert. Have the accompanying text ready. This can be a contents list, or it may be a paragraph or two about the CD or DVD. At this stage do not be concerned about how the text will be arranged.

2 A CD insert measures 12.2cm x 12.2cm (4³⁄₄in x 4³⁄₄in). A jewel case requires a folded sheet to create a front and back so the overall size will be 24cm x 12.2cm (9¹⁄₂in x 4³⁄₄in). To begin with, design the front only. Prepare some thumbnail sketches on layout paper using the title and, if you wish, the text. Do not feel you are bound by the initial idea you select.

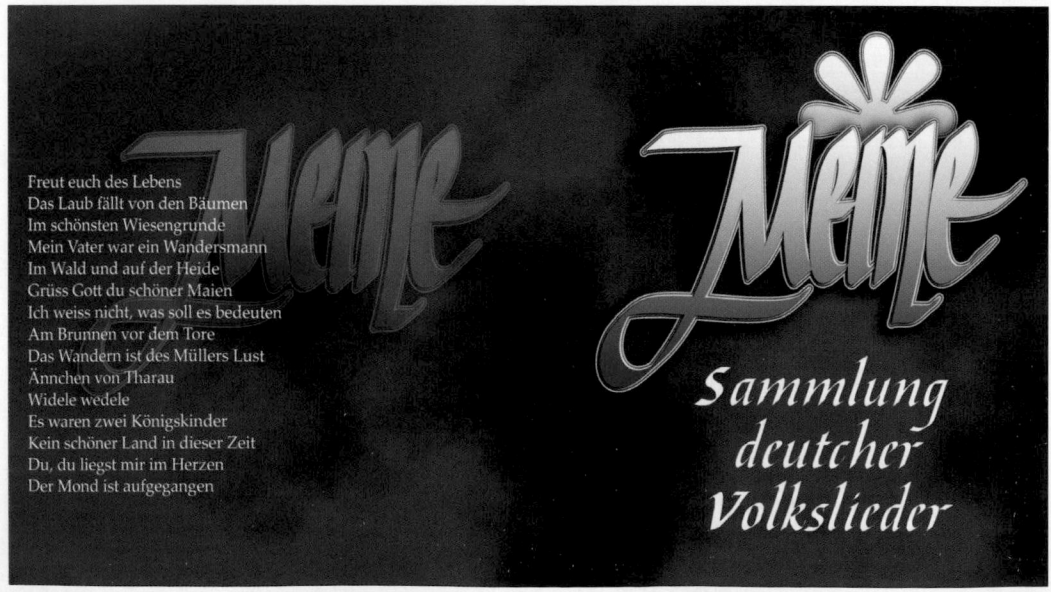

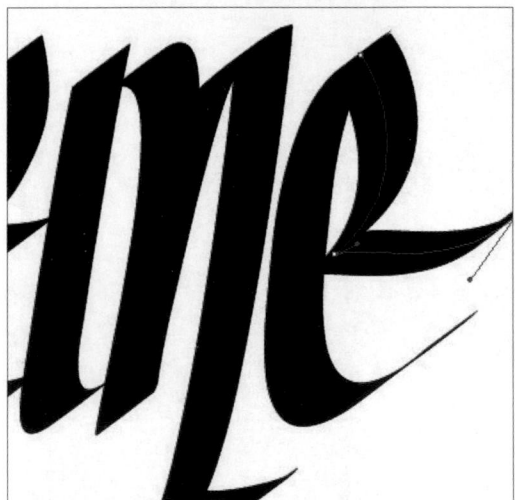

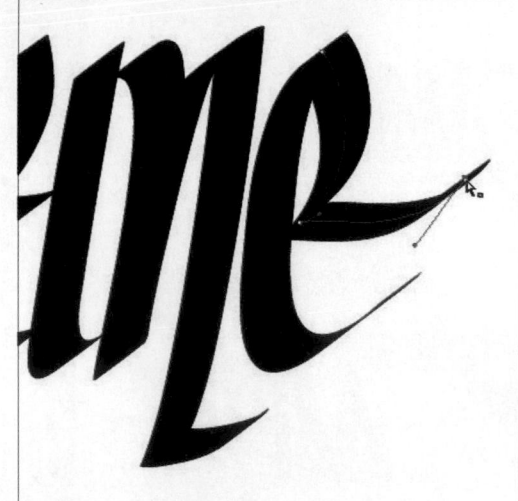

3 Experiment with ideas on the computer for the title lettering using the mouse or a digital pen if you have one. Write very freely. You can write the whole title or selected words. Try varying the line thickness and pen angle to get different effects. Change the height to width proportions until you get a design you would like to use.

4 Modify the lettering using vectors. If you do not have software that lets you do this you will have to miss out this step. To begin with, adjust any parts of the lettering that need adjustment such as the basic forms of the letters or letter spacing. Extend an appropriate part of a letter, a terminal 'e', for example, by dragging it with the selection tool.

Tip: If your software does not have the facility to use vector graphics you can still work through the project but without creating the flourishes on the letters. Some software lets you manipulate text blocks with greater ease and more flexibility than others.

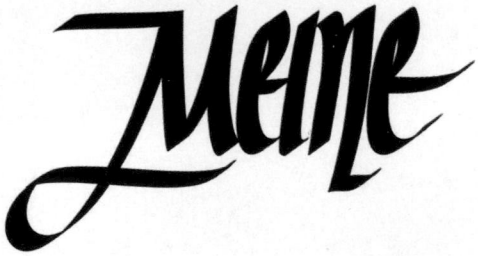

5 Form a more exuberant flourish by dragging a descender or, the first stroke of a capital A, H, M or N. Select the anchor points and drag them down, then to the left and finally back on itself. While you are digitally 'drawing', think about how you would do this with a tradition calligraphic pen and where the thick and thin parts of the line would be.

6 When you have formed these extensions and flourishes, recheck the lettering, especially the letter spacing. Save the vector image in your software's raw format so that you can return to it and make further changes if necessary. Convert the vector image into bitmap format. All vector software gives you the facility to do this.

▶

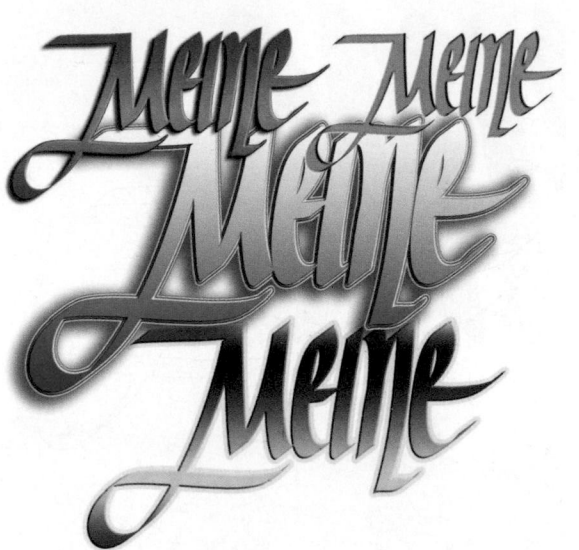

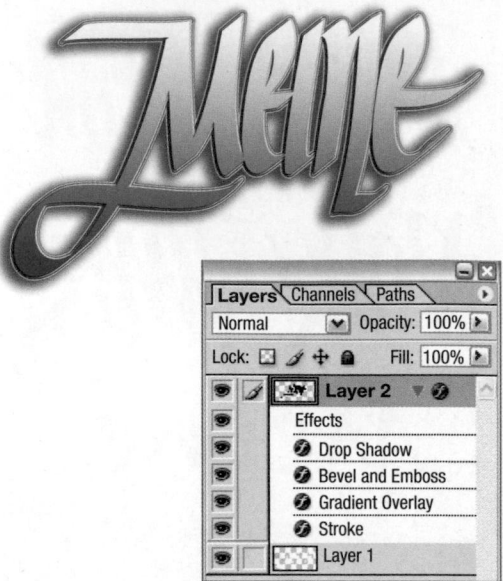

7 Experiment with a range of effects including, fills, filters, styles, drop shadows and so on. Think carefully about colour, as the background that you will be adding will have to work with the lettering. You can let the colour of your lettering determine the overall colour scheme, or modify the colour of the lettering to work with the background.

8 When you have decided on the filter or other effects, save the lettering to file. In this project the modifications and effects are applied to the word *Meine* only at this stage. The rest of the title *Sammlung deutscher Volkslieder* will be considered separately. If your title has more that a word or two it is best not to apply a complex filter to the whole text.

9 Select the background, ensuring that the colour works with the colours of the title lettering. You can choose a simple flat colour fill, a gradient fill, a textured fill or an image. This project uses an image of a blue sky with clouds. However, pure white clouds on sky blue would have too much contrast for a background so the whole image has been reduced in intensity.

Sammlung deutscher Volkslieder

10 Consider the design of any remaining title text – there are still three words left to include. These have been written in a simple italic in black ink on paper. The italic contrasts with the first title word but, being calligraphic, will still work well. This has then been scanned and imported to the graphics software so that it can be applied to the rest of the design.

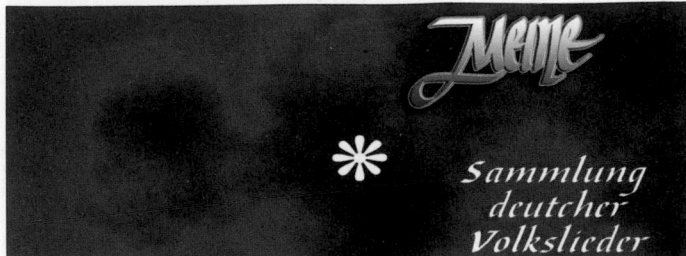

11 Select and add any other image elements. There is not a dot over the letter 'i' in *Meine*. Instead of a simple circle, it would be much more interesting to use an image. A stylized flower shape has been drawn, imported and modified. It can be scaled to any size and used over the 'i'.

12 Type the remaining text or import it from word processing software. This becomes an adjustable 'object'. Select an appropriate typeface. The element in this project will be used on the back of the insert, and not be seen together with the rest of the design. Select a form that you think reflects the nature of the CD's content. Adjust the size of the text block so that it fits within the 12.2cm x 12.2cm (4³/4in x 4³/4in) square.

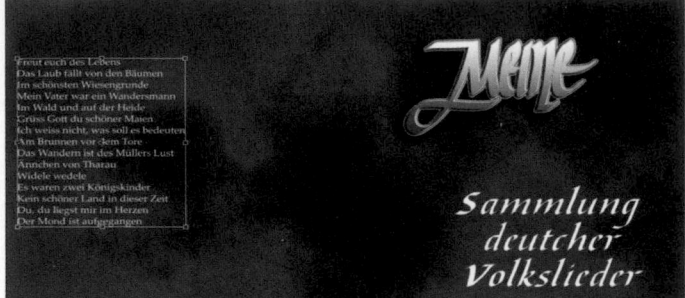

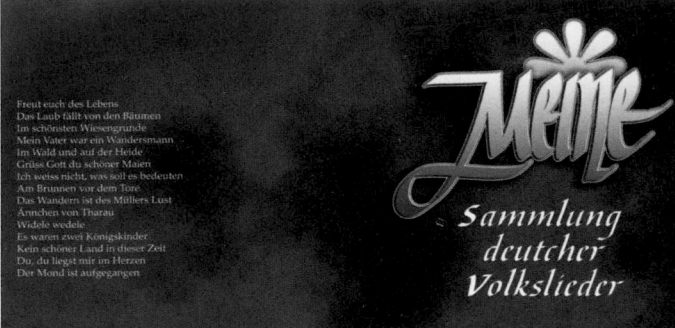

13 Assemble the whole design taking particular note of the position of the fold. Adjust the scale and position of all the design elements, including the title word or words and typed text. The flower shape has been located behind the title lettering and a filter effect added to it. Check that all the colours coordinate well and make any adjustments necessary.

> **Tip:** Inkjet print on most papers will bleed through to the reverse of the sheet. One solution is to print double size and fold the paper to form a front and back.

14 As a final touch the title word *Meine* has been copied and positioned behind the text on the reverse of the insert. The intensity of the colours has been reduced, as it would make the overlaid text less legible. Print the design. Carefully cut out the insert, fold it in half and slide it into the front of a jewel case.

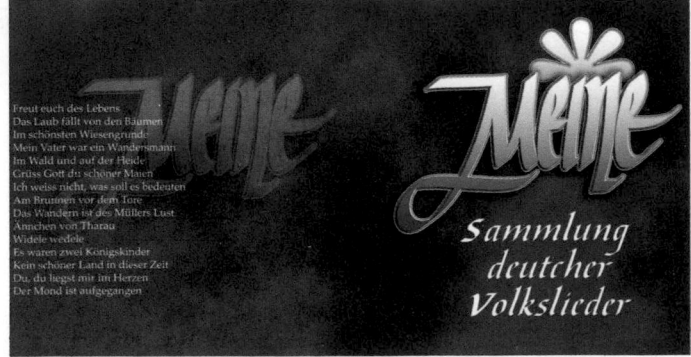

Glossary

Acrylic medium
A modern adhesive that dries clear, used for sticking metal leaf.

Anchor points
In digital calligraphy, the points on or at the ends of a segment or path that control the shape of a vector line.

Arch
The curved part of a letter as it springs from the stem.

Ascender
The rising stroke of the letter which extends above the x-height.

Automatic pens
Poster pens ranging in size from 1 (smallest) to 6A (largest).

Baseline
The bottom writing line on which the lettering sits.

Body height
This is also called the x-height and is the height of the whole letter not including the ascender and descender.

Book hand
Any style of alphabet commonly used in book production before the development of printing. Also called a script.

Bowl
The round or oval part of the letter formed by curved strokes, as in 'R', 'a', 'p' and 'q'.

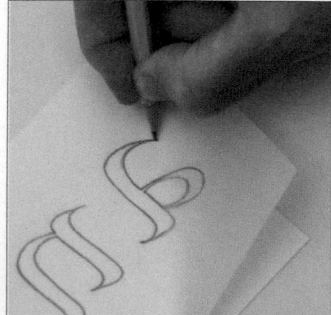

Brause pen
A German-made steep-nib dip pen. Nib size ranges from 1/2mm (1/64in) to 5mm (1/4 in).

Broad-edge pen
A pen with a square-edged nib.

Burnish
To rub a surface in order to make it shiny, normally using specialist burnishing tools.

Codex
A book made up of folded and/or bound leaves forming successive pages.

Cold-pressed paper
Paper with a medium-textured surface.

Counter
The space that is contained within round parts of letters.

Cuneiform
Early script in the form of wedge-shaped signs, used by the Sumerians.

Cursive
Linked or joined writing formed by rapid hand movements creating a fluid effect.

Descender
The tail of the letter which extends below the line, as in 'y' or 'p'.

Diaper patterns
Designs created to ornament a surface with small patterns laid out on a grid. Very useful to illuminators as the patterns can cover plain painted backgrounds, to adorn and enhance painted objects and materials, and to emboss gold surfaces.

Egg tempera
Egg yolk added to ground pigment colour to make paint.

Emboss
To indent a mark on gold or to create a raised or indented surface on paper with a blunt tool through a stencil – from the opposite side of the surface.

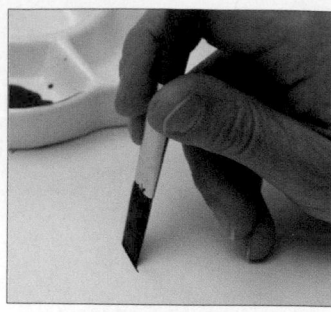

Flourish
An extended or exaggerated ascender or descender which is used to embellish the basic letterform.

Gesso
A compound made from plaster of Paris, glue and white lead. Can be used to form a raised surface on which layers of gold can be attached and polished.

Gild
To apply gold to a surface using either loose leaf, transfer or powdered gold.

Glassine paper
A transparent paper with a non-stick or resistant surface used for protecting gold surfaces. Also called crystal parchment paper.

Gouache
An opaque watercolour paint used when flat, dense colour is required. Also called body colour.

Gum ammoniac
A resin in crystal form that can be activated with hot water to provide a sticky gum base for flat gilding.

Gum arabic
Viscous substance from the acacia tree. Can be used as a binding agent, to aid paint adherence and as a resist.

Gum sandarac
Lumps of gum which, when ground to a fine powder, can be dusted lightly on to paper or vellum to improve the surface.

Hot-pressed paper
Paper with a smooth surface.

Illumination
The decoration of a manuscript, often using gold leaf burnished to a high shine.

Indent
An additional space added to the usual margin at the beginning of a line of writing.

Interlinear spacing
The spacing that occurs between two or more lines allowing sufficient space to accommodate ascenders and descenders.

Layout
The basic plan of a design showing spacing and organization of text.

Logo
A word or combination of letters designed to be used as a trademark, symbol or emblem.

Lower-case
Small letters as distinct from capitals or upper case. Also called miniscule letters.

Majuscule
A capital or upper-case letter.

Manuscript
A handwritten book or document.

Nib width
The width of the writing end (nib) of a broad-edged pen.

Palette
Traditionally, the surface used for mixing paint. In digital calligraphy, the range of colours and brushes that can be used in a graphics application.

Papyrus
Paper-like substance made from the papyrus plant. Commonly used until the 3rd century AD, particularly in Egypt.

Pen angle
The angle that the writing tip of a broad-edged pen makes with a horizontal writing line.

Pointed nib
A nib with a sharply pointed end, such as those manufactured by Gillott. These are used for copperplate writing.

PVA (polyvinyl acetate) glue
A clear adhesive which dries clear and can be used for sticking paper to paper and as gum to attach gold to paper. Also called white glue.

Resist
A substance that prevents paint or ink from reaching the underlying material. When the resist is removed, a pattern or design is left.

Rough paper
Paper with an extremely pronounced texture.

Sans serif
A term denoting letters without serifs or finishing strokes.

Scriptorium
A writing room, particularly that of a medieval monastery in which formal manuscripts were produced.

Serif
The beginning and the end part of the letterform. See also sans serif.

Skeleton letter
The most basic form of a letter demonstrating its essential distinguishing characteristics.

Speedball nibs
American nibs ranging in size from C–0 (largest) to C–6 (smallest).

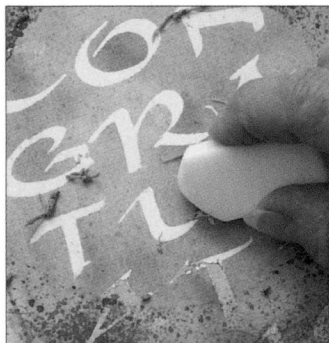

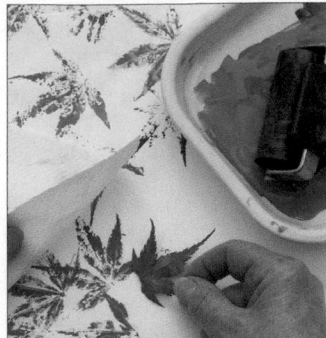

Stem
The main vertical stroke of the letter.

Swash
A simple flourish.

Uncials
A very rounded hand that is composed entirely of capitals.

Vector image
In digital calligraphy, a graphics file that uses mathematical descriptions of lines, curves and angles.

Vellum
Parchment made from calfskin which has been limed, scraped and prepared for either writing or painting.

Versals
Elegant capital letters made by compound pen strokes.

William Mitchell pens
Dip pens with nibs ranging in size from 0 (largest) to 6 (smallest).

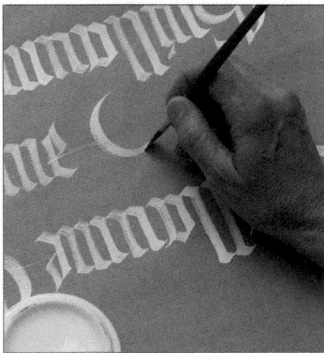

Suppliers

Manufacturers

If you have difficulty finding the materials you require in your local shops, the top manufacturers of pens, paper and other calligraphy materials should have information on your nearby stockists.

UNITED KINGDOM

Daler-Rowney UK Ltd
PO Box 10
Bracknell
Berkshire
RG12 8ST
Tel: (01344) 424621
Website: www.daler-rowney.com

W. Habberley Meadows Ltd (gold for illuminating and artists' materials)
5 Saxon Way
Chelmsley Wood
Birmingham B37 5AY
Tel: (0121) 770 0103
Fax: (0121) 770 6512
Email: gold@habberleymeadows.co.uk
Website: www.habberleymeadows.co.uk

William Cowley
Parchment and Vellum Works
97 Caldecote Street
Newport Pagnell
Buckinghamshire
MK16 0DB
Tel: (01908) 610038
Fax: (01908) 611071

Winsor & Newton
Whitefriars Avenue
Wealdstone
Harrow
Middlesex
HA3 5RH
Tel: (020) 8427 4343
Website: www.winsornewton.com

GERMANY

H Schmincke & Co.
Otto-Hahn-Strasse 2
D-40669 Erkath
Tel: (0211) 2509-0
Fax: (0211) 2509-461
www.schmincke.de

UNITED STATES OF AMERICA

Speedball Art Products Company
(includes paints, inks, calligraphy pens and nibs)
2226 Speedball Road
Statesville
NC 28677
Tel: 800 898 7224
Fax: 704 838 1472
Website: www.speedballart.com

Sanford North America (writing instruments and art materials)
Corporate Headquarters
Sanford
2707 Butterfield Road
Oak Brook
IL 60523
Tel: 800 323 0749
www.sanfordcorp.com

CANADA

Pentel of America (art materials and writing instruments)
2805 Columbia St
Torrance
90509
Canada
Tel: 310 320 3831
Fax: 310 533 0697

NEW ZEALAND

Montarga Art Stamps (manufacturers of rubber stamps, stamp pads, embossing powders, paper and cards)
922 Colombo St
Christchurch
Tel: (03) 366 9963
Fax: (03) 377 7963

Stockists

UNITED KINGDOM

Art Express (hobbycraft, mostly art and craft materials; not gilding materials)
Freepost NEA8739
Leeds
LS3 1JX

Blots Pen and Ink Supplies (UK)
14 Lyndhurst Avenue
Prestwich
Manchester
M25 0GF
Website: www.blotspens.co.uk

'Calligraphity'
(Specialist calligraphy/ lettering books)
Gourock
Scotland
PA19 1AF
1 Broderick Drive
Tel: (044) 1475 639668
Email: info@calligraphity.com
Website: www.calligraphity.com

Khadi Papers
Chilgrove
Chichester
PO18 9HU
Tel: (01243) 535314

L. Cornelissen and Son
(Artists' colourmen for gilders, painters and printmakers)
105 Great Russell Street
London
WC1B 3RY
Tel: (020) 7636 3655
Website: www.cornelissen.com

Stuart Stevenson
(Artists' and gilding materials)
68 Clerkenwell Road
London
EC1M 5QA
Tel: (020) 72531693
Website: www.stuartstevenson.co.uk

T. N. Lawrence and Son Ltd
208 Portland Road
Hove
Sussex
BN3 5QT
Tel: (0845) 6443232
Website: www.lawrence.co.uk

UNITED STATES OF AMERICA

John Neal Bookseller
(books, calligraphy tools and
materials, gilding materials)
POB 9986
Greensboro
NC 27429
Tel: (336) 272 6139
Tel Toll Free: (800) 369 9598
Fax: (336) 272 9015
Email: info@johnnealbooks.com
Website: www.JohnNealBooks.com
Producer of: *Bound and Lettered*
(Publication)
Letter Arts Review (Calligraphy
Publication)

CANADA

Colours Artist Supplies
10660-105 Street
Edmonton
Alberta
Canada
T5H 2W9
Has stores in Calgary, Regina, Saskatoon
and Winnepeg.
Tel: 800 661 9945
Website: www.artistsupplies.com

Curry's Artist's Materials
Has stores in Toronto, Whitby, Barrie, St-
Hubert, QC, Mississauga, Markham, and
Hamilton.
Tel: 800 268 2969
Website: www.currys.com

AUSTRALIA

Janine Mitchell
'Alphabetique'
Calligraphy Shop, Studio, Gallery and
Educational Centre (by appointment)
225 Canterbury Village
Canterbury
Victoria 3126
Tel: (03) 9836 6616
Email@alphabetique.net

The Art Shop
228a Harbour Drive
Coffs Harbour
New South Wales 2450
Email: amleonard@hotmail.com

The Paper Place (Calligraphy Supplies)
Syndal 3149
Melbourne
Tel: 9802 4297

Wills Quills (Australia)
1/166 Victoria
Chatswood
Sydney
New South Wales
Tel: (02) 9411 2500
Fax: (02) 9419 6031
Email: Sales@willsquills.com.au
Website: www.willsquills.com.au

NEW ZEALAND

Gordon Harris (specialist art, graphic
and paper supplies)
4 Gillies Avenue
Newmarket
Auckland
Tel: (09) 520 4466

Gordon Harris
170 Victoria Street
Wellington
Tel: (04) 385 2099

SOUTH AFRICA

ARTXPRESS Cape Town South Africa
(mail-order art supplies)
www.mk34.com

Calligraphy Societies

UNITED KINGDOM

**Calligraphy and Lettering Arts Society
(CLAS)**
54 Boileau Road
London
SW13 9BL
Tel: (020) 8741 7886
Email: info@clas.co.uk
Website: www.clas.co.uk

**Society of Scribes and Illuminators
(SSI)**
6 Queens Square
London
WC1N 3AT
Website: www.calligraphyonline.org

UNITED STATES OF AMERICA

Chicago Calligraphy Collective
PO Box 11333
Chicago
IL 60611
Website: www.chicagocallig.com

The Washington Calligraphers Guild
Merryfield
Website: www.calligraphersguild.org

CANADA

West Coast Calligraphy Society
2225 41st Avenue
Vancouver
British Columbia V6M 4L3

AUSTRALIA

**The Australian Society for
Calligraphers Inc**
PO Box 190 Willoughby
NSW 2068
Website:www.australiansocietyofcalligrap
hers.com.au

NEW ZEALAND

New Zealand Calligraphers
PO Box 99-674
Newmarket
Auckland
Email: info@nzcalligraphers.co.nz

Index

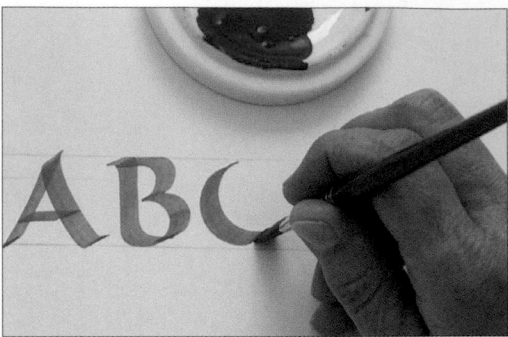

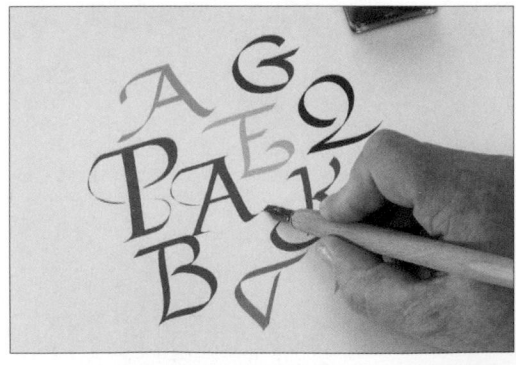

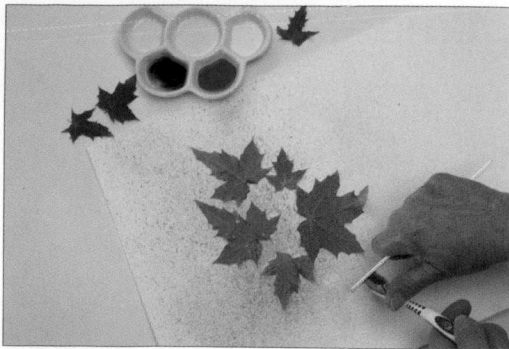

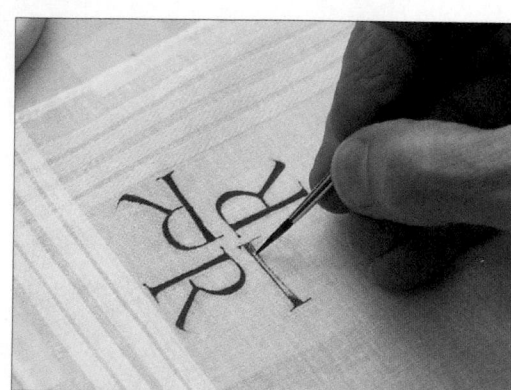

Acknowledgements

Contributing authors

Janet Mehigan first studied calligraphy during her five years training at art college. She holds a BA (Hons) degree in Education and is a Fellow of the Society of Scribes and Illuminators (SSI) and a Fellow and an Associate of The Calligraphy and Lettering Arts Society (CLAS). She teaches both calligraphy and art at all levels in Adult Education and runs numerous workshops for students and calligraphic societies.

Mary Noble started calligraphy 25 years ago. Today she teaches, exhibits and takes commissions. She is a Fellow of both UK national societies, the SSI and the CLAS, and has written and co-authored several calligraphy books, many with Janet Mehigan.

Viva Lloyd studied calligraphy and bookbinding at the Roehampton Institute where she obtained both the Certificate in Calligraphy & Bookbinding and the Diploma in Calligraphy. She is a CLAS Accredited Tutor and travels widely teaching workshops. In 2000 she founded the thriving group of Little Book Makers.

Maureen Sullivan studied Calligraphy, Illumination and Heraldry at Reigate School of Art & Design before studying full-time at Roehampton Institute, London where she graduated with a BA (Hons) degree in Calligraphy & Bookbinding. Maureen is a Fellow of the SSI, teaches workshops, takes commissions, has contributed to publications and is the author of *Craft in Motion*.

Dr George Thomson is a researcher/ practitioner in calligraphy and lettering and exhibits regularly in the UK, continental Europe, USA and Canada. He has lectured throughout Britain and North America. In addition to many academic papers on lettering, he has written a number of books on calligraphy, some of which have been published in several languages.

Jan Pickett originally studied Graphics and she worked commercially as a children's illustrator before training for an art teaching career. Since childhood, Jan's whole life has been a love affair with all forms of art. She enjoys all aspects of calligraphy and its wider applications and regularly teaches Adult Education classes, residential courses and day workshops. She is a Fellow of the CLAS and a Fellow of the SSI.

Janet Mehigan pp. 6–15, 32–3, 52–5, 60–3, 68–71, 86–7, 100–1, 134–5, 182–7, 190–1, 224–35, 250–53; **Mary Noble** pp. 18–31, 40–7, 56–9, 88–93, 132–3, 166–81, 216–23; **Viva Lloyd** pp. 48–51, 64–7, 80–3, 98–9, 102–3, 106–7, 148–57, 200–5, 240–3; **Maureen Sullivan** pp. 36–9, 72–9, 94–5, 104–5, 142–3, 188–9, 192–9, 236–9; **George Thomson** 108–17, 164–5, 210–15, 246–9; **Jan Pickett** pp. 96–7, 158–63, 206–9.

Picture acknowledgements

Photographs are reproduced in this book by kind permission of the following: Bridgeman Art Library 8 (Stapleton Collection), 9 (Musée de la Civilisation Gallo-Romaine), 10 (Bibliothéque Municipale), 11 (Trinity College),12t (Winchester Cathedral), 12b (Fitzwilliam Museum), 13 (British Library), 14 (Bibliothéque Nationale). Janet Mehigan 15b.

Calligraphers' own work supplied for the Gallery. Presentation piece p.129 by Peter Halliday reproduced by permission of The Society of British Neurologists, London. 'Julian's Alphabet' p.122 by kind permission of Julian Barker.

Thanks to **Mike Hemsley** at wg photo for the digital studio photography (wgphoto.co.uk).

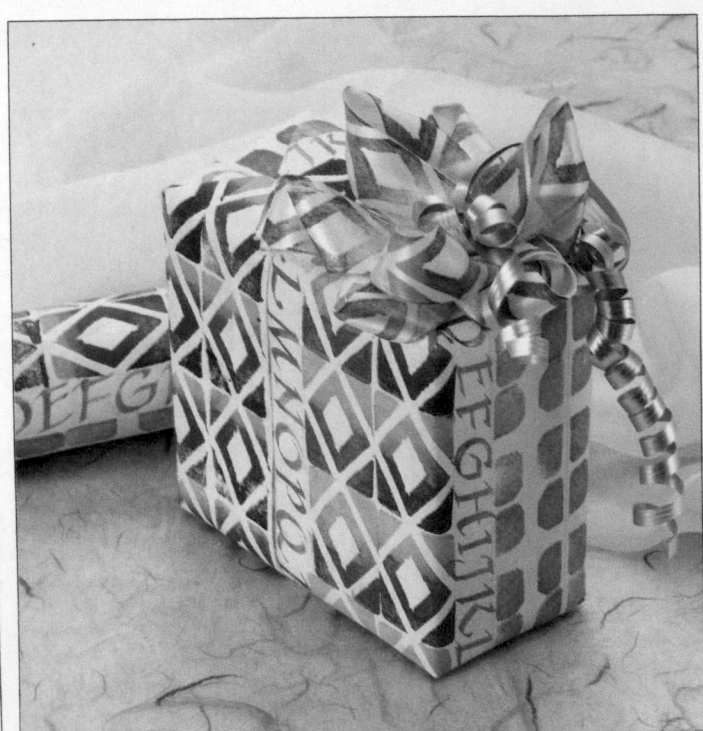

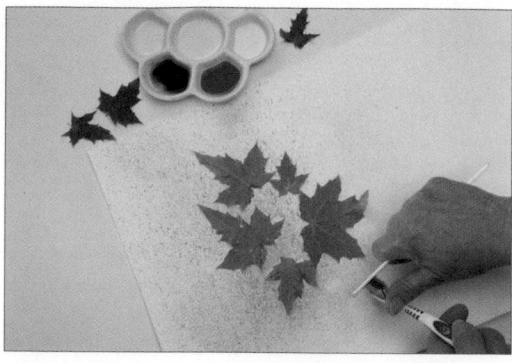
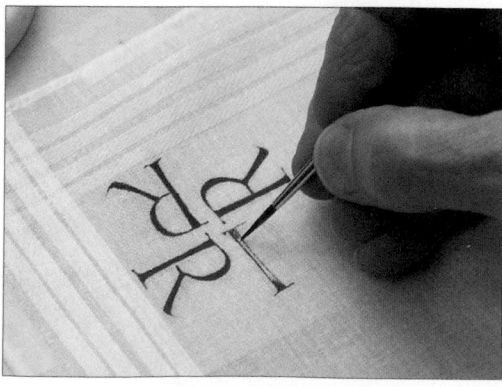

Acknowledgements

Contributing authors

Janet Mehigan first studied calligraphy during her five years training at art college. She holds a BA (Hons) degree in Education and is a Fellow of the Society of Scribes and Illuminators (SSI) and a Fellow and an Associate of The Calligraphy and Lettering Arts Society (CLAS). She teaches both calligraphy and art at all levels in Adult Education and runs numerous workshops for students and calligraphic societies.

Mary Noble started calligraphy 25 years ago. Today she teaches, exhibits and takes commissions. She is a Fellow of both UK national societies, the SSI and the CLAS, and has written and co-authored several calligraphy books, many with Janet Mehigan.

Viva Lloyd studied calligraphy and bookbinding at the Roehampton Institute where she obtained both the Certificate in Calligraphy & Bookbinding and the Diploma in Calligraphy. She is a CLAS Accredited Tutor and travels widely teaching workshops. In 2000 she founded the thriving group of Little Book Makers.

Maureen Sullivan studied Calligraphy, Illumination and Heraldry at Reigate School of Art & Design before studying full-time at Roehampton Institute, London where she graduated with a BA (Hons) degree in Calligraphy & Bookbinding. Maureen is a Fellow of the SSI, teaches workshops, takes commissions, has contributed to publications and is the author of *Craft in Motion*.

Dr George Thomson is a researcher/practitioner in calligraphy and lettering and exhibits regularly in the UK, continental Europe, USA and Canada. He has lectured throughout Britain and North America. In addition to many academic papers on lettering, he has written a number of books on calligraphy, some of which have been published in several languages.

Jan Pickett originally studied Graphics and she worked commercially as a children's illustrator before training for an art teaching career. Since childhood, Jan's whole life has been a love affair with all forms of art. She enjoys all aspects of calligraphy and its wider applications and regularly teaches Adult Education classes, residential courses and day workshops. She is a Fellow of the CLAS and a Fellow of the SSI.

Janet Mehigan pp. 6–15, 32–3, 52–5, 60–3, 68–71, 86–7, 100–1, 134–5, 182–7, 190–1, 224–35, 250–53; **Mary Noble** pp. 18–31, 40–7, 56–9, 88–93, 132–3, 166–81, 216–23; **Viva Lloyd** pp. 48–51, 64–7, 80–3, 98–9, 102–3, 106–7, 148–57, 200–5, 240–3; **Maureen Sullivan** pp. 36–9, 72–9, 94–5, 104–5, 142–3, 188–9, 192–9, 236–9; **George Thomson** 108–17, 164–5, 210–15, 246–9; **Jan Pickett** pp. 96–7, 158–63, 206–9.

Picture acknowledgements

Photographs are reproduced in this book by kind permission of the following: Bridgeman Art Library 8 (Stapleton Collection), 9 (Musée de la Civilisation Gallo-Romaine), 10 (Bibliothéque Municipale), 11 (Trinity College),12t (Winchester Cathedral), 12b (Fitzwilliam Museum), 13 (British Library), 14 (Bibliothéque Nationale). Janet Mehigan 15b.

Calligraphers' own work supplied for the Gallery. Presentation piece p.129 by Peter Halliday reproduced by permission of The Society of British Neurologists, London. 'Julian's Alphabet' p.122 by kind permission of Julian Barker.

Thanks to **Mike Hemsley** at wg photo for the digital studio photography (wgphoto.co.uk).

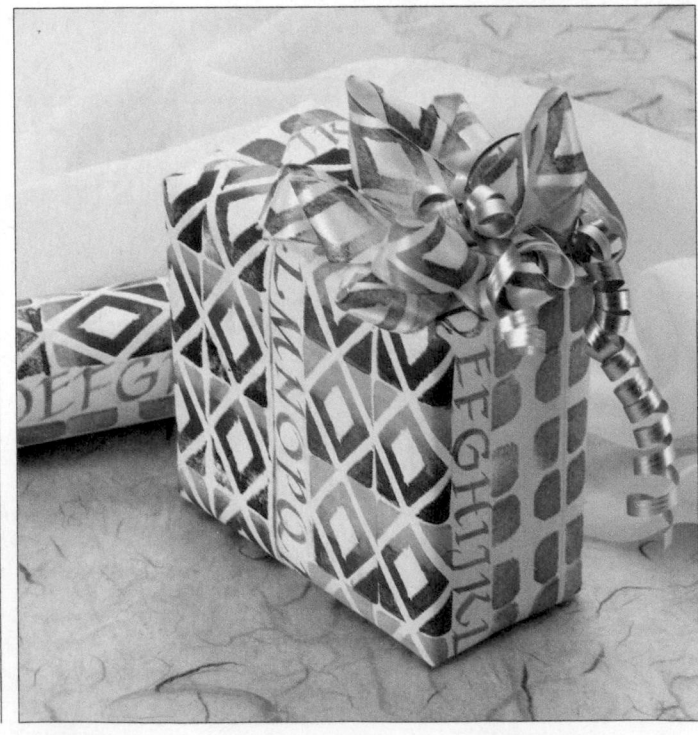